A UNIVERSITY EDUCATION

DAVID WILLETTS

David Willetts (signature)

OXFORD
UNIVERSITY PRESS

OXFORD

UNIVERSITY PRESS

Great Clarendon Street, Oxford, OX2 6DP,
United Kingdom

Oxford University Press is a department of the University of Oxford.
It furthers the University's objective of excellence in research, scholarship,
and education by publishing worldwide. Oxford is a registered trade mark of
Oxford University Press in the UK and in certain other countries

First Edition published in 2017

Impression: 2

Published in the United States of America by Oxford University Press
198 Madison Avenue, New York, NY 10016, United States of America

British Library Cataloguing in Publication Data
Data available

Library of Congress Control Number: 2017950063

ISBN 978–0–19–876726–8

Printed and bound by
CPI Group (UK) Ltd, Croydon, CR0 4YY

A UNIVERSITY EDUCATION

Acknowledgements

I gratefully acknowledge my debt to those many people in the world of higher education who have helped to educate me over the years. Indeed I am a part of that world as a Visiting Professor at King's College London and an Honorary Fellow of Nuffield College, Oxford. Current and former colleagues at King's advised on aspects of the book and kept me in touch with the realities of higher education, including Ed Byrne, David Edgerton, Jonathan Grant, Camille Kandiko Howson, Joanna Newman, Karen O'Brien, Paul Teulon, Christopher Winch, Alison Wolf, and Anna Zimdars. I have learned from my participation in Times Higher's Global Higher Education Summits and conversations with Phil Baty and Duncan Ross on their rankings.

Dean Machin and then Kathleen Henahan provided invaluable research assistance during the long process of writing the book. Nick Hillman of HEPI generously read and re-read the draft. Nicola Dandridge then of Universities UK read and commented on an earlier draft and Julie Tam at UUK helped with the data. The book has also benefited from the discipline of academic peer review by OUP and I am a grateful to their academic reviewers, Chris Wickham and an anonymous reviewer, and also to Matthew Cotton and Luciana O'Flaherty, the book's editors.

The opening section of the book focuses on the university as an institution. The Institute for Fiscal Studies contributed estimates of the RAB charge. Alan Hughes and Robert Hughes contributed new figures on the distribution of our research spend. Adam Kamenetzky of the Policy Institute at King's College London helped research the history of British science policy which was the subject of my inaugural lecture at King's.

The second section of the book is about students. Ian Walker provided generous advice on the economic returns to education and Anna Vignoles read and commented on Chapter 5 too. The Resolution Foundation, particularly Laura Gardner and Conor Ryan, helped me place the university graduate in the wider jobs market. Uta Frith, Sarah Jayne Blakemore, and Michael Thomas advised me on early years and neural plasticity. Mary Curnock Cook of UCAS kindly arranged for me to meet the founding general secretary of UCCA Ronald Kay;

Anne-Marie Watson of UCAS helped with data too. Worcester College, Oxford opened up their archives to investigate a point raised by John Saunders.

The final sections place the university in the wider world and look to the future. Rosa Fernandez and David Doherty of the National Council for Universities and Business, on whose Board I sit, helped with data and advice on links between universities and innovation. David Maguire and Paul Feldman of JISC and Simon Nelson of FutureLearn advised on education technologies. Chip Paucek of 2U where I am senior adviser read and commented on the draft of that chapter. John Claughton the former Chief Master of King Edward's School, Birmingham is a passionate advocate of IB and I drew on his advice in Chapter Fourteen.

The book has benefited from comments and advice of many friends and colleagues in higher education including: Maddalaine Ansel, Janet Beer, John Brennan, Claire Callender, John Douglass, Graham Gibbs, Peter Grus, Gervas Huxley, Paul Klemperer, Tim Leunig, Gordon McKenzie, Stephen Marston, Stephanie Marshall, Henry Morris, David Palfreyman, Miles Parker, Sue Pember, Graeme Reid, Michael Shattock, Neil Shephard, Adrian Smith, Eric Thomas, Peter Urwin, James Wilsdon, and Jonathan Woodhead.

I should also acknowledge my debt to officials in what was then the Department for Business, Innovation and Skills (BIS), the Higher Education Funding Council for England (HEFCE), the Research Councils, and other agencies that I worked with during more than four years as minister for universities and science. They contributed enormously to my university education and I am very grateful to them.

Finally I should also acknowledge a deep debt to my closest intellectual companion during my university education—my adviser and friend Nick Hillman. As a former teacher and a historian he brought a distinctive expertise to every issue and his influence pervades this book, which is dedicated to him.

David Willetts

Contents

List of Abbreviations

ADAS   Agricultural Development Advisory Service
BEIS   Department for Business, Energy and Industrial Strategy
BIS   Department for Business, Innovation and Skills
DEFRA   Department of the Environment, Food and Rural Affairs
DfE   Department for Education
DFID   Department for International Development
DLHE   Destination of Leavers from Higher Education
DWP   Department for Work and Pensions
EEA   European Economic Area
GCSE   General Certificate of Secondary Education
GPA   Grade Point Average
HE   higher education
HEA   Higher Education Academy
HEFCE   Higher Education Funding Council for England
HEIPR   Higher Education Initial Participation Rate
HEPI   Higher Education Policy Institute
HESA   Higher Education Statistical Agency
HMRC   HM Revenue and Customs
HNC   Higher National Certificate
HND   Higher National Diploma
HSCIC   Health and Social Care Information Centre
IFS   Institute for Fiscal Studies
iGCSE   International General Certificate of Secondary Education
IB   International Baccalaureate
IP   Intellectual Property
LA   local authority
MAFF   Ministry of Agriculture, Fisheries and Food
MOOC   Massive Open On-Line Course
NHS   National Health Service
NCH   New College of the Humanities
NSS   National Student Survey

NSSE	National Survey of Student Engagement
NUS	National Union of Students
OECD	Organization for Economic Co-operation and Development
OFFA	Office for Fair Access
Ofqual	Office of Qualifications and Examinations Regulation
OfS	Office for Students
OFT	Office of Fair Trading
OIA	Office of the Independent Adjudicator
OFSTED	Office for Standards in Education, Children's Services and Skills
ONS	Office for National Statistics
PGCE	Postgraduate Certificate in Education
PI	Principal Investigator
PPE	Philosophy, Politics and Economics
PRSB	Professional Record Standards Body
QAA	Quality Assurance Agency for Higher Education
RAB	Resource Accounting and Budgeting
REF	Research Excellence Framework
RPI	Retail Price Index
SAT	college admission test (US)
SATs	National Curriculum assessments (England)
SLC	Student Loans Company
STEM	science, technology, engineering, and mathematics
TEF	Teaching Excellence Framework
THES	*Times Higher Education Supplement*
UCAS	Universities and Colleges Admissions Service
UCCA	Universities Central Council on Admissions
UGC	Universities Grants Committee
UKRI	UK Research and Innovation
UKVI	UK Visas and Immigration
UUK	Universities UK

Introduction

I love universities. You just have to look at the posters stuck to walls and notice-boards. They add up to a picture of the good life—invitations to join sports teams, orchestras, social projects, new drama productions, and charity fund-raising stunts; together with public intellectuals giving guest lectures, performances by indie bands, and of course the occasional student protest against some injustice. I was on the receiving end of a few student protests myself over the years when I was minister for universities and science. Sometimes they were quite unpleasant, but usually well-intentioned young people just did not accept what I was trying to do or why. One incident captured what is special about university, even in those unpropitious circumstances. A group of perhaps forty protesters at Southampton University were shouting denunciations of the Coalition's fees policy. I went over and tried to talk to them but they could not hear my replies so they lent me their loud-hailer to hear my argument better. Then I gave it back so they could broadcast their reply. They returned it to me again and so we carried on the exchanges. Their anger could not suppress their curiosity. It was really rather moving. The university is the institution which, above all, fosters and sustains such intellectual curiosity and openness.

The university is the place where everything we think we know can be challenged and where new ideas are generated and transmitted to future generations so they will be better educated than us. A belief in the possibility of progress is one of the exceptional values of Western civilization and universities embody it because they operate at the intellectual frontier. It is why the university is one of the great institutions of the modern world—as important as the democratic legislature, an independent judiciary, or the joint stock company.

The first part of the book is about how the university has grown to such importance and why it works the way it does. A medieval concept, the independent corporation, has proved to be extraordinarily well suited to one of the most important eighty-five or so major institutions which already existed in

Europe five hundred years ago and still exist now, seventy of them are universities.[1] They are the institutional equivalents of the giant California redwood trees in the natural world—deep-rooted, long-lived, and with the power to shape an entire eco-system around them.

There are now over ten thousand universities, compared with five hundred after the Second World War.[2] They have a range of distinct missions—from fundamental research to vocational education. We in Britain think we know what makes a good university—competitive admission for students with high levels of prior attainment combined with a focus on research. That is the type of university which commands prestige, but it can lead us to assume that other models are 'bad' universities when they may just be different. These attitudes are particularly pervasive in England because of the distinctive history of English universities, uniquely dominated for centuries by Oxford and Cambridge, which have become for many the true idea of a university. But universities come in many more shapes and sizes and together they make up a system of higher education which achieves far more than any one type of institution within it on its own. Universities themselves can be so preoccupied with the differences between them that they can fail to make the case for higher educa- tion as a whole and to acknowledge their interdependence—which arises because of their distinctive roles. This wide range of universities is partly a result of higher education moving from elite to mass, but even whilst we recognize that this has happened we don't necessarily feel that good about it and don't embrace it. But this expansion is actually one of the great achievements of post-war Western societies and crucial to the advance not just of economic opportunity but of liberal values too. We should be proud of it and go still further with more students and an even wider range of universities. This argu- ment matters now because I detect more scepticism about universities and the value of higher education—they are assumed to be either elite and prestigious, in which case they seem to be of little direct relevance to the man in the street, or they are local and accessible, but then risk just being dismissed as inferior. Remote excellence or mundane mediocrity is not a great mix of options. That mind-set does an injustice to higher education as it is today.

Our history has left England with a system of higher education which is much more unusual than we recognize. It has great strengths yet it is responsible for many of the particular challenges facing English education today. And, as in the rest of life, some of the worst problems stem from the very features which are also distinctive strengths. England's strong powerful autonomous institutions protect freedom of enquiry and promote intellectual diversity within them.

They are world-class centres of research. And they compete vigorously with each other. But their very strength can also look to an economist like producer power, with insufficient attention to their students and little competitive challenge from alternative ways of doing things. The challenge I wrestled with as minister and which runs through this account is how to protect their autonomy and strengthen them and their finances whilst opening them up to more challenge and putting them under more pressure to do a better job of educating their students.

The power of our universities rests on England's distinctive system of nationwide competition for admission to university. This is different from most other Western countries where citizens are entitled to go as an undergraduate to their local university provided they pass some minimum standard in a school-leaving exam. But in England nobody has an automatic right of admission anywhere: entry is solely by nationwide application and competition. Each university controls its own admissions and alone decides whom to admit. The incentives they face are to focus on research performance and the prior attainment of their students because these determine a university's position in the league tables and enhance its prestige. That is what many young people and their parents think makes a 'good' university and so do many employers—their high prestige in turn helps their graduates get into the leading professions. The universities which conform to this model have many more applicants than places, so competition is intense. The competition to get into the 'good' universities in turn promotes competition to get into those secondary schools which maximize a young person's chances of getting to these prestigious universities. These schools focus on their performance in A levels so the main function of what is increasingly in practice our school-leaving exam is to assess young people for university entry—indeed A levels were originally created by universities for that very purpose, which is very different from the origins of the school leaving exam in many other countries which can give more weight to a broader education. The influence of this competition to get into university extends even further down the education system. The notorious selection for education by house prices is not just for secondary schools—the effect is as great in the neighbourhoods of those primary schools which feed the secondary schools which feed the universities.[3]

Competition for entry to prestigious universities therefore drives the intense education arms race which now dominates all stages of schooling. This pervades the system because of the expansion of higher education and its crucial role nowadays as the gateway to professions and to the middle class. Up to the

1960s access to university was mainly for a social elite together with some bright hard-working grammar school boys (and a few girls) whereas for everyone else there were many other routes to a decent job and indeed into the professions. Universities did not have the same power of shaping behaviour across earlier stages of education which they have now. Now many more people go into university. This is not the result of some eccentric education experiment in Britain—there has been similar growth across most advanced Western countries and increasingly in developing countries too. But our system of competitive entry to individual universities is unusual, with universities in sole control of deciding who to admit—they are choosing the student. That is why one consequence of expansion has been to make the influence of universities on the rest of the school system particularly powerful in England. It is also the reason for one of the most egregious features of English education—early specialization. University academics prefer to recruit students who already know about subjects related to those they are going to study, so teenagers narrow down to a few subjects earlier than in any other major Western country. It is a vivid example of the exceptional influence of universities over schools as they compete to get their students into the most prestigious universities. Indeed the Coalition introduced a new metric of school performance—getting pupils into the most prestigious universities—which both reflected the assumptions on which this whole model rests and reinforced them.

This model is the result of the very unusual history of English universities and that is what the first two chapters are about. Most Western countries have been slowly and steadily creating new universities in their major cities over centuries. England had two universities early on which then successfully opposed the creation of further universities for the next six hundred years— erecting barriers to entry which, even if they were beautifully carved in stone and covered in ivy, still did real damage to English education. One of the many effects of the Oxbridge duopoly was to create an assumption that one left home to go to university. It also shaped a particular idea of what a university must be like—forming gentlemen by educating them in the liberal arts. The twentieth century saw the rise of mass higher education, but the power of the Oxbridge model meant that civic universities originally created to deliver more vocational higher education then tried to become more like Oxbridge—the first example of the mission drift for which English higher education is notorious.

Mass higher education also has to be paid for, and in Chapter Three we get into the tricky arguments about the Coalition's changes to university financing which I helped to shape. I think they were the right thing to do and try to explain that income-related graduate repayment is a fair and progressive way of financing higher education. One reason the English university looms so large in our national life is that it is the place where most of our research is done. This is something else which is much more unusual than we recognize, and in Chapter Four I explain how we have ended up with more of our publicly funded research based in universities than just about any other Western country. This in turn affects the character of the whole research enterprise in the UK—a point we return to when we look at our weaker performance in commercializing research.

The university is not simply an institution to be admired: it exists so as to benefit its students. Higher education is the main way in which the Western world manages the adolescent's transition to adulthood. It has displaced the classic alternatives—apprenticeships and military service—and changed both individuals and wider society as a result. In the second part of the book I focus on the individual student's journey through his or her education to university and beyond (as the majority of university students are female it usually is 'her' in this book). In particular I want students, worried about money or exams or jobs, to know that they are engaged in what could well be the most valuable, most transformative three years of their lives. Chapters Five and Six investigate the evidence to support these claims and contrast the effects of three years at university with another three years, the first three years of school, which get much greater prominence in today's conventional wisdom. The good news is that we can keep on learning: adult education is exceptionally effective but has lost out because of the widespread belief in the significance of the early years. If a youngster has suffered from poor-quality schooling does that mean they are less likely to benefit from higher education, or conversely will they surge ahead if they get to university? That question is the backdrop to Chapter Seven which looks at how the admission process works and how it could work better. There is more good news: university is the only stage of education in which the performance of youngsters from more modest backgrounds can match those with the greatest advantages.

The crucial moment is when the student and the institution meet, and Chapter Eight looks at what kind of academic experience the student has after she finally gets there. Universities are powerful and respected, with their own purposes, which are different from those of commerce or politics. That is how it should be. The high reputation and deep roots of universities make them particularly powerful protectors of the freedom of academic enquiry. But these very strengths also enable them to trade on their reputations to get away with inadequate teaching or the worst sort of picky scholasticism. The very prestige of Britain's universities, such a source of pride both to them and to the nation as a whole, can also mean that they are not as responsive as they should be to what their students need.

Teaching and research are classic roles of the university. But the university fulfils other valuable functions too. In the third part of the book we look at the other uses of the university. One of these is to deliver vocational training. I often encounter the assumption that academic study in a university is removed from any practical training which requires an apprenticeship. But almost 60 per cent of students are working to get a vocational or business qualification.[4] Many occupations become professions by requiring a university degree. Chapter Nine shows, however, that we have not always done a good job of designing university professional education and this is particularly true in some of our great public services.

Universities are also increasingly important economic players both in their own areas and nationally. This is partly because of their size—a large British university may have a budget approaching a billion pounds and could well be the biggest employer and the biggest exporter in its area. Universities also drive innovation. The process has been summarized very crudely—first money is turned into research and then research is turned into money. Chapter Ten investigates this process. It shows why the strong incentives facing universities in the English model lead them to focus on research performance as measured by citation of academic articles, with weaker incentives for commercial innovation, which anyway may thrive better outside the university.

Some academics are sceptical about these economic roles for the modern university. They attribute the troubles of universities to markets, managers, and ministers. They argue that if only universities were protected from that unholy trinity they could be true to their historic roles. In particular they dislike the forces of 'marketization' and 'consumerism'. Many of the changes they most dislike arise from the transformation of the size and significance of universities as they have become important economic players in their own right. But I would much rather live in a society with big strong outward-looking universities than one where they are smaller and less engaged with our national life. Chapter Eleven reviews these arguments and the recent legislative changes to higher education which place universities in a regulated market environment more explicitly than ever before.

In the final section of the book we look at future trends: changes in where we study, how we study, and what we study. Universities are a distinctive mix of ancient and modern. Graduates dress up in traditional academic robes for a ceremony with perhaps some Latin thrown in to mark their success in disciplines out at the frontiers of knowledge. That mix is very engaging—just observe the pride of students and their families at graduation ceremonies which are still based on medieval academic rituals (and some of these derive from earlier Islamic conventions, a reminder of the flourishing of great institutions of learning in the Arab world). But universities are going to have to change. The two great contemporary forces of globalization and the digital revolution, which have disrupted many key industries, have yet to disrupt our universities but that is starting to happen. They will face competition from big international higher education chains, none of which is British-based. They also face the challenge of disintermediation—completing an on-line course and then adding it to a LinkedIn profile may challenge the significance of that university degree in the job market. But our universities with their distinctive reputations and powerful physical presence can survive and prosper, provided they adapt, in particular by using the power of education technologies.

The final chapter focuses on the biggest single problem in English education, which is specialization far too early. Very few other Western countries expect their 16-year olds to narrow down their education to three subjects, often grouped around either the sciences or the arts. C. P. Snow's two cultures are not the result of some profound conflict between different disciplines: they are the result of the peculiar pattern of English education. Universities have to take much responsibility for it: the way they run their admissions shapes A levels and leads schools to specialize. University academics prefer a prior commitment to their own discipline rather than giving students the space to decide during their first years at university what to focus on later. This has to change. The new arrangements for funding universities through fees and loans provide the opportunity to shift to four-year courses with many more students starting with a foundation year, as they do in Scotland. Instead of government restricting years of undergraduate study to save public funding money we can now expect it to be funded by graduate repayment provided the extra year is genuinely valuable. An alternative is for more graduates to study for a Masters linked to their chosen profession, as they do in the USA. And instead of restricting school funding to cut them down to a maximum of three A levels with the loss of AS levels we should go in the opposite direction with funding for five A levels at sixth form, each with rather less specialization than at present, with the expectation that students study both maths and an arts subject. That would have been good for the country and good for students. It is the main item of unfinished business which is going to have to be addressed as part of a subsequent education reform.

This book has been written over the three years since I stood down from Government. I was optimistic about the future then—not least because university finances were much healthier than for a generation and record numbers of British and overseas students were applying and getting in. But since then Brexit, bringing with it questions about our openness to students and academics from the EU, has created new threats to the networks which enable British universities to thrive. And the General Election of June 2017 cast new doubt over our system of university financing even though I believe it is progressive and fair. There are other challenges too in Britain and around the world. There is rightly a focus on teaching quality but there is not yet a reliable means of assessing it and being confident it is good enough. Public universities in the USA have faced intensifying funding pressures and the Trump administration is challenging the value of research in areas such as climate science where there have been strong Anglo-American partnerships. A media narrative has developed in which we are told it is not worth so many people going to university. And within the university itself freedom of speech and academic enquiry can be threatened, with worrying examples of no-platform policies inhibiting freedom of speech. Despite all this I remain an unashamed believer in growth—growth in knowledge, growth in the number of universities, growth in the number of students, and above all the personal growth which comes as a result of higher education.

Most of my work in politics over the last decade involved education, especially higher education. Although the book is not a narrative of my years as a minister, it draws on those experiences. I have not quite managed to visit every one of the 130 universities in the UK but I have been to most of them—rather like a dedicated (or perhaps obsessive) Scottish mountaineer trying to climb all the Munros. And at every university I visited I learnt something from the people who worked there—the researchers and technicians, the academics and the managers, the students and the Vice Chancellor. By and large they are good, decent people, and smart as well. Almost everyone I met approached their education responsibilities with the belief that this was the most worthwhile and important thing they could do. Whatever our disputes they arose from a genuine disagreement about what was best for their students or their university. The same goes for the excellent officials that I worked with in BIS (The Department of Business, Innovation and Skills) and bodies such as HEFCE (The Higher Education Funding Council for England) and the Research Councils. I was also very fortunate in working with some excellent colleagues in Government. The ministers with whom I found myself dealing on almost all the key issues in higher education policy were David Cameron and George Osborne, Nick Clegg and Vince Cable. David Cameron was one of the few Conservatives who immediately and instinctively sympathized with the aspiration of more people to go to university. George Osborne recognized that our funding reforms made it possible to deliver that by removing the cap on student numbers, one of the Coalition's great social reforms. Nick Clegg was genuinely motivated by the desire to improve social mobility and suffered disproportionately for backing the Coalition's policy on fees and loans. And Vince Cable was throughout a shrewd and thoughtful colleague—we knew that we had to make the Coalition work and we did. I also have great respect for my successors Greg Clark and Jo Johnson who have successfully steered through the legislation which is the logical culmination of the reforms described in this book. But this book is not a politician's memoir and this paragraph says more about individual politicians than the rest of the book put together. Its focus is on the university and the student.

I

The University

ONE

The Rise of the University

Medieval origins

The university is one of Europe's great gifts to the world. There had been sophisticated centres of learning in Classical Athens and Alexandria, in China, and then in North Africa and Spain during the Islamic world's scientific flowering. But it is Europe's universities which gave birth to the humanism of the Renaissance, drove the Reformation, led the rise of empirical science, and promoted the emergence of critical history. They are still extending the boundaries of knowledge today, as part of a global enterprise which is heavily influenced by the European model.

They emerged in the twelfth century. The first wave of a dozen or so, including Bologna, Paris, and Oxford, already comprised different types of university, reflecting their different origins depending on which came first, the chicken or the egg, the teacher or the student. In Bologna, reputed to have been founded in 1088 and hence Europe's oldest university, the student is thought to have come first. Groups of students were looking for training to get qualifications that would help them practise medicine or law and employed teachers to help them. There 'the lecturing staff had to submit to a competitive trial to win the custom of their fee paying consumers . . . teaching was viewed as a commodity like any other and it was logical that new students should sample lecture courses before making their academic purchase'.[1] They were mature students who had probably already started work and knew what extra training they needed to advance in their profession. By contrast in Northern Europe the university began with teachers setting up universities: they had much younger students who were more dependent on them. (They were called masters, reflecting the origins of the model in apprenticeships.) These universities tended to be less vocational as the routes into professions such as the law or medicine were instead via apprenticeships.

Towns gave these new institutions a mixed welcome—and sometimes still do. Tensions between town and gown boiled over into violence. Universities looked to the Church, the major countervailing power of the time, for protection from hostile locals. If their independence was threatened and persecution became too severe they would up sticks and move to a different and more favourable jurisdiction. A greedy council taxing them too much or an internal row within the university would prompt a group of scholars and students to march out of town to a new home. This dynamic of secession and migration drove the second wave of new universities in the thirteenth and fourteenth centuries. Cambridge was founded after such a secession from Oxford in 1209. (Oxford itself emerged when in 1167 King Henry II banned English students from going to Paris to study because France was too strongly linked to his great opponent, Archbishop Thomas Becket.) There were other English secessions too—we nearly ended up with our most prestigious universities in Northampton and Salisbury. These secessions stopped earlier in England than elsewhere because Oxford restricted the right of its graduates to teach elsewhere. (In 2015 the University of Northampton marked the 750th anniversary of being banned and celebrated their 10th anniversary as a university.)

Universities were engaged in a delicate balancing act: they were looking to the Church to protect them from the secular authorities, but also seeking recognition from the Church itself of their distinctive freedoms. Universities enjoyed a very special legal autonomy—a point that is obscured by the widespread belief that 'university' refers to universal knowledge. Dr Johnson defined it as 'a school where all the arts and faculties are taught and studied'.[2] But he was wrong. Newman's great essay *The Idea of a University* repeats this egregious mistake: 'The view taken of a University in these Discourses is . . . it is a place of *teaching* universal *knowledge* . . .'.[3] This error has serious implications because its perpetrators define a university by the type of subjects it teaches, which they distinguish from institutions which just teach contingent and limited knowledge needed for example to practise a trade or profession. But actually a university is defined by the type of institution it is.

'University' means a self-governing corporation, a complete entity in its own right, a totality. In Latin it is a *universitas magistorum et scholarium*—an independent institution of masters and students.[4] Sometimes in Italy an older university may still be called by its full Italian title—*università degli studi*—an independent corporation for studies. As other corporations for other purposes fell away so there was less need to identify specifically when a university was for study.

The modern university has taken over this medieval legal model of the self-governing corporation because it is so well suited to the purposes of higher education today. English universities have unusually high levels of autonomy and we must not turn this feature, however desirable, into a universal truth. Other systems were and still are very different. 'Whereas the chancellor of Paris University was an external official set above the masters' guild and acted as the delegate of the Bishop of Paris, the English chancellors were the living embodiment of guild autonomy.'[5] In France, for example, academics are state employees. From time to time I had to remind the Treasury and other ministers that England's universities were not part of the public sector. (At one point for example the Treasury assumed that policies on public sector pensions applied to universities and it took months of negotiation to correct this error.) Whatever the system, however, a university does have the distinctive power to award its own degrees, whereas a school or college cannot award its own qualifications. This special power of awarding its own qualifications is a privilege which can easily be abused so there has to be some control over access to the status of university. This regulatory function was originally claimed by the papacy, in return for which universities often had ecclesiastical privileges which gave them some protection from the civil authority, though with the disadvantage that they were exposed to ecclesiastical interference instead. They fought this, and Oxford and Cambridge gained full exemption from episcopal jurisdiction in the fifteenth century. (It is sometimes assumed that Oxford and Cambridge must trace their status back to ancient royal charters but actually their original legal recognition came from papal bulls.)

The university is a type of institution whereas higher education is a type of education. An institution providing higher education might not be a university—because, for example, it is a college teaching for degrees issued by a university which is separate. And so could there be a university which does not itself provide higher education? Might the university be issuing degrees but not actually educating anyone? It could be argued this is the Oxbridge model. The college becomes the higher education institution and the degree-awarding body is the university. We turn to this issue later when we consider the external degrees of the University of London.

Italian universities contributed to the Renaissance by promoting empiricism over scholasticism. Medicine, for example, was taught to those demanding students at Bologna with real dissections. The humanism of the Italian Renaissance came from the willingness of Italian scholars to study a wider range of Classical texts and with more critical scrutiny. Galileo's fundamental scientific research was sustained by the Universities of Pisa and Padua. Religious controversies also helped keep universities at the centre of Europe's intellectual life. In Germany universities drove the Reformation. Luther himself was a professor of biblical studies at Wittenberg from 1513 to his death in 1546, never holding any other post and continuing to lecture. Proposing his ninety-five theses exactly five hundred years ago was the classic opening of a medieval disputation—and his action would score quite highly on any modern assessment of academic impact. Many other key leaders of the Reformation were university professors.[6] Oxford and Cambridge were at the heart of the turbulent politics of the English Reformation, with Cambridge more Protestant and Oxford more Royalist or, as Macaulay put it: 'Cambridge had the honour of educating those celebrated Protestant bishops whom Oxford had the honour of burning …'.[7]

Growth, decline, and the English exception

These early universities really mattered: they were engaged with the wider world and helping to shape Western culture. And their numbers grew. By 1400 Europe had twenty-nine universities. Another twenty-eight were created in the fifteenth century and then a further eighteen from 1500 to 1625, making seventy-three after two disappeared. Over those 225 years eight were created in Spain, nine in France, three in the Netherlands, seven in Italy, and fourteen in Germany. Scotland started with none and ended with four.[8] But there is one very significant exception. After the early foundation of Oxford and Cambridge, no new universities were created in England between 1209 (Cambridge) and 1829 (UCL). Six hundred years was rather a long time to wait for a new university. No other European country had such a long period without creating new universities—indeed by 1790 Europe had 143 universities. In 1300 England had a university for every 1.9 million people but by 1800 it had a university for every 4.6 million. Over the same period France went from a university for every 3.3 million people to one for every 1.2 million people.[9] This helps to explain the peculiar position of Oxford and Cambridge in England's national life—they were for most of England's history the national university system. Instead of a network of regional and city universities, as in most other European countries, England had two national universities to which students travelled from across the country. Going away to university was the only way to get higher education. This may have contributed to a more unified national culture in the same way as the national administration of justice or the absence of any local baronial armies.[10] But it did mean that there was little innovation with no new entrants coming in to do things differently. So, for example, the structure of the medieval faculties remained fixed when they had long ceased to reflect the body of knowledge, holding back Oxford and Cambridge from developing any significant role in research.

This long period with just two universities was not because of lack of demand. It was because of barriers to entry policed very forcefully. Oxford and Cambridge imposed a bar on their graduates teaching elsewhere in the country to stop the creation of new universities. This was a conspicuous constraint because the principle, *jus ubique docendi*, was that a university degree was valid across Christendom and enabled a graduate to teach anywhere. But Oxford and Cambridge enforced a much more restrictive interpretation. The last major migration, from Oxford to Stamford in 1334, nearly took root, but Oxford got the King to issue a proclamation that no universities were to be allowed except at Oxford and Cambridge and also imposed a new oath on all new masters that they would not lecture outside the universities of Oxford and Cambridge—an oath that remained obligatory for the next 500 years and maintained England's university duopoly.

There was pressure for new centres of research too, free from the constraints of medieval scholasticism. Francis Bacon proposed a new research institute that, unlike existing universities, would not be 'confined and, as it were, imprisoned in the writings of certain authors'.[11] But Oxford and Cambridge were bitterly opposed. Thomas Gresham left his enormous wealth to fund a new university in London and Gresham College was founded in 1575, but opposition from Oxford and Cambridge was one reason it never got full degree-awarding powers. The Royal Society encountered similar problems. Anthony Wood, the Oxford diarist, noted: 'The Royal Societie instituted this year—the Universitie looks upon it as obnoxious; they desire to confer degrees; the Universitie stick against this.'[12]

Even without the creation of new universities student numbers grew steadily until by 1600 or so England had almost 2.5 per cent of young men going to university.[13] This growth was made possible by the creation of new colleges at Oxford and Cambridge. But the reformers wanted to see more universities created as well to meet this surge in demand. It was one of the Parliamentarians' demands during the Civil War. In 1643 William Dell, Puritan master of Caius College, Cambridge, made the case to the Westminster Assembly of Divines:

> Why universities and colleges should only be at Oxford and Cambridge I know no reason. It would be more advantageous to the good of all the people, to have Universities or Colledges, one at least in every great town or city in the nation as

in London, York, Bristow, Exceter, Norwich and the like; and for the State to allow
to these Colledges an honest and competent maintenance for some godly and
learned men to teach the Tongues and Arts, under a due reformation.[14]

His ambition was eventually fully achieved after more than three hundred years
in 1963 with the creation of the University of York and the University of East
Anglia. But what he was proposing was close to what had already happened in
several European countries, notably Scotland. The Royalists drew a different
lesson. They thought too many people were going to university: it was one of
the reasons for the dissent which had boiled over in the Civil War. Thomas
Hobbes thought expansion of student numbers had been a mistake: 'the universities have been as mischievous to this nation as the Wooden Horse was to the
Trojans'.[15] After the Restoration there was a shift in policy and student numbers
started to decline, falling to a low point in 1760. The total matriculating at
Oxford in 1621, 748, was not to be reached again until 1883. So the pub quiz
question is: which Oxford college was the newest for longest? The answer is
Wadham College, which was founded in 1610 whereas the next wholly new
college, Keble, was created in 1870. (Pembroke College and Worcester College
were created out of older halls on the same sites in 1624 and 1714 respectively.)
The participation rate of 2.5 per cent of young men going to university before
the Civil War was not reached again until the twentieth century.[16]

   The most severe suppression of demand for higher education came from
enforcement of the Test Acts which restricted Oxford and Cambridge to members of the Church of England. You could not enter the university of Oxford
unless you were an Anglican. In Cambridge the interpretation was more liberal:
you could study but could not graduate unless you were an Anglican. This crucial difference helped shape the distinctive characters of the two universities.
Catholics could study on the Continent. Dissenters had an alternative option—
America. They created universities in the American colonies and sent their
children over to study there. Some had links to specific denominations:
Princeton was Presbyterian (1746); Brown was Baptist (1765); Rutgers was
Dutch Reformed (1766). By the time of the War of Independence there were
nine universities in the American colonies, which had a population a third the
size of England's. Dissenters who would have endowed colleges and universities
in their own towns in England instead gave libraries and endowments to
Harvard, Yale, and others. In the eighteenth century 31 per cent of Harvard's
income came from England.[17] America's Ivy League emerged partly because of
the ban on alternative universities in England.

After the excitement and growth of the Renaissance and Reformation the seventeenth and eighteenth centuries saw universities in decline in England and across most of Europe. The chapter of Edward Gibbon's autobiography describing his unhappy year at Oxford, 'the most idle and unprofitable of my whole life', when it was 'steeped in port and prejudice', is a vivid critique of the university at the lowest point in its history.[18] His tutor 'well-remembered he had a salary to receive, and only forgot he had a duty to perform'.[19] On the Continent universities failed to respond to the competitive challenge from another alternative provider—the Jesuits. The Jesuits had pioneered rigorous school education and extended it to a higher level when they were empowered to grant degrees from 1561. They offered a broader curriculum better suited to modern aspirational families—horsemanship, French, dancing. Their boarding houses offered a mix of international students and better supervision and order than the violence, licentiousness, and loose organization of universities.[20]

There was one exception to this dismal picture—Scotland. Here was a vigorous alternative model, based not on endowments and privileges but with high educational standards based on payment of fees to tutors. The Scottish Enlightenment flourished in Europe's best university system. Adam Smith is explicit in his letters that 'In the present state of the Scotch Universities, I do most sincerely look upon them as, in spite of all their faults, without exception, the best seminaries of learning that are to be found anywhere in Europe.'[21] He devotes a fascinating chapter in *The Wealth of Nations* to investigating what has gone wrong with Europe's universities. His critique is very clear and we will return to it in Chapter Eight:

> The improvements which, in modern times, have been made in several different branches of philosophy, have not, the greater part of them, been made in universities; though some no doubt have. The greater part of universities have not even been very forward to adopt those improvements, after they were made; and several of those learned societies have chosen to remain, for a long time, the sanctuaries in which exploded systems and obsolete prejudices found shelter and protection, after they had been hunted out of every other corner of the world. In general, the richest and best endowed universities have been the slowest in adopting those improvements, and the most averse to permit any considerable change in the established plan of education. Those improvements were more easily introduced into some of the poorer universities, in which the teachers, depending upon their reputation for the greater part of their subsistence, were obliged to pay more attention to the current opinions of the world.[22]

Edward Gibbon refers to Adam Smith and offers a very similar analysis of the problem in his memoirs:

> The legal incorporation of these societies by the charters of popes and kings had given them a monopoly of the public instruction; and the spirit of monopolists is narrow, lazy and oppressive. Their work is more costly and less productive than that of independent artists and the new improvements so eagerly grasped by the competition of freedoms are admitted with slow and sullen reluctance in those proud corporations, above the fear of a rival, and below the confession of an error. We may scarcely hope that any reformation will be a voluntary act, and so deeply are they rooted in law and prejudice that even the omnipotence of parliament would shrink from an enquiry into the state and abuses of the two universities.[23]

Universities both in England and across Europe were ripe for reform.

Nineteenth-century reform: Germany, France, and England

Napoleon was the great disruptive force destroying the decayed medieval universities of Continental Europe. In France the universities were moribund and associated with feudal aristocratic privilege. The Revolutionaries abolished the lot of them. Instead Napoleon created Grandes Écoles, delivering practical training in skills like engineering, crucial for winning and maintaining his Empire. The old universities were eventually re-created and are now open to everyone who has left school with a baccalaureate—about 80 per cent. But their allure and status were gone, along with their endowments—the future lay with the Grandes Écoles, which educate the French elite to this day. France is one of the few advanced countries where the elite will not in a strict sense have gone to university though they will certainly have had an excellent higher education.

Napoleon's defeat of Prussia forced it to confront the challenge of how to modernize its failing institutions. Wilhelm von Humboldt, the Prussian Education and then Interior Minister proposed a new type of university that would lead national renewal. He advocated a university which did not just train the elite but also promoted research and an understanding of national culture to strengthen Prussia and catch up with the Industrial Revolution happening in Britain. The University of Berlin was founded in 1810 on these principles. (It was renamed after Humboldt and his brother Alexander by the East German Communists in 1949.) Some of Humboldt's arguments for research-led teaching still sound radical now: 'so the university teacher is no longer a teacher, the student no longer a learner, but the latter carries out research himself, and the professor directs and supports his researches.'[24] Humboldt has gone down in history as the originator of the modern research-intensive university, a model of higher education which Germany was to dominate through the nineteenth century and which was crucial to its industrialization. The institutionalization of research led to the seminar and the laboratory, both German contributions to the modern university, as was the creation of modern disciplines. History, for example, came to mean identifying a sound narrative from primary sources: Leopold von Ranke was excited at the 'still unknown history of Europe' lying hidden in the archives.[25]

The early nineteenth century also saw American higher education taking its distinctive path. It involved one of the most important court cases in American history. Dartmouth College in New Hampshire had been founded under King George III. The trustees had lost confidence in the head of the college and deposed him. The state saw an opportunity to step in, and legislated to remove the trustees' powers to appoint and instead to vest them in the state. The Supreme Court decided in 1819 that the original founding documents were still valid, despite dating back to Colonial times, and that the state had no power to intervene in such autonomous self-governing institutions. It was a ringing endorsement of the autonomy of the university as conceived by its medieval founders. Indeed it was this case that actually confirmed the primacy of the contracts establishing many other types of private corporations too.[26]

Meanwhile English universities were about to change—at last. English Radicals, led by Jeremy Bentham, set up a secular, fee-based college as a joint stock company. It was a deliberate alternative to the Oxford and Cambridge duopoly and heavily influenced by the Scottish model. University College London (UCL) was what we would now call an alternative provider and the abuse it encountered was similar to what we hear today. Setting it up as a limited company and financing it by fees was particularly shocking. Coleridge denounced it as a mere 'lecture bazaar'. Thomas Arnold called it 'that godless institution in Gower Street.'[27] It was not allowed to call itself a university and one newspaper columnist said it was 'a humbug joint-stock subscription school for Cockney boys, without the power of granting degrees or affording honours or distinctions, got up in the bubble season'.[28] Its defenders retaliated:

> Ye Dons and ye Doctors, ye Provosts and Proctors,
> Who are paid to monopolise knowledge,
> Come, make opposition by vote and petition

> To the radical infidel college
> Come...arm all the terrors of privileged errors,
> Which live by the wax of their Charters.[29]

London had at last got a secular liberal higher education institution. That was a competitive challenge for High Church Tories, who responded by creating another London college with a different and distinct Anglican ethos—King's College—in 1829. It was what every commuter recognizes—after waiting six hundred years for a new higher education institution, two then come along together.

These two different colleges then faced the same problem: how could they get university status so that their students could receive full degrees and not merely certificates of completion of a course? The solution was the creation in 1836 of the University of London, putting a university structure above them. This was a solution brokered by the Government, which took a leading role in the new University: indeed, it became a department of state virtually under the management of the Home Secretary and with the Exchequer subsidizing both Colleges.[30] The new university offered external degrees for students at both UCL and King's. That meant examining and teaching were separate from each other, as with Oxbridge colleges. And we can now start referring to 'Oxbridge', coined by Thackeray in his novel *Pendennis* in 1849. Up to then the term had not existed because it would just have meant university, as it still does for Sir Humphrey in *Yes Minister*. 'British democracy recognises that you need a system to protect the important things in life and keep them out of the hands of the barbarians! Things like opera, Radio 3, the countryside, the law, the universities... both of them.'[31]

Access to the University of London's external degrees was extended in 1858 to individual students across the country, regardless of where they were being educated. Then in 1867 University of London external diplomas and certificates were opened to women and in 1878 it became the first English university to admit women to full degrees. A similar federal structure was set up in the North with Victoria University as the external examining institution based in Manchester with affiliates in Liverpool and Leeds. (Durham had become a university in 1832 but degrees were only awarded to Anglicans.) The external degree was Victorian England's most powerful tool for extending access to higher education; it was an ingenious modern version of the Oxbridge collegiate model. You could set up a local college and teach for the University of London external degree. It provided a clear measure of the college's performance against a national standard and an opportunity for local people to get a well-recognized university qualification. Many of our universities today began in this way, gradually earning their freedom to grant their own degrees as they gained credibility—the last to do so was the University of Leicester, which gained its own Royal Charter in 1957. Even whilst the University of London external degree model was disappearing in the UK it took on a new life as a global qualification with students across the world, including Nelson Mandela whilst imprisoned on Robben Island. I long wanted to see the University of London external degree model once more readily available in the UK. This proved frustratingly hard to achieve.

The case for creating new colleges was set out by one of Victorian England's leading intellectuals. John Henry Newman had left the Church of England and had to give up his post at Oxford as a result. His mission was to set up a new college in Ireland devoted to teaching the Catholic population, who had no access to higher education. His Essay on the *Idea of a University* is his prospectus for this new institution. It is for teaching not research—the very opposite of the Humboldt model: 'the diffusion and extension of knowledge rather than the advancement'.[32] Newman was doing the same as Jeremy Bentham, creating a new university college to reach students who were debarred from Oxbridge, but his view of what it should be like was very different. He denounced the idea of students living in digs turning up after work at evening class lectures or 'Minerva by gaslight'.[33] Instead he wanted a collegiate community, devoted to learning for its own sake, which would shape the character of its members. But, whatever type of institution Newman or Bentham wanted, the important first step was to tear down the barriers so it could be created: the Victorians provided such an environment for the first time since the Middle Ages.

All this innovation opened up the question of the future of Oxford and Cambridge.[34] They were deeply opposed to reforming themselves and had created an apparently insurmountable obstacle to it by requiring new college fellows to take an oath opposing change to their statutes. Hence Melbourne had observed, 'universities never reform themselves: everyone knows that.'[35] It would take Government intervention, which began with the establishment of Commissions to inquire into Oxford and Cambridge. They were investigating what funds colleges had, how they were used, and what subjects were being studied. The Cambridge Commission proved to be less controversial, but many Oxford colleges flatly refused to accept the legitimacy of their Commission and refused to answer its questions. But the Commission painstakingly built up evidence of the damage done by ancient restricted fellowships: 'Men who are naturally well fitted to be country clergymen are bribed, because they were born in some parish in Rutland, to remain in Oxford as Fellows, until they are not only unfit for that, but for everything else.'[36] This meant funds were not available for creating new professorships in new subjects. Oxford's defenders lampooned the idea of a 'Government Inspector' to:

> ascertain what steps your college
> Is taking in its useful knowledge.
> Law, grammar, music, diatetics
> Optics with swimming and aesthetics...
> Colonisation, economics
> Brewing, baking and mnemonics...
> Algebra, skating and astronomy,
> With metaphysics and gastronomy.[37]

The Commission replied with a skilful appeal to Oxford snobbery, arguing that 'Unless...the clergy and gentry who are educated at the university are compelled or encouraged to keep pace with the progress of society at large, it is to be feared that from their ignorance of a branch of knowledge so generally diffused, they may find themselves placed below persons in many respects inferior.'[38]

The crucial figure was Oxford University's own MP—William Gladstone. Whilst he remained as opposed as the university to legislation then nothing could happen. But the Commission's report persuaded him and he became a powerful advocate of reform. In 1854 he brought forward his Bill to reform Oxford. Disraeli opposed the measure:

> you will have much to answer for if you place the Universities of this country under the control of the State. I believe that is the great point at question, and I cannot understand how Gentlemen opposite, though they may be University reformers, and though they may be extremely anxious to see great changes, especially in the University of Oxford, for reasons that may influence them—I cannot understand how they can consent to obtain such results at so costly a price as to place a University, which, of all institutions, should be independent and free, under the control and management of the State.[39]

Gladstone's reply was that really he was using state power to set the university free from constraints imposed by unreformed colleges. The Bill recognized:

> the necessity for parliamentary interference; the wisdom of using the instrumentality of a Commission for conducting and regulating that interference...and the necessity, for the interests of the University itself, of providing that the Commissioners shall be armed with sufficient legal authority to give effect to the views of the Legislature.... These are the real principles upon which this Bill has been framed.... it will, above all things, be an emancipating measure. It emancipates the

University from the influence of institutions which of itself it has no adequate power to correct, which came upon it from an extraneous source, and from which it is but fair that the power of the State should relieve it. It emancipates in like manner the colleges of fetters which they cannot of themselves undertake to break, bound as they are by conscience in many cases, and by strong social and personal influences in others.[40]

That argument—the Government as controller or emancipator—has run on ever since, and not just in higher education. Disraeli's worry that the State was a threat to autonomy is understandable. But on this occasion Gladstone was surely right because the universities, great institutions with a noble purpose, had been captured by a small self-perpetuating group and were not fulfilling any higher purpose. That tension between respecting their independence and challenging what we would now call producer power runs through this narrative and through my time as minister. Sometimes it was the most trivial questions which revealed the problem. Should the minister send a Christmas card to every Vice Chancellor? That would mean keeping a database of all their contact details. But it was for HEFCE to deal directly with individual universities, acting as a barrier between them and Government. We did not want to drift into endless ministerial communications to universities, treating them like schools and hospitals. I decided against the Christmas card list.

Gladstone's Bill banned oaths to block all change. The Commission had shown that the collegiate monopoly of instruction had led to decay of professorial teaching so the legislation also gave Government-appointed Commissioners power to merge and rationalize college fellowships to fund new University professorships and lectureships. Some of the most respected Oxford professorships, rich now with the patina of history, were actually created by these Government-appointed commissioners. This in turn promoted research as well as teaching. The Regius Professor of History at Oxford wanted 'men whose investigations could be perpetually adding to knowledge, not as mere conduits to convey it, but as fountains to augment its scantiness and freshen its sleeping waters.'[41] But the opponents of reform thought that something precious had been lost by clumsy Government intervention. Mark Pattison of Lincoln College (and probably the model for George Eliot's Casaubon) regretted that now Oxford was full of 'shop-dons' who were just supplying a demand from students for degrees, not true learning. 'The mischief of the Professorial system is that it implies a different idea of education...a cultivation which from its showy, available marketable character, is really an object of ambition in an age like the present.'[42] Mark Pattison thought deeply about Oxford and subsequently changed his views. But he was expressing fury at the creation of posts such as the Chichele Professorship of Modern History and the Waynflete Professorship of Moral and Metaphysical Philosophy because they were the result of Government intervention: looking back it does seem rather hysterical. One of today's critics of public policy on higher education, Stefan Collini, delicately excludes the role of Government in his account of this period by carefully reporting that 'the colleges of Oxford and Cambridge were reformed'.[43] He understates the role of Government in the nineteenth century and makes later Governments sound more malign and intrusive. As university minister I could not have got away with exercising the kind of power over a university which the Government's Commissioners did in the 1850s. In total there were ten Acts of Parliament regarding Oxford and Cambridge between 1854 and 1880.[44]

This period also saw legislation for the University of London external degree as well so it really was a great period of university reform, shaped at every stage by Government, without which it would not have happened. Reform of Oxbridge also led to reform of the public schools—which were not going to be able to continue to dominate access to Oxbridge unless they responded to this new focus on academic standards. It was an opportunity for them too. As Oxford and Cambridge opened up, the middle classes wanted their sons to go there and public schools expanded to meet that need. This is the era of *Tom Brown's Schooldays*, which was indeed followed in 1861 by *Tom Brown at Oxford*.[45] The impact of university reform on schools went far wider than this as Oxford and Cambridge also agreed for the first time to administer the exams of the Royal Society of Arts for students at local mechanics institutes. This engagement with school exams—which developed into the school certificate—is a further example of the enormous influence of universities on schools, which carries on to this day.

The surge in creation of new academic institutions in Victorian England meant there were several distinct routes to becoming a university. Sometimes it was local business leaders who set up a mechanics institute so their workers could get extra training or perhaps they were just trying to give something back to their community. But we must not be teleological—the institutions were not thought to be on a journey to becoming a university. Nevertheless it is a great story in which many towns and cities across England take pride. Here is the Bradford version:

> In the beginning was the Mechanics Institute . . . and the Mechanics Institute begat the Bradford Technical School and the Bradford Technical School begat the Bradford Technical College. The Bradford Technical College had dual offspring—the Bradford College of Art and Technology and the Bradford Institute of

Technology. The Bradford College of Art and Technology begat Bradford College which grew mighty in stature and became the Bradford and Ilkley Community College...but from the Bradford Institute of Technology issued forth the UNIVERSITY OF BRADFORD.[46]

There was a different route which began with the expansion of church schools which in turn meant more teacher training colleges. They were often linked to cathedrals. That college then became the core of a new university. Today they are revitalizing cathedral cities like Lincoln, Gloucester, Chester, Worcester, Winchester, and Chichester. I could sense within ten minutes of entering an English university whether its origins were as an Anglican teaching college or an urban mechanics institute, perhaps funded by a Methodist businessman. High Church or Low Church remains a palpable distinction between some of our universities.

For England's great industrial cities nothing less than a university of their own was going to be enough. The turn of the twentieth century saw a surge in the creation of these new universities. Manchester and Liverpool were part of federal Victoria University, a kind of University of London for the North. Birmingham leapfrogged them because of the vision and ambition of Joe Chamberlain. Victoria University then split into three—Manchester, Liverpool, and Leeds. Bristol and Sheffield were created as well. The six new civic universities secured an identity of their own when *Redbrick University* was published in 1943. The author was Bruce Truscot, the pseudonym of Edgar Allison Peers, a professor at Liverpool University. You can still see there the vivid red brick of the main building which he used to name the whole group, describing it as 'a hideously cheerful red brick suggestive of something...between a super council-school and a holiday home for children' (see Figure 1).[47] Truscot's popular and influential book was an astute and witty comparison of the big civics with Oxbridge. He argued they should be funded on the same scale as Oxbridge and in particular that they needed dedicated student accommodation so that they too could offer the full collegiate experience—he paints a picture of the earnest student commuting to university from home or from digs which is as different from Brideshead as one can imagine. (One character in Kingsley Amis's Lucky Jim who disappears from later campus novels is the provincial landlady.) Truscot observes that 'though the standards of the highest classes in Honours at Oxford or Cambridge are as high as, or even higher than, anywhere else, the lowest classes certainly descend to a depth reached nowhere else in the country. If he is at Oxford indeed, he need not even suffer from the disadvantage of the statesman who said he only travelled third class because there was no fourth; for

Figure 1. Liverpool University's red brick building.

our most ancient university can display the unique phenomenon of a Fourth Class in Honours.' Oxford and Cambridge were comprehensive universities (intellectually if not socially) which you could get in to 'either by being well-to-do or brilliant'.[48]

Truscot also captures the ambition of the professors at the Red Bricks, many of them Oxbridge products themselves, to escape from what they saw as the demeaning supervision of their universities by local worthies whose power came from the funding they provided: 'a modern university, which starts its life without endowments and on its running expenses generally has a deficit, cannot afford such luxuries as administrative idealism. Since much of the University's income is derived from municipal and commercial sources, municipality and commerce must have a part in university government.'[49] Exchequer funding gradually helped them weaken these local ties. 1889 saw the first Treasury grant of £15,000 for university colleges and the amount grew substantially after the First World War. Walter Moberly, who became the first full-time Chair of the University Grants Committee (UGC) after the Second World War, put the case in a way very similar to Gladstone a century earlier:

> in academic circles, the bogy of State-interference has been much overworked. There are other forms of interference more sinister . . . and these are often tolerated by academic tories. Indeed the State may approach the university as a rescuer

rather than a dragon. Indeed the dogma of freedom from external interference may be, and in the past often has been, used to deny internal freedom…State action is truly a hindrance of hindrances. It does not stifle, but augments or even creates, freedom.[50]

This argument shaped what became a national system with funding from the Exchequer combined with extraordinary freedom at the micro level—such as the academic power over admissions which we analyse in a later chapter—made possible because there was much less local control and supervision than in almost any other country. There were still local representatives on university governing bodies but their power was eroded and they became the dignified not the efficient part of the university constitution. This promoted what A. H. Halsey called Donnish Dominion—as he shrewdly observed: 'it was the nationalisation of funding which undermined the old redbrick and technical college concern for local industrial needs.'[51]

From a German century to an American one

German universities were the dominant force in the nineteenth century. Unlike England, Germany had kept on creating universities to meet new needs and as an instrument of competition between the different states. This in turn made it easier to create new academic disciplines. King George II would have found it very hard to found a new university in England, but back in Saxony he established Göttingen in 1734. England had been able to compensate for its universities being so few and so closed by drawing a disproportionate number of its professionals from the Scottish universities and also by an extraordinary proliferation of learned societies promoting a lively intellectual life outside universities. Nevertheless the lack of the organized research effort of which German universities were capable was one reason why England fell behind in the second science-based Industrial Revolution which got under way in the mid-nineteenth century with new technologies for steel-making, electricity generation, synthetic dyes, fertilisers, etc. German universities did not just excel in utilitarian knowledge: in *Middlemarch* Casaubon's rival says that Casaubon's great project of systematizing all the world's myths is doomed, because he cannot read German:

'If Mr Casaubon read German he would save himself a great deal of trouble.'
'I do not understand you,' said Dorothea, startled and anxious.

'I merely mean,' said Will, in an offhand way, 'that the Germans have taken the
lead in historical inquiries, and they laugh at results which are got by groping around
in woods with a pocket-compass while they have made good roads.'

Casaubon's 'key to all mythologies' is an early fictional example of a certain sort
of academic project—over-ambitious, bogged down in detail, and of course
never published.[52]

America looked to the two most successful European models for its
universities—Scotland and Germany. Johns Hopkins has a claim to be their
first explicitly research-focused university, deliberately based on the Humboldt
model. America's great research-intensive universities are a part of the biggest,
most diverse higher education system anywhere in the world. We tend to focus
on the Ivy League, the elite colleges of New England founded in Colonial
times, but these are, at least when it comes to undergraduates, tiny even compared with many British universities. The eight Ivy League universities have a
total of 60,000 undergraduates so they recruit around 20,000 a year. Manchester
University alone has about the same number of undergraduates as Columbia,
Harvard, Princeton, and Yale combined.[53]

As well as the Ivy League there are the seventy or so land-grant universities
founded by the Morrill Acts of 1862 and 1890. They were formed with the
explicit goal of contributing to the economic development of their home states,
with each state to underwrite 'at least one college where the leading object
shall be, without excluding other scientific and classical studies... to teach such
branches of learning as are related to agriculture and the mechanic arts'.[54] They
include major universities such as MIT and Cornell and Penn State. Both Ivy
League and land-grant universities are bases for extraordinary concentrations of
research. In addition there are liberal arts colleges which focus on teaching a
broad curriculum—the sciences are counted as liberal arts. They may not do
new research but they have an excellent reputation for scholarship—it is a
model which English universities might emulate were it not for the way prestige and rankings and funding depend on research performance. There are also
professional schools, commercial universities, and community colleges focusing
on vocational training. But as many American universities had quite low academic standards in the nineteenth century it was hard for them to offer the
necessary academic training to become a professor—for this ambitious young
American academics looked to Germany, where they studied for their PhD and
then returned to the USA with a qualification that would take them to the
summits of American academia. Figures like Charles Eliot, the great President
of Harvard from 1869 to 1909, had studied in Germany and brought back to

Harvard seminars, labs, graduate schools, and a new, more open scholarly curriculum, making it into a leading research university.

The First Congress of Universities of the British Empire held in 1912 was a response to the fear we were falling behind Germany and the US. Joe Chamberlain had been typically explicit about the challenge: 'university competition between states is as potent as competition in building battleships, and it is on that ground that our university conditions must become of the highest national concern'.[55] One response to the competitive challenge was the Congress's proposal for a postgraduate degree of doctor of philosophy. There was no such option in England, and research students, notably from the United States, were flocking to Germany. The creation of the DPhil in England was evidence that once again British universities had fallen behind and needed to catch up—as we shall see in Chapter Four.

The GI Bill and beyond: California dreamin'

The flight of academics, many of them Jewish, from Nazi Germany provided a profound intellectual stimulus for British and American universities. Nabokov's brilliant novel with its eponymous hero Pnim captures the experience of an accomplished and fastidious intellectual mastering a new language and a new culture, sometimes displaying childlike naivety and using English words in delicious new ways.[56] America then took an overwhelming global lead in higher education because of two great policy decisions. America's post-war GI Bill is probably the best known and most significant extension of access to higher education in history: 7.8 million veterans participated, of whom 2.2 million attended college, with the others getting other forms of training; by 1947 they accounted for half of all students enrolled in college.[57] The Bill did not just discharge an obligation to America's returning GIs: it transformed post-war America. Robert Putnam's important book *Bowling Alone* shows extraordinarily high levels of social engagement by this 'greatest generation'. One major reason is that they benefited from the GI Bill and wanted to put something back in return to help the generations coming after them. This is how the contract between the generations works. The GI Bill had enormous economic significance too—offering university degrees, many in STEM (Science, Technology, Engineering, and Maths) subjects, to young men who had already been fixing jeeps on the front line in Europe or leading platoons in the Pacific theatre gave America a generation of formidable businessmen and public servants with an extraordinary combination of higher education, practical expertise, and leadership skills. The states which had the most developed industries before the war got the big wartime procurement contracts. In these states more young men went straight into jobs in the protected defence industries and fewer went off to fight so they had fewer beneficiaries of the GI Bill. Their lack of graduates cost these very states their industrial lead after the war—an important case study showing that broad access to higher education can be even more valuable than vocational training tied to specific industries.[58] The second decision of equal significance was Vannevar Bush's advice to President Truman that America's great wartime scientific research effort should be continued in peacetime and should be based in America's universities. This combination of mass access to higher education together with university-based research is the origin of America's great clusters which drive American innovation to this day.

Britain did provide some educational opportunities to its returning service personnel. Kingsley Amis's young academic Lucky Jim Dixon has a very different attitude to his older student Michie than to his younger students because

Figure 2. Happy GIs with their admissions papers.

Michie 'commanded a tank troop at Anzio while Dixon was an RAF corporal in western Scotland'. Michie is the only student who actually presses Jim on the quality of his education, asking him for example the kind of question which some students may still struggle to put to their academic supervisor: 'Have you got that syllabus together yet, sir ... You know, sir, the list of stuff for your special subject next year. You said you were going to distribute copies to the Honours people if you remember?'[59] The medieval university of students comes to life if one thinks of it as populated with mature students like Michie not upper-crust teenagers going to Oxbridge. But instead of the soaring ambition of the GI Bill Britain's much less prominent Further Education and Training Scheme was restricted to 'suitably qualified candidates' whose education had been 'prevented or interrupted' by war service.[60] There was a brief surge of extra graduates but they were too few to make much of an impact on British society. 43,000 British ex-servicemen and women went to university, 1 per cent of those who served, whereas in America 2.2 million veterans went to college, 14 per cent of those who served. As previous participation rates were so low, even this modest British number temporarily increased the number going to university by two-thirds. There was one overwhelming reason for the enormous gap in participation between these two countries. America had already achieved widespread access to education up to the age of 18 so it was perfectly placed to transform access to higher education. That gave it pole position in what has been called the race between education and technology, in which educational progress matches and indeed drives technological progress.[61] One reason Britain fell behind key competitors such as the US in the post-war period is that we had fewer highly educated workers than they did.

In Britain the big educational advance of the Second World War was not a GI Bill but Butler's Education Act which for the first time ensured universal, publicly funded access to secondary education. (Some Americans thought it was legislation devoted specifically to the education of butlers—such were their assumptions about English society.) The only time I saw my grandfather in tears was when I passed the entrance exam for King Edward's School in Birmingham, which had become a direct grant grammar school under the Butler Act. My grandfather had passed the exam in the 1920s, but everyone had to pay fees then and his family could not afford to send him so he went out to work instead. Access to higher education only really became a major political issue when the Butler reforms together with the post-war baby boom interacted to create real pressure for places in the early sixties. That is why there is something oddly contrapuntal about the surges in higher education which do not fit into the

classic periods of expansion of the welfare state. The Robbins expansion in
higher education comes as a delayed consequence of the post-war settlement.
Similarly the next expansion of higher education comes in the late eighties and
early nineties, after Keith Joseph had introduced GCSEs in place of the O Level/
CSE divide and the numbers staying on at school after 16 surged.

California in the 1950s and 1960s above all embodies this optimism about the
growth in higher education. Clark Kerr served as President of the University of
California from 1958 until 1967 when he fell out with California's Governor
Reagan. He said he left office as he arrived, 'fired with enthusiasm'. His masterly
book *The Uses of the University* was first published in 1963, the same year as
Robbins, with which it is sometimes compared, as both were optimistic about
the growth of the university.[62] The book then grew by the accretion of lectures
a decade at a time—rather like the American higher education system it was
describing. It was continuously updated with new reports from the front line.
Kerr coins the term 'multiversity' as a description of the diverse roles discharged
by a big modern general-purpose university, sometimes very diverse indeed—
'sex for the students, athletics for the alumni and parking for the faculty'.[63]
Indeed, car-parking is rather a theme, encapsulating this sense of the modern
university as a disparate coalition not a cohesive institution. Universities may
look to outsiders like large, centrally managed organizations but from the inside
they are, in another of Kerr's witticisms, 'a series of individual faculty entrepreneurs held together by a common grievance over parking'.[64] His multiversity
was supposed to be one institution carrying out a multiplicity of roles. This is
hard to achieve because, as we shall see, the pursuit of some goals such as
research excellence or a very selective entry can come at the expense of others
such as more applied research or local recruitment. There is a lot of interest on
both sides of the Atlantic in Arizona State University at present because it seems
to have got closer than most to achieving those disparate and perhaps even conflicting goals.[65] Usually these multiple functions of universities tend to get discharged by different types of institutions within an overall higher education
system such as California's. Actually California's individual universities were not
just one type of sprawling multiversity. The Californian Master Plan of 1960,
which Clark Kerr helped to draft and which remains to this day part of the
legal framework for higher education in the state, allocates distinct roles to different types of institutions, from the research-intensive University of California
taking the top 12.5 per cent of students through the California State University
and then the community colleges, with arrangements for transfers between
these different types of institution. Kerr's account was appealing because he

embraced expansion with such palpable optimism whilst at the same time showing how different types of university would each have their place in his new system. That optimism about the California model is now in retreat.[66]

Successive waves of new institutions in England had distinct characteristics too. After the Oxbridge monopoly was broken in the 1830s England saw the creation of colleges with diverse missions including delivering education and training to meet the needs of the local economy. Many of these new institutions were denounced at the time just as alternative providers are now because they were seen as threats to the established model of a university. But the incomers were then gradually changed by membership of the club—like that long journey taken by some academics from student rebel to membership of the Athenaeum. The Oxbridge model commands such prestige that it has proved hard to sustain a sense of diverse university missions—instead almost all of England's higher educational institutions aim for the prestige which comes from academic research and the rituals associated with it. Our assumptions about what is a good or bad university; the measures used in the league tables; and the link between the class background of students and the prestige of universities all come together to create powerful external forces shaping the behaviour of universities. Just as motor-cars become more similar as different designs are tested in wind tunnels and face the same headwinds so universities facing these same external forces start to look more alike. I would be told, for example, that universities should work much more closely with local employers or deliver higher-level apprenticeships whilst the very people urging such policies regarded the universities which actually did that already as 'bad', unlike the 'good' universities focusing on academic research of global quality. That is why those of us who believe in diversity of missions, as I do, must do everything possible to liberate us from a single scale for judging what makes a good university.

California seems to deliver diversity of missions without the oppressive sense of social and academic hierarchies which bedevils the English universities. Some British academics have advocated the Californian tripartite model with distinct roles allocated to different parts of the publicly funded higher education system and, crucially, far greater flexibility than in England for moving between them.[67] But in California these roles are allocated and enforced by the state's legal framework. English universities have much more autonomy so there is no state-imposed barrier which stops mission creep. The high levels of university autonomy in England are one of the factors exposing them to such pressures to conform with a single scale of values because there are fewer countervailing forces protecting them. The last mechanism we had for this in England—the polytechnics—lost their distinctive status in 1992 and gained university autonomy. There is a trade-off between autonomy and diversity.

The definition of a university and of higher education

Herbert Butterfield described the Whig interpretation of history as writing 'to impose a certain form upon the whole historical story, and to produce a scheme of general history which is bound to converge beautifully upon the present—all demonstrating throughout the workings of an obvious principle of progress...'.[68] This progressive view of history is out of fashion nowadays but it does capture the story of higher education in England over the past two centuries. It is indeed a story of growth and expansion in which more people are brought into higher education, just as classic Whig political history was about the inclusion of more people in our parliamentary democracy.

The growth in the number of students has been accompanied by the creation of new universities both in Britain and around the world. Successive waves of new universities bring more diversity into the system. That is partly because the extra students have different needs from the ones who were going already. It is also because new institutions reflect the values and preoccupations of their time. We can think of today's wide range of universities as successive levels of archaeological deposits with their distinctive identities shaped by their historical origins. But there is a deep tension between on the one hand this growth and diversity and on the other hand a single dominant benchmark of what is best about a university. Whilst new entrants may do things differently their distinctiveness may be eroded under pressure to conform to a single scale of values.

Globally there are around 10,000 institutions calling themselves universities and perhaps around 20,000 institutions of higher education. Of these about three thousand produce at least 200 or more published research papers per year. Two thousand generate a thousand or more per year.[69] British and American universities are at the pinnacle of league tables such as those produced by the *Times Higher* because of the excellence of their research and the prestige which that brings. If we cannot be proud of our universities then there really is not much we can be proud of. But these league tables are organized around one idea of a university. It is the classic residential very selective research-intensive university, preferably with ivy growing on the walls. Enoch Powell captured it rather well: 'A university...is an institution which is peculiar in a precise and definable way. It is a place where there live side by side in mutual intercourse persons whose life is dedicated to the pursuit of knowledge for its own sake, regardless of the consequences or applications of the knowledge thus acquired....It is a place to which resort, during the formative years of early adult life, those desirous and capable of learning how people engaged in the pursuit of knowledge for its own sake go about their business.'[70]

That sort of account captures my own experience of a university education years ago and it was marvellous. It strikes a chord but it also sets a trap. It takes the experience of a certain sort of university education and turns it into the authoritative definition. It starts with our historic and prestigious universities and from them distils the essence of a university. We shift from *is* to *ought*, from descriptive to normative, and that account of a university becomes the standard against which all contemporary universities are judged. Many are then found wanting. That leads straight into narratives of betrayal and ruin, which is often attributed to the very growth of higher education which Whiggish optimists celebrate. It looks as if the critics are uncomfortable with the reality of mass higher education.

We are caught between starry-eyed growthmanship, relaxed about the wide range of modern universities, and bleak accounts of the failings of HiEdBizUK.[71] We need an account of what it is to be a university which is neither so loose that anything counts nor so stringent that it ends up left behind and irrelevant like Pattison's hysterical attacks on Gladstone's Victorian reforms of Oxford. We can already see the outlines. A university is an independent corporation devoted to higher education. It is a community of scholars and students. Its autonomy, evidenced above all in the right to award its own degrees, sets a university apart from other forms of higher education. For education to be higher it must be at the frontiers of knowledge: that does not mean it must include research but at least its teaching needs to be informed by new discoveries and current arguments. A useful definition of levels of higher education emerged from the Bologna exercise in which European governments from Norway to Kazakhstan agreed a broad framework for higher education so that academic credits can be recognized and transferred across their countries (the European Credit Transfer and Accumulation System or ECTS). It is not an EU exercise, though the EU is involved. Britain did not stay aloof, and indeed the then universities minister Tessa Blackstone played a major role in this exercise.[72] As a result of our engagement the definitions reflect our model. A 'first cycle qualification' is a Bachelor's degree awarded to students who 'have demonstrated knowledge and under-standing in a field of study that builds upon their general secondary education, and is typically at a level that, whilst supported by advanced textbooks, includes some aspects that will be informed by knowledge of the forefront of their field of study'. In addition they should have competences such as 'devising and sus-taining arguments and solving problems within their field of study' and 'ability to gather and interpret relevant data to inform judgements that include reflec-tion on relevant social, scientific or ethical issues' and have developed 'learning skills that are necessary for them to continue to undertake further study with a high degree of autonomy'.[73] Then there is a Master's, and above that a doctorate, which are second- and third-cycle qualifications. Behind the flat bureaucratic prose there is an important recognition of a shared European heritage in higher education and a belief that, just as in the Middle Ages, mobility of students and academics between diverse institutions is part of that heritage.

Alternatively one can look to Britain's parliamentary draughtsmen for the meaning of higher education, where definitions have to be unpacked like a series of Russian dolls to discover that higher education is education at more than A level—perhaps illustrating the origins of A levels as exams leading to university.[74] This rather unsatisfactory attempt at defining higher education may be one rea-son why there is no definition of a university in British legislation.

We saw in the Introduction there are about 130 British universities—closer to 150 if you count the individual colleges of London University. There are also other education institutions which are not called universities but provide higher education, such as Further Education Colleges. The UK has 2.3 million students including postgraduate and oversea students, so on average a university may have 20,000 students, though as there are quite a few small institutions the median is closer to 14,000. A small university will have a budget of perhaps £200m, a medium-sized one, £400m, and large ones up to £1bn more.[75]

There is a deep academic literature on the idea of a university. It was prob-ably at its richest in Germany during the late eighteenth and early nineteenth century. Kant envisaged the university as the place where reason and critical thinking could be deployed freely, with pre-eminence for the study of philosophy. Humboldt saw the university as the place where the fundamentals of German nationhood could be understood, notably through the study of the German language as part of philology. In Britain there was a tradition from Arnold to Leavis of placing the study of English literature at the heart of the university and that itself was linked to an idea of the cultivation of a certain type of indi-vidual. More recently the post-modern revolution has questioned the status of any sort of canon and as a result challenges the prestige of the university, though this argument itself emerges from the university—Lyotard's book *The Postmodern Condition* was originally a report for the Council of the Universities of Quebec.[76] I will briefly return to these issues in the Conclusion but the focus of this book is more on the university as an institution.

The focus on the character of the university can come at the expense of understanding the environment within which they function. Autonomy is clearly a prerequisite but it becomes an unreal fantasy if it means operating in a vacuum. We can understand universities better if we understand the environment within which they work and how it shapes their behaviour. My role as minister was to understand universities as part of a system and to try to reform that system so as to bring out the best in them. That is not giving universities orders but understanding the rewards and incentives and peer pressures which influenced their behaviour and trying to improve them. So next we must look close up at how the English system of higher education works and how it shapes our universities.

TWO

Robbins and After

Changes before Robbins

The early 1960s saw the biggest transformation of English higher education of the past hundred years. It is only matched by the break-up of the Oxbridge monopoly and the early Victorian reforms. It will be forever associated with the name of Lionel Robbins, whose great report came out in November 1963: he is for universities what Beveridge is for social security. His report exuded such authority and was associated with such a surge in the number of universities and of students that Robbins has given his name to key decisions which had already been taken even before he put pen to paper.[1]

In the 1950s Britain's twenty-five universities received their funding from fees, endowments (invested in Government bonds which had largely lost their value because of inflation since the First World War), and 'deficit funding' from the University Grants Committee, which was a polite name for subsidies covering their losses.[2] The UGC had been established in 1919 and was the responsibility not of the Education Department but the Treasury, which was proud to fund these great national institutions directly. Like museums and art galleries, higher education was rarefied cultural preservation for a small elite. Public spending on higher education was less than the subsidy for the price of eggs.[3]

By 1962 there were 118,000 full-time university students together with 55,000 in teacher training and 43,000 in further education colleges.[4] This total of 216,000 full-time higher education students broadly matches the number of academics now. Young men did not go off to university—they were conscripted into the army. The annual university intake of around 50,000 young people a year was substantially less than the 150,000 a year doing National Service. The last conscript left the army in the year Robbins was published. Reversing the balance between those two very different routes to adulthood was to change

Britain.[5] It is one of the many profound differences between the baby boomers and the generation that came before them.

Just over half of students were 'county scholars' receiving scholarships for fees and living costs from their own local authority on terms decided by each council. Prospective students had to apply to their chosen university individually, and separately to their local authority for student finance, with no guarantee of success. The Butler Act had made provision for discretionary student support but it was not mandatory: 'it is not unknown for an applicant to be refused an award so near the beginning of the academic year that the university department which he had hoped to enter cannot fill the vacancy thus created'.[6] There were wide variations between local authorities. In the early 1950s, the number of county scholars for every 10,000 people varied from under two in Leeds to over twenty in Cardiganshire and the average award ranged from £96 in Bury to £276 in Gloucester.[7] Such large differences could not be explained solely by the characteristics of the local population. And the Butler Act was not broadening access to Oxbridge: 'as late as 1961–2 just 39% of Oxford undergraduate entrants came from state schools and a mere 25 percent in Cambridge'.[8]

So there were a small number of universities and individuals applied directly to each one with unpredictable discretionary funding for students from local authorities. These three crucial and interdependent features shaped the structure of English higher education. They were all about to change. The system of student funding was the first to be reformed. An official committee led by Sir Colin Anderson recommended a new system in 1960.[9] The Anderson Report was published on the same day as the Beatles first performed under that name and both were in their way to change the lives of young people—though the Beatles are perhaps rather better known.[10] British residents with two A-level passes (or equivalent) admitted to first-degree (or comparable) courses should receive generous awards for maintenance and tuition that were consistent across the country. The Anderson committee reached no conclusion about whether the grants should be administered locally or nationally. Once implemented by the Education Act of 1962, they were administered locally but according to a national formula. Part of the reason for this was to protect university autonomy, as they seemed less directly answerable to Whitehall when some of the public funding flowed through arms-length local government. English local authorities only finally lost their residual role in assessing students for financial support in 2011/12, by which time it had come to look like an unnecessary third administrative function on top of the fee loans provided by the Student Loans Company and the grants to universities from the Higher Education Funding

Council for England (HEFCE). The change from the old discretionary system of student support to a standardized and more generous one improved access to university and also improved the lot of students: 'for a whole generation financial problems became a minor concern of university life'.[11] When older people now say they had a generous grant to fund their time at university they are referring to this system inaugurated in 1960. And crucially this reform happened just before the great expansion associated with Robbins. It was designed generously on the assumption that higher education was a small elite system, even though some growth was expected. It is a classic example of the importance of the order in which decisions are taken in determining the outcome.

For the first time there was a nationally mandated system of student funding. This was matched by another crucial change: university applications were put on a national basis for the first time as well. The Universities Central Council on Admissions (UCCA) was created in 1961. Historically, there had been little need for a centralized admissions service because supply and demand for university were modest and fairly evenly matched. Although each individual could apply directly to as many institutions as they liked, multiple applications were rare before the Second World War. But intensifying competition for places increased the number of applicants making multiple entries. This became unmanageable for applicants and institutions: as one Vice Chancellor complained in 1957, 'no one interested in the selection of students could pretend that the present situation was other than one of deplorable chaos'.[12] One problem was that students did not know if they would get a discretionary grant— that was tackled by Anderson. The other problem was that universities did not know who would turn up at the start of term because they did not know if a student had received a separate offer from another university and was going there instead and that was tackled by the creation of UCCA. Students got a single nationwide application process but in return for that they could not two-time universities any more. The new clearing-house was a big change for universities too. Lord Fulton, the first Chairman of UCCA, later recalled: 'In that critically important decade of the 1950s there was ample evidence of the frustration and injustice suffered by the young as a result of the existing methods of selection for entry. The right to choose their students was generally accepted as one of the three chief pillars of university autonomy. Would the individual universities continue to go it alone or would they find ways of collaborating to ease the burdens on the young without sacrifice of fundamental principle? We know the answer now: but it was not so clear at the beginning.'[13] The scheme took effect properly for entry in 1964. Membership by universities was voluntary but

even Oxford and Cambridge, which had initially stood aloof, joined for the
1966 entry round onwards. By 1968, UCCA was handling 600,000 applications
from 110,000 candidates for eighty institutions. In 2015 its successor, the
Universities and Colleges Admissions Service (UCAS), handled 2,900,000
applications from 720,000 candidates for 370 institutions. This includes 590,000
UK-domiciled applicants to 150 UK universities.[14]

Student demand was growing because of the improved access to free secondary education under the Butler Act. Robbins observed that 'every increase of
educational opportunity at one level leads almost at once to a demand for more
opportunity at a higher level'.[15] On top of that, the baby boom after the war
was clearly going to lead to a further increase in demand in the mid-1960s. The
UGC started detailed work on the merits and consequences of university
expansion long before Robbins. Indeed the idea had been around since the end
of the war. The Barlow Committee of 1945 urged a big increase in science
graduates, and was frustrated that Oxford and Cambridge did not wish to
expand, though the civics were willing, and so in a section entitled 'New
University Institutions' proposed 'early consideration should be given to the
foundation of at least one new University . . . there is some reason to believe that
a number of able teachers from the existing Universities would welcome the
opportunity of re-enacting in the twentieth century the exodus which is said
to have led to the foundation of Peterhouse in the thirteenth'.[16] It was a nice
historical parallel which captures the spirit of Asa Briggs at Sussex or A. D. Lindsay
at Keele, though oddly Robbins failed to make this point.

At the start of the 1960s, the UGC agreed around 170,000 university places
would be necessary by the early 1970s. Although this was a lower figure than
Robbins later proposed, it alone was a massive challenge for the existing struc-
ture because existing universities did not have the will or the means to deliver
all the extra places. New universities were going to be needed—and fast.
Universities were established in Sussex (1961), Keele (1962), East Anglia (1963),
York (1963), Lancaster (1964), Essex (1964), Kent (1965), and Warwick (1965).
These were all planned by the UGC before the Robbins Report: indeed, not a
single further new university was created in England as a result of Robbins.[17]
Previously, universities had emerged bottom up; a college with deep local roots
would seek to graduate to full university status. From 1849 to 1949 every new
university in England had begun teaching for the University of London external
degree before it got its own degree-awarding powers. The UGC's approach was
radically different. According to Michael Shattock: 'This was a unique operation
in British higher education history, where the state intervened to create wholly

new universities, which had no back history of predecessor institutions, on green field sites.'[18] They got university title straight away with no requirement to show any kind of track record—an approach which was highly controversial when the Government permitted probationary degree-awarding powers without any prior record in its 2017 legislation. It could be seen as a conservative measure, however. Some continental European countries met the post-war surge in demand by going instead for massive increases in the size of their traditional universities: this changed them fundamentally, whereas creating new universities alongside existing ones did not.

These three decisions all reinforced each other. Previously civic universities recruited their students locally, students applied somewhat haphazardly to a host of institutions, and you needed local funders to set up a new institution. It was hard to create a new university if you did not know what demand there was or whether local authorities would fund places at it. Now you could immediately slot in to the UCCA process and your prospective students would know they would be funded. And UCCA could only operate efficiently because there was no longer the double jeopardy of not knowing if you would get a means-tested local authority grant to fund a place. Macmillan's Government had created a national system of higher education, but crucially still based on university autonomy and student choice. National government set the terms of the financial support and local government paid it out, but universities still had the power to decide who to admit and so in practice determined who received the support. They had created a single market in higher education, very different from the localist Continental model and from the American state-based system. It is one of the few in the Western world where students have an open, nationwide choice of universities with a uniform and transferable funding entitlement. It is an unusual and surprisingly efficient system, created in a few years in the early 1960s, which continues to function to this day. It all happened before Robbins and with little evidence anyone in Government deliberately designed it as a complete system. To them it must just have looked like the old Oxbridge model writ large.

Robbins and expansion

Many key changes to English higher education which we associate with Robbins therefore emerged before Robbins as the result of a series of ad hoc decisions. There was no account of it as a whole system. It was all very well in practice, but what about the theory? There was a lack of clarity over the status of, and relationship between, universities, colleges of advanced technology, colleges of education, regional colleges, and others. Now that public funding was surging into higher education there had to be better public accountability as well. The official remit to Robbins asked him therefore to look at the 'pattern of full-time higher education...and whether any modifications should be made in the present arrangements for planning and co-ordinating the development of different types of institution'.[19] It was supposed to be about how to manage this new, growing system, which, almost inadvertently, had just been created. Robbins, however, ranges much wider.

Robbins begins by setting out four aims of higher education. First, because it is too often undervalued, is 'instruction in skills'. Secondly, what is taught should be taught in such a way as to 'promote the general powers of the mind' and should operate on a 'plane of generality'. His third principle is 'the advancement of learning'. This is research. It need not be conducted in universities but university teaching is better when it does: 'the process of education is itself most vital when it partakes of the nature of discovery'. The fourth aim is that university should transmit 'a common culture and common standards of citizenship'.[20] Robbins then sets out what we now think of as the Robbins Principle—as important now as it was then—that 'courses of higher education should be available for all those who are qualified by ability and attainment to pursue them and who wish to do so'.[21] The inclusion of attainment alongside ability was his way of sticking to the convention at the time that two A levels should be the minimum requirement for university entry. In the 1980s that formulation was subtly but significantly shifted with the deletion of any reference to qualifying so it just became 'be able to benefit from'.[22] There was a further shift by David Cameron in the 2015 Election to an exuberantly liberal formulation: 'We will ensure that if you want to go to university you can.'[23]

The Committee chaired by Robbins were faced with the key problem of estimating the number of places that might be needed in the future to ensure that their principle was met. They considered two possible approaches. The first, which they defined as 'manpower planning', involved the consideration of 'what supply of different kinds of highly educated persons will be required to meet the needs of the nation'. Such an approach would involve making calculations—or to put it less charitably, guesses—about the future structure of British industry and the sorts of skills companies might need in the future. Manpower forecasting of this sort bedevils many discussions of education and skills. Robbins was a distinguished free-market economist who just did not believe such forecasts were credible. The Committee found 'no reliable basis for reckoning the totality of such needs over a long term'.[24] Instead they opted to look at the problem from the opposite end—considering what the demand was likely to be from suitably qualified young people over the next twenty years. They focused on the number of young people qualified to go to university, not spurious economic forecasts of future jobs. This is a far better approach. It recognizes, for example, that the flow of graduates can itself change the structure of an economy, and indeed we will see in Chapter Five that the latest research does suggest increases in graduates have made possible a move to more decentralized business structures. It puts the individual centre stage. It still seems fresh and radical today. The Report is clear: 'We express our deep conviction that any future estimates of need should proceed from our own basic principle that all who are qualified to pursue full-time higher education should have the opportunity of doing so.'[25] And the research for Robbins' Report showed clearly that they were nowhere near any limit to the pool of ability which would make future expansion undesirable.

The combination of the increase in the number of young people as a result of the baby boom ('the bulge') and the increase in the proportion staying on at school after 16 and getting qualifications making them eligible for higher education ('the trend') drove a big cumulative increase in Robbins' forecast demand for university places.[26] Robbins is being conservative and realistic by assuming that the same proportion of suitably qualified students should get to university and challenges his critics why they believe a lower proportion of school leavers with A levels should go to university in future. Robbins projected that student numbers would almost triple to 560,000 within twenty years (including 350,000 in universities).[27] His bold prescription for expansion is what his Report is best known for. The actual number of enrolments in 1980 was 535,000—pretty close to Robbins' projections. Looking back in 1980 on this growth, Robbins said: 'I doubt very much if there has been any general lowering of admission standards.'[28] He would, however, have been surprised by the distribution of that growth. As Table 2.1 shows, one big difference was where people chose to study. There was less growth in universities and rather more in other higher education institutions than he expected. In 1980–1 there were 39,000 fewer enrolments in universities than his Report projected, and 16,000 more in other institutions such as polytechnics, teacher-training and further education colleges.

The Report makes two key assumptions about this growth which proved hard to reconcile in practice. First, it assumed a substantial proportion of these extra places would be in science and technology. (The growth already planned by the

Table 2.1. Students in full-time higher education, 1938–9 to 2014–15. Full-time students, both undergraduate and postgraduate, from all domiciles (UK, EU, non-EU).

	Universities	Other institutions	All full-time higher education
Pre-Robbins time series			
1938/39	50,000	19,000	69,000
1954/55	82,000	40,000	122,000
1962/63	118,000	98,000	216,000
Post-Robbins time series			
1970/71	235,000	221,000	457,000
1980/81	307,000	228,000	535,000
1990/91	370,000	377,000	747,000
2000/01	1,210,000	77,000	1,286,000
2010/11	1,677,000	62,000	1,739,000
2014/15	1,697,000	115,000	1,812,000
2015/16	1,741,000	110,000	1,851,000
Robbins projections			
1980/81	346,000	212,000	558,000
Difference from actuals	39,000	−16,000	23,000

Source: HESA and David Willetts, *Robbins Revisited: Bigger and Better Higher Education* (Social Market Foundation, October 2013). The big fall in students in 'Other institutions' after 1990/91 is a result of polytechnics becoming universities. From 2010/11 figures for universities are derived from the HESA Student Record. From 2000/01 to 2010/11, 'Other institutions' denotes students studying for HE-level courses at further education colleges. From 2014/15, 'Other institutions' also includes undergraduate students at alternative providers who are studying on a HEFCE designated course, which allows UK/EU students access to the student loan system. These figures only became available in 2016 and are currently classified as experimental statistics. In both 2014/15 and 2015/16 figures for alternative providers exclude postgraduate students and students on non-designated courses, as this data is not currently collected.

UGC was to be two-thirds in science and technology.) Secondly, as women were particularly under-represented at university and their forecasts for growth rested on forecasts of better school attainment, this would mean a particularly dramatic surge in the number of female students (from 68,000 in 1962 to 253,000 in 1980).[29] Together these two assumptions required a massive shift of girls towards science and technology. This may have been right and desirable but it required a change in cultural attitudes and patterns of school teaching which could not be delivered in the time available. In the event, Robbins correctly forecast a big increase in female students but many more of them went into arts and humanities, which is where overcrowding and resource pressures proved most intense. Indeed, successive generations of policy makers underestimated the demand for arts and humanities subjects, which therefore tended to be over-crowded and underfunded. There is a correlation between affluence and pro-pensity to study arts/humanities subjects, with countries with higher per capita GDP tending to have a higher proportion of students in humanities and social sciences. This is the truth behind the vivid personal remark by John Adams: 'I must study Politicks and War that my sons may have liberty to study Mathematicks and Philosophy. My sons ought to study Mathematicks and Philosophy, Geography, natural History, Naval Architecture, navigation, Commerce and Agriculture, in order to give their Children a right to study Painting, Poetry, Musick, Architecture, Statuary, Tapestry and Porcelaine.'[30]

However, policy makers are often keen to encourage young people into STEM subjects because of anxieties about national capabilities in these areas. This was the time of Sputnik and Harold Wilson's White Heat of the Technological Revolution when precisely such anxieties were widespread. Churchill expressed them in his distinctive orotund style: 'In the last ten years, the Soviet higher technical education for mechanical engineering has been developed both in numbers and quality to an extent which far exceeds any-thing we have achieved. This is a matter which needs the immediate attention of Her Majesty's Government...if we are—not to keep abreast—but even to maintain our proportionate place in the world.'[31] The paradox, neatly brought out by Michael Teitelbaum, is that such anxieties can themselves create a boom and bust cycle in STEM subjects which weakens them. The increase in capacity for science and technology went ahead of demand, meaning entry standards fell—affecting perceptions of some of these disciplines which it took years to recover from.[32] Sometimes what the critics are really saying is that they wish the country was a different kind of economy, an argument put by Kenneth Arrow at the time: 'careful reading of such statements indicates that the speakers have in effect been saying: There are not as many engineers and scientists as this nation should have in order to do all the things that need doing such as main-taining our rapid rate of technological progress, raising our standard of living, keeping us militarily strong, etc. In other words, they are saying that (in the economic sense) demand for technically skilled manpower ought to be greater than it is—it is really a shortage of demand for scientists and engineers that concerns them.'[33]

The shift in the gender balance in higher education has carried on. In the 1960s only 25 per cent of full-time students at UK institutions were female. But in 2015/16 they were in the majority—at 55 per cent. The number of women studying has grown by a larger proportion than the number of men across every subject. Women are still under-represented in sciences (maths and physics) and the applied sciences (computing, engineering, technology, and architecture), but the margin has narrowed from the 1960s when only 3 per cent of students studying 'applied science' were women. The most dramatic increase is in medicine: in the 1960s only about 25 per cent of medical students were women, but this has risen to 60 per cent.[34] Now more women enter university than there are men even submitting a UCAS form. This is a remarkable achievement for women, who were outnumbered in universities by men as recently as the 1990s. It is also the culmination of a longstanding educational trend, with white working-class boys in particular finding it hard to recognize that the old manual jobs their fathers did are disappearing and that they need educational qualifications to get a decent job.

The demographic background now is the opposite of the one facing Robbins. There was a mini-peak in the birth rate in the early 1990s after which it fell for a decade, reaching a low point in 2001 after which it recovered. Figure 3 shows we are now in ten years of decline in the number of 18–20-year-olds, which began in 2010 and will continue until the early 2020s. Maintaining the absolute number of people going to university broadly constant is consistent with a slight increase in the proportion of young people going. However, from 2021 onwards the 18–20-year-old population is projected to start increasing again and by 2035 the number of 18–20-year-olds will be almost 200,000 higher than in 2011.

One criticism of Robbins is that he did not think through the implication of his own expansion plans for the balance of teaching and research. If academics maintained their previous balance between teaching and research there would be a big expansion of research too. It would be in disciplines where teaching demand was growing unrelated to any wider research priorities. If that were to be avoided Robbins needed to set out how research priorities could be set separately. Or he would need to show how a new cohort of academics focused mainly on teaching could be recruited. The Report does not get much beyond exhortation on these key issues. The creation of a dual support mechanism for university research (with funding from the University Grants Committee and the Research Councils) in the Science and Technology Act of 1965 was the beginning of an answer to these questions. The creation of UK Research and Innovation is the latest attempt to answer them.

Although Robbins is remembered above all for his advocacy of expansion this is not the whole story. One of the many reasons for meeting this increased demand by creating new universities, not simply expanding existing ones, was the opportunity this provided for innovation in education. Robbins was worried

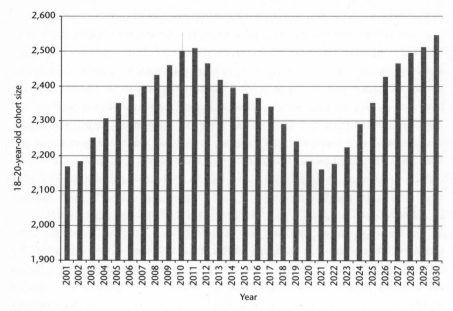

Figure 3. 18–20-year-old cohort size 2001–2030, thousands

Source: UUK-provided figures. Figures to 2012 are based on ONS mid-year population estimates. Figures from 2013 are based on the ONS population projection.

about the quality of teaching and wanted a new focus on this. In particular he was frustrated by excessive specialization in English education and wanted to promote something broader, closer to what was offered at an American liberal arts college. The UGC chairman Keith Murray said of the case for more universities, 'It was one third numbers and two thirds new ideas.'[35] The only new university not created from scratch was the University of Keele, which had been created after the war. When A. D. Lindsay retired as Master of Balliol in 1949 he became the first Principal of the University College of North Staffordshire, aiming to create an experiment in broad education in the liberal arts on the lines of PPE (Philosophy, Politics, and Economics), which he had pioneered at Oxford. That spirit lived on after his death in what became the University of Keele, with a distinctive four-year course, opening with a year's study of Western civilization. Asa Briggs had similar ambitions for Sussex with a curriculum offering 'new maps of learning'.[36] The UGC brought this out in a report of their own a year after Robbins, which recognized 'the need for more experiment in the structure of degree courses, in the content of curricula, in methods of teaching and in university organization: on the academic side, we had declared our main interests to be in the general broadening of undergraduate curriculum, in the breaking down of the rigidities of departmental organisation, and in the strengthening of the relationship between teacher and taught'. The idea was 'to get away from the old single subject honours degree'.[37] Most universities could not afford the Keele extra first year on Western civilization but instead did plan a taught Master's fourth year. But these high hopes for the new universities were thwarted by the student unrest of the later 1960s and then by financial pressures. The trouble was that the UGC and local authorities would not fund this extra year. That obstacle may at last now be disappearing. We will return to this crucial issue in Chapter Fourteen.

How to pay for Robbins—a fifty-year argument

Robbins only devotes seventeen out of three hundred pages of his Report to the question of how to pay for all this—probably one of the reasons his report is celebrated for its civilized tone. Everyone afterwards, persuaded by his eloquent arguments for growth in student numbers, has had to wrestle with the awkward questions of how to fund it. He avoided the problem by assuming 4 per cent annual economic growth—an assumption which solves most financing issues. And he has some vaguely uplifting words that money will of course be found for something as important as this. The Report does, however, consider the pros and cons of a loans scheme. The first argument in favour is about the distribution of burdens: 'The recipient of the subsidy is being put in a position to command a higher income in virtue of taxes paid, in part at least, by those whose incomes are smaller.' So it is only fair to expect graduates with higher incomes to pay back. The second argument is an appeal to 'morals and incentive': 'It is said that the student financed by grants is sometimes apt to take his privilege for granted: and that this may have as a by-product the lack of any particular sense of obligation and need to work. By contrast, the student financed by loan is likely to have a greater sense of individual responsibility.'[38]

The Report also sets out two counter-arguments. First, Robbins argues, 'the connection between higher education and individual earning power can be overstated'. This is actually an argument for income-contingent loans, which graduates only pay back if they are earning above a minimum level. The second objection is the effect on young people if they 'emerge from the process of education with a load of debt'. He is particularly worried 'that British parents would be strengthened in their age-long disinclination to consider their daughters to be as deserving of higher education as their sons'. The Report concludes this discussion by pointing out: 'If as time goes on the habit [of going into higher education] is more firmly established, the arguments of justice of distribution and of the advantage of increasing individual responsibility may come to weigh more heavily and lead to some experiment in this direction.'[39] The committee's minutes reveal that they came close to including a line in the Report stating that loans might become 'acceptable in about ten years' time'.[40]

A number of economists made submissions to the Robbins Committee recommending graduate contributions. A submission by the economist A. R. Prest was particularly pertinent. Prest outlined five options for making funds available to students and the possible recovery of those funds from those who benefited: unconditional grants; loans with generous repayment terms; subsidized saving schemes; income tax deductions for fee payments; and finally students entering into a contract to repay a specified proportion of their lifetime earnings. Even though he described the second option as loans with 'low interest and/or generous repayment terms' he was clearly considering mortgage-style loans rather than loans whose repayments were income-contingent. He ruled out this mortgage option on the grounds that the potential burden of repayment would deter those from poor backgrounds, given that the size of each monthly repayment would be linked to the size of debt rather than salary. Thus repayment terms would be the same for low-earning graduates and someone who becomes a millionaire. Prest dismissed the first four options and advocated the fifth as the most promising option. This had the merit of linking repayments to earnings. The income-contingent loan scheme we have ended up with is somewhere between Prest's second and fifth options: it is limited by the actual cost of higher education like the mortgage model, and it is related to earnings like the equity stake in earnings model. We will look at this further in the next chapter.[41]

In a lecture the year after the Report came out Robbins admitted: 'I have little doubt that, as time goes on and the advantages of higher education are more generally perceived, and the burdens of financing its expansion are more severely felt, there may easily come a change in attitudes such that the equitable arguments for a considerable replacement of grants by loans will become practically relevant.'[42] And in his 1980 book *Higher Education Revisited* he explicitly backs an income-contingent loan policy, saying: 'It is a matter of regret to me, personally, that I did not at the time sufficiently appreciate the advantages of the Prest scheme, in spite of the fact that it had already been promulgated. My own inclination tended definitely against the policy of subsidy.' And he warns: 'the post Second-World War mythology of the bottomless public purse dies hard'.[43]

Polytechnics

Robbins envisaged a big, diverse network of universities. Clark Kerr, running the California system at that time, and another of higher education's great heroes, had a similar vision. But we have seen how the California system explicitly allocated distinctive roles to different types of university. This requires a constraint on university autonomy which would have caused real problems in England: it would have risked universities being incorporated in the public sector. Indeed, one reason why Robbins did not include teacher-training colleges in his university model was that he feared they were under such high levels of supervision from the Department of Education that they could pull higher education into the public sector. If that happened a small number of independently funded universities, certainly including Oxbridge, would have opted out, leaving England with a higher education system divided much like our schools are. Robbins believed in university autonomy and this was reinforced by his aim of keeping a single national system of higher education—keeping Oxbridge in was, as it remains to this day, one of the biggest protections of autonomy for other universities too. But the dilemma is that an autonomous system with the cultural power of the Oxbridge model was unlikely to deliver the diversity which Robbins also wanted to see. Autonomy and diversity are in tension. This was the very astute criticism by Martin Trow in California, who argued that Robbins had created 'an inverted pyramid with the elite institutions [shaping] the characteristics of the bulk of British higher education' in which all universities were to aspire to be like Oxbridge instead of carving out space for other models.[44] That was to lead to the biggest challenge to the Robbins model in the creation of an alternative type of institution outside his model, an alternative type of higher education so significant that to this day its demise is regretted by some—the polytechnic.

The Robbins Report was published in November 1963, just at the time the Conservative Government was convulsed with the succession to Harold Macmillan. One of Alec Douglas-Home's first decisions as Prime Minister was to endorse the Report, as did Harold Wilson, then the leader of the Opposition. But when Labour entered Government the following year and Tony Crosland became Education Secretary they broke one of Robbins' crucial recommendations and included higher education in the Department for Education for the first time— with a complicated arrangement of a separate Permanent Secretary which did not last for long. This was the high point of national planning and scares over skill shortages. The Robbins model of forecasting future student numbers with a sublime disregard for supposed national economic needs for specific skills was very frustrating for the incoming Government. Every minister for universities must have thought at some point that the job would be so much easier if you could turn a tap and produce ten thousand extra engineering students or five thousand more students learning a foreign language. Indeed in some countries you can, but you can't do that with English universities. So one can see why it was very tempting for Crosland to create a new parallel form of higher education within the public sector, doing all the things ministers wanted them to do. In particular they were to deliver technical and vocational higher education on a model very different from Oxbridge. That is why in a speech at Woolwich in 1965 Tony Crosland announced a binary divide in higher education with public sector polytechnics alongside the autonomous universities. He astutely identified the weakness of a higher education monoculture shaped by the prestige of Oxbridge.

> The Government accepts this dual system as being fundamentally the right one, with each sector making its own distinctive contribution to the whole. We infinitely prefer it to the alternative concept of a unitary system, hierarchically arranged on the 'ladder' principle, with the Universities at the top and the other institutions down below. Such a system would be characterized by a continuous rat-race to reach the First or University Division, a constant pressure on those below to ape the Universities above, and a certain inevitable failure to achieve the diversity in higher education which contemporary society needs.[45]

To give polytechnics a fair chance of recruiting new students no new universities would be created for at least ten years. Robbins had recommended the creation of six new universities in addition to those already planned before his Report. His proposals were abandoned only eighteen months after his Report was published.[46] Only one new university was created directly as a result of his Report—Stirling in Scotland, though Colleges of Advanced Technology were also converted to university status.

The polytechnic was to be a distinctive form of higher education. It would belong to the local community and the local authority and so meet their local employment needs. It would be more vocational and practical. As part of the public sector polytechnics could be asked to comply with national training priorities. The binary divide and refusal to allow further colleges to complete the long journey to university status was an English attempt to create a version of the California system, in which different roles are allocated to different players in the higher education system. The trouble is that you can't describe this for England without thinking of John Cleese, Ronnie Barker, and Ronnie

Corbett in the Class sketch, which was broadcast within a year of Crosland's announcement. Its three individuals represent three classes but it could equally have been about three types of higher education—Oxbridge, the rest of the universities, and polytechnics. Indeed, this is the burden of a powerful speech by Lionel Robbins in the Lords on the issue:

> I regard it as a supreme paradox that a government which is pledged to abolish artificial hierarchy and invidious distinctions in the schools, should, at the same time and under the same Secretary of State, be actively engaged in preventing the elimination of artificial hierarchy and invidious distinctions in higher education... Is it not extraordinary that a minister who is bending his powers to the diminution of the anxieties of the 11 plus should at the same time be pursuing a policy which must make the anxieties of the 18 plus even more formidable than they are now?...I would appeal to him to think again...before continuing on a course which can bring no pleasure or benefit but to a few snobs at the centre and bullies at the periphery.[47]

That powerful Augustan epigram at the end is still relevant to the bring-backers today.

The polytechnic model was eventually abandoned by Kenneth Baker and John Major and polytechnics secured university status in 1992 with the power to award their own degrees. That decision is still controversial and I was regularly urged to bring them back—usually for other people's children. But even if polytechnics had survived they would have faced the same competitive pressures as the rest of higher education—with status coming from research and with student demand for STEM courses not matching their interest in the humanities and social sciences. The binary divide was obstructing that progress to incorporation as a university which the polytechnics aspired to. I concluded that instead of arguing over the name 'university' we should recognize that there are different types of university and they come in different shapes and sizes. There were times when this seemed hopeless—when a media commentator or ministerial colleague just assumed an ex-poly was a bad university when I had been there and knew how well it taught its students and how effective its vocational courses were. Often the very people who said they wanted to bring back polytechnics dismissed those universities which were like polytechnics. They could not look behind the name and see the value of the work they were doing. Sometimes I thought that paradoxically the polytechnics had not all lost out to Oxbridge—their values of engagement with the needs of the local economy and practical vocational training were spreading to other universities

just as the challenge of the Redbricks changed Oxbridge. The trouble is that it
is hard for outsiders to see how much of what happens in universities is vocational.
That is partly because all these vocational courses end up with an honours
degree as against other forms of higher education qualification. The OECD
says we are weak compared with other countries in our post-secondary vocational sub-Honours offer—10 per cent of young people doing qualifications
such as HNCs and HNDs as against 20 per cent in the US and more than a
third elsewhere.[48] This is the result of a funding system which rewards degree
study. It is one of the reasons why I wanted to promote alternative providers
delivering these sorts of qualifications—an issue for Chapters Ten and Eleven.

It is not easy to achieve any kind of public recognition of a distinctive 'polytechnic' mission for universities. The excellent Janet Beer, then Vice Chancellor
of Oxford Brookes University, formerly Oxford Poly, was asked about this by a
Commons Select Committee when she appeared before them in 2009 together
with the Vice Chancellor of Oxford University.[49] They were asked if 2:1 degrees
in history from their two universities were of equivalent standard. Janet Beer
could not really answer because she was not going to say one was inferior but
neither could she say they were the same—a university degree is not like an
A level and uniform across the country. What could she have said? She could
have said that there is not a standard national university leaving exam and that
degree classifications were not intended to imply a uniform standard, though the
External Examiner system was intended to maintain basic standards. She could
have accepted that the prior attainment of her students tended to be lower and
this influenced their absolute levels of performance but this did not mean that
they did not advance as much as students at that other university in Oxford. She
could have explained the diversity of missions: Oxford Brookes is a different type
of university from Oxford and actually more like an American liberal arts college.
She could have gone on to say that her only regret is that there are no metrics
which capture what Oxford Brookes does to high standards for its distinct
mission—there is more than one way to be world class. BMW has its Mini plant
in Oxford. It also makes BMW luxury saloon cars in Munich. A Mini is not a
bad BMW: it is a different kind of car and the same goes for our universities.

Policy since Robbins

We have seen that Robbins had been set the challenge of coming up with a
better model for managing higher education as a system—after the brilliant but

rather haphazard improvisation of policy over the previous few years. The higher education system was supposed to work with a model of rational five-year planning—the quinquennial review. But that system collapsed under financial pressures—the periodic fiscal crises affecting successive Governments together with high inflation eroding the value of the allocated funding. This led to swings in policy between growth and retrenchment. In fact policy after Robbins looked more like the behaviour of an impatient man in a shower who alternates between freezing and scalding as he tries to get the temperature right.

The optimists who saw the value of higher education went for growth in numbers. The most conspicuous of these was Margaret Thatcher, who as education minister in the Heath Government put forward probably the most expansionary plan ever proposed by the Education Department. Her White Paper also had the unusual merit of looking at higher education as part of the wider education system.[50] She closed more grammar schools than any other education secretary and hoped that the new comprehensives would increase the number of young people able and eligible to go to university. She aimed at nothing less than the continuation of the Robbins expansion for another decade—expecting that about 22 per cent of 18-year-olds would be going into higher education by 1981 compared with 15 per cent in 1971 and 7 per cent in 1961.[51] But things were very different in the early years of her premiership. Her successor as education minister, the anguished Keith Joseph, was not interested in growth. He was the only Conservative education minister to propose and try to deliver a fall in student numbers. This partly reflected the fall in the birth rate from its peak in 1964 to its low point in 1976. But also he was trapped in a funding model which held the resource per student broadly constant, and therefore he controlled public spending by reducing numbers. Kenneth Baker as Education Secretary broke this log-jam by shifting to a model in which universities just received the marginal cost of extra students. He unleashed another great surge in student numbers in the late 1980s and early 1990s.[52] But expansion came at the cost of a significant fall in the funding available for each student. The result was a decline in the standards of higher education. This created increasing desperation amongst Vice Chancellors as they saw governments happy to preside over increases in student numbers but unwilling to pay for them. It threatened to become an awkward issue in the 1997 Election and so the then Education Secretary Gillian Shepherd agreed with David Blunkett, her opposite number, to commission Ron Dearing to review the whole subject, reporting after the Election. We will pick up the messy story of how these financial issues were addressed in the next chapter.

There was one other issue on which Robbins had robust views—where responsibility for universities should lie in Whitehall. Universities had long had a special status and fallen under the Treasury rather than the Department of Education. There was a buffer between the individual universities and Whitehall—the University Grants Committee set up in 1919 which eventually became the Higher Education Funding Council and was finally abolished in 2017. This served to keep ministers out of invidious and sensitive decisions about how much funding should go to individual universities. The obvious option has always seemed that universities should be part of the Education Department. But Robbins did not want them to be bossed about as if they were schools. Instead he saw them as part of the cultural fabric of the country and envisaged that they might go into a department rather like today's DCMS (The Department of Culture, Media and Sport) alongside museums and art galleries. However, the incoming Labour government gave the Department for Education responsibility for universities in 1964. Almost half a century later, Gordon Brown, as Prime Minister, transferred them to the short-lived Department of Innovation, Universities and Skills, after which they found themselves included in the new Department for Business, Innovation and Skills. That decision was endorsed by David Cameron and then reversed by Theresa May, who put universities back in the Department of Education. There is no right way of doing this. But the research and innovation role of universities is of growing economic significance and is not properly understood by the Education Department so it remains with the Business Department. This means that responsibility for the work of universities is now split between two departments—not a happy arrangement.

What might have been?

What if different decisions had been taken in those crucial years in the early sixties when our current system of higher education was taking shape? We have seen that one distinctive feature of our higher education is that it is predominantly a boarding-school model—and might indeed have been influenced by the tendency of the English elite to send their children away to public school, so it would be rather peculiar to come back home for their university study. Instead students are on average 91 miles away from home.[53] The national maintenance grant put every student in a similar financial position to a scion of the English gentry: 'if students were not of independent means the State had to make them appear to be so by giving financial support... which would enable them to conduct themselves as gentlemen . . . with the most expensive system of residence in the western world'.[54] This has long been an unusual and expensive feature of the English system—with the recent shift from maintenance grant to loans significantly reducing public spending but maintaining the cash support to students. In response to this two low-cost solutions are regularly proposed. First we are told students should stay at home and go to their local university. But given the diverse missions and prestige of our universities it is hard to see why parents and students should just settle for being allocated to their local university, which may not teach the course you are after. (You can't, for example, train to be a vet in Wales.) Then we are told, in that case can we at least have a two-year course, and in 2017 the fee regime was made more flexible to permit this. But our higher education is already rather cursory compared with most other countries: individual students are doing too little not too much (a point we will return to in Chapter Eight on the student academic experience). Perhaps, however, it could be an American model in which you do two years at a college and then the second two years at a full university. Some finish after two years with a qualification well short of an honours degree.

Behind these policy options there is indeed a different route which we could have taken. Most systems have choice at some level. Ours comes when the young person chooses both university and subject of study—a very unusual combination of big decisions which we will consider further in Chapter Fourteen. But what if instead of inventing UCAS we had instead invented a credit transfer system? We went for a highly efficient nationwide system for one big decision about where to go to university and what to study. Neither decision need be so big and final. You could start by going to your local university but build up credits which are themselves recognized and usable across the system. You could do a foundation degree or a two-year degree at your local university and then transfer on. This is the holy grail of some education reformers such as the late David Watson. It has proved hard to introduce. One reason is that it requires some universities explicitly to accept a subordinate role in the system as two-year colleges sending their best students somewhere else for an honours degree: few would voluntarily choose that role given the way prestige shapes our system. But there are other reasons too. At the moment the current system provides a crucial moment of decision for a student about where to apply, but after they have been accepted the university holds all the cards: it is harder to change institution than in most other countries. In fact the power is even more specifically with the academic department which recruited you, as it can also be hard to change subject. The university will be reluctant to relinquish this power. This raises difficult questions about how interchange-able courses at different universities really are. It is another example of that dilemma which runs through this book. Are we looking here at producer power erecting a tiresome barrier to competition and mobility—a similar issue as moving from one energy company to another? Or is it instead a genuine reflection of differences between different institutions? Surely in this case it is the latter.

Without the concurrent decisions of the Macmillan Government to imple-ment a national grant system and of universities to institute a proper national admissions system, the UK could have gone down the Continental route of local higher education, with grants determined by local authorities and with universities mainly serving their local communities. Instead, what developed was a national sector of autonomous universities with nationwide recruitment patterns and national student support rules: you could apply for full-time undergraduate study relatively easily anywhere in the country, with a generous LEA grant in tow. It was a crucial divergence from the localist and regionalist models common in many countries, including the USA, France, and Germany. England remains an outlier compared to its European neighbours in this and other respects.

Above all, before Robbins it was not clear whether or not England even had a national *system* of higher education. After Robbins, no one doubted it. And it is a system which can still be seen today. This was the basis for the further expansion with which his Report is associated. Although there have been various twists and turns in the half century since (including the temporary establish-ment of the binary system), the system of English higher education today is clearly recognizable as the one Robbins and his immediate predecessors devised, with one mass university system populated by highly autonomous institutions deciding who to admit and on what terms. The key question he had not resolved was how to pay for this expanding higher education system and that is what we must now turn to.

THREE

How to Pay for it

The problem of paying for higher education left by Robbins

Paying for university education has been one of the most acute and politically fraught challenges in public policy. Both the Blair government and the Coalition had some of their smallest Parliamentary majorities for votes on this issue, such as the emotions it arouses.[1] It sparked violent protests in November 2010 (see Figure 4) and was seen as one of the issues boosting support for Jeremy Corbyn in the General Election of June 2017. It touches such a raw nerve because people worry that we are imposing costs on the younger generation which previous generations of young people did not have to bear. Having written a book myself about the importance of fairness between the generations I well understand why this matters so much.[2] One can only tackle this anxiety if the new way of funding higher education is better for the younger generation than any likely alternative. When I was Opposition spokesman before 2010 I said that the test of any changes we brought in would be if they were in the interests of students and that is the test I tried to apply throughout my time as minister.

Through the 1970s, 1980s, and 1990s higher education faced persistent financial crises. Higher education was one of the public services facing particularly rapid growth of demand. For the amount of public spending per student to be maintained there would have to be very large increases in total public spending on higher education. Expecting such big increases in spending for any programme was difficult enough. But at the same time higher education was not a political priority. Indeed this view was reinforced by universities. I would encounter protesters on university campuses demanding free higher education whilst inside the university's own social scientists repeated the conventional wisdom that it was the early years that really mattered and the Vice Chancellor told me he could not do any better on access for disadvantaged students unless

Figure 4. Students protesting, 2010.

schools improved and that should be the priority. Moreover, as it is usually the quality of its research that makes a university's reputation, pressures to maintain research funding were greater than for teaching. Teaching quality is also harder to measure so it was difficult to see if funding cuts were doing damage. All this added up to a dangerous tendency for teaching in universities to be very vulnerable to public spending cuts. The Dearing Report estimated that during the period 1976–96 public funding per student in higher education fell by more than 40 per cent.[3] The powerful pressure for more young people to go to university was not matched by any great willingness from governments or taxpayers to fund them so the resource for teaching each student was falling. This trend worked inexorably over the last forty years, though it was particularly acute when student numbers doubled in the late 1980s and early 1990s and funding for students halved. By 2005, when Blair's fees and loans came in, the resource for educating each university student was a third of what it had been in 1965. Students lost out as a result—with a university education that was overcrowded and underfunded.

Kingsley Amis famously declared in advance of the Robbins Report that 'more will mean worse'. Had he just been talking about the pressure of student numbers on university finances he would have been right—more did mean worse. By contrast the far more popular school budget increased steadily over this period. The IFS (Institute for Fiscal Studies) estimate that during the 1980s and 1990s 'primary school spending per pupil grew by about 2.2% in real terms per year on average, whilst secondary school spending per pupil grew by about 1.5% per year'. And over 'the 2000s, the growth in primary and secondary school spending per pupil significantly accelerated to around 5% per year in real terms'.[4] Table 3.1 shows the contrasting trends. Whilst funding per school pupil more than doubled over the fifteen years from 1990, the funding for a university student fell by a third, before the introduction of fees halted and then reversed the decline.

These cuts in public resource behind each university student, year after year and decade after decade, meant larger and larger seminars, more crowded

Table 3.1. Resources per student in real terms, 2012–13 prices

	HE spend per student (Grant + fees)	Spend per primary school pupil	Spend per secondary school pupil
1989–90	£9,400 (after which steady decline)	£2,100	£3,500
1990–1	£8,700	£2,100	£3,500
1991–2	£8,200	£2,200	£3,500
1996–7	£6,300 (low point after which it stays in mid-£6,000s)	£2,300	£3,400
2004–5	£6,600	£3,800	£5,000
2005–6	£6,800 (start of increases)	£4,000	£5,100
2006–7	£7,000 (when fees come in)	£4,100	£5,300
2007–8	£8,000	£4,200	£5,500
2008–9	£8,500	£4,400	£5,700
2009–10	£8,500	£4,400	£5,700
2010–11	£8,400	£4,300	£5,700
2011–12	£7,900 (Coalition low point before fees come in)	£4,700	£6,300
2012–13	£8,200 (Coalition fee increase starts to come in)	£4,700	£6,400
2013–14	£8,500	£4,800	£6,300
2014–15	£9,000 (highest real resource per student since 1991–2)	£4,900	£6,300

Source: HE figures derived from institutions' reported income and student numbers, FTE, accessed through Higher Education Information Database, Higher Education Statistical Agency, January 2017. They include HEFCE grant and also fees and loans funding higher education which are not public spending. They exclude capital funding. Chris Belfield, Claire Crawford, and Luke Sibieta, 'Long-run comparisons of spending per pupil across different stages of education', Institute for Fiscal Studies (2017), figure 6.1a.

Table 3.2. University student–staff ratio (SSR) and school
pupil–teacher ratio (PTR) over time

	University SSR	School PTR
1980/1	9.1	18.2
1990/1	11.4	17.3
2000/1	18.1	17.9
2010/11	17.4	15.6
2013/14	16.2	15.4
2014/15	15.4	15.5

Source: SSR and PTR 1975/6–2003/4: 'Further, higher, better' (Section 26) UCU
Submission to the Government's second comprehensive Spending Review
(September 2006), 138. SSR for 2004/5–2014/15: UUK-provided based on HESA
HEIDI data covering all of UK. The PTR relates to all LA maintained primary
and secondary schools in England. PTR for 2004/5–2014/15: 'Table 17a: Pupil:
teacher ratios and pupil: adult ratios in state funded schools', Main Tables
SFR21/2016 School workforce in England: November 2015 released June 2016.

lectures, less well equipped laboratories and libraries, minimal direct engagement with academic staff, and less academic feedback. The deterioration in
student–staff ratios in universities compared with improvements in pupil–
teacher ratios in schools shows what was going on: 2000/1 was the year the
number of university students to staff overtook the school ratio (Table 3.2).
But the table also shows how Blair's funding reforms and then the Coalition's
stopped the decline and the university student-to-staff ratio became once
again slightly better than in schools (not that the absolute figures are really
comparable: it is the trends which are significant).

This was a betrayal of the younger generation in which almost everyone was
complicit from governments (who boasted of increasing students but did not
properly fund them) to universities (who got on with their research) and sometimes even students themselves (who did not mind being left to their own
devices so long as there was a well-paid job when they graduated). That was the
real crisis in higher education. And to their credit it led universities themselves
to press Government for a better way of funding them. The campaign began in
the run-up to the 1997 General Election. The universities came to recognize
that they needed a source of funding which was not public spending and hence
not always at risk of cuts. They threatened to introduce their own emergency
top-up fees of £300 per student in 1997 unless something was done, which
would have turned higher education into a sensitive election issue. That is why
the Dearing Enquiry was set up on a cross-party basis by the then Education

Secretary Gillian Shephard at the end of the Major Government. It proposed for the first time a graduate contribution of about £1,000 to cover 25 per cent of the costs of higher education, structured as a loan to be repaid as a proportion of the graduate's income ('income-contingent') rather than the fixed repayment mortgage-style loans which had been introduced on a small scale already. There were also maintenance grants for low-income students together with a loan scheme as well. David Blunkett tore up Dearing's key proposals on the day the report was published, proposing instead a means-tested fee of up to £1,000 payable up-front without a loan to cover it, though increasing the maintenance loan by a matching amount. (This peculiar move was partly driven by the fear that EU students could claim fee loans. But they faced a more stringent residency test to be eligible for maintenance loans. The NUS also pressed hard for fees to be means-tested.) This failure to provide a loan explicitly to cover the fee was a major defect. It set back the higher education funding debate because it made the fee an amount actually paid by a student rather than a way of defining a subsequent graduate contribution. Tony Blair finally grasped the nettle with a £3,000 fee covered by an income-contingent loan after he had been persuaded by the universities that they needed a new financing model. Gordon Brown was opposed and despite being Chancellor promoted opposition to the Government's own Bill. Blair only bought him off with a promise not to fight a third Election—a promise he subsequently broke. The Conservatives voted against the reforms in what was one of the low points of our years in Opposition. Labour fought back with the formidable ministerial team of Charles Clarke and Alan Johnson, launching a charm offensive ('I'm the charm and he's offensive', said Alan Johnson). There was a genuine fear that young people would be put off by these 'fees' but fortunately the evidence came in to show the fear was misplaced.

The model of income-contingent loans introduced by Blair is not unlike the one which Robbins came to wish he had implemented all those years ago and which the Coalition then extended in our own reforms. Indeed as soon as the financial crisis broke in 2008 it was clear to the more far-sighted Labour figures—such as Peter Mandelson—that there were going to be more public spending cuts and higher education would not be exempt from them. So he wanted to repeat Gillian Shephard's device and set up a review which would identify a way forward and straddle the Election due in 2010—moreover the 2004 Blair legislation required one after five years. He consulted me as the Shadow Secretary of State and I cleared my approach with David Cameron and George Osborne. Peter Mandelson and I agreed the terms of the reference of the review and that John Browne should chair it. I recognized that this could well mean that fees would have to go up. The National Union of Students (NUS) were worried about this and were trying to get parliamentary candidates to sign up to a pledge not to increase fees.[5] The Liberal Democrats were signing up to it—as their policy was to abolish fees despite several of their senior members, such as Vince Cable and David Laws, recognizing that this was unaffordable. My worry was that Labour would double-cross us and their candidates would all sign up to the pledge too: I discussed this very frankly with Peter Mandelson, who assured me that this would not happen and he stuck to his word. I wrote to Conservative candidates strongly advising them not to sign the pledge.[6]

The Liberal Democrats may well have gained a few seats from both major parties as a result of their willingness to sign this pledge when neither of the major parties would.[7] After the Election as the Coalition Agreement was negotiated we recognized that the Lib Dems had a serious problem because of the pledge they had signed earlier and so this was one of the very few areas of Coalition policy from which they got a special exemption.[8] We thought they would deploy it and just stay out of the whole issue. But there was a particular problem for Vince Cable as the policy was led by the Department for Business, Innovation and Skills (BIS), where he was Secretary of State, and indeed higher education was a substantial part of the total BIS budget. It would have been peculiar for him—and very uncomfortable for me—if I had been bringing such controversial proposals to the Commons with him sitting silently beside me and not voting for them himself. And over that summer of 2010 all the senior Liberal Democrats came to understand that, faced with pressures to cut public spending, increased fees and loans was the best and fairest way of financing higher education. I very much regret that they suffered such political damage from doing the right thing. I still can't quite understand why they did not activate the Coalition agreement from early on—they may have thought there was some ingenious alternative option and got sucked into the policy discussions before they discovered the inescapable truth of what had got to be done. But we are now in the position that all three parties when faced with the dilemma of how to finance higher education have ended up with this model first proposed fifty years ago. Churchill's observation when America entered the Second World War could equally apply to the political parties when it comes to funding higher education: 'eventually they do the right thing, but only after first exhausting every other possibility'.

Lord Browne's report was crucial in shaping the debate.[9] He had identified how we could save public spending without universities losing money—about

£4,000 per student of the teaching grants which HEFCE paid to universities could be replaced by higher fees and loans. The question was how high fees and loans should go. I argued for a high figure as I believed university teaching was underfunded and this was an opportunity to put more resources into it. It would mean we would stay true to the promise only to make changes which benefited students if the result was more cash for their education—and also more cash for their maintenance—none of which they would have to pay up-front. I also wanted to get on with it briskly as my experience was that these kind of decisions only got harder. Moreover we were under pressure from the Treasury to deliver the cuts early and were already at risk of imposing funding cuts on universities before the extra fee income came through.

There was an objection that this shift from grant to loans disadvantaged Humanities as all their public funding went whereas some other disciplines kept some teaching grant. But actually the Humanities in particular benefited from the changes. There were four different bands of grant funding to cover teaching costs of different subjects. They were not a judgement on their relative value but just compensated subjects which cost more to teach than others—labs are required for teaching chemistry but not for philosophy. The lowest-cost courses were in Band D, disciplines such as History or English, which only received a HEFCE teaching grant of £2,325 per student. Adding in the fee loan of £3,375 (the original Blair £3,000 up-rated for inflation) made £5,700 of teaching resource for Humanities students under the old system before our changes. Removing all their grant and substituting a fee loan of £9,000 meant extra money for teaching the Humanities, even after allowing for the allocation of about £1,000 of fee income for access programmes. The other bands received more teaching grant under the old system, up to about £13,335 for B and A which covered medical and veterinary teaching costs. These other bands all lost about £4,000 of grant each. They too gained from a fee income of £9,000: their fee loan income went up by more than the grant they lost but they did not gain as much as the Humanities because they lost more grant. Overall between 2010/11 and 2014/15 HEFCE teaching grant for all subjects declined from £4.7bn to £1.5bn, delivering a saving in public spending of over £3bn. At the same time the income of universities from fees rose by almost £5bn, from £2.6bn to £7.3bn.[10] So we were able to deliver one of the biggest single cuts in public spending of the Coalition whilst at the same time increasing the total cash going to universities for teaching and access by £1.5bn. That's not bad.

We have at last ended up with a model which properly delivers and funds what the great reformers of the early sixties envisaged. Unlike many other

systems it has student choice at its heart. It leaves with universities the responsibility of deciding who they should admit and allocates funding according to
the choices of students. And as it is a graduate repayment scheme it does not
count as public spending—this is not some strange device but reflects the reality that the money provided by the Exchequer should be repaid later. As it
took most funding of higher education teaching out of public spending, it
made it possible to boost funding per student. It also meant the Coalition
could afford to end student number controls and at last deliver the Robbins
principle of access for everyone with the aptitude to benefit from higher education. This model has been endorsed by the OECD as one of the few that
ensures a sustainable system. Andreas Schleicher, director of education and
skills at the OECD, describes the English system thus: 'The higher education
financing system, I would say, is certainly efficient, probably fair and the returns
to individuals are still very, very substantial. Despite its heavy reliance on private financing of higher education, the UK has made a wise choice—it works
for individuals, it works for government.'[11]

The new English system of funding higher education: graduate repayment

There is substantial private payment but it is not direct private payment up
front by students. It is a graduate repayment scheme which requires no up-front
payment by students for their tuition. There are fees but these are paid for with
a loan which never actually goes through the student's hands—it is provided
direct to the university by the Student Loans Company. In addition maintenance
loans help with living costs. These loans for fees and maintenance are not like
commercial loans. They are a means of setting an amount that graduates will be
expected to pay back at the rate of 9 per cent on earnings above £21,000 per
year. This repayment threshold is substantially higher than the £15,000 set
under the previous Blair reforms. Increasing the repayment threshold significantly reduced a graduate's fixed monthly outgoings, though of course graduates are expected to pay back more in total and will do so for longer. If, for
example, a graduate is earning £25,000, the repayments are 9 per cent of the
£4,000 she earns above the threshold—i.e. £360 per year or £30 per month.
On the old formula it would have been 9 per cent of the £10,000 of earnings
above the old threshold—i.e. £900 per year or £75 per month. The Blair
arrangements were front-end loaded—with repayments coming from young

graduates whereas our new arrangement shifted repayment out into more prosperous middle age.

If you just tried to use commercial loans to fund higher education you would face the problem that a bank would lend to Janet, privately educated and on her way to a well-paid career in banking, but not to John, a care leaver who wants to be a social worker. They might also want to know what financial assets a student and perhaps their family could pledge as security for the loan. Indeed, banking regulations require banks to assess the risk of lending to each potential customer and exclude those they think are risky. This is very different from the approach we should take to funding higher education: it should, in principle, be available for all citizens who have secured a place at university. The current arrangements are close to that principle (the major exception is students who already have an equivalent level qualification). The original Student Loans Company is called a company because it was originally set up in the late eighties with the expectation that the clearing banks would co-own it and lend the funds. They backed out because the universal scheme was so different from their usual commercial lending practices.

Although this graduate repayment scheme is based on something called a loan it is nothing like a commercial loan. If a child of mine left university owing £25,000 on credit cards or bank overdrafts I would be very worried indeed. On the other hand graduates leave university with the prospect of paying on average around £800,000 of tax during their working lives and that does not worry us.[12] The difference is that the overdraft is a fixed stock of debt that has to be paid back come what may. By contrast we think of income tax as a flow of future payments that will only have to be paid if and when our income rises, making that flow of payments manageable. The graduate repayments are much more like the future income tax payments than the overdraft, but people don't always realize that. The crucial step is to think of it not as a fixed pile of debt but as a flow of payments because they are so responsive to what happens to your earnings. So, for example, I was regularly told that this so-called debt would damage a graduate's ability to get a mortgage as some of her borrowing capacity would have been used up already. But it isn't a fixed loan that has to be repaid and mortgage lenders do not treat it as such. Instead it is usually covered by lenders in their calculation of fixed outgoings, like energy bills or income tax.

Our changes in 2012 raised the repayment threshold to lower the fixed outgoings with the deliberate aim of easing the burden on young graduates getting started in the housing market. And I never had a single constituency case of a graduate coming to see me to complain about her repayments even when set at the lower limit of £15,000. It is the repayment threshold and rate which matter. As the independent money expert Martin Lewis put it: 'There's too much focus on the headline amount being borrowed—a mostly irrelevant figure. What really counts is how much needs repaying and that depends solely on what's earned after university.'[13] So if for example a Government cut the maximum fee to £6,000 or £3,000 but did not change the repayment terms they would not be changing the repayments and hence the disposable incomes of any young graduate. They would simply be enabling them to pay off their loan sooner in their working lives.

If you accept the argument so far then you might observe with some exasperation that we made a rod for our own backs by getting ourselves trapped in the misleading language of fees and loans when it is really a graduate contribution scheme. The Australians have done better, calling their programmes HELP (Higher Education Loan Programme) or HECS (Higher Education Contribution Scheme). We did look at this in government but the language of fees and loans had already taken hold. It was how the structure we inherited was described. If we had tried to change it we would have been in danger of having an official name and a separate colloquial description. I did not wish to go back to the days of the poll tax, which ministers were supposed to call the community charge so the audience on Question Time would give a ragged cheer if a minister forgot and lapsed into talking about the poll tax.

That prompts a further question. Why have all this palaver of fees and loans at all? Why not just have a graduate income tax as a fair way of expecting graduates to pay back? But this takes you back to all the problems of funding higher education out of public spending. And hypothecating a tax has always proved hard to sustain. Moreover, universities would have no funds for a decade or more whilst the Government waited for the graduate tax to come in, as it would be hard to tax people who had already graduated and with the tax authorities not knowing which taxpayers were graduates anyway. If you introduced it for all graduates today you would first need to identify the nation's graduates—an intrusive and cumbersome process. Finally, you lose the direct financial link between the university and the student. Under the fees and loans system the student is bringing resource with him or her to the university of their choice. That direct link is one of the biggest single prizes of this model. It is a kind of repayable education voucher. It is impossible for the university to say they cannot afford to educate a student properly—she can point to the fee being paid on her behalf. It gives her a kind of consumer power—an issue we will consider further.

Our scheme is carefully designed as a middle way between a fully public and a fully private scheme. Spending on universities is not public spending—competing with popular public services and controlled by the Treasury. Nor is it conventional commercial lending as then financial regulation kicks in and you risk losing its universality. It is surprisingly difficult to avoid getting impaled on the horns of this dilemma—in my experience almost every alternative model ends up rather nastily skewered by one horn or the other, and either becomes public spending or loses its universality. A non-commercial repayment arrangement is the only practical way to avoid the dilemma.

In some classifications of higher education systems this English model appears indistinguishable from the American system which does often require private payment up front by students. The OECD, for example, treated our system as private payment like the US. But regarding our system as just another example of private payment fails to capture what is special about the English arrangements. Our system of income-contingent repayment by graduates is very different from payment up front by students, even though both may be categorized as private payment. It is different because it has universal access for full-time students and repayments depend on your earnings. These two key features make it very different from a commercial scheme, even one with Federal guarantees.

This answers the challenge of those who say we need to do more for poor students. They tend to be influenced by American evidence and ask why we can't offer generous means-tested remission of fees like in the US. The Sutton Trust, for example, claimed that poor students could not afford the arrangements or were being put off—neither statement being correct, thank heavens—and advocated American-style fees exemptions for them. But when it comes to paying for higher education it is graduates' current earnings which matter, not their previous circumstances. It would be absurd and indefensible that two university graduates should be working side by side and earning the same amount, perhaps even having studied the same course at the same university, but with one having 9 per cent less deducted from her salary than the other because she came from a poor background. There is an important principle here: what matters are your circumstances as an adult. That is what income-contingent graduate repayment is all about. If you end up in a low-pay job you do not pay back: if you can afford to, you do. Determining your graduate repayment by your family circumstances when you were a student would be stretching the concept of social justice to breaking point. By that point it really shouldn't matter where you came from: it is your circumstances when you are repaying that matter.

Repayment is based on where you are, not where you came from. That is what makes the scheme progressive—graduates only pay back if their income is high enough for them to afford to, just like income tax.

Nevertheless the critics kept on maintaining that people from disadvantaged backgrounds were being put off. I remember a Q&A session with young people in the East End of London shortly after we had announced our fees policy and one of them, clearly smart and responsible, said to me, 'I want to be a doctor but I can't afford to go to university now.' Nobody should believe that. It would be a tragedy if any young person did not go to university because they actually believed that they could not afford it. One of the great strengths of our system now compared with many other advanced countries is that there are no up-front payments for any full-time first-time student. By contrast there are real up-front payments by students or their families of up to €2,000 in France, depending on the status of the university, €1,500 in Italy, and €2,000 in the Netherlands.

We tried to communicate the facts as best we could. We did not have an advertising budget for wider communication of our policies. But we did recruit a team of about forty recent graduates who went to every school and college explaining the facts of our finance system and answering any questions prospective students had about university. They were excellent ambassadors for higher education. The pattern of applications suggested that all this worked. The year before the new regime came in (2011–12) there was an artificial peak in applications with fewer prospective students taking gap years as they tried to get in under the old regime. That surge meant there was then an artificial dip in the first year of the higher fees (2012–13). The second year of the new system was the crucial test. It was my most anxious time as minister for universities. A further fall in applications would have meant we had a real problem. But we got back on track with strong growth in applications in 2013–14 and subsequently that growth has continued, even whilst the size of the age cohort has been falling. It is particularly encouraging that applications from poorer groups have been rising strongly. It comprehensively rebuts the claim that our reforms were going to put poor students off.

The real problem facing low-income students is not fees but cash resource at university—one of many occasions when the NUS, beneath the rhetoric, had a shrewd assessment of their members' interests. In their meetings with me they focused above all on cash in the pockets of students at university. Even during the General Election campaign of summer 2017 it was issues such as the high cost of rents which aroused the anger of students. That is the real pressure point—not payments decades later if they are in well-paid jobs. That is why we increased the total value of the maintenance grant and loans. We also created a National Scholarship Programme which was rather clunky and ineffective and soon abandoned. In fact many of the students protesting about the fees were actually most unhappy about the cut in Educational Maintenance Allowance for 16 to 18 year olds which did reduce their cash income even whilst we were increasing it for university students. The further shift from maintenance grant to loans in 2016 was accompanied by a further increase in the value of the total support worth about £500 a year to a low-income student.[14] Perhaps there is more that can be done here, especially in London, where students report less satisfaction, probably linked to much higher living costs.

Amidst all this controversy we were not focusing on what economists would regard as a true calculation of the cost of higher education which includes income forgone. The real up-front cost for a young person of going to university is not a fee which they don't pay unless and until they are well-paid graduates. The real cost up-front is the three years or so of earnings they forgo when they are studying. That is much more significant economically. This cost is diminished when earnings of non-graduates are low. Indeed you could argue that the real cost of going to university has fallen in the past few years as the pay of young non-graduates has performed so badly. But if you are a potential mature student who might have to give up a job or reduce your hours to go and study the costs look higher and riskier during tough times.

The logic of the English system: the equity principle

Even if you accept that this graduate repayment scheme is a good structure you may think we pushed the boat out too far in expecting graduates to repay fees of £9,000. Higher education brings a mixture of private and public gain so you could argue that it makes sense to fund it out of a mix of payment by the graduate beneficiaries and the Exchequer. One approach would be to go for a mix of public and private payment that roughly matched the balance of private and public benefits. Despite its apparent logic this approach is not widely used across public services some of which are free at the point of use even though there are direct private benefits too. Health care or schooling bring private as well as public benefits but that is not the basis for a mixed funding model. At the other end of the scale many vocational training qualifications for specific jobs are exclusively privately funded, even though the wider economy gains as well. It appears that Governments do not regularly combine public and private payment for public services in a way that matches public and private benefit. We actually went further in applying this principle in higher education than elsewhere. The Coalition estimated it was broadly shifting the balance of funding from 60/40 public/private to 40/60 and this is not far from some of the heroic estimates of the balance of private and public gains which we will consider in Chapter Five.

The pursuit of that kind of balance between private and public payment is trumped by the principle of fairness. Repayment of the full cost of their higher education by graduates who enjoy above-average earnings as a result of their university education appears fair—otherwise lower-income non-graduate taxpayers would be meeting the costs of university education propelling graduates into much higher incomes than the non-graduates themselves are likely to enjoy. Moreover, given that public spending is limited, a system which depended on substantial levels of public spending per student is likely to ration student numbers, but turning away people who wish to go to university and could benefit from it is bad for them and bad for the economy.

A better way of thinking of the English system is that it is a graduate repayment balanced by public spending to deliver equity between different types of student. Imagine that you are a student not doing a high-cost subject and coming from a middle-income family. You are eligible for a fee loan to cover the £9,000 annual cost of your university teaching. You are also eligible for a maintenance loan to cover your living costs of up to £10,700.[15] After university you then go into reasonably well-paid work and you can be expected to repay in full the money that was provided for your higher education by the time you reach prosperous middle age by virtue of what is in effect a 29 per cent rate of income tax instead of 20 per cent. People may say you left university with almost £50,000 of debt, but that payback during your working life is modest compared with the £800,000 of income tax you are likely to have paid in the same period. Your total cash payments on an average mortgage could be another £500,000 as well. This version of the model is essentially one where the Government smooths your resources over the life cycle—providing finance when you are a student and collecting back when you are better off. It is an example of ultimately 100 per cent private payment, though with the opening loans a universal entitlement which can only be delivered if the Government funds them initially. But not every student falls so neatly into the system. There are four important pressure points where a public contribution is needed to ensure the system is fair and progressive.

First, there may be extra teaching costs for certain sets of students and we meet these extra costs so as to equalize the graduate repayment. So, for example, we saw earlier that there are some subjects which clearly cost more to teach—Medicine or Engineering compared with Philosophy or English. Governments make no evaluative judgement about the relative merits of these different disciplines but do try to provide extra public funding for the higher-cost subjects so that the remaining funding via fees is broadly the same. There are separate payments for strategically important and vulnerable subjects. There are also some funds to reflect the higher costs of teaching students from disadvantaged backgrounds who may require more teaching support—a modest version of the pupil premium at school. That is why in 2015–16 there continued to be grants of just over £1bn to universities via the Higher Education Funding Council to meet this range of extra teaching costs, notably about £640m for high-cost subjects.

Secondly, there is direct funding to students from low-income backgrounds or who have special needs. The biggest element was maintenance grants, though these have now been replaced by maintenance loans. But there is still help with childcare costs for students who are parents. There is also help with the higher costs facing disabled students. This added up to about another £300 million of public spending in 2015–16.[16]

The third category of spending is capital. In the past universities used to get public grants for their capital investment. One reason for increasing the fees up to £9,000 was to provide a stream of income which enabled universities to borrow more for capital investment. Indeed the financiers always used to advise that university balance sheets were very conservative and they could borrow more. But universities have very different capital endowments and needs so there is a good argument for some continuing public support for teaching capital so that students in universities with less capital do not lose out. The programme was significantly enhanced and has been running at approximately £200 million per year.

These three categories add up to continuing public finance for higher education alongside graduate repayment to ensure equitable treatment of students. They deliver public as well as private funding for benefits which are both public and private. Some critics think we failed to understand the public value of university education—they think that if we had we would have gone for a different balance of public and private payment. But actually the equity principle is a perfectly sensible way of funding higher education—it does not have to depend on a formula linking the balance of benefits.

The RAB charge and the
inter-generational contract

There is a fourth and final category of spending. There will be some graduates who do not earn above the repayment threshold for long enough to repay the full costs of the loans for their education. Some increase in net public borrowing will arise when these loans are written off. This possible future cost is identified in the so-called RAB charge—the Resource Accounting and Budgeting charge which forecasts the percentage of the value of loans which may not be paid back. Writing off loans is a deliberate feature of the system to make it fair and progressive. It has however caused much confusion so we must now consider it in more depth.

Graduates have thirty years to repay the costs of their higher education—both fee and maintenance loans. At the end of that period the loans they have not repaid will be written off. Nobody can know now what these write-offs will be. But the Whitehall Department responsible, BIS and now the Department for Education, estimates—and re-estimates—this sum and identifies it as part of the departmental accounting process. These speculative calculations, made with heroic assumptions about future earning and future policy, are the RAB charge. It is one of the more esoteric corners of public finance. It has become just about the most controversial aspect of the scheme.

Government loans to students are not public spending because the loan outlay is matched with an obligation to pay it back. The RAB charge is not public spending either: it is an estimate of possible future write-offs. We can only count as public net borrowing that part of the loan which is written off when it actually happens—everything else is speculation. But it is good practice within government for BIS to estimate future write-offs and include them in its internal departmental accounts so that they can be monitored by the Treasury. If there were not this monitoring then Departments would blithely make loans without worrying about the chances of getting the money back. But these estimates are for internal Whitehall purposes and do not feed through into the national accounts, the overall Treasury arithmetic measuring actual public spending. It is common sense to treat as increased net borrowing the write-off when it actually happens. It would be very peculiar if, for example, the Government actually cut spending on a real programme now because of a speculative estimate of possible loan write-offs in thirty years' time. That also means the RAB charge is not money available to be somehow reallocated to spend on something else today.

To estimate the RAB charge you also have to make heroic assumptions about the distribution of graduate earnings over thirty-five years after someone entered university. The first students under the Coalition's new scheme entered university in 2012: some started their graduate repayments in 2016 and could be repaying up until 2046. A crucial issue in forecasting their repayments is what will happen to women's earnings. At the moment the Government expects to write off a higher proportion of female graduate loans because women's earnings are forecast to be lower than men's. One of the big challenges for our society is tackling this injustice of lower female earnings—forecasting the RAB charge involves reaching a judgement on where we will have got to by the middle of the century. The pattern of earnings also matters in another way. If you have parts of your career when you earn a little and others when you earn a lot then you are likely to be paying back at least some of your student loans. However, the same overall averages for graduate earnings could involve a different pattern in which some graduates get sustained high earnings whilst others are stuck on much lower pay—this combination reduces total repayments. These are the sort of issues which also affect the long-term prospects for the graduate premium. They are inherently uncertain and debatable: they are not the same as the facts of public spending this year but we have to make heroic assumptions about them to estimate the RAB charge.

The RAB calculation also assumes that the details of the scheme are fixed until 2050. But the guide to terms and conditions which the student receives when they take out the loan states: 'The regulations may change from time to time and this means the terms of your loan may also change.'[17] In order to make a forecast some very specific assumptions have to be made. The assumption that its parameters are unchanged for thirty-five years in turn makes the estimate of the RAB charge very sensitive to one particular set of data—namely, earnings. The value of the £21,000 repayment threshold was assumed to be fixed relative to earnings indefinitely at whatever level it had reached in 2016. This is a very peculiar feature of the estimates of the RAB charge. When we fixed it in November 2010, the proposed £21,000 threshold represented about 75 per cent of projected average earnings of £28,000 in 2016. But then earnings did not grow as rapidly as the Office of Budget Responsibility forecast and by 2016 average earnings were more like £26,000, which meant that the £21,000 threshold had in effect risen to about 80 per cent of projected earnings. It was assumed, for the purposes of estimating the RAB, that it would stay at this higher level relative to earnings for the next thirty years and this is why the RAB estimate increased so much during my time as minister—because earnings were growing less than forecast, making the repayment threshold more generous. The repayment threshold would have to be about £19,500 to have the same value relative to average earnings as was expected in 2010 when it was set. That is one reason why the new Government rightly decided in the Budget of summer 2015 to freeze the repayment threshold. The critics saw this as a breach of faith, tantamount to a bank changing the repayment terms of a loan after you have taken it out. But a loan is not a commercial contract—which is why we were explicit about our power to alter its terms. Looking back, however, I regret that we did not signal the basis for the repayment threshold more explicitly at the time by just adding in brackets, 'i.e. 75 per cent of average earnings'.

This is incidentally not just an issue which arises just with this system of financing higher education. Conceptually exactly the same issue arises with a graduate tax. You could ask the advocate of a graduate tax to specify the rate and the graduate tax threshold. You could then use those assumptions to estimate the revenues from a graduate tax relative to the long-term cost of higher education and then announce every few months whether or not by 2046, thirty years after repayments began, your graduate tax had swung into a massive deficit or not. If the advocate of the graduate tax comes back and says it is not supposed to be as rigid as that then you can reply that no system of funding any public service is supposed to be that rigid, but it doesn't stop the use of such peculiar calculations for the RAB charge in the graduate contribution scheme. Sometimes the same people who advocate a graduate tax also argue that the detailed terms of the graduate repayments in the current scheme should be fixed in legislation. But income tax rates and allowances change so it is hard to see how the details of a graduate tax would be fixed.

We can trace these possible loan write-offs to the origins of the modern graduate repayment scheme in human capital theory—the idea that we can consider education as investment in our human capital and that this capital is increasingly important both for individuals and economies. But a toddler cannot waddle into a bank and get a loan for a quarter of a million of pounds or whatever is needed to pay for his or her education. So it makes sense to provide them with this capital investment for them to repay later in some form or other as tax-paying citizens. It is the best way to address the problem of under-investment in human capital which is a consequence of either limits to public spending or to personal resources. Milton Friedman set out the argument very clearly:

> Individuals should bear the costs of investments in themselves and receive the
> rewards, and they should not be prevented by market imperfections from making

the investments when they are willing to bear the costs...A government body could offer to finance or help finance the training of any individual who could meet minimum quality standards by making available not more than a limited sum per year for not more than a specified number of years, provided it was spent on securing training at a recognized institution. The individual would agree in return to pay to the government in each future year x per cent of his earnings in excess of y dollars for each $1,000 that he gets in this way. This payment could easily be combined with payment of income tax and so involve a minimum of administrative expense.[18]

An ingenious solution to the challenge of funding university studies was therefore developed by Milton Friedman and Gary Becker and most ambitiously applied at Yale Law School in the 1970s. This was the first modern graduate repayment scheme. Students pledged that for every $1,000 they borrowed from the university, they would repay 4 per cent of earnings for thirty-five years or until the whole cohort paid off its debt. This scheme had good intentions—Yale wanted to increase their numbers of public school (in British parlance, state school) students. The Yale Tuition Postponement Option had no external subsidies: all the costs were met within the cohort and so some paid more when others could not pay back. But there was increasing anger from affluent graduates who ended up paying far more than the actual cost of their education to cover the cost of their contemporaries with lower earnings. Yale had to abandon the scheme and write off the debts of their low-earning graduates. One participant in the Yale scheme was Bill Clinton.[19] He learnt from this experiment and put a federal graduate repayment scheme to fund access to university in his 1992 presidential platform.

Every subsequent version of a graduate repayment scheme has had to confront this question: to what extent are low earners in a cohort to be paid for by high earners in the same cohort or should they instead be financed by the whole of society? There are deep questions about the social contract here. There is an argument that it is equitable for those graduates who have gained the most to pay back more and subsidize those who have done least well. However, my view is that it is not fair to expect all the burdens of sustaining the less advantaged members of one generation to be borne solely by their more affluent contemporaries.[20] Governments spread risks and costs across different generations and so the generality of taxpayers can and should meet the costs of those graduates who, it turns out, cannot afford their full repayments. Moreover the scheme is voluntary, and if it demands too much of highly paid graduates those students who can expect to earn a lot might not join the scheme at all.

The English graduate repayment scheme is based on a loan for the cost of a student's education so that each graduate can see they pay back for the cost of their own education. That is why it is right for taxpayers eventually to pay to write off the loans that are not repaid. Wider society picks up the bill for those who end up with lower earnings.

Paradoxically therefore this RAB charge, the most controversial feature of the scheme, is actually the answer to the most fundamental challenge to the scheme. The critics say that the scheme breaks the inter-generational contract because instead of all of us paying for the education of university students we are expecting them to pay for it themselves, albeit in later life when they are prosperous. But other generations do pay for that cohort's education in our scheme, and in the most progressive possible way. They pay for the university education of people who, for whatever reason, do not earn much in later life and they pay through writing off their loans. The RAB charge is how we ensure we do not impose an unfair burden on one generation by expecting them alone to bear the cost of their low-paid contemporaries. The RAB charge is how we discharge the inter-generational contract. So when a critic says, 'the RAB charge is too high so the whole system is unsustainable', they are actually saying, 'the amount which all of us are expected to contribute to the education of this cohort of students is too high'. (And how sustainable do they think the old scheme was with outright grants which effectively meant it had an RAB charge of 100 per cent?) If that is what they really think they should not also object that our system breaches the obligation we have to younger generations as they want any such breach to be bigger. In fact it is how we are setting the balance between public payment by all of us and private payment by graduate beneficiaries.

The scale of the write-off and how much we can expect graduates to pay back can be decided as part of setting that private–public balance we discussed earlier. It is a genuine and important democratic decision what this balance should be. It is decided by the level at which we set the repayment threshold. Indeed, one of the advantages of this structure is that it is flexible. This system of financing higher education in England is sufficiently flexible to reflect different balances of private and public benefits and different balances between payment by the generality of taxpayers and individual graduates. It can do this without compromising its key principles. That is why the way the debate went on the RAB charge was so misleading—the forecasting model assumed parameters were fixed out to 2046 even though no policy maker would make such a commitment in this or any other area of public policy. That appeared to make the structure far more inflexible than it really is. The structure can be calibrated in many different ways to give a different balance of payment between taxpayers and graduates. Governments can respond to changes in political opinion about, for example, the mix of public and graduate payment within this overall structure. It also enables the system to respond to changes in the real world—for example, if there were to be a fall in returns to graduates.

We need a framework explicitly to adjust the parameters to keep it flexible and sustainable whilst keeping the basic structure. Such a framework should also avoid endless ad hoc adjustments. I have therefore proposed that once in each Parliament the Government should assess the latest evidence on the costs and benefits of education and set the key figures for the graduate contribution scheme.[21] This could be done within Government or by an outside panel of experts and interested parties or some combination. It is emphatically not a review of the whole system. It is not a Robbins or a Dearing or a Browne. Its purpose is not to change the structure of higher education funding. All three political parties, when in office, have recognized its strengths. And structural changes can distract us from uncomfortable trade-offs. Instead the aim is to calibrate the structure in the light of new evidence and any change in political views on the right balance to strike. That review would in effect be deciding on the right balance of payments between the generations.

This exercise could happen alongside the Government's public expenditure decisions or follow on from them. An outside advisory panel could include representatives of the universities, the NUS, and other key players. Its framework would be set by the Government, which also has to have ultimate power of decision. The aim would be to operate the graduate contribution scheme on a stable basis five years at a time. Both universities and the NUS say they want stability in the system and this gives substantial stability for five years within a framework that lasts much longer. If you tried to fix every variable for longer than five years you would actually get a brittle and unsustainable system. The system is supple enough to adjust the balance between the generations without tearing it up and starting again.

There are several good reasons for the five-year review. It matches the life of a Parliament and increasingly in turn that matches the main public spending reviews. It is very similar to the system of setting national insurance contribution rates for five years to match expected spending on contributory benefits over the same period. Another consideration is that there are limits to how much change and complexity the Students Loan Company can handle, even with the new IT system. Universities themselves used to be funded with a five-year

Table 3.3. Effect on RAB charge of illustrative changes in repayment terms

Up-rate repayment threshold every five years instead of annually	−3%
Hold at £21k for five years and then up-rate annually at lower level	−5%
Increase maximum interest rate from 3% to 4%	−4%
Increase maximum repayment period from 30 to 35 years	−8%
Increase repayment rate from 9% to 12%	−9%
Reduce repayment threshold from £21k to £18k	−8%

Source: First two options are author's estimates. Latter four are IFS estimates for author on baseline estimate for RAB charge of 31%.

allocation of funding as this was thought to be the right way to finance autonomous institutions that needed to plan for the long term. That collapsed in the 1970s under the combined weight of high inflation and public spending crises. The model of funding universities with a quinquennial review has a certain historical legitimacy. It would be great to bring it back.

Here is a cut-out-and-keep guide to some options which would reduce the RAB charge (Table 3.3). I am not advocating them: some are undesirable or politically unacceptable or both. But others are quite close to what the Government did in 2015. Between them they give an idea of the sort of flexibilities in the scheme and the kind of reductions in the RAB charge which might result.

Alternatively Governments could reduce annual graduate repayments even more by raising the repayment threshold or cutting the 9% repayment rate. An open assessment of these kind of options and a decision on them every five years seems to me to be the right way of deciding these things rather than Government just exercising its discretion to change the terms in an ad hoc way. We have already seen that the claim that somehow these changes are illegitimate is misplaced—but this objection gets some emotional force when changes are unexpected and ad hoc whereas the open and regular assessment would also be harder to object to.

There is another option which could be considered in the light of the summer 2017 Election campaign in which Jeremy Corbyn reopened the issue of student finance. One widespread grievance is about the high interest rate of up to the RPI plus 3 per cent on outstanding debt. This does not affect actual monthly repayments by graduates but it does extend the period a graduate is paying back. We introduced it to make the scheme as progressive as possible: it enabled us to extract as much money as possible from well-paid graduates. Nevertheless it is clearly unpopular—perhaps for the very same reasons as that earlier Yale model was. It would be possible to reduce the interest rate or remove it altogether. This would reduce the total amount repaid and hence increase the RAB charge but might be a price worth paying to maintain the overall scheme which has done so much to improve the resources available for student teaching and was paid for in a progressive and fair way.

The RAB charge is, of course, an average. It opens up the wider question of whether to fund 'good' students and 'good' universities with low RAB charges as against 'bad' ones with a high RAB. That is part of a wider debate about diversity of fees to which we now turn.

Differential fees?

When I announced our policy in the Commons in November 2010 I claimed that fees of £9,000 would be 'exceptional'.[22] That was a mistake—a wrong forecast based on a false analysis. I stopped making the claim soon afterwards but by then it was too late—it was thought that our reforms should generate price competition or they would have failed. My only defence can be that this assumption was widespread across Whitehall. However, as soon as one recognized that what really mattered for students was the repayment formula not the fee level then it was clear that there would not and should not be much price competition. A student who had said, 'I am going to Leeds because its fee is £7,750 and I can afford it more easily than York at £8,750' would not understand the basic features of the scheme.[23] The only significant scope for price competition was for some providers coming in at under £6,000 because then the university would face less onerous obligations and the student could see that their graduate repayments would finish significantly sooner than someone with the full £9,000 × 3 to repay. £6,000 was an important step-change as higher education institutions below it were not required to spend funds on access. There could be no-frills options, from alternative providers for example, at this level.

I was increasingly sceptical of achieving widespread price competition. First, it requires a change in the structure of repayments so that students were more sensitive to the level of the up-front fee and that could well be damaging. Secondly, it is not clear why some fees should be higher than others. It is assumed that the 'top' universities should charge more—they would be 'reassuringly expensive'. (Frank Lowe's brilliant advertising slogan for Stella Artois. The expense of Stella arose partly from Government regulation—higher duty because of its greater alcohol content. There is a parallel as John Browne's proposed higher levy on high-fee universities would have had a similar effect.) But these universities tend to take the students with more advantaged backgrounds who may require less educational support. In schools we tend to apply the opposite argument—that there should be a pupil premium which boosts resources for the schools taking students from disadvantaged backgrounds. On this argument it is the less prestigious universities which should be able to charge higher fees to get more resource for their tougher students. These arguments seemed to balance each other out and favoured level fees.

There is, however, a significant strand of thought that the lack of price competition is a terrible let-down and we need to promote it. In his review John Browne himself envisaged price competition, but he recognized that fees would race up as the Exchequer would be funding them and graduates would not worry much, providing their repayment formula was unchanged. With typical clarity and boldness of thought, he proposed therefore that universities should pay a levy on their loans which covered the likely RAB charge—the higher the fee the greater the risk of the Government having to write off some of the loans and the higher the rate of the levy to cover this risk. The trouble was that when he wrote his report we did not have the data to know the right RAB charge for individual institutions so his levy would be based on a national average. This meant that the levy on, for example, Oxbridge if they put up their fees would be much higher than the actual risks that their graduates would not be able to pay back their loans. Indeed both Oxford and Cambridge lobbied hard against the proposal for precisely this reason. We ended up with the cruder fee cap instead. It was one reason why I encouraged research which would enable us to understand better the earnings and hence repayment prospects of different graduates doing different courses at different institutions. That would also enlighten the wider debate on social mobility, which is far too dependent on studies of birth cohorts from 1958 and 1970. It could also be the basis for setting a variable levy that was higher if we had good grounds for expecting less of the fee loans to be repaid because graduate earnings were lower. It was hard to get the project going because the researchers, the excellent Anna Vignoles and Neil Shephard, needed access to HMRC earnings data and this was difficult to obtain, but we won through in the end.[24] The results were finally published in 2016.[25] Moreover new legislation has removed some of the barriers so now we also have more detailed LEO data (Longitudinal Educational Outcomes) which goes even further in linking education tax and benefit information.

The findings are very significant. There are indeed big differences in graduate earnings. Interestingly subjects matter more than institutions—so, graduates in LEM subjects (Law, Economics, and Management) earn most, followed by STEM students, with performing and creative arts showing the lowest earnings. But looking behind the headlines one could see how difficult it would be to use the diversity of earnings to justify differential fees and levies between universities. The family background of students is a big factor in their future earnings. So is the location of the university—if it is in a high-pay area its graduates earn more. In the words of the report, 'Mean difference in earnings across most institutions are not sizeable once we take account of the fact that different types of students sort into different institutions.'[26] So universities would not be rewarded for their excellent performance—they would instead be rewarded for operating in the South-East and taking students from affluent backgrounds who go into banking but would be penalized for being in a poorer region and taking people from state schools who become teachers or nurses. This is not a good basis for differential fees. Once again we face the problem that widespread assumptions about good and bad universities have little to do with educational quality. On the Browne logic the levy should vary by discipline rather than university—and that is the approach they have tried in Australia. But then we are back into the argument whether we want people to study some subjects not others, and would we be trying to put up fees for high-paid subjects such as medicine which are clearly of high social value too? And I remain very wary of a Government trying to intrude in this way into a personal decision. Moreover our real problem is that we have to take these type of decisions so young—far too much specialization too young is the real problem, which we will look at it in Chapter Fourteen.

The Government tried to break out of this log-jam by linking fees to educational gain to reward high-quality teaching. That is in principle a much better way to do it. But it does depend on reliable metrics of teaching excellence—an issue we return to in Chapter Eight.

The prize—end of number controls and extending access to loans

The system of fees and loans has now been operating for over a decade. It has been a conspicuous success—broadening participation in higher education, bringing in more funds to university education, and saving public money. Taking most of higher education out of public spending has led to the removal of direct controls set by Government on student numbers university by university.[27]

Sweeping these absurd controls away is one of the great social reforms of the Coalition Government and it was fitting that we should announce that policy in 2013, the year of the fiftieth anniversary of the Robbins Report. The Conservative Manifesto of 2015 stated that: 'This year, for the first time, over half a million people have been admitted to our universities, including a record proportion of students from disadvantaged backgrounds. From September, we will go even further, abolishing the cap on higher education student numbers and removing an arbitrary ceiling on ambition.'[28] That was only possible because the public spending constraints on growth of student numbers had finally been resolved and at the same time there is no student up-front payment either. English higher education is one of the few systems across the world to have achieved this. Abolishing fees would jeopardize this great social reform because once again Governments would need some mechanism for controlling public spending by controlling the number of students.

We can see the effect of the English financing model by contrasting it with Scotland. Carved in stone outside Heriot-Watt University is Alex Salmond's statement that: 'The rocks will melt with the sun before I allow tuition fees to be imposed on Scottish students.' One of the benefits of devolution is we can now compare different policies across different parts of the UK and see which works best. And it is clear that the English model of higher education does much better for low-income students than the Scottish model. UCAS figures show the proportion of young people from the lowest-income fifth of the population going to university in Scotland has risen from 7.3 per cent in 2011 to 9.7 per cent in 2015. In England the figure has gone from 13.8 per cent to 17 per cent over the same period. The UK average has risen from 13.4 per cent in 2011 to 16.6 per cent in 2015. The Sutton Trust makes a similar comparison but by area and reaches a similar conclusion: 'Scottish 18 year olds from the most advantaged areas are still more than four times more likely to go straight to university than those from the least advantaged areas. In England, those from the most advantaged areas are 2.4 times as likely to go to university as those from the least, and three times as likely in Wales and Northern Ireland.'[29]

Scotland's Auditor General reported in July 2016 that offer rates are higher for other UK and non-EU students than for Scottish and other EU students. And the trends are diverging too, with Scottish universities offering unlimited places for students from England and fewer to students from Scotland because their numbers are limited. This is because there is a cap on funding for Scottish students whereas an English student brings her funding with her in the form of the loan to pay the £9,000 fees levied on students from England. It is this constraint on numbers of Scottish students that is the reason why fewer poor students get in.

Scotland is entitled to make these choices, though its claims for moral superiority are rather hollow. And the comparison confirms the crucial point that public funding and rationing go together: if you wish to escape rationing you have to escape dependence on public funding as well.[30] That is why the main focus of public policy has increasingly been on extending entitlement to loans more widely. There are three main areas for progress.

One of my great regrets looking back on my time as universities minister is that the number of part-time students fell so sharply. We thought we were offering them more help by, for the first time, extending loans to them to cover their fees. But this offer was actually quite restricted as many of them were barred by the previous Labour Government's ELQ policy excluding from public support students who were studying for an 'Equivalent or Lower Qualification' to one they already had. I was able to take a first modest step to remove this bar by announcing in 2013 that part-time students in certain STEM courses would be entitled to fee loans even if they already had a degree. The Conservative Government then took this much further with a further broadening of entitlement and for the first time providing maintenance loans for part-time students.[31] The next step is completely to remove the ELQ restriction and to provide loans to all part-time students. The exemption of STEM subjects from ELQ constraints is the only actual example of a policy bias in favour of STEM subjects. I do not like such subject bias, but it was easier to get the policy through for STEM subjects as the caricature was that mature students in the Humanities were rich bankers who wanted to study the history of art in their retirement. Actually one of the courses hardest hit was theology, as many people train for the priesthood having already had a different career. When eventually we once again provide loans to mature theology students a historic mistake will finally have been reversed.

The second group who are increasingly covered by these loans are postgraduate students. There are various Master's courses which have had a range of ad hoc funding arrangements including Personal Career Development Loans. Participation in these programmes is the new frontier in the battle for social mobility as an increasing number of jobs now expect some postgraduate qualification as well, so it is important that they are now brought within the scope of the student loan scheme. From 2016–17 students resident in England under the age of 60 on Masters degrees (taught or research, including on a part-time basis, provided it is at least 50 per cent intensity) became eligible for a postgraduate loan of up to £10,000. The loan can be spread over two to three years and, unlike undergraduate tuition fee loans, is provided directly to the student to cover both fees and maintenance costs, though it does not cover these costs

in full. As with undergraduate loans, the minimum income threshold for repayment is £21,000, though students pay 6 per cent of their income as opposed to
9 per cent. Graduates would repay undergraduate and postgraduate loans concurrently. While the sector broadly supported the proposals, both the IFS and
Nick Hillman of HEPI warned that as, unlike with undergraduates, the loan is
not linked to fees there is potential for tuition fee inflation.[32] The Government,
in their impact assessment, noted the possibility of providers raising fees but
sought to avoid a fee cap at the postgraduate level and stated that competition
would likely stave off significant fee increases. The official impact assessment
projected demand of 60,700 in 2016–17 and estimated that within those 60,700
there would be 7,600 students who would have otherwise not undertaken a
Master's degree.[33] This funding for Master's courses also opens up the option of
a broader undergraduate education followed by more specific postgraduate
professional study, as they do in America.

Doctoral students can get a stipend as part of their funding from a Research
Council but not all doctoral students can get a Research Council grant. In the
2016 Budget, the Government announced plans for PhD loans to plug this gap.
From 2018–19 anyone under the age of 60, resident in England and accepted
onto a PhD programme in the UK without Research Council funding, would
be eligible for a loan of up to £25,000. As with postgraduate loans, the repayment rate is 6 per cent above the £21,000 minimum income threshold.[34]

There is a further group who could participate in the scheme as well: British
students studying abroad. This is a group for whom we offer less help than most
other countries, who see it as a good way to broaden the horizons of their
young people. We discuss this further in Chapter Twelve. One could even go
further and imagine this model of funding higher education being extended
to vocational training too. There would have to be a way of defining eligible
schemes.[35] The RAB charge on some of these loans might be high, however.
The substantial graduate premium makes higher education particularly well
suited to this form of finance because it is expecting beneficiaries with above
average earnings to pay back.

Conclusion

So we have seen that we have delivered well-funded universities at a time of
austerity financed by the generality of taxpayers and graduates in well-paid jobs.

It is recognized around the world as a fair and effective way to finance higher education. Andreas Schleicher of the OECD describes our system as 'the most scalable and sustainable approach to university finance'.[36] It includes continuing public support—through grants to universities both for some subjects and for some students. But these forms of support are not visible and hence not appreciated. Moreover the most important way in which the generality of taxpayers contribute—by not expecting less affluent graduates to pay back for their higher education—is seen by some as a defect rather than the deliberate policy it is. But these forms of public support are more effective than a general subsidy to higher education which has not proved sufficient to fund it to an acceptable standard and has obstructed social mobility by leading to restrictions in student numbers.

I hope that at last we have achieved a viable and progressive way of financing higher education. Of course it needs to adjust in the light of political and economic pressures and a five-year review makes that possible. If we want graduates to pay back less we can change the parameters by cutting the interest rate on graduate 'debt' for example, or increase the repayment threshold above £21,000. If we believe graduates should pay back more, we can instead lower the repayment threshold. If we want to help students themselves with their cost of living we can do more on maintenance loans or grants. If there is a willingness to increase public spending on higher education it could go as extra grants for high cost subjects such as engineering where the extra cost of up-to-date equipment may not be reflected in the funding formula. Or there could be increases in the grants to help universities with the costs of more disadvantaged students, like the pupil premium in school funding. All these options and more are possible without destroying the basic structure of graduate repayments. It is better to use these flexibilities than tear up the system and start again. Our criterion should be the crucial one—what is in the best interests of students. Reducing the funds to teach them or restricting the number of young people who can go to university is not helping young people, it is betraying them.

FOUR

The Research–Intensive University

Origins in Germany and the US

Professor Liebig of Giessen University is looking back with pride on his career in organic chemistry and his keen young team of researchers in their lab 'almost exclusively devoted to the improvement of organic analysis... The only complaints were those of the attendant who in the evenings, when he had to clean, could not get the workers to leave the laboratory.'[1] All quite typical—except that he is describing a laboratory he created in 1826. It was the first research laboratory based in a university. There were a few other laboratories but they were usually sponsored by learned societies (you can still see Michael Faraday's laboratory at the Royal Institution) and were nothing to do with universities. Professor Liebig knew the significance of what he was doing: 'there began at the small university an activity such as the world had not yet seen'.[2] It was the birth of one of the most important institutions of the modern world—the research-based university systematically creating new knowledge—and it was conceived in Germany, as we saw in Chapter One. Wilhelm von Humboldt wrote a short policy paper which proved to be one of the seminal documents in the emergence of the modern university, proposing that the university should become a centre of research. Underneath the idealist Hegelian prose he wrestles with issues which are still live today. He argues that research based in the university is enhanced by teaching, compared with the alternative model of research in a separate academy:

> If one declares the university as destined only for the teaching and dissemination of science, but the academy to its expansion, one clearly does the former an injustice. Surely, the sciences have been just as much—and in Germany more so—expanded by university professors as by the academy members, and these men have arrived

at their advances in their field precisely through their teaching. For the free oral lecture before listeners, among whom there is always a significant number of minds that think along for themselves, surely spurs on the person who has become used to this kind of study as much as the solitary leisure of the writer's life or the loose association of an academic fellowship. The course of science is evidently quicker and more lively at a university, where it is continuously mulled over in a large number of strong, robust, and youthful minds. . . . Moreover, university teaching is not such an arduous business that it should be regarded as an interruption of the leisure for study rather than an aid to the same. Also, at every large university there are men who, by lecturing little or not at all, only study and research by themselves in solitude. For that reason, one could surely entrust the expansion of the sciences to the universities alone, provided the latter are properly set up, and for that purpose dispense with the academies.

That statement, more than 200 years ago, still makes the case for teaching enhancing research—though without betraying much interest in whether research enhances teaching.[3]

This new role for the university had started to emerge in eighteenth-century Germany, partly driven by competition between fragmented local states for prestigious new universities because of their unwillingness to see their smartest minds leaving their state for a rival. (Universities are to this day a crucial tool in demographic and economic competition between American states, one reason why they invest in them.) Much of this research initially was in the humanities, especially philology, which drew on both classical humanism and the Romantic Movement's fascination with national identity expressed in national languages. The fundamental shift in thinking, however, is Humboldt's proposal that universities create new knowledge by systematic research—previously it was individual geniuses such as Aristotle or Newton who were thought to be the sole creators of new knowledge.

The great universities of the nineteenth century were places such as Halle, which invented the seminar at which a student presented a dissertation, leading on to the emergence of the PhD. Göttingen was the first German university to break free from religious censorship and establish philosophy as the dominant discipline. Kant's essay *The Conflict of the Faculties* uses this pre-eminent role for philosophy to place academic study above censorship.[4] British thinkers such as Thomas Carlyle understood the significance of what was happening in Germany. So did Matthew Arnold, who reported in 1870 that his German friends called Oxford 'a great Gymnasium' (an advanced secondary school) but not of course a proper university because of the lack of research.[5] T. H. Huxley observed in 1892 that 'The medieval university looked backwards, it professed to be a storehouse of old knowledge.... The modern university looks forward, and is a factory of new knowledge.' This quotation in a letter from Huxley of 1892 is cited by Clark Kerr as part of his own response to left-wing critics who argued that the post-war American university had sold out to the military-industrial complex and become a 'knowledge factory'. He was showing how unhistorical such critics were.[6]

The research-intensive university now flourishes in the US and the UK and increasingly in emerging economies too. The traumas of Nazism and then Communism played their part in weakening that model in Germany. You can see the results at Humboldt University, founded by Humboldt himself in 1810 as the University of Berlin and now named after him. It is located in what was East Berlin. I remember walking up the main staircase to give a lecture, past photographs of some of their twenty-nine Nobel Prize winners. Helmholtz, Einstein, and Max Planck were all there. But the portraits come to an end in the 1930s. Nazism, the war, and then Communism killed Humboldt's model—literally. I asked about the pock-marks in the walls of the inner courtyards and they explained: 'that is where the firing squads were'. The marks were indeed at chest height.

Under West Germany's constitution universities were the responsibility of the individual Länder and, to stop the federal Government subverting this, it was specifically forbidden from funding them directly. The only way the national Government could fund research was via separate federal institutes until they amended the Constitution in 2015 to permit federal funding of university-based research as part of their effort to boost their universities through the Excellence Initiative.[7]

Germany's shift away from research based in the university had already begun early in the twentieth century however. Thomas Mann's *Magic Mountain* explores the tension between academic detachment from the world and engagement with it. Herman Hesse's novel *The Glass Bead Game* is one of the most powerful modern accounts of scholasticism in which arguments and observations become counters in an endless and sterile game; they cease to refer to anything in the wider world. It can be intoxicating but it becomes claustrophobic. By the beginning of the twentieth century many German universities were thought to have succumbed to this scholasticism. In response the German Government created separate Kaiser Wilhelm research institutes which were to be closer to business and practical applications, shifting away from university-based research even before the horrors of Nazism. Germany created the research university and then turned away from that model, passing the baton to the US. Now Germany conducts more of its research, which is of exceptional quality, in its network of Max Planck, Leibniz, Helmholz, and Fraunhofer research institutes with a range of distinct missions ranging from pure to applied research. The Max Planck Institutes with their eighteen Nobel Prizes since the war rival our leading universities for their research quality—and indeed are matched only by Harvard for their research output—but their excellent work does not propel German universities up the rankings.

The German university still does a lot of R&D, funded by the state governments or by research-intensive companies. So a state (a Land) with a big agricultural sector may well sponsor agricultural research in its local university. This on its own enables German spend on R&D in universities broadly to match Britain's and some of Germany's universities have done well in the research rankings even without federal support. But their work is part of a much wider research effort and is proportionately less significant. With our unusually low R&D spend Britain has ended up backing one model—the research-intensive university winning prestige through global rankings. The benefits of Germany's Research Excellence initiative are now coming through. There are now seven German universities in the *THES* global top hundred, including Humboldt University. If the UK messes up with ill-thought-out policies and if our research effort is weakened by Brexit then German research-intensive universities will once more be the best in Europe within the next twenty years.

America's first research university, Johns Hopkins, was deliberately created on the German model in the 1870s. As America had very little by way of postgraduate study the way to develop an academic career was to go to Germany to study for a PhD and then return to the US. Germany had a massive impact on the development of the American graduate school in the late nineteenth century up to the First World War. Harvard's curriculum reform in that period, for example, was led by Charles Eliot, who had studied in Germany, as had nine of twenty-three professors on the faculty.[8] The crucial moment, however, was in 1945 when Vannevar Bush's notable report, *Science: The Endless Frontier*, was submitted to President Truman.[9] Having harnessed science and technology for the Second World War, Bush argued that America needed to maintain its intense research effort in these fields. He proposed that America's leading universities should be the base for this work:

These institutions are uniquely qualified by tradition and by their special characteristics to carry out basic research...It is chiefly in these institutions that scientists may work in an atmosphere which is relatively free from the adverse pressure of convention, prejudice, or commercial necessity. At their best they provide the scientific worker with a strong sense of solidarity and security, as well as a substantial degree of personal intellectual freedom...critical linking of support for basic research with the advanced education of aspiring scientists and engineers.[10]

The rise of the American research university, now at the heart of the great research and innovation clusters of America's East and West Coasts, can be traced directly to that crucial Government decision about the direction of its peace-time research effort. Vannevar Bush is America's Humboldt—though after victory not defeat. By the 1960s it was said that it had become difficult to tell whether MIT was 'a university with many government research laboratories appended to it or a cluster of government research laboratories with a very good educational institution attached'[11] America's 'private' universities now get as much of their money from Government as in the UK: it comes in enormous research grants for work across the disciplines from physical sciences to humanities and social sciences.

The First World War and after: British universities catch up

England lagged way behind these developments in Germany and the US. Newman, for example, explicitly opposed the idea that universities are for research: 'If its object were scientific and philosophical discovery, I do not see why a University should have students.'[12] Our tradition was research by the learned amateur outside the university—the gentleman with the time to think freely. Darwin was not attached to any university. And that model worked because these gentleman scientists created networks as good as any within a modern university and its surrounding cluster. The historian Joel Mokyr argues that one reason why the Industrial Revolution—which was also a science and technology revolution—happened in late eighteenth-century Britain was that it then had the most efficient system of information exchange the world had seen.[13] The UK had a network of newspapers and journals, coffee houses, local clubs, and professional societies from Birmingham's Lunar Society to the Royal Society so that new ideas and information about new technical advances could be widely shared and, just as importantly, freely challenged. Instead of being a private club dedicated to the secret investigation of mysteries, the Royal Society when it was created chose open publication based on an early version of peer review: it was a historic moment in the advance of science.[14]

Britain had nothing comparable to Germany's research-intensive universities through the nineteenth century: just restoring standards of teaching had been the main focus of the Oxbridge reforms of the 1850s. The technological challenges of the First World War finally prompted a surge of policy initiatives because of a recognition of how far we had fallen behind Germany: 'many of our industries have since the outbreak of war suffered through our inability to produce at home certain articles and materials required in trade processes, the manufacture of which has become localised abroad, and particularly in Germany, because science there has been more thoroughly and effectively applied to the solution of scientific problems bearing on trade and industry'. That Government report, published in 1915, is a classic critique of our business performance which could have been endorsed by Joe Chamberlain, Harold Wilson, or Michael Heseltine. It goes on to propose new Government support for research, so a new Department of Scientific and Industrial Research was established in 1916. The report observes: 'A great part of all research will necessarily be done in Universities and Colleges which are already aided by the State'.[15] This is very similar to the argument which Vannevar Bush used in his report after the Second World War. That shared Anglo-American assumption of the university as the best place for such research, provoked in both cases by the experience of a world war, is the origin of the dominance of the Anglo-American research-intensive university.

For the early part of the First World War Germany and Britain were competing for the support of neutral America. Britain's weak point was German influence through their educational leadership. The crucial moment came in 1916 when a British academic returned from a lecture tour of the US to report in *The Observer* that 'The enormous educational machine in America, which is so much more important than anything of the same kind we have in Europe, is almost entirely run from Germany. A very large proportion of the staffs of the colleges and universities has received all its educational training, or at any rate its postgraduate training in Germany.' It was one of those occasions when a vivid point made at the right time prompts a media and political storm.[16] Within two days the Foreign Office had started an exercise on 'German educational influence in America'. Foreign Office pressure was crucial in getting English universities to develop courses which would attract overseas students from America and challenge the influence of Germany. (By contrast I found the Foreign Office largely unwilling to engage on this issue a century later—leaving it to BIS to fight endless battles with the Home Office.) The DPhil was eventually introduced in Oxford in 1917 as an alternative for American graduate students after America had joined the war and Germany was closed to them. Within three years the PhD had become a new national model, though Oxford insists to this day on calling the DPhil what almost everyone else calls the PhD.[17] But the American universities needed a counter-party representing Britain's universities as a group so that they could arrange student admissions. Once again the Foreign Office led the way in what was called their 'summons to the universities' in the following letter from Balfour in March 1918:

> There appeared to be, rightly or wrongly, an impression that there exists among British Universities, as compared with German or French, a degree of local inde-pendence and variety, combined with a lack of any common organisation or even meeting ground for consultation, which made it very difficult for Americans who might desire to finish their studies abroad to find out what work was being done in Great Britain and what University could best provide for their needs. I am ven-turing now to invite representatives of all the Universities of Great Britain and Ireland to meet Mr Fisher and myself at the Foreign Office and confer upon the whole subject.[18]

As a result of this meeting the universities prepared a memo on 'action taken to encourage immigration of students from foreign countries and from the King's dominions overseas'. The need to work with Government on this and other projects led to the creation of the Committee of Vice Chancellors and Principals, who met for the first time in 1918, the forerunner of what is now Universities UK. However, Sir Oliver Lodge of Birmingham University made a crucial inter-vention at the Foreign Office meeting arguing that the real problem was not just information, it was the lack of qualified university teachers and suitable facilities for any influx of overseas students, so if the Government was concerned about the problem it should help fund the remedy. This gave impetus to the creation in 1919 of the University Grants Committee, the forerunner of HEFCE, to distribute public funding to universities—a body which functioned as the sponsor and funder of universities until the Government legislated in 2017 to replace it with the Office for Students and UK Research and Innovation (UKRI).

Just as Robbins came after a spurt of activity rather than prompting it so the Haldane report on the Machinery of Government produced at the end of the First World War brings all this together. It sets out the structure of the modern British state, allocating Departmental form to underlying function in a way that had not been done before. It gives a prominent role to the organization of research by Government. It proposes that there should be both research directly commissioned by Government Departments and also separately the promotion of 'Intelligence and Research for General Use'.[19] It was a crucial moment in the creation of what David Edgerton neatly calls the Warfare State and which he dates from 1920 to 1970, a period of sustained and close Government activity to promote R&D, above all for national defence.[20] The report is also seen as the origin of the Haldane Principle that ministers do not decide which research projects should be funded out of the Science Budget, though the principle is not set out explicitly in the text. Within four years therefore Britain created the Department of Scientific and Industrial Research (DSIR) with a science research budget, the DPhil, the Committee of Vice Chancellors and Principals, and the University Grants Committee. The Government had finally recognized how far we had fallen behind Germany and the US in research. The catalyst for all this activity was the war and in particular the Foreign Office's recognition of the need to offer postgraduate research opportunities to rival Germany's.

The interwar years saw attempts at creating separate networks of national research labs, sponsored by the DSIR, but they rarely lasted whereas the universities' research functions have. After the Second World War there was a fear of science unconstrained by the ethical framework of the humanities and Sir Walter Moberly, the head of the University Grants Committee, argued that scientific research should therefore best be conducted on a multidisciplinary university campus.[21] The University Grants Committee grew in power and significance, with its grants to universities covering both research and teaching costs. A network of over fifty Research Associations was also created after the end of the Second World War but they were largely closed down in the 1970s and 1980s—either because the industries they served had disappeared or because they were privatized and then subsequently absorbed into other companies. The Department of Scientific Research acted as sponsor of the different public sector research establishments. Burke Trend's report of 1963 identified two key problems with this structure: first, 'the various agencies concerned with the promotion of civil science do not, in the aggregate, constitute a coherent and articulated pattern of organisation; second that the arrangements for co-ordinating the Government's scientific effort and for apportioning the available resources between the agencies on a rational basis are insufficiently clear and precise'.[22] The old Department of Scientific and Industrial Research was abolished in 1965 when the Wilson Government created the modern structure of Research Councils as part of its pursuit of what Wilson called 'The White Heat of the Technological Revolution'. Each Research Council enjoyed a high degree of autonomy under a minister of science—an arrangement which survived until the individual Research Councils lost their individual accounting officers and were subsumed in UK Research and Innovation in 2017.[23]

Research outside or inside universities: Germany and Britain compared

America is so big and rich it can sustain both a network of great research institutes and of research-intensive universities. Indeed, Vannevar Bush's vision was not accepted by America's big departments of state, which insisted on sponsoring their own networks of research labs. But within Europe two medium-sized innovative economies, Germany and the UK, have ended up with very different models: Table 4.1 shows Germany has a lower proportion of its research in universities than Britain, where it is unusually high.

It is not that spending on university R&D in Britain is high as a percentage of GDP—it is just that other types of R&D spending are very low, as Table 4.2 shows.

Having come rather late to the idea of the research-intensive university, long after Germany and the US, Britain has now ended up as the outlier with an unusually high proportion of research happening in universities, and concentrated in a world-class group of elite research-intensive universities. This has happened for several reasons. We have already seen how England has national

Table 4.1. Higher Education R&D spending (HERD) as a percentage of total Gross Expenditure on R&D (GERD) 2014

Country	HERD%GERD
China (People's Republic of)	6.9
Korea	9.1
Japan	12.6
United States	14.2
Germany	17.3
France	20.6
Finland	22.9
United Kingdom	26.1
Sweden	29.0
Norway	31.1
Denmark	33.2

Source: Data provided by Robert Hughes, Centre for Business Research, University of Cambridge from the OECD Main Science and Technology Indicators. Figures are for 2014 except for the US (2013).

Table 4.2. Types of R&D expenditure as a percentage of GDP 2014

	United Kingdom	France	Germany	United States
Total Gross Expenditure on R&D (GERD)	1.7	2.26	2.84	2.74
Business Sector R&D (BERD)	1.1	1.46	1.93	1.94
Higher Education R&D (HERD)	0.44	0.46	0.49	0.39
Government R&D (GovERD)	0.13	0.3	0.42	0.31

Source: Data provided by Robert Hughes, Centre for Business Research, University of Cambridge from the OECD Main Science and Technology Indicators.

competition for entry to individual universities whereas Germany has local comprehensive universities with the presumption that students would go to their local university at least for undergraduate study. The German model is only possible because most students don't think there is much difference between universities—they just go to the one which is nearby and quite possibly live at home. The fact that Germany's teaching-based universities are not ranked on their teaching performance shows how hard it is to develop reliable metrics of teaching quality. But there are widely recognized metrics of research performance so research excellence is a basis for universities to be compared, to be ranked, and to compete. The German Government has now identified some universities as centres of research excellence. As they do so they create a status ranking of their universities and I expect students will care more about which university they go to. Local university recruitment and less internationally prestigious research on university campuses go together in a mutually dependent system. In England by contrast we have already seen that we have an unusual system of nationwide competitive entry to university. That means that doing well in the main driver of university rankings—research—matters to our universities because it helps attract students. It matters as much as the performance of the college football team does in the US. Those British parents competing to get their child into a good secondary school to get good A levels are doing so to boost their chances of getting their child to a university with a high reputation and that in turn will have been heavily shaped by its place in the research rankings. So competition for students and competition in research complement each other and shape the whole English education system.

It is not just that universities face intense competition for students, driving them to pursue research excellence. The way research funding is allocated further strengthens the position of our universities. A successful funding system has to balance two different principles. On one hand finance for new research projects should not favour incumbents so the bright new kid on the block can get a chance. On the other hand you need strong institutions with core funding which provide some stability and protection. This dualism is embodied in two distinct flows of research funding in the UK—project funding from the Research Councils and funding specifically for universities according to their historic research performance. This is the classic British 'dual funding' system. We will look at these two types of funding in turn and see how they have combined to drive our universities to the top of the research league tables whilst disadvantaging research institutes outside universities.

Research council funding and opportunities for young Principal Investigators (PIs)

The Research Councils allocate about £3bn per year. They use some of this for sponsoring their own research institutes but this role has tended to be squeezed out by competitive funding for specific projects much of which goes to universities. The Research Councils argue that research institutes may ossify and get stuck in old research programmes whereas project funding is more nimble. They focus on competitive, transactional, low trust allocation of funds for future research in which status and history should count for little—you are only as good as your next bid. Some of this funding is responsive mode (an academic has a bright idea; they apply for funds to investigate and the Research Council evaluates and responds to their proposal). The rest is challenge mode when one or more Research Councils invite bids for funds around a specific problem or challenge. This distinction is not quite the same as that between fundamental and applied research—tackling a big global challenge may lead to fundamental research.

There is no regard for age or the country of your birth in the allocation of Research Council funding. Research networks are best when they are open and international not hierarchical and exclusive. Forty per cent of our researchers come from abroad.[24] By contrast 97 per cent of Italian researchers are Italian—94 per cent in Spain are Spanish.[25] Of our 120 or so Nobel Laureates a third were born abroad, including half of the last ten.[26] Only 28 per cent of our researchers have never worked outside the UK.[27] I go round labs talking to smart young researchers from across the world—France or Italy, Germany or China—and try to find out why so many of them come from abroad to work in a British university. One answer comes up quite often. In Germany or Italy you slowly work your way up under the patronage of a baronial Professor at the head of a department of a research institute or perhaps in a university. Herr Doktor Professor sets the research agenda and younger staff have to accommodate to it—it is the academic equivalent of Germany's apprenticeship system. In England younger academics can develop their own research programme and will be encouraged to bid directly to a Research Council and other bodies for funds. (They used to say that in Germany you were Bunsen's man whereas in England you were a Balliol man, and loyalty to a college or a university independent of your discipline can be intellectually liberating.) Prestige is not the criterion of success and is (usually) not relevant when research work is attributed. There are subtle differences in the listing of authors of academic papers—one of the esoteric but crucial aspects of modern research culture. In Britain the person who did the key work is likely to be named first, regardless of their status, whereas in some other countries the dominant professor will come first. In some highly egalitarian countries and disciplines it is alphabetical order. In Asia informal ties of deference and reciprocity mean that status plays a more important part in allocating authorship. (The way conventions on authorship differ between disciplines, institutions, and countries is a fascinating example of how even the physical sciences are susceptible to cultural influences.[28])

I had the privilege of going to the Nobel Prize ceremony in Stockholm in 2010 when the UK had four Nobel Prize winners but only one had actually been born and educated in Britain. They had come from Cyprus to the LSE and from Russia to Manchester University via the Netherlands because we provided the best environment for doing their research. (And ironically the British-born winner, Robert Edwards, was the only one not to have received Research Council funding.)[29] But there is a wide gap between the elite researchers in the lab recruited from across the world and the products of an English education system which results in too many people knowing too little about science or indeed the humanities because of excessive early specialization. Our open system with recruitment from around the world is one reason why the inadequacies of our own education system do not do more damage—we recruit researchers with a broader education. Brexit poses a potential threat to this model and the science community attaches great importance to ensuring that we keep open movement of researchers—which means funding for collaboration with researchers abroad and attractive, flexible arrangements for moving into Britain. And we must hope that Brexit leads us at last to address the defects in our own education system.

In return for that freedom to develop their own research ideas young academics in Britain are at greater risk of being booted out if they don't win the funding. On the Continent you gain security and perhaps a slow-maturing wisdom but at the price of a loss of enterprise and initiative when you are young. It is a micro version of the wider contrast between different economic systems, with those systems which offer the greatest opportunities to youth being the most innovative.[30] If you are young and exceptional you can advance further and faster in the UK than in most other countries. Even in the US a doctorate takes much longer than in the UK—six or seven years rather than four. And it comes after a longer period of study at Master's level to cover ground which might already have been covered in England as part of an undergraduate course because of our early specialization. Young American academics are rather like American soldiers in the World Wars: they may arrive a couple of years late but they are very effective when they do turn up.

You should not get funded because you are senior or well-connected or even because your previous project was successful. The occasional senior academic, spluttering over a rejection—'Don't they know who I am?'—may blame the Government because they assume that their proposal must have been academically excellent so some other requirement, such as showing impact, must have been the problem. But even this does not remove full bias against younger researchers' bids as the peers doing the peer review may indeed literally be peers, belonging to the same generation and interested in the same problems, whereas a different problem preoccupies a different generation. The age of Principal Investigators (PIs) winning grants is an important indicator of the dynamism of research and is shown in Table 4.3.

The danger is that cuts in staff at Research Councils means they economize by handling bigger bids, fewer in total, and this favours older, more long-established researchers. This approach is particularly bad for the humanities, where the best use of money may be a small grant to cover the costs of a researcher to fly abroad to spend a week in an archive. One of my concerns as a minister was that we were driving gigantism in research projects because it looked more efficient, when it was not. (Funding direct to learned societies

Table 4.3. Research grants awarded to PIs aged under 40

Year	Total number of research grants awarded	Number and % of research grants given to under-40s
2011/12	3135	755 (24%)
2012/13	3210	775 (24%)
2013/14	2970	780 (26%)
2014/15	3095	810 (26%)
Total number over four years	12,410	3120 (25%)

Source: Data extracted from Tables 2, 4, 6, 8, 10, and 12 of *Research Councils Diversity Data* (RCUK, March 2015 and March 2016). Fellowships excluded.

such as the Royal Society and the British Academy is intended to counteract this by enabling them to fund promising young researchers and run discretionary schemes to help with modest research costs.)

There are still considerable frustrations among younger researchers, especially post-docs. There is an argument that some of the most deep-seated problems in our science base go back to poor career-planning for younger researchers. Why is there so much focus on numbers of journal articles and their impact factors? One reason is that a university needs some system, however crude, for winnowing out 200 applicants for a post. This problem in turn arises because the increase in the number of doctoral students and post-docs over the past decade has not been matched by the expansion of permanent posts higher up the system. Using these metrics also intensifies the pressure on researchers to come up with positive results, which are what get published. I had a very bright private secretary who had done a PhD at Cambridge but she had not been able to take her academic career further because the bit of DNA she had analysed for a potential link to cancer had turned out not to have a significant role so she had no result worth a journal article. She was facing an incentive system in which only good news gets reported and there is no room for a journal of negative results. This is very different from the reporting of politics: often the frustrated minister feels there is only room for reporting policies which do not work and little space for a success. In both cases the media believe they are doing their job but it is possible that in the long run science is ill-served by a system with such powerful incentives to accentuate the positive—this may lie behind the growing concern about the non-reproducibility of results.

University funding delivered through the Research Excellence Framework (REF)

There is one type of British institution which does get core funding in the expectation that it uses this to stay at the frontiers of research: universities as institutions get about £1.6bn of annual high trust core research funding which historically came from the Higher Education Funding Council. It can be thought of as compensation for lack of endowments, and indeed Bruce Truscot's original argument was that the Redbricks should get public funding to compete with Oxbridge, which had the advantage of substantial endowments. This funding is more likely to be used for blue skies research.[31] Whilst our research-intensive universities get core funding for their research, there is no comparable core support for research institutes outside universities. The conventional account of a dual funding system can imply a satisfying completeness to the model but actually it leaves a significant gap—core funding for research outside universities. This gap is one reason for the dominant role of universities in Britain's research system.

This second strand of research funding is allocated through the Research Excellence Framework (REF) and before that the Research Assessment Exercise (RAE). Originally the grants from the University Grants Committee to universities for their research were not separate from the funding for teaching—they were all included in a single university grant. They were then disentangled in separate grants in the 1980s.[32] The specific evaluation of research was introduced in 1985 and research was to be funded selectively by the UGC on the basis of these confidential assessments of quality. A. H. Halsey identified this as a crucial moment in what he called the Decline of Donnish Dominion, as research performance had to be appraised for the first time.[33] The new University Funding Council which replaced the University Grants Committee introduced explicit rankings of research overall which were first published in 1989. The research performance of specific departments and indeed individuals was then identified. This model, operating over thirty years, has transformed the performance of British research by putting academic researchers under greater pressure to perform than in any other national system. The funding is allocated on the basis of previous research excellence as judged by subject panels of academic experts and is allocated for periods of about six years. Universities have discretion in how to spend it, so even if, for example, they get research funding because of their world-class historians they could if they wish then use the funds to beef up the physics department—it gives universities a bit of space to build up teams or shift the balance between departments. But now it is clear how individuals are ranked this can constrain the discretion of universities to shift funds around. And, contrary to Halsey's claim, it has had the effect of strengthening the power of the star researchers who can calculate how much funding they individually bring into their university. One reason for the defensiveness of some scholars in the humanities may be because they are unlikely to bring in funds on the scale of researchers active in big science—though this is not intended to diminish their intellectual worth. The autonomous university becomes the place where all kinds of tensions around research funding are played out. Should universities, for example, use their funds to invest in historic success or to support the new insurgents doing something different?

The REF has succeeded in transforming the output and efficiency of the research community. But there are a range of concerns about it. For a start it is now big and onerous. The scale of the REF is enormous—assessing 200,000 papers by 50,000 academics. The time and effort involved is high. They say the REF is the closest the academic community gets to a General Election. Jonathan Grant at King's College London estimates the costs at £250 million. But it is used to allocate more than £10 billion of research funding over six years (from 2015/16 to 2020/21) so the REF is an efficient way of allocating performance-related research funding. The costs of the REF work out at about 2.5 per cent of funds allocated. By contrast the overhead costs of Research Council grants are about 13 per cent of the value of funds being allocated. Moreover the REF estimates include as a cost time which academics devote to reading and assessing these papers. This is the rigorous economist's way of estimating costs and is rarely applied across Whitehall. What would the overhead cost of the tax system look like if it included the time spent filling in tax returns? Compared with most of Whitehall's arrangements for allocating public spending the REF actually has very low overhead costs.[34] There are always hopes that it can be modified to save on these. There are two options. Would the result be very different if, instead of this lengthy process, a dozen leading academics in a discipline got together for dinner in the Athenaeum and agreed a ranking of the best performers in their field? The reply is that there were hidden gems uncovered by the process and anyway such discretionary judgements are not really an acceptable way of allocating public money any more. Another option is metrics—using measures such as citations to reveal who is doing the best work. We do not yet have measures which are sophisticated enough to do this though there are some disciplines where we are getting close.[35]

Academics sometimes resented a new requirement introduced in the 2008–14 REF to show impact from their research: they feared it brought the barbarians even closer to the gates of academe. Impact was actually a response to worries about the kind of behaviour which might be promoted by the relentless pressure on academics to produce more papers. An academic can get onto a treadmill where the task is just to keep on churning out the papers for the peer-reviewed journals without looking up and asking oneself that most challenging of questions—what is it all for? (The REF itself only asked for a maximum of four papers to be submitted but promotion may depend on rather more.) Impact assessments were not introduced to change the type of research undertaken but to encourage researchers to think about the potential contribution their research can make to economy and society. I myself had doubts about the impact case studies, fearing they would be time-consuming for little practical benefit, so I delayed the REF to see if we could find a better way, but when I negotiated with the Treasury in the summer of 2010 for cash protection for the science budget, one of their conditions was that we should go ahead with the impact exercise within the REF. HEFCE asked that just one in ten of the researchers submitted for assessment as part of the REF, which concluded in 2014, should show impact, defined as 'demonstrable effect on, change or benefit to the economy, society, culture, public policy or services, health, well-being, the environment or quality of life beyond academia'. Those impact assessments did turn out to be of value. It was significant that the humanities, having been most wary of the implications of this whole exercise, ended up with excellent examples of impact—if a new interpretation of an author leads to an innovative production of a play, that is genuine and worthwhile impact.[36] These criteria were however interpreted rather narrowly and Lord Stern's Review in 2016 sensibly proposed a broader interpretation of impact.[37] One of the most important forms of impact can be better-informed teaching, and it would be very welcome if this factor were introduced into impact assessments. The Research Councils also ask that applications for a research grant explain what the impact of the research might be. But these are not and cannot be forecasts of exactly what will be achieved.

The REF may now be having perverse effects because it favours competition over collaboration. Whereas with teaching standards the problem is that the fixed number of places per university weakened competitive pressures, the intense competition for research funds may have penalized collaboration across institutions and across departments. The REF is based on the one researcher whose name appears first on the list of authors: this focus on the one individual may not promote collaboration with others within or across disciplines. In the words of one Oxford University report: 'current measures of quality and success, and competition for restricted funds, have created behaviours in the best researchers and research institutions that are not optimised to deliver the large scale cross-disciplinary research required to make significant progress that is significant on the global scale'.[38] Perhaps there is a parallel with football: we could say that our teams compete so hard domestically that we have the best league but as a nation we do not win the World Cup. The competition stops our individual teams getting big enough to take important research all the way through to full commercialization. That is why my view as minister was that when it comes to university teaching we needed more competition but when it comes to research we needed more collaboration. Practical measures to improve things include giving a higher weighting to interdisciplinary work and recognizing more than the first name on the research paper.

The combined effect of these two funding streams help to explain the extraordinary position which universities enjoy in our research system. HEFCE provides core funding to universities for research but there is no equivalent core funding for research institutes. The Research Councils may operate and fund some, but it comes out of a single budget which could also be used for individual research projects. Some Whitehall Departments also sponsor research institutes devoted to specific issues for which they are responsible—animal health, for example. But there is a crucial difference between these research institutes and university research activities: universities are part of the private sector whereas research institutes are in the public sector. This gives universities a further significant advantage because the public sector has proved to be an inhospitable and unstable environment for research. I observed, for example, the problems caused by the application of public sector pay rules which made it hard for research institutes to recruit internationally mobile scientists, while such rules did not apply to universities which are not public bodies. Cabinet Office rules on procurement were also written for organizations buying standard supplies, not for research bodies which wanted to collaborate with outside bodies to develop innovative new kit and where the very prestige of the environment where they were being used was a handy negotiating tool. I came to suspect that the Cabinet Office wanted to make life so difficult for research institutes in the public sector that they would be driven to privatize themselves out of sheer desperation. Departments were poor custodians of their own research institutes as well—frequently running them down or trying to privatize or close them. I therefore introduced the 'Manchester guidelines' (based on work we commissioned from Manchester University) to ensure that Departments across Whitehall could not do this without a proper review shared with the science minister. With such a perilous existence in the public sector, our research institutes seek the protective embrace of our universities, which look like strong and friendly patrons. And the universities have an incentive to take over a high-quality team of researchers in an independent institute because it adds to their research output and pushes them up the rankings. One can see why we have ended up with such an unusually high proportion of research done on university campuses. But individual universities may not prove to be reliable custodians of what should be seen as national assets. If nationally significant facilities fall under the management of a single autonomous university they can be vulnerable to a change of intellectual fashion, a temporary decline in research performance, or even just the arrival of a new Vice Chancellor, and a research institute is lost. The counter-argument is that this restless instability is just what is needed to keep our research at the cutting edge.

This model also leads to high levels of concentration of research, with both of Britain's leading funding streams concentrated on our prestigious research-intensive universities. Britain's top ten research-intensive universities get about half of the total public research budget and, narrowing down even further, the UK's top five research universities get about 35 per cent of the public research budget.[39] This concentration is greater than in the US where the top ten get 23 per cent and the top five get 15 per cent of public research funds.[40] Britain has nothing like Germany's local funding of research or America's network of federal research laboratories. We have all our eggs in one basket.

The Haldane Principle and the success of the British research model

Both funding streams are protected from political interference by the Haldane Principle but it was hard to pin down exactly what it meant. The Campaign for Science and Engineering, CASE, had written to David Cameron in Opposition asking about his policies for science and he had replied with a commitment to Haldane. When I arrived in BIS I commissioned an excellent official, Graeme Reid, to work on this. It was an opportunity to publish an authoritative statement of the principle but subtly updated, making it clear, for example, that there was a role for ministers in major capital spending decisions. It proved to be useful in heading off attempts to intervene in the detailed allocation of the science budget. I stated that

> The Haldane principle means that decisions on individual research proposals are best taken by researchers themselves through peer review. This involves evaluating the quality, excellence and likely impact of science and research programmes. Prioritisation of an individual research council's spending within its allocation is not a decision for Ministers ... This statement on the Haldane principle applies to science and research which the Government funds through the research councils and national academies.[41]

There is a further specific legal protection for these freedoms when it comes to university funding: 'The Further and Higher Education Act 1992 states that the Secretary of State may not attach conditions on grants to HEFCE which are framed by reference to: particular courses of study, programme of research, the criteria for the selection and appointment of academic staff or the admission of students.'[42] This crucial principle can be traced back to the great Humboldt, who put it in rather more Hegelian terms than would normally be used in Whitehall: the state 'must not demand from ... [Universities] anything that relates directly and straightforwardly to itself, but must nurse the inner conviction that when they achieve their final purpose, they will also fulfill its purposes'.[43] The one place where you will not find his principle is in Haldane's own report of 1918—apart from a discussion of funding of medical research. David Edgerton has argued that the principle was invented by Britain's first science minister, Quintin Hogg, in 1963 to challenge Harold Wilson's 'White Heat of the Technological Revolution' by arguing that his plans for a Ministry of Technology threatened deep constitutional principles of institutional autonomy for universities.[44]

We may take this principle for granted but there are many countries—including some in the West—where compliance with any form of the Haldane Principle is by no means assured. These high principles are also tested in Britain as well, as the boundaries are fuzzy—big capital projects, for example, clearly require ministerial involvement as the science community cannot just award itself a new facility for £250m. An ambitious Asian country is trying to recruit a Nobel Prize winner and most of his team with a $50m offer that includes a new purpose-built lab: can and should we respond fast enough to keep them? A friendly country wants us to join their major science capital project and in return we want them to bring current spending to an under-resourced British facility: can we negotiate a deal? A facility is jointly funded by the Research Councils and external charities—should it comply with public sector pay rules and lose out in the international competition for talent or recruit the best (and most expensive) manager, which the charity funders see as their priority? We are bidding to lead a major global scientific project but a rival country is about to win the HQ partly because of fears that our visa regime will impede the movement of researchers: what can we offer to win the competition? These are the sort of issues which I got involved in: the public funding of scientific research inevitably brings ministers into these type of public policy decisions. Then there are the deep questions about the social acceptability of certain strands of science research—from GM crops to mitochondrial DNA. It is not possible to conduct science completely outside the realm of politics and democratic government. The Haldane Principle is right but it does not fully resolve the task of finding the right and respectful way of linking university research and public policy.

This model of research funding does however succeed triumphantly in delivering world-class research. The UK has won around 120 Nobel Prizes since they were created at the beginning of the last century.[45] This is an area of human accomplishment where we are still emphatically world class. The ranks of British Nobel Prize winners are not lots of bearded Edwardian gentlemen looking like W. G. Grace. We won twelve in the decade from 2005 to 2015. The greatest total volume of high-quality research comes of course from the US. Their national research effort is massive compared with us and not just because their economy is bigger. The USA embraces the role of the public sector and public funding more enthusiastically than we do, maybe because they recognize this is an area where public spending does not crowd out private spending but crowds it in. Their economy is five times bigger than ours, yet their total public and private spend on R&D is ten times ours and their Government spend on R&D outside universities is fifteen times ours, as Table 4.4 shows. But we get forty-three citations per $m of public spend on R&D and America gets sixteen.

That America, the world's most productive science base, channels a high proportion of its funding via universities is powerful evidence of the importance of the modern research-intensive university. One study found that publicly funded research has bigger economic impact than privately funded and of that it is research in universities which has the biggest impact, with a 0.17 multiplier for publicly funded versus 0.13 for private.[46] The performance of our universities in the league table is artificially boosted because they get so much of our research funding and activity compared with universities in other countries, which do not play such a prominent role in research. However, even after

Table 4.4. Total spending on R&D and breakdown, UK 2014, US 2013

	GERD ($bn)	BERD ($bn)	HERD ($bn)	GovERD ($bn)
United Kingdom	44	28	11	3
United States	457	322	65	48

GERD is Gross domestic expenditure, BERD is Business expenditure, HERD is Higher education expenditure and GovERD is Government expenditure on public agencies, in each case on R&D.

Source: Data provided by Robert Hughes, Centre for Business Research, University of Cambridge from the OECD Main Science and Technology Indicators. (For abbreviations, see Table 4.2.)

allowing for this our system also delivers an extraordinary range of high-quality academic research for relatively low levels of public spending. The global rankings of the performance of national university-based research systems broadly match the proportion of national output devoted to R&D—except for us. We are ranked twelfth on inputs (if it's any comfort that is actually up from 26th and before that 28th for spending relative to our GDP per head) but when it comes to outputs we are second.[47]

UK Research and Innovation (UKRI): the balance of disciplines and interdisciplinary work

This success is one reason why many sceptics were wary of the creation of the UKRI in 2017. International observers would not say that Britain's problem is that our research base underperforms and is crying out for reform. Yet it is a wide-ranging reorganization. The seven Research Councils, each of which used to have their own accounting officer, are now brought together under a single chief executive of UKRI, Sir Mark Walport, who is the sole accounting officer. Moreover from 1919 there was a single funding body with responsibility for universities as a whole, but HEFCE is now abolished with its research funding brought under UKRI alongside the Research Councils whilst teaching funding goes to the separate Office for Students. Innovate UK comes under UKRI as well. This goes against the argument that one reason for the success of British science has been the diversity of organizations funding it so that no one single set of values dominates.

UKRI, however, had powerful advocates in Paul Nurse, the outgoing President of the Royal Society, George Osborne, the then Chancellor, and Sajid Javid, the then BIS Secretary of State. Even before they got involved there was clear hostility to the Research Councils from the Cabinet Office, which did not like this network of public bodies staffed with people who count as public sector employees, so I was frequently pressed to review them. The Cabinet Office was not alone. Scientists did not like it when Research Councils turned down good bids for research projects: the real reason might be that money was tight but they could easily imagine that it was a failure by administrators to grasp the unique value of their particular research proposal. And Research Councils loyally enforced the Coalition's policy for holding down top pay levels, which got them into conflict with outside funders like the Wellcome Trust with whom they shared funding for research institutes and who wanted to pay the going rate for people of an internationally high standard. So the Research Councils had their critics. That was the backdrop to George Osborne commissioning Paul Nurse to review the Research Councils.[48] Paul Nurse argued that it was cumbersome and bureaucratic for each of the seven Research Councils to have their own accounting officers so they should be brought together under one person. He also wanted to see greater co-ordination of research on big strategic priorities and greater recognition of interdisciplinary research. Sajid Javid, the then Secretary of State in BIS, had set himself the aim of reducing the number of partner bodies with which a slimmed-down BIS would deal, and the merger of seven Research Councils and Innovate UK into one body helped in this. In addition UKRI could absorb the REF funding responsibilities of the old HEFCE which needed a home if they were not to be part of the Office for Students. I myself doubted the need for organizational change on this scale. It looked to the sceptics like a solution in search of a problem. The advocates of the changes argued, however, that there were problems—both in getting the balance right between different disciplines and also in promoting interdisciplinary research—which UKRI could address. We will look at these arguments in turn.

Most medium-sized economies are world class in a few specific areas linked perhaps to the particular strengths of their economy or their natural resources. We are exceptional in being world class across so many different disciplines. One measure of the quality of research is the number of citations per paper, relative to the world average, weighted by subject area as some fields cite more than others. A field-weighted citation index of 1.5 means a country gets 50 per cent more citations per paper in that discipline than the world average. The US ranges from 1.27 to 1.58. The UK's index ranges from 1.44 to 1.78. No other country in the G7 has a range as high as that.[49] This range is important because big global challenges are not going to be solved by one discipline on its own. The German term *Wissenschaft* covers all the disciplines, not just physical or biological sciences but also the social sciences and the arts and humanities;

that is the broad interpretation of 'science' in our ring-fenced science budget: it rightly includes humanities and social sciences. There is no hierarchy in which particle physics is more or less valuable than history. Tackling ebola involves biological science but also an understanding of burial practices in West Africa from anthropology and social science. Whilst the UK is not going to solve global challenges on its own, our capacity to absorb advances across the world is greater if we have real strength across a wide range of disciplines.

The British system, with so much research activity in universities, gives students themselves a significant and underestimated role in the balance of our research activity because the distribution of academics partly reflects students' choices about which subjects to study. As we saw in the discussion of the Robbins Report, English students steadfastly continue to show a strong desire to study humanities and social sciences and this helps offset a preference for STEM subjects in parts of Whitehall. The university has a lot of academic staff in humanities and social sciences because lots of students want to study them, and as university staff are usually assessed for promotion on their research performance it means they need to do research as well and so the university sponsors a lot of research in these areas. As a result REF funding for universities is more weighted towards humanities and social sciences than Research Council funding. This means the balance of research activity is significantly influenced by the subjects which 18-year-olds apply to study—and because in England we specialize so young, that means the subject preferences and A level decisions of 16-year-olds. Critics argue that it is wrong for the distribution of public resources for research to be influenced by the interests of a bunch of teenagers. It is certainly an unusual way to shape the national research effort and one of the odder consequences of the concentration of our research on universities. But it appears to work. It is one reason for the vigour of the humanities in Britain. The irony is that the humanities tend to be particularly wary of 'marketization' but student choice is one of the best protections that the humanities have got.

One of the arguments for the creation of the new UKRI was that it brought decisions about the balance between different disciplines out into the open, and that stable distribution of funding between Research Councils was evidence that we lacked any strategy. Now we can have an explicit strategy on this for the first time. But as minister of science I did have the power to shift the balance of funding between the different Research Councils and other bodies. I was presented with this option in the summer of 2010 after the Comprehensive Spending Review. I commissioned the shrewd Adrian Smith, then the senior official responsible for science in BIS, to consult our learned societies and other bodies on whether there was a case for this. He reported that the academic community did not believe the broad balance of funding should be changed. It was also my political judgement that there was little reason for redistributing funding within a flat cash total—you would be robbing Peter to pay Paul. Faced with the decision in the summer of 2010 whether to change the balance of funding between the Research Councils, I decided not to do this and maintained cash spend on the arts and humanities and the social sciences just as on the physical sciences. Indeed, combined with the particular gains they made from the reforms to student funding the humanities and social sciences have quite rightly been well-supported through difficult times.

Behind this there was a strategy, though not always set out as clearly as it should be. That strategy has been quite simply to maintain Britain as a major scientific player with strengths across a very wide range of disciplines including humanities and social sciences as well as life science and physical sciences. That is our science strategy and it remains a good one. Both of our two strands of funding have been harnessed to that goal of conducting research of global standard across a wide range of disciplines. The day might come when we would have to decide we could not afford a research base covering the full range of disciplines and were going to have to specialize. My nightmare was that funding would become so tight that we would face such a scenario, but so far that moment of crisis has been avoided and indeed the substantial increase in funding announced in the 2016 Autumn Statement makes this moment of crisis less likely.

With so much prestige and research activity concentrated in autonomous universities and protected by the Haldane Principle, the critics argue that the balance of power is with the university 'providers' not the Research Council funders, which means that ministers require a certain amount of ingenuity to deliver any more detailed strategy than excellence everywhere. This could be a useful role for UKRI. However, science ministers such as William Waldegrave, David Sainsbury, or myself were able to shape a science policy whilst working with the consent of the research community. For example every couple of months I would convene a meeting of all the research bodies for which I had responsibility—the Research Councils, HEFCE, Innovate UK, and other specific agencies such as the Atomic Energy Authority and the Met Office. We would talk very informally about what we were up to. I would be able to report that, for example, the Government was very interested in the challenge of Alzheimers because of the long-term growth of the elderly population and without giving anyone an instruction they would assess the case and, if it was strong, develop a new shared research project that met the highest academic standards. Those informal arrangements worked rather well, though perhaps we now need something more structured and formal and that is what UKRI is likely to deliver.

Strength across a wide range of disciplines is not the same as being good at interdisciplinary work and there is real frustration amongst academics that they work within structures which make this harder than it should be. The critics say that the structure of seven different Research Councils militates against interdisciplinary working, though they do share funding of big cross-disciplinary challenges. But the Research Councils did work together to assemble joint funding streams focused on big challenges. The Engineering and Physical Sciences Research Council, for example, reckon they spend £50m a year on social science as many of their technology projects involve understanding how humans would interact with their innovations. A useful study by the British Academy suggests that individual Research Councils are funding research projects across the full range of the thirty-six disciplines represented within the 2014 REF—with the Economic and Social Research Council funding work in every single one and the Engineering and Physical Sciences Research Council a close second with thirty-one.[50] The Royal Academy of Engineering reports that 'The research councils are regarded as having been successful at funding challenge-led interdisciplinary consortia, but the support of interdisciplinary activities does not satisfactorily extend to the smaller responsive mode grants, which play a particularly important role for those starting out in their interdisciplinary research careers'.[51] It does not look as if Research Councils are the source of the problem: if there is one we should look elsewhere.

Britain's lack of serious well-funded interdisciplinary public research institutes outside universities may be a crucial weakness in promoting interdisciplinary research. One might hope that the big research-intensive university should promote interdisciplinary research. The idea is that in the Senior Common Room or by the coffee machine a moral philosopher gets into lively conversation with a computer scientist programming a new robot and together they realize that Asimov's three rules for robots do not solve every ethical problem. Or at least you might find a physicist talking to a chemist. Big universities covering many disciplines at the heart of city clusters can be powerful creative institutions. However, universities tend to be organized in departments which reflect teaching responsibilities and traditional disciplines. Some of the most powerful advocates of reform—such as Paul Nurse and Mark Walport—wanted to free more research from teaching-based university structures so it could be more interdisciplinary and innovative. That is an understandable ambition. Those student choices which admirably protect the humanities may also be inhibiting the growth of interdisciplinary research because student preferences, shaped by early specialization, can be very conservative. The British Academy report found that 'fewer than 1% of undergraduate degrees in the UK are truly interdisciplinary—although a higher proportion are joint honours'.[52] It is not just the preferences of students. The most prestigious journals are rooted in established disciplines. This raises deep questions about how to assess quality in a piece of interdisciplinary research which may not fit neatly into the established structures of the canon. Indeed the British Academy concluded that the main obstacle to interdisciplinary work is the structure of evaluation of research, notably in universities. The university should be the classic multidisciplinary environment breaking down barriers between disciplines and it is a pity if it is not. This is the real challenge for universities and UKRI may help them address it.

There are other arguments for UKRI as well. First, the Treasury clearly liked the new model and the significant extra funding secured in 2016 would not have been possible without UKRI. Indeed, the creation of UKRI has put research funding on a new upward trajectory which is very welcome indeed. Second, Brexit poses a whole series of new challenges in organizing British research activity so that it can still access international networks and funding streams. We need a body which can do deals on research funding with the EU and with research agencies across the world. UKRI is crucial to that. It is the challenge of Brexit to which we now must turn.

Brexit

Overall Great Britain remains extraordinarily open and well-connected and our universities are at the heart of these networks. Some of the networks are very real indeed—Janet (the inter-university IT network funded by JISC) is an underestimated resource for the exchange of data between our universities. They are also international networks—the flows of researchers into and out of the UK are exceptional. We are second only to Canada (with its close links to US) for the proportion of researchers who have come from abroad and stayed more than two years.[53] Thirty-nine per cent of full-time research-only academic staff at UK HE institutions were from nationalities outside the UK, as Table 4.5 shows.

Table 4.5. Nationality of UK-based academic research staff 2014/15

Nationality	Academic Employment Function (FPE), 2014/15	
	Research only	Teaching + Research
Non-European Union	18.8% (84,560)	9% (90,180)
Other European Union	20.1% (90,255)	10.4% (105,095)
United Kingdom	57.9% (259,850)	77.7% (782,325)
Not known	3.2% (14,485)	2.9% (29,080)

Source: HESA Staff Record 2014/15.

That is why the research community was overwhelmingly in favour of our remaining in the EU. The argument during the Referendum came over as all about money and we did indeed do well out of competitively allocated EU research funding. But often the condition for winning these funds was that they had to be spent in a partnership across more than one EU country. This promoted research networks which were as valuable as the funding and we must aim to remain in them. One way to achieve this is to stay within the framework of Horizon 2020 and its successor. This would probably involve our paying a direct contribution to the EU to participate—as do other non-EU countries such as Switzerland and Norway and Israel. If this is not negotiable a fall-back could be for the British Government to set up a parallel fund to shadow EU research and finance British research activities which link up to the programme. Finally British universities and research institutes may set up new operations within the EU which could themselves individually be eligible for EU funding and participate in EU networks. The best single argument for UKRI is that a single body should be a powerful voice for British science and better able to steer whatever changes are necessary as Brexit approaches.

Conclusion

These four chapters have looked at the rise of the university. Nothing exemplifies this rise better than the way in which British universities now dominate publicly funded research more than in any other major university system. It has led to a characteristic British model of research which is strong on autonomy and good for university rankings but can be weak on application and commercialization. We will turn to this challenge in Chapter Ten.

Our universities do excellent research. That is good for all of us. It is how they compete with other. It also reinforces their prestige. This gives them strength and authority and the power to protect the freedoms of the academic community. But it can weaken the focus on teaching the student, and in the next four chapters we look at the university from the perspective of the student.

II

The Student

FIVE

Why it's Worth Going
to University

Introduction

You may well have gone to university. If so, would you do it all over again? I expect so. One survey of recent graduates found 96 per cent of them would do it again.[1] If you haven't gone but are thinking about going to university you should almost certainly go for it. You won't regret it. It may well turn out to be one of the most rewarding and transforming experiences of your life. But what is it that makes more and more of us go to university when the media are full of stories of graduates who are unemployed and the usual clichés that too many people go to university? And why are record numbers of young people going even after the changes in student finance, which I helped to bring in, mean that graduates are likely to be paying back more over their working lives?

Just look at the newspaper headlines:

> Thousands of new graduates out of work, figures show.[2]
> Expansion of the university sector has destroyed its status.[3]
> UK graduates are wasting degrees in lower-skilled jobs.[4]
> Today's university students are being sold a lie.[5]

Is College Worth It? is a very fair question, and the American book with that title answers with a clear 'No' for many people, many courses, and many institutions.[6] The conventional wisdom is that going to university is often an expensive waste of time. But for most students the truth is the opposite. For most young people it is a deeply rewarding, life-changing experience. And it matters particularly if you come from a poor background because then it really could transform your chances in life.

I meet parents who think that too many people go to university but definitely want their own child to go—it is the other parents' kids who aren't supposed to go. But the other parents might not see it that way. A survey of mothers of children born in the year 2000 showed that even for the mothers with the lowest qualifications 96 per cent wanted their child to go to university.[7] These are levels of support for higher education which sound like election results in a one-party state.

The sceptics reply that, however widespread this aspiration, it does not make sense to fulfil it. And then the advocates of university disagree about what makes it worthwhile. Some point to the economic benefits, but that is then denounced as a narrowly utilitarian account of what should be a deeply rewarding intellectual experience. The purists dislike any talk of benefits, even ones that are not economic, because they are 'instrumentalist'—making the university merely a means to something else. So instead they say that the university is worthwhile in its own right. But just asserting that—however true—does not win over the sceptics. Universities are home to the most stringent minds, rightly probing and challenging every proposition, so it would be peculiar if they then tried to justify themselves in a way that was impervious to investigation. The value of universities must be explained and argued for. We should welcome the challenge of showing that higher education brings wider benefits—it means investigating evidence that could back up the intuitive case for higher education.

The purists have a point, though. Education is worthwhile in its own right, not just as a means to something else. Knowledge is better than ignorance. Understanding is better than a mind confined by prejudice. 'Knowledge is capable of being its own end. Such is the constitution of the human mind, that any kind of knowledge, if it be really such, is its own reward.... That further advantages accrue to us and redound to others by its possession, over and above what it is in itself, I am very far indeed from denying; but independent of these, we are satisfying a direct need of our nature in its very acquisition.'[8] That was Newman making the case for a Catholic University in Ireland in his great Victorian essay on the *Idea of a University*. But he then goes on to argue that this education should change us into different and better people: 'it is more correct to speak of a University as a place of education, than of instruction, though, when knowledge is concerned, instruction would at first sight have seemed the more appropriate word. But education is a higher word; it implies an action upon our mental nature, and the formation of a character...'.[9] As our basic material needs are met we seek to make something meaningful of our lives and a university education is the most powerful route to that fulfilment in the modern world.

At its simplest the case for higher education is really just the case for education. The value of education does not suddenly stop when you are aged 11 or 15 or 18. We would think it very peculiar now if someone said—as they used to—that primary school education was a good thing but secondary school was an unaffordable luxury. The value of higher education is particularly clear if you are on the outside looking in. In Ireland higher education had been reserved for Protestants so Newman looked at what Protestants got and Catholics were deprived of. 'Protestant youths, who can spare the time, continue their studies till the age of twenty-one or twenty-two; thus they employ a time of life all-important and especially favourable to mental culture...a youth who ends his education at seventeen is no match for one who ends it at twenty-two.'[10]

We now have evidence to support his bold claims about the benefits of those extra years of education. The figure below summarizes that evidence by dividing it in two different ways. First, there are gains for the individual from going to university as distinct from gains for wider society. Secondly, there are economic gains as distinct from non-economic gains. Draw these as two axes and you get four quadrants, each of which shows a real positive benefit. Too much time and effort is wasted arguing about which quadrant matters most. If you point out that the individual gains financially then you face the charge that you fail to recognize that higher education is really a public good—valuable to society as a whole and not just for an individual's economic gains. But citing any one type of gain should not exclude the others. The quadrants below give equal space to each different type of benefit but everyone can give their own personal weighting to each of these types. We will look at them in turn.[11]

Figure 5. Quadrant of the benefits of university.

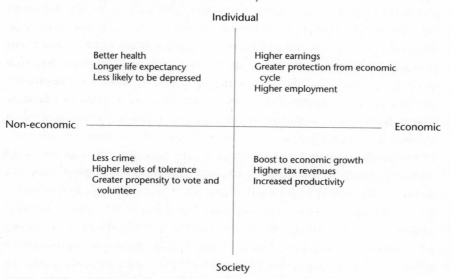

Note: Also see David Willetts, *Robbins Re-Visited: Bigger and Better Higher Education* (Social Market Foundation, 2013), 20.

Benefits to individuals which aren't economic: but are they just selection effects?

We are so preoccupied with the economic effects of behaviour that it is right instead to start with non-economic effects, which are just as important. We will begin with individual effects and the most notable of these is personal health. Whatever students might get up to, university does not set them up for a life of high alcohol consumption. Graduates are less likely to drink heavily, to smoke, and to be obese.[12] 1.6 fewer cigarettes are smoked per person per day for every extra year of schooling. We exercise an extra seventeen minutes each week for every extra year in college.[13] Going to university improves your life expectancy too. Estimates vary but one is that a graduate lives 2.5 years longer than someone who completed upper secondary education. That is roughly the length of the course, so students use up none of their allotted lifespan whilst they are at university: it really is free time.[14] In the US a 25-year-old graduate will on average live a further fifty-seven years as against fifty years for a non-graduate—lower obesity is a key reason.[15] Graduates are more likely to drive safely and to live in a house with fewer accidents.[16] Going to university buffers the impact of disability as well.[17] Graduates reap psychological rewards from these patterns of behaviour: 77 per cent of adults with tertiary education are satisfied with their life as against 66 per cent of adults with upper secondary and 63 per cent of those educated below this level.[18] Graduates are less likely to be depressed—especially men, where there is a 55 per cent difference for those with a degree as against those with A levels.[19] Graduates also have greater interest and involvement in politics; more positive attitudes to immigration and immigrants; more tolerant perceptions of welfare benefits and benefit recipients—differences which are still apparent even after allowing for other key characteristics such as income. The increase in the number of graduates has itself become a major factor driving changes in social attitudes.[20]

The sceptics try to argue these effects away by saying that what we are attributing to university is actually caused by something else. They say that going to university does not change people: it is rather that the type of people who go to university are also likely to be the sort of people who will anyway be likely to vote more or smoke less.[21] There could well be such an effect but it is not the whole story. The crucial question is whether there is any impact after you have allowed for this selection effect. That is what the more sophisticated studies are trying to investigate. Different studies have different methodologies but modern social science does try to adjust for other factors to separate out, in this case, the distinctive effect of more education. Whenever possible they are trying to compare what happens if you go to university as against people of otherwise similar characteristics who do not go. Natural experiments such as twin studies or lotteries, in which some go to university and some do not, show a real effect from higher education.[22]

There does appear to be a genuine effect from going to university. After all, we are looking at how young people spend a crucial three years of their life, probably the first time they have lived away from home as a semi-independent adult. For many it is a particularly intense experience. Perhaps for the first time you shape a social group away from your neighbourhood and your family. You can suddenly live the way you want, with friends you choose, and study what really interests you. For many young people it is a moment of extraordinary liberation from a home town that has become tedious, a family you are growing apart from, and too many exams which penalize genuine intellectual curiosity. It would be very odd if those crucial years had no effect on you. It would be like saying National Service or three years in prison had no effect on people. Experiences of this scale and significance do have an effect. People would have to be unusually thick-skinned and hard-baked if something that looms so large in a person's life did not change them, especially as these years are particularly important in the development of a person's identity. Politics starts to matter both as expressing who you are and as one of the important ways an individual relates to the world. So, for example, when asked about the most significant political events that have happened in their lifetime, people are disproportionately likely to refer to an event when they were aged 17 to 25.[23]

Does going to university change you for the better? Some critics do accept that going away to university is a big life experience but then they say it is a bad one. This was Henry Brougham's criticism of unreformed Oxford in the 1820s: 'The plan of sending young men of eighteen or nineteen to live together for the three most critical years of their lives, at a distance from their parents or guardians, subject to no effectual or useful control, and suffered to drink, dice, and wench as they please...is one of the most extravagant follies that ever entered in the minds of men.'[24] That objection goes back to the seventeenth century: 'parents sending their children far from them, young and hopeful, have for all their care and cost, after several years received them back again with their tongues and Arts, profane, wicked, abominable and incorrigible wretches'.[25] It can happen. But the evidence for the benefits is strong and the reason is that going to university is a well-managed transition from childhood dependence to adult independence. You are free from school but not yet in the world of paid work. You are free from your parents but not yet with all the responsibilities of adulthood. In the past you used to leave home to live with a new master as you learned a craft or worked as a domestic servant. Going to university is the true heir to that tradition of apprenticeships. This could be why one of the reasons going to university has such a beneficial impact—it is how modern societies best handle that transition into adulthood.

So going to university makes you more healthy and boosts your wellbeing. We haven't got through all the other benefits yet, but already there is a danger of getting far too smug. That is why there is a decent reticence about arguing that graduates lead better lives and contribute more to society. It can easily come across as just the sort of arrogant self-regard which people associate with graduates. The argument is even more distasteful if it comes wrapped up with educational scepticism suggesting that graduates have these qualities innately rather than their being linked to the power of an institution to shape behaviour. This is one reason why the evidence that it is not just a selection effect matters. We are not saying graduates are inherently better people. It is rather that going to university is a big experience and people who go through this experience are changed by it.

This argument for the wider benefits of a university education is ironically rather similar to what was a widespread criticism of Oxbridge. Nineteenth-century critics argued that Oxford and Cambridge were just a finishing school for the upper classes and lacked the intellectual seriousness of, for example, Germany's universities. Newman conceded that his critics would say his Idea of a University 'will result in nothing better or higher than in the production of that antiquated variety of human nature and remnant of feudalism as they consider it, called a "gentleman"'.[26] And, especially in Asia, this is something they still associate—and rather like—about an English education. But there has been some progress. A university nowadays is a far more diverse community than anything which young people are likely to have come across before. (It is where I met my first Etonian and my first golfer.) Our schools are often very homogenous whereas our universities can be a refreshing contrast to that. And the social capital is no longer just to ensure you can fill your hereditary role in society: instead it is the so-called soft skills which modern employers value. Universities can democratize access to these skills. They can be learned in unexpected ways as was pointed out by a former student protester: 'I spent significant periods of my first degree course in occupation of college premises.

It taught me skills of organising, public speaking, and publicity that I would not have learned in lectures and that have stayed with me since.'[27]

Economic benefits to individuals

The Robbins Report of 1963 is often cited as a civilized and humane document, resting on wider values than the narrow focus on economic returns which is all we are supposed to understand nowadays. But Robbins put the economic benefits of higher education very clearly, whilst softening the message by getting Confucius to deliver it for him: 'Confucius said in the Analects that it was not easy to find a man who had studied for three years without aiming at pay.'[28] The more fastidious university heads tend to explain the economic returns from university education in a rather coy manner. Dean Gaisford of Christ Church, Oxford managed to be particularly unctuous: 'the study of ancient tongues . . . not only refines the intellect and elevates above the common herd, but also leads not infrequently to positions of considerable emolument'.[29]

Aiming to boost your earnings is not an ignoble ambition which we have to apologize for. Nearly 80 per cent of students say that one reason they are in higher education is to 'enable me to get a good job' and over 50 per cent have as their main reason either long-term career plans or getting a good job.[30] If that is their goal they are right to want to go to university. The evidence is stark. Ten years after their graduation, 'women graduates earn three times as much as women without a degree, while male graduates earn around twice as much as male non-graduates'.[31] Table 5.1 summarizes the data from the Labour Force Survey, which is a different data-set and hence with slightly different figures.

Compelling new evidence showing the scale of the earnings gain from going to university was published in 2013. We start with the net present value of the lifetime earnings of a non-graduate who is in all other respects like a graduate: for men it is £606,000 and for women it is £475,000. On top of that male graduates will earn a further £168,000 (a graduate premium of 28 per cent) over their working lives. For women the return is an even greater £252,000 (an earnings boost of 53 per cent).[32]

All these figures are net of the higher taxes you pay and of graduate loan repayments including the new higher loan repayments. The cost of graduate loan repayments on higher fees of £3,000, £6,000, or even £9,000 is relatively low compared to the big economic gains from going to university. They are not even the biggest overall cost of higher education. What economists would rightly

Table 5.1. Wages: postgraduates, graduates, and
non-graduates, 2015

Young people: aged 21–30	Median Wages (£)
Postgrads	28,000
Grads	24,000
Non-grads	18,000
All working age: 16–64	
Postgrads	39,000
Grads	31,500
Non-grads	22,000

Source: Graduate Labour Market Statistics for England, 2015, wages
rounded to nearest £500. Published April 2016.

regard as the biggest real cost of higher education barely appears in the public
debate—that is the opportunity cost, the three years of earnings you forgo by
going to university. As the real earnings of young non-graduates have been falling, the true cost of going to university was probably declining at the very time
of the controversy over our fee changes.[33] Even as the number of graduates has
continued to rise, the gap between graduate and non-graduate earnings remained
wide and maintained the same pattern of widening with age.[34]

One recent challenge to this evidence came from the Bank of England.[35]
Their analysis showed that graduate earnings fell over the last twenty years,
relative to the earnings of those with no qualifications. It did also find that
rising levels of education amongst the UK workforce have, since the mid-1990s,
added nearly half a percentage point to wage growth each year. Nevertheless
their key finding was that while in 1995 having a degree would on average
increase wages by 45 per cent over those with no qualifications, that premium
had dropped to 34 per cent by 2015. The Bank suggests that one reason for this
apparent reduction in the wage premium could be an oversupply of graduates.[36] But this is very different from the findings of the Institute for Fiscal
Studies (IFS), which compared graduate wages against those of school leavers
and found that the median wage difference between graduates and school leavers 'has essentially stayed flat at around 35% over the past two decades for 25- to
29-year-olds'.[37] Moreover the IFS traced wage premiums by education level for
different birth cohorts (e.g. 1965–9, 1975–9, 1985–9) and found that at different
stages of life the median graduate wage premium held up for successive cohorts,
despite an increasing number of graduates. It is worth getting to the bottom of
this. The IFS explains that the difference between their findings and those of

the Bank of England arises because the IFS compares actual wages between different education categories and birth cohorts. Graduates tend to work in higher-paid occupations and getting a higher education is one reason for this. The Bank assumes that graduate earnings are boosted because of the occupations they work in. It lowers its estimate for the graduate premium by excluding this effect. The IFS approach seems to capture better the reality of what being a graduate does for one's options in the labour market.[38]

The real cost that matters is the cost of not going to college: this is what has been rising. A study in the US conveys the point in its title: *The Rising Cost of Not Going to College* looks not just at earnings but at the real net worth of American households after including all their debts, including the substantial education debts of American graduates. It is bad news: since 1984 the real net worth of a household headed by young graduates has fallen by 12 per cent or nearly $3,500. But for non-graduates it has fallen by 73 per cent or $8,500.[39] The figures for declining net wealth of young people as a whole are an issue which I tackled in *The Pinch*.[40] This is evidence of how the decline in the wealth of young people is distributed—going to university is clearly one way to protect you from the worst effects. The study also shows median annual real earnings for young graduates in America rose by 17 per cent to $45,500 between 1965 and 2013. This increase in graduate earnings is after a big expansion in the proportion of the working population with a degree from 13 per cent in 1965 to 34 per cent in 2013. Meanwhile the earnings of young American adults without a college degree actually fell in cash terms over this period: nowadays to share in the American Dream you have to get a degree.[41]

There have been a series of research papers going back a decade which, even though they use different methods, all tell the same story of a substantial graduate premium in the UK in the £120,000–£160,000 range.[42] If anything the more recent British study by Walker and Zhu shows even higher returns than some previous estimates. One reason is that it counts all the extra earnings of a graduate even if that is not their final qualification because, for example, they go on to get a doctorate. These postgraduate options do add even further value. But the justification of this approach is that it better captures the choice which a young person faces: choosing whether or not to go to university is a very significant fork in the road.[43] Moreover this argument cuts both ways as amongst the non-graduates with two A levels are people who then go on to get many other types of post-A-level qualification rather than a degree—including apprenticeships. Indeed it includes among non-graduates with two A Levels over a quarter who have some higher vocational qualifications.[44]

It is striking that the result is so strong even by comparison with the apprenticeships, whose long-term returns are significantly lower than for graduates. Graduate earnings are expected on average to grow about 0.5 per cent a year more than those of non-graduates.[45] Over time across most major economies there has been a widening of the gap between graduate and non-graduate earnings.[46] Apprentices start off ahead as they do not have those three years of earnings forgone and may be as well paid as a graduate straight out of university. But what matters is not so much your starting income but the far better lifetime trajectory through the labour market if you are a graduate. It is a race between the hare and tortoise in which the graduate steadily catches up and then overtakes the apprentice. The key graduate attributes are generic and enable graduates to ride through big changes in the type of work they will do over a long career whereas apprentices are more tied to specific industries which can make them more vulnerable to risk and lowers long-term rewards. An IFS analysis confirms the point: 'this earnings gap between the high- and low-educated grows throughout adults' 20s; in other words, earnings tend to rise more steeply with age and/or experience for the more highly educated...the recession brought real earnings growth to a complete standstill for the low-educated born in the mid-1980s, as they approached age 25; in contrast, their graduate contemporaries continued to see clear increases in their real earnings at this point (but less sharp increases than graduates would normally expect early in their careers).'[47] The deep recession from 2008 hit the incomes of non-graduates more than graduates. It looks as if the wider range of skills of graduates offer them greater protection against the vagaries of the economic cycle and restructuring and this extra protection against adversity means, as the economists put it, 'that the spread between graduate and non-graduate human capital is higher than is typically reported in labour economics which often ignores the pricing of this type of risk exposure'.[48]

The pessimists fear that as the number of students goes up the average boost to their earnings shrinks. To some extent we would expect this because of composition effects as, for example, people with lower academic abilities become graduates and hence depress the earnings of both graduates and non-graduates. Imagine a school with accurate setting by intelligence, where the brightest pupil from the lower set is promoted to the upper set. Average intelligence in both sets falls.[49] But overall the argument that more graduates means returns to higher education fall is one of those propositions which looks right in theory but has not happened in practice. The growth of graduate numbers over decades seems to have been matched with more demand for graduates so returns remain high. So, for example, there was a spectacular doubling in the proportion of people going into higher education between the mid-1980s and the mid-1990s, when it went up from under 15 per cent to over 30 per cent in just a decade.[50] But a study of the impact of this particular surge shows no fall in the graduate premium even in these extraordinary circumstances.[51] It looks as if successive governments, perhaps more by accident than design, have delivered an increase in graduates that roughly matches the increase in demand for them with the result that returns have remained broadly stable. This helps to explain why the graduate premium has remained so high when market economics tells us that these high returns to certain qualifications should be competed away. Richard Blundell has an ingenious explanation which does not just depend on the happy accident that the expansion of student numbers matched technological change which was increasing demand for them. He argues that an increase in the number of graduates makes a more decentralized form of business structure possible. The United States had more graduates than the UK and was able to make this shift first, but the surge in the number of British graduates in the 1990s enabled us to do something similar. This is not unlike my own argument in *The Pinch* that the shift in Britain's industrial structure was only possible because of the decline in the number of apprentices trapped in the old industries and the increase in the number of young graduates available to move into new industries. The twist in the tail is that Blundell suggests that this effect could be a one-off and after it the demand for graduates may not increase at the same pace.[52]

Another challenge, as we saw earlier when looking at non-economic benefits, is that people who go to university are more able and therefore more likely to get good earnings anyway. That is why the key British analyses such as by Walker and Zhu compare graduates with people who could have gone to university but did not: that is why many have gained some other qualification. Their estimate of the graduate premium is not for graduates compared with everyone else but specifically compared with people with two A levels who could have gone but did not go to university. Whichever way you look at it going to university makes a real difference to earnings—it is not just picking out the people who would have earned a lot anyway.[53]

There are other ways to ensure it is a fair comparison. One way is that stalwart of modern social science, the twin study. Unless there are special circumstances this removes many of the usual problems of comparison as you can assume that they have broadly similar abilities and childhood experiences. The only UK study shows that every extra year of education adds 8 per cent to earnings—so three years should be worth 25 per cent, which is roughly what other researchers obtained with very different approaches.[54]

The gains are clearly bigger if you get a good degree, with employers increasingly recruiting graduates with a 2.1 or better. A good degree has a significant further effect on earnings—a further 8 per cent for men and 7 per cent for women on top of a lower second or below, which raises male earnings by 17 per cent and female by 23 per cent compared to a control group of 2+ A levels. A good degree is worth an extra £76,000 for men and £85,000 for women.[55] That might be a motivation for a bit more revision in the run-up to Finals. It looks as if the premium to a good degree as against a lower class of degree may have risen as more people go to university. This may in turn explain the impression of many fifty-something parents that our children work harder at university than we did—it is because it matters more what class of degree you get. It is all part of the wider picture of more access to education intensifying competitive pressures on students.[56] There are of course exceptions to this pattern, neatly caught by President George Bush in an address to graduates of his old university: 'To those of you who received honours, awards and distinctions, I say well done. And to the C students, I say you too can be President of the United States.'[57]

The sceptics argue that averages hide very high returns to elite groups of graduates and much less for the rest. But the UK data show 'how much less inequality there is amongst graduates, particularly women, than there is amongst the non-graduates'.[58] One researcher has looked at the effect of college (i.e. university in the US) on students who just scraped into the poorest-performing state college in Florida compared to those who just failed to get in—these two groups are almost identical in terms of their high school scores but those that scraped in earned a lot more, 22 per cent more, than those that didn't—and they earned about the same as those that easily got in.[59]

More research is now being done on returns to different subjects and to studying at different institutions. We saw in Chapter Three that the highest financial returns appear to be to medicine, law, finance, and business studies: these professional courses are the ones which lead most directly to well-paid jobs—they are up-market vocational training. The highest graduate premium is medicine, where it stands at over £400,000.[60] Then in the middle are STEM. The lowest returns tend to come to some arts subjects. And there is a small minority, especially in the creative and performing arts, whose earnings are very low—so the latest sophisticated analysis shows that Noel Coward was right all along about Mrs Worthington not putting her daughter on the stage

('The profession is overcrowded, | And the struggle's pretty tough').[61] Although the interest tends to be on the universities with low graduate earnings, research shows that the subject you study matters at least as much as the institution. The critics point out that the returns to some courses at some universities look very low. But that depends on where the student started and what they would otherwise have done. If going to university means that you end up working as a pharmacist rather than in your parents' newsagents then it may have transformed your life even if your earnings are a fraction of an Oxbridge-educated lawyer. And whilst there are big differences in economic benefit between different courses, the non-economic benefits are more evenly spread.

Sceptics also argue that the graduate premium has stopped rising in absolute terms—it is just that the earnings of non-graduates are falling. So the alternative to a university education has got even harder.[62] That may be true: the hollowing out of the labour market means there are fewer reasonably well-paid non-graduate jobs. This makes the case for going to university even more compelling—for many young people there is, as they say, no alternative. This is even more acutely true for women than for men. It does look as if the returns to women from higher education are significantly higher than for men. This is not because female graduates are even better paid than male graduates: it is rather because female non-graduate jobs are not well paid whereas a group of non-graduate jobs—electrician, plumber, long-distance lorry driver, etc.—are still predominantly male and quite well paid. This tends to confirm our argument earlier about the importance of thinking of the cost of not going to university. For women their higher risk of very low paid non-graduate jobs mean that the opportunity cost of going is even lower and this could be one reason why more women than men go to university.[63]

The evidence on employment is as clear as on earnings, as Table 5.2 shows. So how come there are all these stories in the media about unemployed graduates? (Figure 6 captures what many people think.) Some of the figures they cite do not look so good. And it is worth explaining why—it all goes back to the difficulties of collecting good reliable statistics. We are too dependent on figures collected by universities showing what their graduates are doing six months after graduating. This has the advantage that most universities are still in contact with their graduates then. But this is more than offset by the disadvantage that it is not a very useful measure as students might still be doing nothing or doing temporary work whilst they look around for what they really want. The anxieties can't all be explained as misleading interpretation of inadequate statistics however. For a start, the route

Table 5.2. Employment: postgraduates, graduates, and non-graduates 2015

Young people: aged 21–30	Employment rate
Postgrads	87.3%
Grads	86.6%
Non-grads	71.6%
All working age: 16–64	
Postgrads	87.5%
Grads	87.1%
Non-grads	69.8%

Source: Graduate Labour Market Statistics for England, 2015, published April 2016.

Figure 6. A graduate premium—or not?

Source: 'Graduate' by Jamie Charteris, © Paperlink 2017.

from graduation to that well-paid job and career is more complicated and slower than it used to be with more compromises on the way. There is a genuine fear about what is happening to graduate jobs—are there fewer relative to the number of graduates, a trend disguised by redefining some pretty mundane work as now requiring graduates? Our analysis at the Resolution Foundation think tank (of which I am Executive Chair) is that there is a hollowing out of routine jobs in the middle but no increase in the number of low-skilled jobs—instead all the increase is in the high-skill jobs. So the change in the pattern of jobs is not so much a U-shaped curve—it is more like a Nike Swoosh.[64] These high-skills jobs are likely to be done by graduates. But what exactly do we mean by a graduate job? Some jobs previously done by non-graduates are now being taken over by graduates. Is this just qualification inflation or is the real character of the work changing?

The experts try to define graduate jobs, but it is not at all straightforward. The Prince of Wales is a graduate, but is being heir to the throne a graduate job? Is setting up a small business a graduate job? Is being a Cabinet Minister a graduate job—after all, John Major (who left school at 16 with three O levels) led a Cabinet which included two Fellows of All Souls. One approach is to classify occupations and take the top three of the hierarchy of nine standard occupational classifications as graduate jobs. On this definition 79 per cent of younger graduates were in graduate employment in 2015. This can then be refined by going through lots of different jobs and assessing whether they require graduate skills—so, managing a hotel is a graduate job but not managing a pub.[65] The process whereby jobs become graduate jobs is often mocked as unnecessary qualification inflation but it may also be driven by changes in the type of work—there is more technology, more regulatory compliance, and more complexity in many jobs than a generation ago even if the job title has not changed. So 40 per cent of the recent increase in graduate jobs was due to up-skilling of previously non-graduate jobs.[66]

However, it is worrying that 30 per cent of recent graduates, asked if a degree is needed to do their job, say no.[67] This may be a measure of job dissatisfaction, not necessarily of skills needed, but that may not be much comfort to the graduates involved. Making work meaningful and rewarding remains a real issue which some modern employers ignore.

The most realistic response to these anxieties about graduates who are not in good, well-paid jobs straight after graduating is that the whole process of finding the job that suits you may take longer than before but you are on a track to a better job. It is not just what you are doing at 25 but what you are likely to be doing aged 40. Graduates have steeper age-employment profiles than non-graduates—something else shown by Walker and Zhu. These longer-term effects are not just because of what graduates know when they start but because they keep on learning. Graduates of both sexes report more skill improvement over the past ten years than people with lower qualifications.[68] Moreover being a graduate is by far the best track to the jobs of the future. The OECD say 80 per cent of new jobs require a graduate qualification.[69] And we do not have to rely on speculative forecasts. It is an observable fact that 'the fastest growing occupations in the US today, such as medical staff, systems analysts and software engineers depend on graduate recruitment'.[70]

Overall, the evidence is overwhelmingly that graduates are more likely to be in graduate jobs and better paid for doing them, with an even greater gain for postgraduates. Now we must turn from economic benefits for individuals to the wider economic impact.

Wider economic benefits

When the Chancellor of the Exchequer, George Osborne, was preparing the Autumn Statement of 2013 he was looking, as always, for measures to raise the growth rate. I had just written a pamphlet for the fiftieth anniversary of the Robbins Report updating its arguments for more people to have the opportunity of going to university and I pressed the case for more places for students. The Chancellor told me that of all the measures which the Treasury reviewed the one which had greatest impact on the long-term growth rate was more graduates. It was just one example of a wider economic proposition—the expansion of higher education 'has helped to fuel economic growth around the world'.[71] When the ten poorest American states modelled what they could do to bring their economic performance up to the American average the top measure was increased student enrolment.[72] Indeed, the OECD say that when they are trying to forecast the long-term growth rate of an economy one of the measures they use is how many graduates there will be in the workforce.[73] However, one study failed to find the effect the OECD claims, though there was a positive effect on growth from having a higher proportion of researchers in the workforce, perhaps because they were better able to absorb and implement technological advances.[74]

There is a direct Exchequer benefit from more graduates. As graduates earn more they pay more tax and claim less in benefits. The latest estimates are that male non-graduates will generate about £406,000 of Government revenue with graduates contributing a further £264,000 on top. Female non-graduates will pay income taxes that bring the Government revenue of £287,000 whereas female graduates pay more than double, adding a further £318,000 for the Exchequer. It makes sense for the Exchequer to invest in its tax base by having

more well-paid workers who will pay lots of tax over their careers. So go to
university and pay on average £300,000 more tax: it puts into perspective the
worries about graduate debt.[75] Compare these Exchequer gains with the earlier
figures from the same research for the financial returns to individuals, and one
observes a striking result: the Exchequer gets more revenues out of graduates
than graduates get as higher earnings. The Exchequer gets back more than the
maximum rate of income tax rate as VAT is also included and graduates spend
a higher proportion of their higher incomes on goods subject to VAT. There is
also a saving on spending on unemployment benefits which is included in these
estimates.[76] These calculations are for Government tax revenues and ignore
wider effects through, for example, higher economic growth or less crime.
Even so the public returns are higher than the private returns.

We can also estimate the impact of more graduates on the growth rate.[77]
Around 20 per cent of UK economic growth between 1982 and 2005 came as
a direct result of increased graduate skills accumulation. They are an important
part of the nation's capital: graduates represent 26 per cent of all those in
employment, but account for 35 per cent of the UK's human capital stock.[78]
A 1 per cent increase in the share of the workforce with a degree increases
long-term productivity by between 0.2 per cent and 0.5 per cent, so a third of
labour market productivity growth from 1994 to 2005 can be attributed to
rising number of graduates in the workforce. International evidence bears it
out. Out of fifteen advanced countries we enjoyed one of the highest rates of
growth of output per hour between 1982 and 2005, which is linked to the rapid
rise in the share of our workforce with a degree. I like to think Robbins, a high-
minded, eminent economist, would be dancing a jig and whooping with delight
if he knew the long-term benefits we have enjoyed from his expansion of student numbers. The whole Thatcherite transformation of the British economy
depended on the surge of young people into the workplace after the second
peak of the baby boom of the early sixties, and their economic impact was then
reinforced with the expansion of university places for them. That expansion
provided the educated, flexible workers needed for new and very different
jobs as Britain went through deep structural change. The then Conservative
Government was very sceptical of apprenticeships because they were seen by
contrast as entrenching old skills for old industries. Indeed, when comparing
Anglo-American and Continental European models of capitalism one of the key
differences is that flexible Anglo-Saxon labour markets are linked to more participation in higher education and less apprenticeship-based training, which
tends to be associated with protection for stable industrial sectors.

The surge of young graduates, flexible young workers, into the jobs market was key to Margaret Thatcher's transformation of the labour market.[79] Britain enjoyed a surge in productivity when they entered their age of peak earnings and performance. The baby boomers would have graduated, aged 21, between 1966 and 1986. During this period three times as many people graduated with a first degree—1.24 million—compared with the previous twenty years. These graduates would then have entered their most productive working period (inferred from where their salaries peak aged 30 to 45) from 1975 to 2010. That long run between the deep recession of the early eighties and the Crash of the late Noughties is one of Britain's best sustained periods of strong economic performance.[80] For a century the British economy was in relative decline, with its per capita GDP underperforming compared with the US or Germany or France. In the past thirty years that decline has been reversed and one recent paper analysing this has the expansion of higher education first on its list followed by greater competition in product and labour markets.[81] The recession after the financial crash saw an unusual mix of high employment and lower wages and low productivity. This has put the slowdown of productivity growth back on the agenda. There is a lively debate about the 'productivity puzzle': most of the explanations focus on the structure of the labour market and lack of vocational skills among non-graduates.[82]

New graduates bring with them knowledge of new research and techniques. They are one of the most important single mechanisms whereby university research and new technology reach the wider economy. This may be one reason why productivity of industrial plants 'in cities that experience large increases in the share of college graduates rises more than the productivity of similar plants in cities that experience small increases in the share of college graduates'.[83] This filters through into higher wages for everyone. It is not just that graduates themselves secure higher wages: the rest of the workforce gain too. There are regional effects here as well as national. They are important further evidence because if one compares different regions of the same country the effects are not complicated by wider differences in national policies or cultures. British researchers looked at wider productivity gains beyond those captured in the higher wages of better-educated workers and found that 'an increase of 1 percentage point in the proportion of the workforce with an academic level 4 (degree+) from those with just A levels or equivalent leads to an increase in productivity of 0.5 percent of which 0.075 percent may go in earnings and the remainder to the employer'. This is the spillover effect from university-level qualifications on wider productivity—and the researchers found no such spillover effects on productivity from vocational qualifications.[84] One study from the US found 1 per cent more graduates boosts earnings of high school drop-outs by 1.9 per cent, high school graduate wages by 1.6 per cent, and college graduate wages by 0.4 per cent.[85] So one of the best ways of boosting non-graduate earnings is for them to be working in a place with lots of graduates.

These benefits come not just from the effects of lots of graduates: there seems to be an effect from the university as an institution: 'a 10% increase in the number of universities (which means adding one more university in the average region in our data) increases that region's income by 0.4%'. That is a global finding but the researchers then apply it to UK data in particular: 'In the UK we estimate that if one university were added to each of its 10 regions, this would lead to about 0.7% higher national income (£11billion based on 2010 figures). This is higher than the likely annual cost, which based on average university expenditure is more like £1.6billion. The large margin between benefits and costs suggests that university expansion remains beneficial.'[86]

Wider non-economic benefits, including better cities

The dividing lines between these different types of benefits are not sharp. We began with non-economic gains to individuals—but if a graduate has better health that means an economic benefit from savings in NHS costs and this is a saving from which everyone gains. Our fourth and final category of non-economic collective benefits is a good example of this blurring of divisions—these wider benefits are closely linked to non-economic gains to individuals.

Graduates commit less crime, for example—and we all gain from lower crime. Areas with more students see lower crime rates. There are 1.06 fewer total conviction rates per 1,000 university students (whereas police data suggest secondary schools are if anything likely to be crime hot spots). This lower crime rate is found for offences like burglary, theft, and criminal damage but not for violent crime.[87] A 16 percentage point increase in those educated to degree level is associated with £1bn of savings in the costs of crime.[88] There is evidence from the US that completing high school reduces the chances of incarceration by about 0.76 percentage points for whites and by 3.4 percentage points for blacks.[89] These are useful savings in public spending. We will see in the next chapter that savings in incarceration rates are surprisingly important in some of the estimates of high returns for childcare programmes whereas many of the estimates for returns to higher education do not even include any figures for such effects, despite the clear evidence of graduates having lower crime rates.

Graduates are on average more socially engaged. Graduates are one and a half times more likely to be members of a charitable organization than those whose education ended at A level.[90] The OECD has found that each year of schooling is associated with an increase of 0.8 per cent in volunteering rates.[91] Graduates are more likely to vote and less politically cynical.[92] Sixty-one per cent of adults without A-levels vote as against 81 per cent of those with a degree. This effect is most dramatic amongst younger adults, with a 32 percentage points gap among 25–34-year-olds.[93] It links to evidence that graduates are more likely to think their participation in politics is worthwhile.[94] This is not just true for Britain: it is a wider effect. Each additional year of higher education in Europe increases levels of interpersonal trust by 3.1 per cent, political interest by 15 per cent, and party membership by 2 per cent.[95]

Perhaps the most vivid single effect of a university is not on the individual or the national economy but on the city. Richard Florida has powerfully shown that what matters is not just what you do with your life and who you do it with but also where you do it. Place matters. And universities transform places. One way they change them is through their demographic impact. Western cities are in an increasingly intense battle for shrinking numbers of young people. Universities are key in attracting young people to a place and changing its character as a result. Cities like Portsmouth, Lincoln, Worcester, Winchester, and Chester which had lost their traditional industries or were just facing genteel decay are being transformed by dynamic new universities. Now towns and cities like Shrewsbury and Hereford want to emulate their success and are actively campaigning for their own universities. Were it not for planning restrictions, Oxford and Cambridge would already be major cities attracting more investment from around the world. London is a centre for so many activities we forget its role as the global centre for higher education and research, with more elite universities than any other city in the world. Imagine the West Coast of the US without Stanford and CalTech or the East Coast without Harvard and MIT. We do not fully appreciate the extraordinary global advantage we get from the golden triangle of Oxford, Cambridge, and London. Edinburgh, Manchester, Birmingham, and Bristol are also examples of major clusters of research universities shaping a region. Universities change the character of all these places—and for the better.[96] There are boosts to output in these places as a result of the investment in higher education. So non-graduates are better off in these cities as a result of more graduates. These are externalities of education.

One global study found that higher university presence in a region is also associated with pro-democracy views among individuals. They add that the 'striking thing about this result is that it persists even when we control for an individual's own education, suggesting that there could be some kind of externality associated with universities through the diffusion of ideas into their surrounding areas'.[97]

Taking stock

This recognition of the wide range of benefits from higher education—public as well as private and non-economic as well as economic—should satisfy even the sternest critics of economic reductionism, such as Stefan Collini, who warns: 'we need to show that there is a public not merely a private benefit from higher education that can be characterised in various, not merely economic, terms'.[98] However, the economists are remorseless and deploy the tools of economics to measure benefits even when they are not economic in character. Walter McMahon has led this application of human capital theory to higher education, trying to estimate all the different ways in which higher education contributes to living a good life. Imagine that earning an extra £25,000 a year boosted your life expectancy by two years and imagine that for any given level of earnings a university graduate also lives on average two years longer than a non-graduate. We can then say that the direct effect of going to university on life expectancy is equivalent to earning £25,000 more per year. Going to university also boosts your earnings and that yields a further impact on life expectancy, an important indirect effect which can then be added in. You may object in principle to measuring extra life expectancy this way but it is a well-intentioned attempt to establish a common currency which makes it possible to compare the scale of these effects. And the results are rather striking: what we are treating as the non-economic effects are actually larger in scale than the conventional economic effects. In particular the gains in health and social capital appear to be even greater than the value of the wage premium.[99]

This adds up to a compelling case for more people to go to university. It is why the removal of controls on student numbers will count as one of the great social reforms of the Coalition Government of 2010–15. But now we need to consider two types of objection to all this—each with a distinguished and prominent protagonist.

Kingsley Amis: 'more will mean worse'

Lucky Jim is one of the great campus novels. Set in a provincial university just after the war it is both a great comic novel and brings to life some of the classic criticisms of modern universities, notably that standards are declining as too many students are being let in:

> 'It's the same everywhere you look; not only this place, but all the provincial universities are going the same way. Not London, I suppose, and not the Scottish ones. But my God, go to most places and try and get someone turfed out merely because he's too stupid to pass his exams—it'd be easier to sack a prof. That's the trouble with having so many people here on Education Authority grants.... You can see the Authorities' point in a way. "We pay for John Smith to enter College here and now you tell us, after seven years, that he'll never get a degree. You're wasting our money." If we institute an entrance exam to keep out the ones who can't read or write, the entry goes down by half, and half of us lose our jobs.'[100]

Those are the words of a fictional character, but Amis continued to make the point in his own words too:

> The trouble is not just illiteracy, even understanding this as including unsteady grasp of the fundamentals of a subject as well as unsteadiness with hard words like *goes* and *its*. But for the moment I want to drum the fact of the illiteracy into those who are playing what I have heard called the university numbers racket, those quantitative thinkers who believe that Britain is *falling behind* America and Russia by not producing as many university graduates per head, and that she must *catch up* by building *more* colleges which will turn out *more* graduates and so give us *more* technologists (especially them) and *more* school-teachers...MORE will mean WORSE....I am quite sure that a university admissions policy demanding even less than it now demands—for that is what a larger intake means—will wreck academic standards beyond repair.[101]

These are arguments we are familiar with to this day, though no one else has expressed them so vividly. But when did his character say an exam to keep out the ones who cannot read or write would reduce the intake by half? *Lucky Jim* was published in 1954 when 3.4 per cent of the population went to university. And when did Amis himself claim that universities were 'already taking almost everyone who can read and write'?[102] That was in 1960 when about 5 per cent of people went to university and about 40,000 people got university degrees every year.

Nowadays almost 50 per cent of young people go to university and about 400,000 British people get university degrees every year. I doubt if even those most opposed to university expansion actually believe we should cut student numbers by over 90 per cent to get back to the 1950s. And anyway Kingsley Amis clearly believed the rot had set in by 1954. Today's sceptics are often rather keen on the 1950s, believing that standards were higher then, whereas Amis is saying that things were bad even then, in the days of grammar schools and before Robbins. Those students on local authority grants who he says are lowering standards are the influx of grammar school students who got their fees paid for them.[103] Indeed, the social phenomenon behind *Lucky Jim* and which Amis sees as lowering standards is the arrival of provincial grammar school boys at university, which is now celebrated by some nostalgists as a triumph of post-war social mobility. So even they can't really accept Amis's argument was true when he put it forward. Nor did the creation of universities like Warwick and York in the early 1960s cause a descent into barbarism as Amis feared. If Amis was wrong then it is quite possible the same argument is also wrong now.

The pessimists will reply that this time it is going to be different—this time the fears are going to be justified. There is a very tricky philosophical puzzle: how you prove things aren't true—green up to now and blue in the future.[104] Some of the pessimists are setting such a challenge. We can reply that we've heard these warnings before but it did not turn out as bad as they feared so they have to show why this time it is different. The pessimists claim it is obvious that if more people go to university then returns must fall. We have already shown that is incorrect. Demand for graduates has also increased and returns have remained high. But there is another version of this proposition which must be arithmetically true. As there are more and more graduates in the national average so it is harder to show graduates rising above the average. And the comparator group of people with two A levels who do not go but could have gone must shrink. But we can still show graduates doing better than non-graduates. And in a way this just shows that university education becomes so pervasive that not having gone itself becomes increasingly unusual—like being a smoker or being married by the age of 20 and all the other behaviours which were widespread in the old days before mass higher education.

We can concede something very important to Kingsley Amis, however. Setting aside his anxieties about their effects, he was the first writer to observe one of the great educational and social changes in post-war Britain—the shift from elite to mass higher education. It is a crucial change in the character of the university which is not widely appreciated or understood. When we see photographs of the M1 in the years immediately after it was opened we are amazed at how quiet and empty it looks and perhaps dream of being the solitary driver cruising past Luton in 1960. The M1 was expected to carry 20,000 cars per day and is now taking 140,000—growth on a similar scale to higher education. But we know that there is no going back and that if we were such a solitary driver we would be in a country that was actually very different and deeply impoverished compared with what we all now enjoy (or we would think an epidemic had broken out and nobody had bothered to tell us). We don't just have more university places and more cars—we also have more TV channels, more foreign travel, more supermarkets, more information, more books, and more films—the shift from elite to mass is one of the features of modern capitalism and we cannot and should not stop it in higher education any more than anywhere else.

Alison Wolf's objection: it is just signalling

There is a rather different and rather more sophisticated critique of this growth of education, especially higher education. A clever book by Alison Wolf, *Does Education Matter?*, argues that the purpose of education is not to learn things but to signal you are clever by getting through exams and getting in to selective universities.[105] So it does make sense to go to university because that is how in a modern economy you signal you are smart. But you don't actually learn much—there is no real improvement in human capital behind it. This argument recognizes there are private gains in going to university but argues it is a fallacy to aggregate these and regard them as overall gains: instead they are the private gains that come from access to a positional good. The argument has a certain appeal and it is quite hard to challenge as it also predicts that graduates will earn more—it just disagrees about the reasons why. There is a genuine concern about the quality of the actual educational experience you get at university. Perhaps universities can get away with it because the benefit of going to university is getting your CV onto the desk of a good employer, not because of any stuff you might actually learn.

Alison Wolf's argument also gained some credibility because it matches the careers of the great tech entrepreneurs. Steve Jobs, Bill Gates, and Mark Zuckerberg all dropped out of university. Indeed, Steve Jobs is supposed to have recommended to university students that having shown they were smart enough to get in they should then drop out and do something more worthwhile. But the experience of those great American entrepreneurs actually shows what is wrong with this argument. As another American entrepreneur recently out of college put it: 'they all thought of those ideas in college. That environment of intense collaboration and camaraderie and community within the setting of a more formal educational environment creates a kind of alchemy.'[106] And would we have that beautiful Apple script if Steve Jobs had not dropped in on a calligraphy class at Reed College even after dropping out?

Other studies show how more education and training do raise productivity across firms because better-educated workers actually know more useful stuff and have more valuable skills. Even more encouraging, these gains in human capital yield benefits across the whole business. A one percentage point increase in training is associated with an increase in value added per hour of about 0.6 per cent and an increase in hourly wages of about 0.3 per cent. It is more evidence that even non-graduates gain from working alongside graduates—and these improvements in productivity are real: they cannot be from signalling.[107]

The signalling thesis was empirically tested by Ian Walker when the English school-leaving age was raised from 15 to 16 years. If staying on beyond the compulsory age was just a signal that you had something special then you would expect no gain to earnings from more compulsory education. Instead there would just be another round in the education arms race with people having to stay on beyond the new compulsory age to get any kind of earnings boost. But that is not what happened. Instead there was a compression of the range of education received and more was earned by those who stayed on to the new compulsory minimum leaving age.[108] Another ingenious way of testing the signalling thesis is to look at the self-employed, where you would expect there to be less signalling as there is no employer to signal to. But there is no significant gap between their earnings and employees with a similar level of education doing similar work.[109]

A further crucial piece of evidence is the contribution of education to growth in Asia. South Korea is the classic case study showing the gains from education. In 1950 its GDP per capita was $850. This was comparable to Nigeria's of $750. But by 2005 South Korea's GDP per capita was $17,500 while Nigeria's languished at $1,350.[110] South Korea has clearly moved from a developing to a developed country. As part of this process the percentage of young South Koreans going to university has gone up to 64 per cent. This is the highest percentage of any OECD country and has risen from just over 30 per cent since 1990.[111] This has not just enabled them to transform their economy by making possible the rise of high-tech firms like Samsung. It has also transformed their culture and given it global reach. Gangnam style comes from the district with Korea's greatest concentration of education institutions and which sends the highest proportion of young people to Korea's elite universities—hence the ironic self-mockery which is crucial to Psy's appeal. Psy's video 'broke' YouTube in early December 2014 when viewings went over two billion or so, the maximum number in the original 32-bit computer architecture. Boris Johnson pronounced it the cultural masterpiece of 2012: 'the Koreans are so darned clever that not only can they make cheap and efficient cars. They can also make number one smash hits.'[112]

The case for going to university

Signalling effects are part of the benefits of educational qualifications. But they are nothing like the whole story. The evidence is that education does matter and it matters because you learn stuff and develop skills which don't just boost your earnings but may well make for a more fulfilled life. Going to university is more beneficial for your health than a five-a-day diet.[113] And unlike the five-a-day diet, the beneficial effects of higher education reach others too. Parents of students live longer, even after allowing for other factors such as their own education. It looks as if investing in young people transmits benefits back up to older generations too—strengthening the contract between the generations. Well-educated children may keep parents up to date with the latest information about healthy living.[114] But that may not be the whole story: parents may attach more value to the future if they have a well-educated child or expect more support from them in their old age, which in turn affects their behaviour. There are deep issues here about the value we place on our future and our family's which we will pursue further in the next chapter.

Whilst the evidence of the benefits of higher education is as compelling as for a healthy diet it is harder to communicate and get it accepted. One reason is consideration and courtesy—it can easily become educational snobbery at the expense of fellow citizens who have less education. That is deeply distasteful. We all know of people who have raised their families well, served bravely in the armed forces, or built up successful companies without going to university. In particular we think of the dignity and wisdom of older people who may not have had that opportunity. That is why there can be an understandable caution about setting out some of this evidence. But remember who loses out from this reticence. It is not the middle-class kids who are on the highway to university anyway. It is the kids from more disadvantaged backgrounds who do not get the message unless it is broadcast loud and clear.

The trouble is the media headlines tend to be very different. Kingsley Amis was one of our great post-war novelists and he got to write the narrative. Ironically the shift to graduate employment has been particularly dramatic in the media. That article you read about how graduates are going to be unemployed is likely to have been written by a graduate. Journalists almost always reply to this by saying that media studies does not get you a job in journalism so it is evidence of how irrelevant university study is. Media studies may not be a preparation for a career in journalism but it does lead to careers in advertising, PR, marketing, web-based services—modern service industry jobs which for some reason are supposed to be less worthwhile than physically making things. But whatever the specific value of media studies, actually journalism has been transformed from a non-graduate craft-based job entered via an apprenticeship to an overwhelmingly graduate job, often after studying English or History at university. Those old journalists clearly included some larger than life characters. But the character of journalism has changed and probably for the better—more sceptical and more analytical. I do not believe these changes would have been possible but for the shift to graduate recruitment.

There is a further reason why we hear less about these benefits from higher education. Until recently universities had their student numbers capped. Many of them still have many more applicants than the places that are available. So there has been little incentive for many universities to put in the effort of communicating the benefits of higher education. Indeed, over-subscribed universities sometimes oppose more students going to university as they fear an increase in students will divert funds away from them towards the universities which would recruit the extra students. Those less prestigious universities take more students from disadvantaged backgrounds and transform their lives, but as they have fewer graduates in Westminster and Whitehall they do not command attention in the same way. The prominent universities who particularly influence the debate have no particular interest in making the case for more people to go.

I find, however, that students themselves get these arguments pretty well. When I meet a group of students and suggest that another group of young people in the same city who aren't going to university will probably earn less over their working lives than you guys, the students tend to agree. Then I suggest this is true even if they have roughly similar A levels to them. Again the students can see this. They also recognize that a lot of the benefit comes because they are learning stuff and developing skills which it would be much harder to get outside university. Most students, however, do stress that there is more to university than getting a job—above all it is just the most fantastic experience. And they are right.

The evidence we have set out for the benefits of higher education may be true but that does not mean it is the whole truth. There is more to university than all those benefits, non-financial as well as financial, which we have identified. Universities are not just a means to an end: university scholarship is an end in its own right. That is why for some of the purists this focus on benefits misses the real point. It is like laboriously proving there are benefits to Christmas or to a summer holiday or to marriage. These are experiences which do not feel like transactions to earn a return. That is not what studying may feel like.

Stefan Collini neatly mocks instrumentalism: 'if we do slide into making the development of [transferable] . . . skills appear to be the defining purpose of our disciplines then we again run the risk of the reply that there are surely more direct and reliable ways to do that than by having someone decipher thirteenth century manorial records or examine the metrical patterns in Gerard Manley Hopkins' poetry. If our purpose really *is* to enable people to write good memos to their sales force, then those look like pretty funny places to start from.'[115] It is a lively passage and of course he is right but its effect comes from his mockery of the suggestion that banal business skills are the 'defining purpose' of great intellectual disciplines. Such an idea is clearly nonsensical. Evidence showing how university study helps make life better does not mean that these types of betterment are the reason for choosing to study at university. When economists calculate benefits and costs they are looking at consequences: they are not psychologists offering an account of human motivation. Many academics and students are driven by pure intellectual curiosity. It is a deep human instinct. People can and should study subjects they love because they love them. The evidence they reap personal benefits from studying a subject is not a claim that those benefits are the reason they do it. However, it is legitimate to be motivated by practical consequences. Imagine your mother died of some horrible disease when you were young and ever since you wanted to research it so this affliction is lifted from humanity. If someone said you were really doing this out of pure intellectual curiosity and not for any wider benefit you would find it hard to agree with their idea of what makes enquiry high-minded. We argue ourselves into a very peculiar corner if bringing attention to the practical benefits of great intellectual disciplines is seen as some sort of betrayal.

These benefits can accrue indirectly in disciplines very different from medicine. So, for example, we should be allowed to say that Shakespeare is a boost to tourism in the Midlands. That certainly does not mean you become a Shakespeare scholar to boost the local tourism industry. But when it comes to trying to get funding for Shakespeare studies is it really a betrayal to show that there is this economic benefit? And it may be that flows of funds from tourism help to sustain the finances of local theatre companies which are as a result able to perform a play with a fresh interpretation influenced by new scholarship. These circles of mutual connection help make the world go round. It would be perverse to refuse to draw attention to these effects even when they exist.

As a politician and a minister I was always, rightly, being told of the importance of the evidence-based policy. That requires rational empirical analysis. It would not be acceptable if doctors or museum directors or generals just said that their particular service was inherently worthwhile and should not be analysed for benefits and costs. (Indeed the expert analysts of health economics or military effectiveness themselves are to be found within universities.) So universities should not be afraid to analyse their own value using tools they themselves have developed for others.

One way that ministers can exert influence is by commissioning independent research that can influence thinking even without a clear clarion call from universities themselves. Some of the evidence on the wider benefits of learning which I cited earlier was commissioned by David Blunkett. During my time as minister BIS published a lot more research which showed the value of going to university. It was a long, slow battle but eventually BIS itself came to realize that it had in higher education one of the most powerful instruments for improving productivity and boosting innovation, its key economic objectives. And universities embraced this role—provided, of course, we did not reduce them to this as their only role. But there were Liberal Democrats who had reconciled themselves to their absurd policy of abolishing fees and loans by arguing too many people were going to university and their policy would be affordable if there were fewer students. Some colleagues in my own Party opposed to producing more intellectuals, who were either useless or dangerous, and did not want more graduates. But right from our discussions in Opposition David Cameron was an expansionist. He saw, quite rightly, that the aspiration to go to university was in many ways an aspiration to join the middle class and should be welcomed as such, just like the desire to own one's own home. For my part I always hated controls on student numbers because it meant that volunteers hungry for education who came knocking on the doors of universities and could benefit from higher education were being turned away. I saw the abolition of number controls as a key part of a strategy to spread opportunity. But to do that we had to have reformed university finances so that expansion no longer came with a big bill for the Treasury—as we saw in Chapter Three.

There was another reason for this wariness about higher education. It is a very different three years, the first three years, which have caught policy makers' imagination. But which three years is it that really matters? And why has the case for higher education been so unpersuasive compared to the case for the early years? That is the question to which we now turn.

SIX

Which Three Years?

The different stages of education

I meant it when I said that I loved universities. But attitudes to universities are mixed. Other stages of education do better in winning hearts and minds, and politicians react accordingly. The target of three million apprenticeships was celebrated as a popular policy whereas there was little celebration of the reality of two million students in British universities. Telegenic rows of students serve as a backdrop for politicians' speeches on any subject—apart from higher education itself. Legislation on schools was seen as popular use of parliamentary time but there was reluctance to devote any parliamentary time to sorting out an incoherent legal framework for universities which lagged way behind our reforms. Above all the early years of childhood were seen as far more important than later stages of education in shaping life chances and improving social mobility.

I do not begrudge these other stages of education their political appeal—honest! Anyway politicians and their advisers are just reflecting a wider conventional wisdom. Universities themselves helped shape this view of educational priorities. I would go to university meetings where protesters outside demanded more public funding so higher education could be 'free' whilst inside earnest public policy students and academics told me that actually public funding should be shifted to the early years or that primary school literacy and numeracy programmes were the real educational priority.

These attitudes are influenced by the tendency of educators at whatever level to blame the previous stage of education for their problems. Universities say they would love to recruit someone from a disadvantaged background but prospective students have been let down by their schooling so their A level grades just aren't good enough and the university cannot gamble on their being able to catch up at such a late stage. Colleges say it is hard for them to focus on helping students get good A levels when they are also expected to provide remedial education for 16–18-year-olds who have failed at secondary school. Secondary schools say it is hard for them to deliver good GCSE results when too many kids arrive from primary school without the basics of reading and writing. The primary schools say it is hard to get up to the required standards of literacy and numeracy when 5-year-olds-have never held a crayon or seen a book because instead they spent all their early years sitting passively in front of screens. The nurseries say that now they get 3-year-olds who have not even been potty-trained. And just about everyone says the first three years are crucial for your chances in life. You end up with hard-pressed parents buying educational toys for their newborn babies and a pregnant woman who fears that unless she plays Mozart and recitations of French irregular verbs to her baby in the womb it will not get a place at Oxbridge. The English education system seems to operate on that worst of management principles—kiss up, kick down—in which activity is shaped by the competition to get to the next stage, with university as the ultimate goal, whilst at the same time previous stages of education get the blame, which ends up falling on the hard-pressed parent or nursery with a toddler. With all this in the background, it looks like common sense to tackle our education problems not at the university end but where they start—at the beginning.

Early years determinism

This is reinforced by a widespread belief that early interventions have high impact because our brains are shaped in the first three years. The intellectual guru behind this consensus is a very distinguished and very courteous economist—Professor James Heckman of Chicago University. He is a Nobel Prize winner, though he won that for his development of rigorous microeconomic statistical techniques rather than for his work specifically on early years education. And of course he is not and does not claim to be a neuroscientist. In a series of influential papers through the first decade of the century he formulated a coherent model for evaluating investment in human capital at different stages of the life-cycle and argued particularly that American society under-invests in the very young and over-invests in mature adults. He explicitly challenges Gary Becker's model of investment in human capital because that ignores the way returns are cumulative whereas he argues returns on education at later stages depend on investment in earlier stages. In particular he analysed and re-analysed the data from two early years projects—the Abecedarian and Perry Pre-school programmes—showing headline returns of a massive 16 per cent.[1] That was the time when Labour was legislating for university fees, sometimes linking that measure with the need to invest more public funds in early years instead: 'If I was a proper socialist, I'd move all higher education funds to early years', said Charles Clarke.[2] Since then Heckman has halved his estimates of the returns to these early years programmes as a more long-term assessment of educational achievements and careers for participants became possible. There appears to be a kind of half-life effect in which early improvements are eroded as other children who did not participate in the programme catch up. There are still significant wage returns for girls but the latest estimates show negligible effects for boys. At first Heckman speculated that the gains came from neurological stimulation boosting cognitive skills, but in the light of the growing evidence of few long-term cognitive gains from the programme he now attributes the main benefits of the programme to non-cognitive effects—to put it crudely, the effects now are on attitudes and behaviour, non-cognitive skills, rather than on intelligence. This in turn has helped to create the fashionable interest in character and resilience. It is an important shift and helps to explain why now Heckman estimates the big gains from the programme are not private gains enjoyed by individual participants as higher wages; they are social benefits enjoyed by the rest of society, notably through lower crime.

The biggest component (60 per cent on some estimates) of the social benefit from these American early years programmes is reduced costs of crime and savings in the rate of incarceration of young males because they are less likely to commit crime. If young American men from poor backgrounds did not commit so much crime in the first place and get incarcerated quite so much these gains would be much smaller. This in turn depends on some very specific effects indeed. Economists do not like murder because it is costly, and a significant source of the social benefits of the whole programme is that participants in the programme committed one murder whereas a control group of non-participants committed two.[3] But the one murder by the person in the programme was a murder of a younger person who had a lifetime of earnings ahead of him, and if you include this in the calculations the entire social return of the early years programme falls significantly. It is to Heckman's credit that he himself analyses this scrupulously in a paper five years after his initial paper claiming high returns. But if the economists evaluating the programme are discussing the economic significance of the age of one murder victim this suggests that the economic and social benefits of these programmes may not be quite as reliable and substantial as is claimed. It also suggests that this programme's returns may depend on the backdrop of a high crime, high incarceration environment—i.e. inner-city America. Heckman's results are much more culturally specific than many economists have recognized (there is a wider lesson here for the economics profession).

It is significant that the benefits feed through in reduced crime because this has long been the hope for education. Invited in 1930 to envisage life in 1950, this is what the US National Education Association proposed: 'Crime will be virtually abolished by transferring to the preventive process of school and education the problems of conduct which police and courts and prisons now seek to remedy when it is too late.'[4] We continue to believe early intervention somehow prevents later social problems when these hopes are regularly dashed. I sat in Cabinet Committee meetings where Treasury ministers, usually beady-eyed sceptics about any spending programme, agreed that we should spend more on early years as it would save money later: a claim that could be made with equal validity for many other areas of spending and would normally leave the Treasury completely unmoved.

All this matters because in the words of Heckman and his collaborators: 'The economic case for expanding preschool education for disadvantaged children is largely based on evidence from the High/Scope Perry Preschool program, and early intervention in the lives of disadvantaged children in the early 1960s.'[5] Whilst these studies have had the biggest influence, not least because of the respect in which James Heckman is rightly held, a major English programme, Sure Start, has also been appraised. It also shows some benefits, but not as big as hoped and not really in improved educational performance by participants. Instead the main gains have come from higher earnings of women who are able to do more paid work if their children are in childcare.[6] This is a good thing and a more prosperous household will indeed be good for the children. But it is not the kind of gain by a direct impact on young children and their neurological development which the early years advocates claim.

The big expansion of public funding for early years education was launched in Britain in 2005 and eight years later those youngsters went through their Key Stage 2 assessment—it showed little impact.[7] Meanwhile a Skills for Life programme helping poorly educated adults improve their English and Maths showed a high return. However, the returns to vocational programmes run by FE colleges looked to be very low. One influential paper actually showed returns were negative to some NVQs, and this heavily influenced Alison Wolf's Report on vocational skills.[8] It looked like a case study in the signalling theory but working negatively as these qualifications appeared to be signalling there was something wrong with you. However, it now appears that these survey-based studies did not properly allow for the fact that learners on these programmes were so disadvantaged that their prospects without these qualifications were very poor indeed. One revised estimate is that a learner who achieves a Full Level 2 (equivalent to GCSEs) or equivalent will earn 11 per cent more than a similar person who has the same learning aim, but who did not achieve the qualification. Other basic remedial qualifications at Levels 1 or 2 which further education colleges delivered to young unemployed people also appear to have useful returns in the 5 per cent to 10 per cent range.[9] Some further education programmes are very much focused on disadvantaged people. That is why they are worthwhile. It was a particularly cruel irony that the failure of some studies fully to capture how disadvantaged these students were meant that their returns appeared low and they were disproportionately cut.

So we now have returns to vocational programmes for young people aged 16+ being revised up and returns to early interventions being revised down, but long after the conventional wisdom has been fixed and the funding re-allocated. Public and political support for the early programmes remains massive while it is minimal for adult education. The reason is the apparent power of early years determinism and that in turn depends on popular neuroscience, to which we now must now turn. When his initial evaluations appeared to show high returns from the American early years interventions Heckman speculated that the mechanism could be neurological—through re-shaping the brain in what used to be called its critical period.[10] A famous image on the cover of a pamphlet co-authored by Iain Duncan Smith MP and Graham Allen MP shows the brains of two different 3-year-olds. One is a big, brash, healthy, stimulated brain on its way to stardom and the other a shrunken weedy runt of a brain that has not been stimulated and so is condemned to welfare dependency. If they were characters in *Blackadder* one would say it is the difference between Rik Mayall's Flashheart and Tony Robinson's Baldrick. The image is interpreted to show that if we want kids smart enough to get the most out of education we have to start at the beginning in the crucial three years when their brains are literally taking shape.[11]

This is where a second Nobel Prize comes in—for Medicine and Physiology, awarded to David Hubel and Torsten Wiesel in 1983. Their research programme, which has yielded enormous advances in our understanding of the brain, investigated how sensory stimulus was linked to brain development. Their most famous experiment was to show that if one eye of a kitten were sewn up for the first three months after birth it would be permanently blind in that eye. It provided the scientific impetus for the need to treat glaucoma in a newborn baby in the first six weeks as otherwise its sight could be permanently impaired.[12] Findings like these supply the neurological foundations for early years determinism. But that original experiment on the kitten's eyes was part of a much richer research programme which investigates which of our faculties depend for their development on sensory stimulus and when. It is not the case that all our faculties depend on such a stimulus. Indeed, if both the kitten's eyes are sewn up and then released the kitten does develop sight. If only one eye is sewn up the neurological functions for sight are all diverted to the working eye whereas if both are closed there is available capacity when they are both opened. Nor does it appear that the effect of any sensory stimulus or deprivation is via synapses. Researchers have removed the retinas from some foetal rhesus monkeys while providing unusually high levels of visual stimulation after birth for others. Overall there is no big difference in the number of synapses in the brains of monkeys with these very divergent experiences.[13] There are other faculties which are so primed to work that it looks as if no further sensory stimulus is necessary.[14] The right hand of an infant monkey is put tight-fisted in a leather mitten for the first four months with no sensory input. When the glove is removed it is soon able to use that hand to distinguish size and texture as well as a normal monkey.[15]

Moreover, old dogs can learn new tricks, contrary to what the pessimists—and Homer Simpson—predict. When Marge suggests an Adult Education Course Homer complains 'every time I learn something new it pushes some old stuff out of my brain. Remember when I took that home wine-making course and forgot how to drive.'[16] I would have enjoyed participating in the imaginative experiment in which a neurologist taught 60-year-olds to juggle. They could do it, and there was a change in their brain structure very like what occurs with younger jugglers. Their performance was not as good, however, because of deterioration in their motor skills which meant they were not always nimble even though their brain had learned the new trick.[17] These changes in the brain can happen very quickly indeed. Studies have shown that in just five days the sensory and motor areas of the adult brain can adapt according to how they are used. Non-piano-playing adults learned a five-finger exercise on the piano for two hours a day over the course of five days. The area of the brain responsible for finger movements became enlarged and more active in these participants compared with control participants who had not learned the piano exercise. So a relatively short amount of practice can make a significant difference to the brain.[18] There are some sensitive periods for some capabilities—especially when there is competition for use of neural tissue, such as a strong and a weaker eye. But when it comes to cognition and education there do not appear to be critical periods and instead our brains remain plastic through our lives.

That image of the two different brains was supposed to show the effect of stimulus or lack of it on brain structure but there is little support for this claim. Indeed, no reputable neurologist regards that brain image as an accurate representation of the effects of brain stimulation—they say the smaller brain must have some kind of disease or special medical condition. I asked the neuroscientist Professor Sarah-Jayne Blakemore about the image and she said: 'I have seen no evidence from scientific research that...a kind of shrinkage of the brain so significant could be a consequence of neglect or abuse of any level...it's more likely that the child with the very small brain had pre-existing genetic congenital problems like microencephaly.... To say that that shrinkage of the brain is a consequence of neglect is really a step too far from that image, and the problem with that image is that it undermines the really excellent scientific work on the effects of neglect and abuse on the developing brain, which does show that bringing children up in neglectful or abusive environments or chaotic environments does affect the brain, but in much more subtle ways than this extremely significant shrinkage.'[19]

John Bruer shows in a masterful analysis that three propositions at the heart of early years determinism are wrong. First, the process of synaptic pruning is itself part of improving brain function: there is no particular benefit in leaving more synapses un-pruned. Second, there are some critical periods for some faculties but they vary and for many faculties their development is not shaped in some critical period. In particular it looks as if many cognitive and life skills remain quite plastic over a lifetime. Thirdly, extreme sensory deprivation does inhibit neurological development but there is little evidence that enriching the environment beyond what most children have across time and culture yields special neurological benefit. It is an example of excessive faith in one particular scientific model at one moment in history. The great wartime scientist Patrick Blackett warned of such scientism, and after listing some contemporary salutary examples ended with a remarkably prescient fantasy: 'We cannot look to the scientists for salvation....Perhaps soon we will be told to pin our hopes on a dictatorship of midwives.'[20]

It is the evolutionary refutation which I find most persuasive. Something would have gone terribly wrong with human evolution if human development were so dependent on the first few years and could so easily go wrong. Actually we were endowed with faculties which are programmed to develop. It takes a lot to stop them. Years chained to a bed in an old Romanian orphanage would tragically inflict long-term damage on a child, but a wide range of types of childhood across most cultures do not. Colombian boy soldiers who had no education at all were successfully educated and reintegrated into society as young adults—and their brains changed as a result.[21] We are incredibly resilient and can catch up if given half a chance. We can recover from knocks and blows—and not just metaphorically but literally. After the amputation of a limb the brain rapidly reconfigures to get extra work and data from the limbs that remain. The brain of a blind person even uses the visual cortex to analyse data from Braille dots. In deaf people who lip-read the auditory cortex is redeployed so that it can 'respond to mouth movements'.[22]

Something else about our development is also very important for education. Humans take an unusually long time growing up because we have a lot to learn. We eat a wide range of very high value food, for example, which takes a lot of skill and training to track down and identify. Learning all that takes time.[23] It is not just that we spend a long time learning: we use that extra time to get more efficient at learning as we deploy higher-order faculties—a child may start just observing the berries which its mother picks but as it gets older it can be taught explicit rules: 'never eat berries from a plant whose leaves have four fingers until after the rains have come.' This is a much more efficient way of learning than the all-absorbing induction practised by young children. They may learn their first language without having to master the concept of the irregular verb but that is only because they are immersed in the language morning, noon, and night—learning about irregular verbs is a much less time-consuming way of learning a second language. Higher education is a particularly efficient stage for learning. This is one reason why the returns from going to university which we saw in the previous chapter are at least as high as the estimated returns from early years programmes.

What this means for the balance of funding

This is all very relevant to public policy. We assume that the right moment to tackle a problem is early. That is supposed to be preventive. But what is 'early'? There is no particular reason why that should be when a child is under 3. The crucial years for development of schizophrenia, for example, are when someone is aged 17 to 22: those early adult years are when we should aim for early diagnosis but sadly often fail to deliver it. It should mean the right time given the nature of the problem and the available remedies. You have to balance the risks and costs of delay as against the costs of acting before you can be sure there really is a problem—the risks of a false positive. The right time to intervene may be when a problem definitely presents itself if that is more effective than indiscriminate attempts at early prevention, especially if there is little evidence they are effective. It is frustrating how these elementary principles of good public policy are suspended when it comes to the different stages of education.

Imagine there is a social problem of unemployment and depression which manifests itself amongst some 18-year-olds. You have a choice—you can spend money trying to assess which 3-year-olds may suffer these problems in fifteen years time and then try to deliver a programme which prevents that. Or you can tackle the problems when they arise. This has to be a rational decision based on risks and benefits. It is possible that more education for prisoners would be a better targeting of resources than supposedly preventive early years programmes. It is not a dereliction of duty to conclude that the most effective use of limited public resource is to spend it when the problem presents itself and can be directly addressed.

Successive Governments have shifted the balance of public spending on education towards earlier stages. Funding for adult education has been reduced most severely—we now spend substantially more public money on education in the first three years than on all adults. Higher education has seen a big reduction in public spend, though offset with more spending financed by graduate repayments. Spending on those sadly unloved 16–18-year-olds is being cut back compared with 11–16-year-olds. Primary schools do best of all. The Coalition, following on from the previous Labour government, protected real spending on schools and cut public spending on over-16s—priorities which reflected both popular attitudes and a cross-party policy consensus. Institute for Fiscal Studies' (IFS) figures accurately captured relative priorities of public spending over the decade 1998 to 2009. Under-5s spend was up 6.1 per cent per year; primary 3.9 per cent; secondary 5.0 per cent; and HE 2.3 per cent. For the first time in the history of English education policy public spending per student in schools overtook spend per student in HE in 2005–6.[24] A more recent analysis in Table 6.1 shows the downward trend in adult education spend compared with protection for pre-primary education.

This striking and unusual English policy experiment made us an outlier amongst OECD countries for the distribution of our public spending. Compared

Table 6.1. £billions spent on adult education and pre-primary education

	2009	2010	2011	2012	2013
Adult skills	4.5	4.3	3.7	3.6	3.4
Pre-primary	5.3	5.2	4.9	5.2	5.3

Source: Adult skills figures from R. Lupton, L. Unwin, and S. Thompson, *The Coalition's Record on Further and Higher Education and Skills: Policy, Spending and Outcomes 2010–2015*, CASE Working Paper 14 (January 2015), 26. The figures for adult skills may be overstated by including some vocational training for 16–18-year-olds. Pre-primary figures from 'Education spending in the UK', House of Commons Standard Note SN/SG/1078 (10 December 2014), 4. NB: Adult skills figures are in 2009/10 prices; pre-primary figures are in 2013/14 prices, uprated to 2016 prices.

to other OECD countries, spending per pupil on primary education is high in Britain relative to spending on other phases. We spend 10 per cent more per pupil on secondary education than primary education, whereas the OECD average is 20 per cent.[25] The OECD breakdown of the distribution of education spending tells us very clearly the priorities of the English political class and the policy community compared with other advanced countries. It shows that, before the introduction of £9,000 fees and loans, our spend on tertiary education was 1.3 per cent of GDP as against the 1.6 per cent average across the OECD. (In the US it is 2.6 per cent, in Sweden 1.8 per cent.)[26]

Imagine that this balance of public funding across education remained broadly stable and then you as a parent were given a discretionary pot of, say, an extra £5,000 which you could spend at whatever stage of education you thought most important for your child. How would you spend it? I would spend it on extra tuition for 16–18-year-olds to get them decent A levels or the International Baccalaureate or some other respected vocational qualification like a BTEC or an HNC. These are the first qualifications which really stick with you through life and are crucial in determining your chances of going to university. And with the plasticity of the adolescent brain this period really matters. But currently it is education provision for 16–18-year-olds which is losing, especially in further education and sixth form colleges. I have always had a real regard for Principals of these colleges, who do a tough job without complaining and enjoy less public recognition than head-teachers or Vice Chancellors. Vince Cable, to his credit, understood and cared about further education and softened the blow when he could.

There is one other explanation of the appeal of these early years programmes. They are either universal or specifically targeted on poor people. But higher education is different. It is seen as above all for students from advantaged backgrounds, and then the graduates themselves are likely to go on to prosperity and success. This is what holds back the case for higher education: people ask why public money should go on the haves rather than the have-nots. It is why we can indeed ask graduates in well-paid jobs to pay back. It is another reason why broadening access is so important—as we shall see in the next chapter. But there is another implication as well. It is why if we are to spend public money on higher education it should be clearly on equalizing measures which help those who for some reason or another do not have these advantages—as we saw in Chapter Three.

It is tempting to argue that we should invest more at every stage of education. Education is not a zero sum game and the high-minded argument is that every stage of education should gain. James Heckman argues that spending at different stages is complementary and if you spend more on early years you will also have more university students capable of benefiting from going to university later. But resources are limited and public policy is about priorities within whatever that total is set. And my argument is that there is less complementarity of the sort the advocates of early years suggest because you can get benefit out of later stages of education even without enriched early years. The important line of causation might even go in the opposite direction: one of the explanations for the poor impact of Sure Start on the development of young children is that the staff were not well enough trained. You need more people to go to college and university to raise the quality of early years provision. It might also be that it is best to concentrate the help on those children in the most deprived circumstances.[27]

There is another problem with this focus on early years. It leads to a belief that these years should be educationally enriched, and so early years are schoolified—an ugly word for an ugly phenomenon. The evidence is that the countries with the best education outcomes for the basics like literacy and numeracy leave their young children to play and experience the world in 3D. The Nordic countries may not, however, just leave their children to a nostalgic world of Swallows and Amazons. There is a lot of parental input and supervised play in those longer pre-school years. However, it is when children are 6 or 7 that they go into the classroom for formal education. It is only then that their brains are actually going to be receptive to more formal learning and can benefit most from it. They say education is wasted on the young—well, schooling is certainly wasted on the very young. This 'schoolification' of early years, followed by early specialization and then leaving university early, is a peculiar English model. Our educational problem is that we do everything too soon: it is bad for a high-quality, broadly based education.

There is a very frustrating paradox here. In the previous chapter we saw a large amount of economic evidence that going to university is worthwhile, but that argument meets a lot of scepticism. When it comes to the first three years the position is reversed—there is modest and limited evidence but the view of the special significance of these years is embraced with great credulity. One reason is that it fills a hole so neatly and appears to deliver a compromise between so many awkward and apparently irreconcilable positions. Early years determinism is handily placed in the middle of very fraught debates about education and intelligence. If you maintain IQ is already fixed at birth by your genes there is a Calvinist harshness which people don't like. But if we can adjust to our environment indefinitely then there are some very subversive challenges to the widespread explicit and implicit use of selection though education. The message that if we are nimble we have a brief opportunity to improve things seems like a safe mid-point. Labour got the creation of a new public expenditure programme extending the role of the welfare state. The Treasury were happy as it was funded out of savings in later stages of education. Conservatives get a kind of defence for selection later, as by then selective schools and universities can say it is too late to expect students to change—adding that if only we had done more earlier it might have been possible to take more people from disadvantaged backgrounds. I sometimes detected a fake ruefulness which goes like this: 'OK so these young people have had a tough time and it may have been unfair but the fact is that by the time they are aged 18 it is too late. They have not got good A levels and they have not got the study skills to gain from going to university. We must hope that schools eventually will all be as good as the elite but until then they have missed the boat and should do something different.' Every stage of education leaves the student or the parent feeling as if they are confronted by a receptionist at a fashionable restaurant who sucks her teeth and sighs when you turn up without a reservation and says, 'You just missed the last table—if only you had come ten minutes earlier I might have been able to squeeze you in', but you never quite know if that is the real reason or they never really wanted you anyway. That is licensed by early years determinism and amateur neuroscience. But it is wrong. Verbal and non-verbal IQ can change by up to 20 points in the teenage years—there is still plenty to play for.[28]

Deep down it is a very bleak argument—saying that there is nothing to be done for an 18-year-old now and we must hope to do better with the 2-year-olds. But even if we do not like the argument we have to consider whether it really is too late for a badly educated 18-year-old. There are deep questions here about how malleable we are. We are not just a shapeless clay that can be moulded to become a Nobel Prize winner or a Fellow of All Souls. Clearly there are limits shaped by our genetic inheritance and our experiences. But different advanced Western countries with which we share a lot seem to have very different views about how much people can rise to the challenge of a new environment. And what we think of as exceptional inner gifts may actually be the result of lots of study and training, as Matthew Seyd shows in *Bounce*.[29] In particular the university may have more power to change us—and for the better—than we recognize. Universities argue that prior attainment is the barrier that stops them recruiting a wider range of students. Some highly efficient forms of teaching do clearly require large amounts of prior knowledge and can then move forward at great speed and very effectively. But that is not the only form of higher education and it is possible for people to change and advance as a result of the university experience. Higher education also needs to cater for them. This argument might be easier to win if there were a good account of how university can change us which is as plausible as the neuroscientific claims of early years activists. So here goes.

How universities change people

The last chapter summarized the evidence for the many benefits of university. Now we need to dig a bit deeper to see how universities achieve this. The evidence of better health amongst graduates is a good test of whether we can really show how university changes you. Is there really an account of the effect of higher education which matches the boldness of the narrative about the significance of early years? We have already seen that one obvious explanation is that it is just a selection effect—people from more affluent backgrounds go to university and they tend to be healthier so there is a correlation. But social scientists do seem to have shown there is more to it than this. Perhaps if you received more education you are more likely to receive health education messages. That sounds plausible but is pretty mundane and actually knowledge of health issues is only a small part of the explanation of the better health of better-educated people.[30] Is there a deeper and more satisfying account of the impact of the university on the individual?

A third Nobel Prize winner can help us here. Gary Becker was a truly great economist who specialized in education and the family. He speculated that education really works by changing the way we value the future. At university our minds are trained to think things through, which means we look ahead and the way we behave changes the more we are oriented to thinking about the future. 'Schooling focuses students' attention on the future. Schooling can communicate images of the situations and difficulties of adult life, which are the future of childhood and adolescence. In addition, through repeated practice at problem solving, schooling helps children learn the art of scenario simulation. Thus educated people should be more productive at reducing the remoteness of future pleasures.' This gets us closer to understanding how university changes us.[31]

One of the most famous studies of our ability to defer gratification into the future was conducted by Walter Mischel. He presented 4-year-olds with the choice of one very real cookie now or the promise of two cookies in the future. The capacity of the children to control their appetites and go for two cookies later proved to be a powerful predictor of lifetime success. But there is an important twist to his argument which got lost from sight. We can all learn techniques to help make it easier to reject that immediate cookie now—such as treating the cookie in front of you as a mere image of a cookie and thinking of something completely different you will do in the future.[32] These are not techniques you can only learn when you are 4; they apply equally when you are 14 or 24. In fact the period from adolescence through into the early twenties is crucial for the development of skills in assessing risk, broadening one's perspective, and taking a decision.

There is evidence for going to college having precisely this effect. It comes from the natural experiment of admission decisions in a public college in Mexico determined through a lottery. The researcher found that after getting to college, and compared with those who did not get a lottery place, those 'individuals who were successful in the admission lottery were, on average, more patient'—i.e. more likely to wait a year for a seven-day all-expenses-paid trip rather than a five-day trip on similar terms now. This is the kind of effect that is claimed for early years education but it is for students with an average age of 21.[33]

I have argued that one way we learn to invest in the future is through an inter-generational contract in which we receive from older generations and in turn give to younger generations. We have some fascinating evidence that university influences behaviour this way. Robert Putnam has studied the social capital of successive cohorts and has found the generation who fought in the Second World War to be the most willing to give back to society through getting involved in charities—especially for the young. But why? They might easily have thought they had contributed more than enough by fighting in the war and were entitled to take it a bit easier after that. The most persuasive explanation attributes their behaviour to the GI Bill. This massive and unprecedented investment in them left them determined to give back in return for this life-changing experience. As the author of the key study puts it: 'My central finding is that the G.I. Bill's education and training provisions had an overwhelmingly positive effect on male veterans' civic involvement. Those veterans who utilized the provisions became more active citizens in public life in the postwar years than those who did not.'[34]

The university embodies the exchange between the generations. Older generations invest in the future through supporting the education of younger generations, and that in turn prompts the beneficiaries to want to give something back themselves. Indeed, one of my concerns about a widespread misunderstanding of our changes in higher education funding is that students might think there is no public investment in them and hence their sense of reciprocal obligation will be eroded. But actually, as I tried to explain in Chapter Three, there is still, quite rightly, public support for university education—there could be a regrettable loss of social capital if we fail to explain that.

The university has been created over generations to invest in young people and slowly build up the coral reef of human knowledge—which is far bigger than any one individual but to which an individual can make a worthwhile contribution. A university itself embodies the inter-generational contract. And so does an individual discipline, as students learn about an intellectual framework developed over centuries which is still growing and changing. Getting some understanding of the shape of the canon of a discipline and where it is contested or advancing is a wonderful thing. This kind of understanding of a discipline changes people. One piece of evidence is from students playing roles in classic challenges in game theory, such as the Prisoners' Dilemma, in which the best outcome is for neither prisoner to betray the other but there are strong incentives for them to betray each other. The good news is that there is a tendency for students to reach more co-operative solutions as they move closer to graduation. But there is one exception which itself shows how university changes us. Economics students exhibit no such tendency—if anything they shift to less co-operative solutions. In the Prisoners' Dilemma 60 per cent of economics students betray as against 40 per cent of students in other disciplines. Economics students are less likely to cite fairness and more likely to predict selfish behaviour by others. These effects develop over time: they are not just prior selection. This American research shows that 'exposure to the self interest model does in fact increase the self-interested behaviour'. We may not welcome this but it is at least evidence of the power of university study to change us—and the power of specific subjects.[35]

One could even copy the effective advocacy for early years and inject some layman's neuroscience into the case for higher education—and neuroscience adds to the authority of any argument.[36] The pre-frontal cortex, the part of our brain responsible for rational agency, long-term thinking and planning, develops out into our early twenties. That is why teenagers have a different view of risk and value the future less than adults do. There is a sensitive period when this key neurological function is developing. It is strengthened if young people are engaged in projects which promote this capability. These young adults need to experience the slow build-up of skill in a sport, understanding of an intellectual discipline, or mastery of a craft through training: in all these cases they find that putting in the hours and deferring gratification can yield results beyond what they thought possible. This training best takes place in a semi-supervised environment where they are neither treated as children nor as fully independent adults, so they can take controlled risks. Over the centuries we have created institutions which do this—the army, organized sports, apprenticeships, and universities. Of these the one which is by far the most significant in the lives of young people nowadays is the university and we should value it accordingly.

Lotteries, selection effects, and motivation

Lotteries provide powerful evidence to challenge arguments that universities don't have any effect apart from selection or signalling effects. The Americans ran a lottery for the Vietnam draft. It had a particularly complicated structure which gives some exceptional opportunities for education research. If you drew a low number you were at risk of being drafted but could avoid it by staying on in education. Those who got a higher lottery number were not at risk of being drafted and so did not have the same incentive to get more education. And in some years there were groups who faced a risk of being drafted and so increased their education but then nobody in that range of lottery numbers was drafted after all so there is no veteran effect in the group. Those who did extra education in these unpropitious circumstances show a 6.5 per cent increase in weekly earnings per additional year of college as against those with similar backgrounds who got a high lottery number and therefore did not have the same incentive to stay on in education.[37]

We have this lottery evidence because other countries, such as the US, use them much more than we do. We make painstaking attempts to select the right people with the right aptitudes. But in the US they are more willing to use lotteries to allocate people to oversubscribed schools or colleges and then expect the institution to do its work. Our approach looks scrupulously fair. The Eleven-Plus is but the most vivid and controversial example of this way of thinking. It can be seen as ensuring the greatest possible efficiency in delivering education by making sure it is best tailored to the individual's abilities. But what if the individual's abilities are not completely fixed and will themselves change in response to their education? Then these selection devices instead look like examples of producer power—choosing the individuals who make life easiest for the education provider institution they join. And the very prestige of some of our universities with their many applicants puts them in a strong position to do just that, which in turn can put some groups at a disadvantage.

America is much more willing to assume a stronger institutional effect on individuals, to whom they attribute greater potential than we do—that is why Walter McMahon, the author of the leading American book on the benefits of higher education, does not devote much attention to selection effects. By contrast English social science is much more aware of the risk of selection effects. This is an admirable commitment to rigour, but just occasionally one detects an underpinning assumption that institutions—from marriage to universities—can't really make a difference and all they can do is take people whose prior behaviour or abilities suits them anyway.

There is a further twist to this argument. Your belief about whether abilities are fixed or malleable itself affects behaviour. Carol Dweck shows that to some extent these beliefs are self-fulfilling.[38] She shows the negative effects of a belief that skills are fixed early on—and this is particularly bad for girls. The belief that their abilities are fixed reduces the amount of work adolescents do. Instead we should embrace the kind of philosophy supported by Matthew Seyd's evidence that what looks like extraordinary flair to the observer may actually be the result of hours and hours of training.[39] So let me advance a hypothesis now which we will test later. I propose that as selection into higher education is particularly strong in England and as it rests on a particularly strong belief in fixed abilities then there should be lower hours of study than in higher education systems resting on a different philosophy. We will test this hypothesis in Chapter Eight.

The Flynn effect

There are other ways of showing the extraordinary capacity of the brain to advance, even without the power of higher education. Professor James Flynn has given his name to the striking observation that IQ has been going up for a century across the developed world. At any one point of time IQ levels may differ a bit between countries (when he last checked, British IQ was about three points higher than US). And rates of improvement may differ (American IQ has been growing faster than British). But the overall trend is clear. So, for example, between 1980 and 2008 the average IQ of British 5–15-year-olds grew by 6.23 points or 0.22 per year (as against 0.36 per year for US kids).[40]

Flynn is not claiming that a newborn baby has a physically different brain now than in 1900. Instead it is evidence of neural plasticity. And it is not just in the early years that this occurs. Flynn's explanation is about the effect of interacting with the modern world in all its sophistication. As he puts it: 'If the question is "Do we have better brain potential at conception, or were our ancestors too stupid to deal with the concrete world of everyday life?" the answer is no. If the question is "Do we live in a time that poses a wider range of cognitive problems than our ancestors encountered, and have we developed new cognitive skills and the kind of brains that can deal with these problems?" the answer is yes.' He goes on to speculate about the reasons for these improvements—'more formal schooling, more cognitively demanding jobs, cognitively challenging leisure, better ratio of adults to children, richer interaction of parent and child'. And as a result of these processes, which extend way beyond the early years, 'our brains may well be different from those of our ancestors'.[41]

He pins down the different components of IQ tests. We seem to have made the biggest gains in fluid intelligence—pattern spotting and quick logical problem solving. This has seen massive improvements of 20 points for adults and 24 for children. We have made big gains in moving from analysing concrete situations to the ability to generalize and conceive of hypotheticals. Flynn goes on to draw out a crucial implication: 'This habit of mind is a prerequisite for higher education.'[42] So there is no fixed pool of ability. We are getting smarter so more of us can benefit from going to university. Moreover, this capacity gets better as we get older: we draw on a wider range of experiences and can apply deep pattern recognition to problems as they present themselves.

The evidence is that our children have greater intellectual stimulus and demands than ever before and as a result are smarter than ever. This is what modernity is all about. Flynn even has an ingenious explanation of why we may not appreciate this. It is because more parents have been to university. This has had an effect on our appraisal of our children's education standards which is not properly recognized. The parents of the baby boomers were unlikely to have gone to university so boomers had personal experience of educational progress, overtaking the education level achieved by their parents. But now many parents are graduates themselves and so have more education than their 18-year-olds, and gains in IQ are greater for adults than for children—partly because of the effects of tertiary education. For such parents it may be shocking that 18-year-olds appear less well-educated compared to them, when at that stage of their own upbringing they were already better educated than their parents. That can feel like a decline in educational standards but really it is a reflection of how education opportunities have already expanded.[43]

Conclusion

Early years determinism represents an advance on stark forms of genetic determinism because it argues that we are not born with everything about our brain or our character fixed. It does not fall for those ingenious arguments about signalling and selection because it does not claim that sending a child to a pre-school is just to signal she is smart already. The trouble is that it does not apply this insight as boldly across education as it should, trying to draw too tight a boundary line after which everything is fixed and the clay is set in the mould. Imagine that everything positive they say about the first three years is actually true for the first thirty-three years—or even after that. That is a better guide to education policy.

It is tempting to say that regardless of whether early years determinism is justified by the latest neuroscience at least it is harmless. Nobody can reasonably object to better early years provision and I certainly agree that quality childcare is a good thing. But we have seen there are at least four reasons why early years determinism needs careful scrutiny—it influences patterns of funding when the total available for education is limited; it justifies subsequent selection decisions; it can erode individual ambition; and it can lead to over-structuring of early education. Above all, however, we have offered an alternative explanation of how education at all ages, including at university, can change you. So getting in to university is not just a matter of identifying who is already well-educated. That is the issue to which we now must turn.

SEVEN

Getting in to University

The unusual English model

Our system of university admissions is medieval—and was created in 1961 when UCAS, originally called UCCA (the Universities Central Council on Admissions, now the Universities and Colleges Admissions Services), was set up. We have a single national system of competitive application to university, based on the assumption that most students will move away from home. It is very different from the classic Continental and American model in which you go to your local college or university for a tertiary education, which is neither highly selective nor highly specialized. Nearly half of American undergraduates study at a two-year college and then obtain what we would have called an ordinary degree. If they have higher ACT or SAT scores they are more likely to start at a university providing a full four-year course from the beginning but this is still likely to be in their home state and open to students who can arrive after two years at a college.[1] Then if they really have an aptitude for academic study and wish to specialize or need to get a professional qualification they do a post-graduate Masters course: perhaps at this point they may move out of the state. Ask an American professional where they went to university and you will be told which business or law or medical school they went to as a postgraduate. But they may well have started their undergraduate studies somewhere very different and much closer to home. And their whole time in higher education is likely to have been longer than in England.

The English system by contrast is the medieval model of a young gentleman leaving home (or boarding school—meaning it would be very peculiar to return home for university) to go to Oxford or Cambridge. It has been shaped by a long history as a unitary state with very few universities and nationwide migration of students to get to them. It is so deeply embedded that the decision to set up the nationwide admissions system provoked very little discussion or challenge. So that medieval model now applies to a million English undergraduates and over a hundred universities. The ordinary degree has largely disappeared and most students study for an honours degree.

Students come in many shapes and sizes—you do not have to be young and you do not have to move away from home to be a student. Nevertheless it is no accident that the 18-year-old leaving home is our most powerful image of university education. That is what a third of 18- and 19-year-olds now do. At a motorway service station in late September you can see the cars come in, loaded with pot plants, musical instruments, bean-bags, and even a few books. It is a mass migration—all it needs is Sir David Attenborough to provide an excited commentary as the convoys of heavily laden estate cars roll by. He would, however, find this migration rather unusual—it is a migration *north* in the autumn. Our prestigious universities are well distributed across the country, unlike our most academically successful private schools. That is why they say their students travel south to school and north to university.[2]

In England the university chooses whom to admit in a nationwide competitive allocation of places. This puts all our universities in the unusually strong position of deciding who they wish to educate. The autonomy enjoyed by English universities in determining their own admissions in turn means the balance of power within the university matters. Here we find another striking feature of our universities—individual academic departments have significant power to decide on admissions. Students are admitted to study a specific subject. If a student were to arrive as a generalist for the first year or two with no subject preferences then she would not be applying for a specific academic department and there would be no departmental power over admissions—it would be a university-wide decision. In England the prospective student identifies what subject she wants to study and then the academics in that department decide if they want to admit her. This power is reducing—not least because of university-wide monitoring of the social background of students. And the less selective universities have less power to specify prior aptitude in particular disciplines—they are 'recruiting', not 'selective'. Nevertheless this system of selective entry based on aptitude for a specific subject remains the dominant model and departments set their criteria even if they do not decide individual cases.

In America decisions on who to admit are all part of a single university-wide operation with no significant role for individual academic departments in admissions. The prospective student may indicate some broad area of interest but she will choose her courses after she arrives and the different academic departments will have to market their discipline to her. The most popular subject offered to get in to an American university is 'Undeclared'—American students only have to decide their Major by the second term of their second year. The opening weeks of an American academic year see students trying out different lectures and seminars to decide which they will stick with. In England the prospective student has to market herself to the department and having committed to a specific subject cannot easily shift to a different one. One academic who had taught both at Oxford and at Harvard told me a key difference was that at Harvard the first he knew of his students was when they turned up in their first week whereas at Oxford he had been closely involved in who should be admitted. (He went on to say that academic staff could be released from this heavy burden if instead places were allocated by a lottery of students above a certain grade, perhaps with some adjustment for disadvantage. He argued this could have the double benefit of both softening the blow to the Oxbridge reject and diminishing the occasional arrogance of those who do get in.)

American Ivy League universities are explicit about 'molding the class'. They recognize that they provide much of the American elite and are heavily over-subscribed but that leads them to take a very different approach to selecting their students than in England. This is partly to do with the extraordinarily sensitive issue of race in America, where universities had maximum limits (for Jewish students) and minimum targets (for Black students). Racial quotas have been struck down by the Supreme Court but they still 'mold' the class. They think they have an obligation to try to ensure America has a good mix of future leaders. Of course their candidates need to have achieved high standards in the SAT but one Harvard academic told me that if they just took the people with the highest SAT scores they would end up producing middle-rank programmers for IBM, not shaping America's future. They are looking for students with something else. These decisions are possible because the decisions on undergraduate admission are not taken by subject specialists in departments but by the university's central admissions department. This incidentally is how they are able to build up substantial endowments. There is a widespread misconception that American tax reliefs are the reason but they are not much more generous than ours. The real difference is that universities offer explicit donor preference schemes so that you can increase the chances of a son or daughter getting a place by a big donation. In the coy and convoluted words of Lawrence Summers, former President of Harvard, 'It is not realistic to expect that schools and universities dependent on charitable contributions will not be attentive to the offspring of their supporters.' It would not be acceptable to say that in England.[3]

America's elite universities can recruit someone because the orchestra needs a good oboeist, or he got a respectable SAT score from a poor school in the toughest part of Chicago so he must be really bright and motivated, or her parents will give $10m to the scholarship fund, or his father hit a home run for our baseball team in the finals thirty years ago and it will be great to welcome his son here too. All of these considerations are possible. Indeed, the social compact which underpins the system depends on all of these being valid considerations. They can get away with letting in the daughter whose parents are going to give $10m partly because they also let in that disadvantaged student from Chicago with lower grades.[4] And out of this mix emerges a ruling elite who may be community organizers or generals or entrepreneurs. Increasingly they are applying these criteria to applicants from around the world too. The selective English university is also likely to staff our elite but they are more reluctant to acknowledge this and, partly for that very reason, focus more narrowly on academic excellence. Academic staff in individual departments, especially in our more selective universities, identify those whose A level marks and personal statement suggest they have the greatest aptitude as a historian or a physicist, plus probably nowadays some kind of allowance for disadvantage. We have ruled most of the other criteria out—and there would be a media storm if most of the criteria used in the American Ivy League were ever applied here. After investing all that effort in getting their children good A levels it is understandable that parents regard a place at a good university as a legitimate reward for A level performance. The American system is more like the English one when it comes to applying for graduate school—that is where the academics do have a greater role in deciding who to admit.

Many American universities belong to the states and they too shape admission policies on principles very different from ours. In England nobody has a right to study at university because no public authority has the power to enforce any such claim on autonomous universities. In some US states if you get above a certain mark in a school-leaving exam you have a right to go to the university in your state—though which one will depend in part on your SAT/ACT score. Republican Governor Jeb Bush guaranteed all high school students in the top 20 per cent of their class a place at one of Florida's public universities and colleges. California guarantees a place at university for the top 9 per cent in each high school, subject to a minimum grade. I explained to a right-wing Republican that in England such schemes would be regarded as the worst sort of left-wing social engineering, undermining meritocracy and the autonomy of our universities. He replied that if you just measured their performance in exams at the age of 18 'no kid from South Central Los Angeles would ever go to university' but there were bright kids there and they needed a chance. It was all part of the American dream. They should not be the victims of failing state schools. Given that bright kids were to be found all over the place it was much more effective to take the top performers from each school rather than to take the best-educated ones, which would favour some schools over others. He wanted to focus on the individual not the school. That is an argument it would be hard to win in England. It is the difference between American faith in resilience and endeavour, and the English tendency, reinforced by early years determinism, to assume that these disadvantages cannot be overcome.

When England was creating UCCA the US was creating credit transfer—a system of interchangeable study credits which make it easier to move from university to university, so weakening the commitment to a specific university and hence its producer power. In America choice happens within the system—movement between universities and between courses at universities—not through a single big first decision of the university to try to get to and the course to study, after which you are committed. Some Americans look enviously at our system as they think a single national system is more comprehensible and easier for disadvantaged students to access than individual application to specific universities. Indeed, one attractive 'Nudge' idea for broadening access in England is that every student in the sixth form should fill in a UCAS application form—and then they just have to decide whether to click *Send*.

Our exceptional open national competition for entry to universities and their sheer diversity creates an appetite for the ranking of universities. The rankings in the media both reflect and shape student preferences. Two main criteria push research-intensive Russell Group universities to the top of the rankings—prior attainment of students measured by A level grades and research performance. These prestigious universities often give their graduates access to the best jobs because employers follow the rankings too. This means that really employers are selecting on the basis of A level grades as transmitted via university admission decisions. All this makes it unusually important what A levels you get and which university you get to at age 18 and this in turn shapes our schools system. Schools are judged on their performance in getting their students into university, especially the most prestigious ones. That is why the Oxford University reforms in the 1850s, opening up admissions by ending many closed awards for students from specific public schools, prompted the great public school reform movement. And today parents, ambitious for their children, want to know to which universities a school sends its students. As a result, what schools teach and how is heavily influenced by what universities are looking for. Indeed, the role of the A level has always been to help universities select students. Given the unusual way that university admission works in England that means that schools need to know what the historians or the physicists deciding admission to their university department are looking for. The answer is what you would expect: they are looking for students who already know quite a lot of history or physics and display a real aptitude for it. When Michael Gove as Secretary of State for Education summoned university academics to advise on A levels they are reported to have said how shocked they were by how little their prospective students knew in their specific disciplines. The truth is the opposite. Eighteen-year-olds going to study physics or history, for example, at an English university probably know more physics or history than any other group of 18-year-olds in any other major Western country—the real problem is that they know less about almost everything else. We are beginning to see why we have ended with more academic specialization at school than any other Western educational system. It is because of the power of university departments and our admissions system. No other Western country expects 16-year-olds to restrict their academic subjects so narrowly and indeed explicitly funds its secondary schools on the basis that post-16s study three academic subjects—an issue we will return to in Chapter Fourteen. In the US the SAT/ACT score is a measure of academic aptitude, not a specific exam in particular disciplines, and this crucial difference emerges from the different way American universities recruit.

Our single transparent national competitive entry means that a school can be assessed by how many of its students get through to our most prestigious universities. That is what independent schools and our most academic secondary schools focus on and is now set by the DfE as an explicit measure of school performance. Schools themselves are then keen to recruit those students who are likely to do best at A level and get to the universities ranked by parents and the DfE. This drives the many subtle ways in which parents and schools select at 11, from house prices to religious observance, which are pervasive though much less overt than the old Eleven-Plus. This in turn drives high levels of social segregation in secondary schools—unusually high for an officially non-selective Western school system. That leaves behind a long tail of underperforming schools caught in a vicious spiral of low prestige and decline—which can be escaped, but not easily.

The clearest evidence of parental preferences comes from the behaviour of fee-paying private schools. 65 per cent of independent school students go to Russell Group universities as against 26 per cent of state school students. They achieve this by investing all their efforts in securing the good A level grades in the key subjects which are the be-all and end-all of university admissions. Indeed, their students are flattered by their A level results. Economists have come up with an ingenious measure of this effect. They tracked how a private school education enabled a student to 'outperform at A level—i.e. get better grades than their subsequent degree class for any given university'. They found that 'A male student who previously attended an independent school is about 6.5 percentage points less likely to obtain a good degree than is an otherwise equivalent student who attended an LEA school.'[5] You could see this as a measure of the underperformance of state schools whose students then go on to do better at university. But some of the enhanced performance depends on access to limited positional goods such as teaching staff with exceptional academic qualifications—who are expensive and in short supply. This account is supported by the finding that there is even a correlation with the exact level of fees: 'Increasing fees by £2,000 leads to an approximate 1 percentage point reduction in the probability of a "good" degree for males.'[6] Parents are paying for their children's A level grades to be boosted so they can get into the most prestigious universities and the more you pay the more they are boosted. This is vivid evidence of the power of universities on school behaviour. The private schools do have a response to this evidence—that they serve up a high-grade product in good condition which the universities then fail to nurture by failing to deliver the kind of pastoral care which their students need. But as this finding is about relative performance it is still necessary to explain why this problem affects privately educated students more. I believe that this is a vivid example of wider behaviour across secondary education—shaped by our university admission system.

How many people go and from what background?

This unusual structure and incentives has an enormous influence on English education. But now let us turn to the numbers flowing through these structures. Tony Blair set a target in 1999 for 50 per cent of young people to go to university by 2010.[7] We came very close to meeting Tony Blair's 50 per cent target in 2011–12 when there was an artificial surge as students dropped gap years to get in before the new higher fees. 2012–13 saw a drop. My most anxious time, which I believed would determine the fate of our higher education reforms, was waiting for the figures for applications in 2013–14. If the decline had continued then our reforms would indeed have been putting off students, which would have been a tragedy. But instead there was a healthy recovery in student applications which fed through into record numbers of places. In particular there were more applicants from low-income families. That was the moment we knew our reforms had taken root. The participation rate continued to climb, reaching 48 per cent in 2014–15.

The Coalition never endorsed Blair's target as we thought the number going to university should emerge from the choices of prospective students and the decisions of universities. That is why we removed the limits set by Government on the number of students going to university. It was a major education reform, transforming opportunities for young people. Until then there were students keen to learn, doing the right thing and applying for university, and the university was willing to educate them, but they were being turned away because of Government control on numbers. This was the only stage of education where the Government deliberately restricted access, requiring that capable volunteers be rejected. Number controls were removed for the 2015–16 academic year and pent-up demand was released. It was not quite like shoppers outside Harrods on the first day of the sales but certainly a solid increase. Table 7.1 shows the Higher Education Initial Participation Rate (HEIPR), which is the percentage of 17 to 30 year olds going to higher education.

Table 7.1. Higher Education Initial Participation Rate (HEIPR) (%)

	Male	Female	All
2006–7	38	47	42
2007–8	39	48	43
2008–9	41	51	45
2009–10	41	51	46
2010–11	42	51	46
2011–12	45	54	49
2012–13	39	47	43
2013–14	42	51	47
2014–15	43	53	48

Source: UK Government statistics on-line: participation rates in higher education 2006–2014 published 2 September 2015, and note 'Participation in higher education in England and the UK, Paul Bolton, House of Commons, SN/SG/2620, 2016.

Table 7.2. HE application rates, 18–19-year-olds,
English students only

2009	36.7%
2010	39.7%
2011	42.2%
2012	41.8%
2013	41.3%
2014	47.9%
2015	44.4%
2016	44.7%
2017	45.2%

Source: Cohort application rates by age 19, England, UCAS
2017 Application Cycle: UK application rates by the January
deadline, UCAS, data tables for figure 21, February 2017.

Many young people go straight from school to university. The application
rates of English 18- and 19-year-olds are in Table 7.2. Not all of these applicants
would have secured a place.

Just sometimes, in those moments of paranoia which afflict every minister,
I would think there were only two media stories about university applications—
either too many were going to university or too few were because our fees were
putting people off. The figure could never be OK. Then every year UCAS would
come to brief me on the figures and it was clear the growth was carrying on. That
is why I came to believe that there is a deep-seated trend for more young people
to apply for university: we should accept it and welcome it. It is all part of a parent's
hope that their child will have a decent, well-paid job, own a house of their own,
and settle down with a partner and raise their children well. We saw in Chapter
Five that these aspirations are indeed all associated with going to university. One
survey showed 68 per cent of 14–19 year olds are planning to go to university,
broadly in line with the 75 per cent of under 25s who want to own a home.[8] It
would be foolhardy for any political party to set itself against these aspirations.

Some rough and ready estimates give the absolute numbers behind these
percentages. We have a population of just over 60 million people. Imagine them
distributed in cohorts evenly spread across the different ages and it works out at
about 800,000 people per year. Half of a cohort going to university means
about 400,000 per year. (The birth rate was falling in the 1990s so at present
there are fewer 18-year-olds in each successive cohort. That means the pessimists
can sometimes claim there has been a fall in the number of 18-year-olds applying
whilst the optimists can reply that it is a higher proportion.) The average degree
course lasts three years so that means around 1.2 million undergraduate students

at a British university. Add in students from overseas and students doing postgraduate courses and that doubles up to over two million students. These numbers, far bigger than anything envisaged even twenty years ago, are a measure of the central role of the university in modern Britain.

Many more women are going to university than men. That is why this book usually refers to students as female. This is very different from the plight of women so vividly captured in Virginia Woolf's *A Room of One's Own*: 'I was actually at the door which leads into the library itself. I must have opened it, for instantly there issued, like a guardian angel barring the way with a flutter of black gown instead of white wings, a deprecating, silvery, kindly gentleman, who regretted in a low voice as he waved me back that ladies are only admitted to the library if accompanied by a Fellow of the College or furnished with a letter of introduction.'[9] Girls have gradually been overtaking boys: girls were always better at GCSEs than boys though boys kept their lead at A level but that lead has now been reversed. Females overtook males in university places in 1996. Table 7.1 showed that women have now achieved Tony Blair's much mocked target of 50 per cent participation—with men some way behind. The same proportion of women get Firsts as men, so increased numbers of women have not led to lower standards. More women do postgraduate courses than men. Already more women get Masters. They have not yet overtaken men in getting doctorates but that barrier will be the next to fall.[10] One explanation for the gender gap is that boys have more well-paid non-graduate job options than girls, as we saw in Chapter Five. Equivalent but preponderantly female jobs such as teaching and nursing have meanwhile become graduate-entry. In addition the Eleven-Plus gave boys a special boost as there was often a 50/50 gender balance of grammar school places despite girls doing better at primary school, so girls needed a higher mark to get a grammar school place than boys.

As well as gender there is also a clear influence from income and class. The good news is that the percentage of children from the poorest quintile going to university is double what it was a decade ago—when it was 10 per cent. The bad news is that it is still just a third of the applications from the most affluent quintile. About 20 per cent of children from low-income households go on into higher education as against 60 per cent of children from affluent households. We can also compare participation rates in the richest and poorest areas between the first half and the second half of the 2000–10 decade. Participation in the richest quintile of areas has gone up from 56.0 per cent to 57.6 per cent, a 3 per cent increase. For the poorest areas it has gone up from 13.6 per cent to 16.1 per cent, a 19 per cent increase. Participation rates are lowest in the North-East, Yorkshire, and the Humber Estuary.[11]

There are significant ethnic divergences as well, as shown in Table 7.3.

Table 7.3. Entry rates to higher education for
18-year-olds in English state schools 2015

Chinese	57.9%
Asian	42.9%
Black	37.5%
Other Ethnic	37.0%
Mixed	33.0%
White	28.7%

Source: UCAS End of Cycle report: Analysis and research,
December 2016, data tables and figure 60.

One ethnic group above all has a problem. White British is the only major ethnic group under-represented in higher education, as the Table shows. Putting together race, class, and gender there is one group which clearly ends up at the bottom of the pile—white working-class boys, whose chances of going on to higher education are as low as 10 per cent.[12] But only two higher education institutions set targets for recruiting more male students in their 2016/17 Access Agreements.[13] However, these boys are followed by similarly disadvantaged girls, who are not far behind. And whilst some ethnic groups do better at getting in, they then do rather worse at getting a job afterwards, so there is scope for a continuing argument about the exact balance between disadvantage by class, gender, and ethnicity.[14]

I was regularly told that too many people go to university. But it appears to be a very unusual social problem because it is rife in the very parts of the country we associate with prosperity and economic growth. It is a problem which is to be found not in Hull or Bolsover or Great Yarmouth, where 20 per cent or fewer of young people go to university, but instead is most acute in Harrow, Kensington and Chelsea, and Richmond-upon-Thames, where over 60 per cent of young people are going to university.[15] These areas with high participation contain schools which appear to pride themselves on doing twice as well as Blair's target and sending close to 100 per cent of their intake to university. If we are to reverse this trend for so many people to go to university we don't need to worry about 'bog standard comprehensives' in the poorer cities: pupils there are clearly doing an excellent job of resisting the blandishments of university life. Nor should we worry about white working-class boys: they, above all, are the group who are immune to the dangerous lure of higher education. Instead we should worry about middle-class children in the prosperous Home Counties where rates of going to university exceed 70 per cent. But I have

Table 7.4. HE participation rates by parliamentary constituency

City of London & Westminster	73%
Richmond	67%
Wimbledon	65%
Leeds Central	15%
Bristol S	14%
Nottingham N	13%

Source: *Polar3 Participation Rates of those who Turned 18 between 2005–2009 by Parliamentary Constituency*, HEFCE, October 2012. The top three constituencies are Conservative whereas the bottom three are Labour. A separate UCAS analysis measures participation specifically at age 18 and shows that just in that one year 63% of 18-year-olds in Wimbledon went to university, putting it top of their table. See UCAS, *End of Cycle Report: Analysis and Research*, December 2016, data tables and figure 17.

never come across local campaigns to tackle this supposed problem in the prosperous London suburbs and shire towns where it is most acute. Indeed, whilst the 50 per cent target was set by a Labour Prime Minister it is actually Conservative areas which are delivering it, as shown in Table 7.4, which gives figures for highest and lowest participation rates by constituency.

Governments should not decide how many people should go to university. Instead that should emerge as a result of the free decisions of students applying and universities deciding whom to admit. For too long Government got involved in setting limits in order to control public spending: our funding reforms have meant that constraint has gone, as we saw in Chapter Three. This at last opens up the opportunity to transform participation. For over twenty years I was proud to represent Havant, a mainly urban area between Portsmouth and Chichester. It includes a large council estate and indeed was for a time the most working-class Conservative constituency. It has a higher education participation rate of 23 per cent. Meanwhile Vince Cable represented prosperous Twickenham with a participation rate of 62 per cent. I pointed out to him that I wanted to see more of my constituents going to university but not at the expense of his. That means more university places in total. Disadvantaged groups will have a very long wait if is a zero sum game and improved participation from poorer areas can only be achieved by somehow reducing the number of people from more prosperous areas going to university. That is why the only reliable way to improve university participation of disadvantaged groups is to have more people going to university in total. And we are making progress as university

participation gradually spreads wider across society from the most advantaged
to the least advantaged. In the old days, boys from elite backgrounds were the
main group going to university. The Butler Education Act of 1944, the surge in
the birth rate after the war, and the raising of the school leaving age meant that
universities were opened up and expanded in the late 1950s and early 1960s.
Table 7.5 shows the growth of participation. The first beneficiaries of this were
middle-class girls in particular, whose participation was behind lower-middle-
class boys but then overtook them. Six per cent of males born in 1958 from the
20 per cent lowest income had a degree by age 23—as did 6 per cent of females
from the middle 60 per cent of income. For those born in 1970 this had risen
to 8 per cent for low-income males and 15 per cent for middle-income females.[16]
And as we get closer to saturation for young people from prosperous backgrounds so increasingly we can see the growth in numbers coming from young
people from more disadvantaged backgrounds.

With such high participation rates in prosperous areas and from some schools
it is understandable that society's movers and shakers can't imagine there could
be anyone left who does not go to university yet could benefit from it. That is
because the groups who are missing out are living in a very different part of town,
having a very different childhood, and going to very different schools. Sometimes
their lower rate of going to university is justified by the argument that their role
in life is to do the jobs that don't involve going to university. That argument has
been expressed for centuries, regardless of how many people actually go to university. It was the argument in the gruesome letter in which Thomas Hardy's Jude

Table 7.5. Higher education participation
rates since the war

1950	3.4%
1970	8.4%
1990	19.3%
2000	33%
2010	46%
2014	48%

Source: Education: Historical statistics, House of Commons
SN/SG/4252, 27 November 2012, p. 14 and Paul Bolton,
'Participation in higher education in England and the
UK: social indicators', House of Commons SN/SG/2630,
September 2016. There is a discontinuity in the series after
2000 with a shift from the Age Participation Index, which
looked at entrants under age 21 in Great Britain, to the
Higher Education Initial Participation Rate, which looks
at 17–30-year-old first-time entrants domiciled in England.

the Obscure is rejected by Biblioll College, Oxford, despite all his efforts to educate himself: 'Sir,—I have read your letter with interest; and, judging from your
description of yourself as a working-man, I venture to think that you will have a
much better chance of success in life by remaining in your own sphere and sticking to your trade than by adopting any other course. That, therefore, is what
I advise you to do. Yours faithfully T Tetuphenay.'[17] Here is the point made by one
seventeenth-century Oxford academic: 'There is an opinion commonly receiv'd,
that the Scholars of England are overproportion'd to the preferments for letter'd
persons, and that those whom Nature or Fortune had determin'd to the Plough,
the Oar, or other Handicrafts were being diverted to the study of Liberal Arts.'[18]
You can still find that argument in the pages of our newspapers today.

Groups which already have high rates of university participation are more
sceptical about more people going to university than groups with low participation. Thirty per cent of graduates support a reduction in the number of university places, compared with 11 per cent of those without formal qualifications.
Twenty-six per cent of those from professional and managerial backgrounds
think opportunities should be reduced, compared with 10 per cent of those
in traditional working-class jobs. The analysts offer the following explanation:
'The middle classes and existing graduates are more likely to seek to protect the
value of their investment in higher education by restricting access to it, while
those in manual occupations and without a university degree are more likely to
wish to reduce barriers to participation.'[19] Restricting participation may be trying to ensure that a university education is more valuable for those that already
get in: it is educational Nimbyism. And politically it suggests that the policy of
more places at university is actually more attractive to lower-income outsiders
than higher-income insiders. Sometimes Tory strategists thought that more
places at university was a policy for middle-class intellectuals that did not appeal
to less affluent voters: the truth was the other way round—it was the groups
who were missing out who, quite rationally, were most keen on expansion. The
groups who are missing out look at what the most privileged obtain and want
the same too. As we saw in Chapter Five, this approach prompted the charge
from Kingsley Amis that 'More Will Mean Worse'. His argument was neatly
challenged at the time by comparing degree results from areas sending more
young people to university with the results secured by students from areas
which sent fewer to university. It showed that sending more students did not
lead to a proportionate decline in performance by students at university.[20]

Imagine what would happen if participation for everyone else reached the
levels already achieved by groups with high participation. What if boys did as

well as girls? An extra 400,000 young men would have gone to university between 2008 and 2015. What if everyone else did as well as ethnic Chinese? Britain's ethnic Chinese have an amazing 57 per cent participation rate at the age of 18: if all ethnic groups enjoyed the same rate there would be an extra 190,000 18-year-olds going each year.[21] What if 18–30-year-olds across the country achieved the same levels of participation as in the most prosperous areas? That was the calculation I used in a pamphlet which marked the fiftieth anniversary of the publication of the Robbins Report in 2013 and which influenced the Whitehall debate on student number controls. Then we would be talking of a university participation rate of about 75 per cent (even higher than some of the earlier figures because this includes a wide age range up to 30). It would mean across Britain 600,000 out of each year's cohort going to university by the time they were aged 30 as against about 400,000 now—an increase of almost 50 per cent.[22] If you simply extrapolate trend growth over the past twenty years this figure could be achieved in approximately 2040. Historical precedent suggests we can expect something like this to happen.

Alternative routes

The 18-year-old's route through A levels to university and on to adulthood has all the reliability and familiarity of a Jumbo jet rolling down a runway to take off. But it is not the whole story. There are other types of student and other routes to university. As well as the flow of new young students there is the stock of adults who may have missed out on university first time round and want to study as mature students. It is the Polish plumber whose business is growing fast and would like a proper understanding of business practices and company legislation. It is the lone parent who dropped out of school when she got pregnant aged 15 but now aged 30, with her kids at secondary school, wants to do something with her life and thinks she could be a social worker. It is the fifty-something who has started emailing in order to communicate with a grandchild in Australia and has discovered she has a gift for story-telling. These are the kind of mature students I met and I developed enormous respect for their determination to get higher education. In fact their stories help bring to life the evidence assembled in Chapter Five and reveal just how much higher education can change people's lives. Some mature students may already have a job but realize that to move on and get promotion they need more qualifications. They may just have hated school and the prospect of A levels and dropped out of education at 16 and now deeply regret missing out on university. Sometimes it is people who have already got a degree but want to study something different (there was a flurry of publicity for retired judges going back to university, though it would have been rather worrying if they were going to study law). They may have followed family pressures and trained as a pharmacist or an accountant but as they grew more confident they knew that really they wanted to be a teacher. They may well have family obligations or need to keep on earning, so often these mature students are also part-time students.

One of my biggest regrets looking back on my time in office is that we presided over a big fall in numbers of part-time students. This particularly affected Birkbeck College and the Open University, as they focused on mature students, but other universities had extension colleges and adult learning centres to help these kinds of students which have been cut back or even closed. It was not supposed to be like that. What happened? As grant funding for universities fell we actually extended fee loans to part-time students to help with their costs but there was much lower take-up of these loans than we expected. Potential students may have worried about increasing their borrowing, and because they weren't in school or college it was hard to reach them to explain that the system was much less onerous than they may have feared. The financial incentive for universities is much greater for recruiting a full-time student, who will bring £9,000 a year and probably won't drop out, compared to a part-timer who will bring lower annual fees and is at greater risk of dropping out. Public services were major sponsors of part-time study among their staff, and they cut back on training budgets. Applications may also have been affected by the policy introduced by the previous Government in 2008 of no public funding to universities for students who were studying for a qualification at a level equivalent to or lower than one they already had. This left two-thirds of would-be part-time students without an entitlement to fee loans and offset our attempts to provide more of them.[23] As we saw in Chapter Three, we should extend entitlement to fee loans to more part-time students.

If a university takes more mature or part-time students or ones from poorer backgrounds they are likely to have a higher drop-out rate: if your child is ill or your partner loses their job you may not be able to carry on studying. We should not expect all universities to have the same drop-out rate. Our average is about 6 per cent of under-21-year-olds who do not continue their course into the next year—the rate is 8 per cent for students from poor areas.[24] This non-continuation rate is low by international standards—indeed, you could argue it is too low and evidence of a risk-averse selection processes. A university taking on more mature and part-time students will find that it is higher. It is also a reason for credit transfer, which also gives the student something to show for a shorter period of study.

The extraordinary range of mature students opens up the question of what kind of qualifications you need to get to university. In England we have a combination of intense academic selection for our most prestigious universities and no official minimum standard of entry to university. At the moment some universities will admit students without any A levels or equivalent qualification. Imagine we said you needed a minimum of two Es at A level to go to university. We would be excluding, for example, that lone parent who dropped out of school at 16 to raise her children and now wants to study to be a nurse or a social worker. But it may not make sense to tell these 30-year-olds that they have to start by doing two A levels. Ministers—and the media—like calling for street-wise parents to be social workers and nurses etc. and it would be silly to erect new barriers to precisely such groups. They may have the ability to benefit from university provided they get some help to prepare—a one-year access course, for example.

Even some of the young people who go straight to university may not have conventional A levels. Indeed, there will be more of them as a consequence of the policy that A levels should be harder and revert to being an elite qualification rather than morphing into the school-leaving exam for 18-year-olds. At the same time we have seen more young people wish to go to university and many universities want to take them. So we are heading for a wider range of qualifications being offered by 18-year-olds to get to university. Many applicants have a mix of A levels and other qualifications. Some have BTECs. If you add together the mature students and these younger ones as well, one finds that fewer than half the people from the poorest areas going to university do so on the basis of A levels as against 64 per cent in the richest areas and 58 per cent on average.[25] (And these alternative qualifications are not necessarily second best, especially if you look at future job prospects. BTEC plus degree appears to score slightly better on employment than A level plus degree.)[26]

Access for this wide range of individuals and for a wide range of alternative providers are two sides of same coin. The gap in the market is not well-educated middle-class youngsters with good A levels—they are quite well served. It is all the others who can fall between the cracks. The challenge they set leads to important innovations in higher education. Local FE colleges can often help. But also these alternative students may turn to alternative providers—as we shall see in Chapter Eleven. They may also be most likely to benefit from opportunities for on-line learning, as we shall see in Chapter Thirteen.

Behind all this there is a deep question of how forgiving an education system should be. Is it one strike and you are out? Or can you get back on track? (I messed up my A levels but still got to Oxford because I sat the separate entrance exam in my seventh term. The system would not be so tolerant of such a slip now.) The classic account by Goldin and Katz linking America's educational performance to its economic success in the twentieth century argues that one of America's advantages was that its education system was more flexible and forgiving than European models: falling at one hurdle did not mean you were out of the race. Instead, in the wise words of Jerome Kern's song, you picked yourself up, dusted yourself down, and started all over again. They show how important it was that the US education system was 'open, forgiving, and gender neutral'.[27] America is similarly forgiving for companies which get into difficulties—Chapter Eleven of the US Bankruptcy Code is less punitive than Britain's bankruptcy laws. There is a parallel between how we treat people and companies who underperform.

European education systems have tested schoolchildren at several different stages and promoted only the best, a system which was seen as both meritocratic and efficient as we selected those who could most clearly benefit. This was very different from what looked like a wasteful American system in which one could advance to higher grades and institutions even if one failed to perform adequately in lower grades. America is more aware of the incentives for schools to appear to do well by just selecting the students it is easiest to educate. That is why lotteries for school entry are widely used in the US as a way of weakening producer power, whereas in England lotteries have proved very controversial. The American system was also possible because of the absence of national standards in what was a local system. 'In England, France and Germany admission to publicly funded schools beyond the elementary years, or in a later period beyond the age of compulsion was by examination, generally at the national level.'[28] As a result, in 1960 15 per cent of British 17-year-olds were at school whereas 70 per cent of US 17-year-olds were. The GI Bill was another example of how forgiving US policy could be as it did not set high barriers to entry to university, unlike the British equivalent. The shift from an elite to mass to universal higher education is also a shift to a more forgiving model of education and that involves a big shift in attitudes to how an education system should work. But how far can we expect this shift in attitudes to be delivered through changes in recruitment practices to elite universities?

Access: where should they go? Top universities and good universities

So far we have considered participation—the numbers of people from different backgrounds going on to higher education.[29] But then there is the question of access—getting to the most prestigious universities. We saw that people from affluent backgrounds are three times more likely to go to university, but when it comes to getting to the most prestigious universities the gap is even wider, with young people from better-off families six times more likely to go. Less than 4 per cent of young people from the poorest areas get to study at the most highly selective institutions as against over 21 per cent of young people from the most affluent areas.[30]

The issue has been with us for a long time. 'Of all the criticisms passed upon modern Oxford, none can compare in the earnestness, amounting often to vehemence, with which it is urged, or in the interest which it excites, than the complaint that neither the education, the endowments, nor the social advantages of the University are sufficiently open to the man of humble means.'[31] That was the then Chancellor of Oxford University, Lord Curzon, over a hundred years ago. The argument had already been rumbling on for centuries. It is Latimer's complaint to King Edward VI: 'There be none now but great men's sons in colleges.'[32] Ingenious research by the historian Gregory Clark shows these forces are still at work: 'If I just know that you have a rare surname shared with someone who was wealthy in 1800, I can predict now that you're nine times more likely to attend Oxford or Cambridge.'[33] I do not believe that now there is a single Vice Chancellor sipping port and puffing at a cigar whilst muttering that they must keep the working man away from the dreaming spires and the research labs of their university. But we still have deep structural obstacles to social mobility and rightly worry whether education impedes or enhances it.

Twice in my political career I experienced how fraught these issues are—the arguments about grammar schools in 2007, and around the appointment of Les Ebdon to OFFA in 2012. The change in the composition of grammar schools is a vivid example of the process whereby parents try to get their children to the schools that will get them into a top university and the arms race which then develops. Grammar schools do well at getting children into the most prestigious universities so parents want to get their child through academic selection at age 11. As a result areas with grammar schools have unusual concentrations of private primary schools. Or you buy a house in the catchment area of the primary schools that do best at getting their children into the grammar school—and that means selection by mortgage. Indeed, the high house price effect is actually most acute for primary schools which feed the most academic secondaries (which are not just the ones in areas with grammar schools). But it is not just grammar schools. Everywhere parents are looking for the primary schools which get their children into the high-performing secondary schools that get them the A levels that get them to elite universities.[34] Of those from selective schools who went to university, 6 per cent were from the poorest background and 36 per cent from the most affluent. Of those who went from comprehensives 9 per cent were poorest and 32 per cent most affluent.[35] This is important evidence of how the intensifying competition for entry into university drives competition and selection at earlier stages of education.

The competition is to get to the most prestigious universities. Three events in quick succession crystallized the issue. First, in 1992 polytechnics acquired university status, giving us a more diverse range of universities than ever before. Then in 1993 the *Times* launched the first British university ranking—its 'good' university guide with A level entry grades a key measure. And then, in 1994, the first distinctive mission group, the Russell Group, was created, followed by others. The prestigious universities at the top of the *Times* league table which those parents are aiming at are often referred to as the Russell Group, the most prominent of the mission groups within British universities. It is named after the Russell Hotel in Bloomsbury, where representatives of universities with medical schools used to meet—those universities tend to be the ones which do the most research and which require the highest A level grades to enter: the two key measures which shape the rankings. The Group has grown by admitting other universities such as the LSE which meet these criteria even if they do not have a medical school. Some universities with distinctive research strengths are, however, not in the Russell Group. The Vice Chancellor of Leicester University was invited to join the Russell Group when it was created but he did not think it would be right to join one specific mission group when he was representing all of Britain's universities as president of Universities UK—little did he realize that membership of the Russell Group would become a shorthand for the quality of a university. The Russell Group is ultimately a members' club which can choose to admit new members on its own terms. In BIS we preferred to use more objective criteria like universities in the top 30 per cent for grades of students on entry.

Other universities fulfil different missions. There are universities which may not be research intensive but have high prestige and very selective entry—the conservatoires, for example. Some may have research strengths in specific areas in which they take students with high A levels. The former colleges of advanced technology (Aston, Bath, Bradford, Brunel, City, Loughborough, Salford, Surrey) still have a distinctive character: they developed sandwich courses and include a spell in industry as part of their courses which shows up in their strong links to business and their excellent graduate employment performance. Others have very good links to key regional industries, such as the University of Northampton and the shoe industry. The Universities of Hertfordshire and Oxford Brookes both have strong departments training motor engineers for the world-class automotive engineering cluster near them. One English university achieves the exceptional treble of being in the top twenty for ethnic diversity, for widening participation, and for employment after six months—the University of Huddersfield. Other universities began as Anglican teacher-training colleges and are now focused on training people for public service—teachers, nurses, and social workers. These are all missions in which it is possible to be world class but they are not recognized in the rankings and they are unlikely to be seen as a 'top' university.

Research by Vikki Boliver suggests our universities come in four clusters—Oxbridge; Old, i.e. pre-1992; New, i.e. post-1992; and fourth a sub-set of New universities, about a quarter of them, with particularly wide access and the usual challenges that go with that. Her analysis is subversive because she suggests that once you exclude Oxbridge there is little difference between the Russell Group and other research-intensive pre-1992 universities. She also stresses that overall there is less divergence in quality of teaching.[36]

Malcolm Gladwell looked at the ranking of American universities in an essay in the *New Yorker*.[37] He argued that a ranking could cover a heterogeneous group of universities if it just assessed them along one measure of performance. But it could not both cover such diversity and provide an overall comprehensive ranking. That is why it is so pernicious to take the conventional measure and assume it ranks universities from good to bad when they are just different. A football club is not a bad rugby club: it is, literally, a different ball-game and they both have their place.

This is even more important when one discovers the metric which really lies behind the conventional rankings. It is a very revealing list of our universities. It starts with Oxford and Cambridge at the top. Then there are Durham, Bristol, Exeter, Imperial, and the Courtauld. The Royal College of Art, Warwick, York, and Nottingham are close after. Shortly after them come Sheffield, Manchester, Leeds, Birmingham. Then in the middle you find Keele, Kent,

Portsmouth. Finally down at the bottom are Bedfordshire, London South Bank, London Met, Bolton, Wolverhampton, and Bradford. It pretty much matches the informal prestige rankings which in my experience politicians, commentators, and parents carry around in their heads. But it is not some careful ranking of quality of research or teaching. It is simply measuring the social composition of the student body. It ranks our universities by the percentage of UK students from the less advantaged socio-economic groups, starting with 10 per cent for Oxbridge, 20 per cent or so for most of the Russell Group, 30 per cent for new universities in cathedral cities, down to more than 40 per cent if you are a modern university in an industrial town and more than 50 per cent for the last ones on the list, which are mainly universities in the East End of London.[38] Stefan Collini says that 'In Britain, entrance to a university is almost the only widely desired social good that cannot be straightforwardly bought.'[39] Nominally that is true. But if you look at the actual distribution of access to the most prestigious universities the result is pretty much the same as if it were allocated by parental income—mediated via private education or expensive houses in areas with good schools. That is why it is right for the Government to focus on this key issue in social mobility. The great prize is credible measures of performance which dislodge the deep implicit and informal ranking by social background. That is why there are lessons to learn from three well-regarded research-intensive universities which stand out for their social mix—Liverpool, King's College London, where I am a visiting professor, both on 26 per cent of students from less affluent backgrounds, and Queen Mary University of London, with an extraordinary 37 per cent.

This opens up one of the key challenges of our system—ensuring heterogeneity. A whole range of types of higher education can be called universities. Our last attempt at sustaining an alternative name for some of them—polytechnics—was abandoned in 1992. That makes it even more important that we recognize that there are diverse university missions. If we think there is one type of university and they are in a single range from good ones to bad ones then we will sacrifice what should be a crucial strength of any HE system—diversity. We should be proud of our top universities with their patina of history, global recognition, and world-class research. They often command high rankings not just domestically but in the international league tables. Their students are smart, highly motivated, and well educated. They are ambitious for themselves and often with a social conscience too. They are a good reason for being optimistic for the future of our country. Their students may come from a relatively narrow social background, but that is not a crime, and anyway the universities are just reflecting prior attainment of their applicants. Perhaps we should not be surprised or shocked if our elite universities reflect our class structure. But we can't just settle for things as they are. For a start the rankings obscure the distinct characteristics and strengths of the range of our universities—and penalize some of the very missions which pundits and politicians claim they want universities to focus on. The rankings do not reflect the quality of teaching—the metric which is conspicuously absent and which we will turn to in the next chapter. They protect incumbents because they reward prestige as reflected in demand from students with high prior attainments. And the metrics behind the rankings are a barrier to social mobility because they penalize recruits with mediocre A levels and so deter universities from assessing applicants on future potential rather than prior attainment. This is where we face a trade-off which opens up some the most difficult issues in higher education. These research-intensive universities have enormous prestige and admirable self-confidence and they carefully and legitimately select who they admit. But at the same time the economist cannot help but see them also as examples of producer power protected behind barriers to entry, both for other universities and for students.

An ingenious proposal by the late John Vaizey shows how these barriers work. He was temperamentally a radical on a journey from the Left to Thatcherism. He was an expert on education, and a fellow and admissions tutor at Worcester College, Oxford. Oxford colleges are ranked academically in the Norrington Table and the dons were discussing how Worcester could move up the league. He proposed in the 1960s that they take more state school pupils, even with 10 per cent lower grades, because the evidence was that they went on to do better in their finals than students who had been privately educated.[40] The Franks Report a few years earlier had indeed shown that students from independent boarding schools had the lowest proportion of Firsts and highest of Thirds out of their Oxford intake.[41] As we saw earlier in this chapter, the same phenomenon can be observed now. In the words of one expert: 'students from independent schools perform less well than do students from state schools with equivalent entry grades'.[42]

There are obvious sensitivities around this specific example, but it could just as well be any other metric which proved to be a better indicator of future degree performance than prior A level grades. But a university adopting John Vaizey's proposal and accepting students with lower A level grades who they expected to out-perform in Finals would encounter two problems. First, the only league table which mattered for Worcester College, Oxford was the Norrington Table at the end of the student's course: Oxford colleges are ranked against each other by results not by the prior attainment of their new students. But almost all the rankings of our universities give a heavy weighting to the A level grades of entrants. A Vice Chancellor who tried the Vaizey approach would see his university fall down the league tables. (It looks as if the Vice Chancellor of Bristol is, to his credit, risking it.) Indeed, some of the very same newspapers with passionate leading articles about social mobility then construct university league tables which block it by using entry grades as a key measure of quality. (The *Guardian* have gone further than most in including a measure of value added.) There is a second problem too. Worcester College could measure its final performance in comparison with other colleges whose students were all sitting the same Oxford University exam. But universities award their own degrees. If they do get smarter students who do better they can award more Firsts, but there is a well-established trend for more of these to be awarded anyway so it is hard to signal a genuine improvement in performance against an external measure. And if you are a less prestigious university, no student however excellent may be able to signal quite how good he or she is if that university's degree is not eminent. So there are penalties for taking these students on and few rewards if they perform better.

Imagine a university that was doing the equivalent of, for example, the Mossbourne Academy in Hackney—taking students with poor prior attainments and then through excellent teaching really adding educational value. The two factors obstructing the Vaizey solution stand in their way: they would stay down the league table because they would be taking students with poorer grades and nobody would know the high standards that lay behind their degrees. We are familiar with the idea of a coasting secondary school. Perhaps it is located in a prosperous area or in subtle ways selecting the students who are easiest to educate. It will appear to do a good job but may not be adding as much value as a school in a tough area taking children with lower levels of prior attainment. Successive Governments have developed metrics which try to capture the distance a child travels educationally as a measure of school performance. It enables bold challengers to outrank comfortable incumbents. But the conventional ranking of universities by prior attainment of students and the absence of a single national higher education exam makes it much harder to do this in higher education. So incumbency is rewarded in our higher education system and so is selection by prior attainment.

Employment outcomes of different universities are not the be-all and end-all but they can illuminate this debate and the evidence they provide is striking. Men (women) who graduate from an old university earn 12 per cent (7 per cent) more than a similar graduate from a new one and a Russell Group graduate earns a further 4 per cent (2 per cent). However, once you allow for the father's education and A level performance the gaps between types of university become statistically insignificant.[43] So it is not clear there is added value on top of a classic selection effect. Even though overall going to university adds real value, when it comes to the contrast between individual universities the results appear to be largely selection effects. This sort of evidence makes one wary of conventional rankings. It also reinforces the case against variable fees.

There is one further ironic twist to this story. Whilst the Department for Education (DfE) absolutely understood the importance of measuring value added for schools, that very department started measuring schools by how many of their students went to the Russell Group. A university which was doing the equivalent of an academy school in a tough area and moving students on and up by high-quality teaching would not be recognized in the DfE's own destination measures. The Department should not have placed such an obstacle in the way of improvement at the university level. The very same ministers who lauded Mossbourne created barriers to its equivalent university, a bold new challenger, by rewarding schools that sent their students to Russell Group universities. It was a frustrating example of the Government betraying its own professed belief that it should be on the side of challengers instead of strengthening incumbents.

This is ultimately about the routes into the key jobs that shape the character of our country. It is about who will govern us, judge us, perform to us, heal us, manage us, report on us, and represent us over the next half-century. The Sutton Trust starts with the fact that going to a Russell Group university is a clear route into Britain's elite. They then identify the '3,000 missing students' each year who had good GCSEs and might have been expected to go to a Russell Group university but did not. They then aim through summer schools and other access initiatives to raise the chances of those students getting in to the prestigious universities. It is the same philosophy as their belief in assisted places for low-income students at leading private schools and also why they have advised grammar schools on how they could become accessible to low-income students. It rests on a frank recognition of where power and prestige rests in the English education system today. It says Britain is always going to be run by people from a small network of schools and universities—and the challenge is to broaden access to them. The DfE backed this approach with public funding for the Trust to run summer schools aimed specifically at Russell Group universities.

There is an alternative approach—to try to open up doors that may be currently closed to students who did not go to the most prestigious universities. It does not accept that routes into the elite are or should be so circumscribed. I have sat at plush dinners with bankers and lawyers complaining that they simply cannot find the talented recruits they need, which sometimes turns out to mean that they have been looking at about four 'top' universities or the Russell Group at most. Is that the only group to recruit from? Indeed, are the missing 3,000 really missing? They may know what they are doing: issues such as cost of living and distance from home matter more for students who choose not to apply to most selective universities. The very middle-class identity of the most prestigious universities can put off students from other backgrounds—for example, because the level of personal spending required to participate fully in social activities is an expensive barrier. We are assuming we know what is the right decision—shaped by the assumptions of parents who are intensely conservative both about institutions and courses of study.

I worked with DfE ministers on what we might say to 16-year-olds with good GCSEs but at a secondary school which did not send many students to the most prestigious universities. We rapidly realized that we could not just say, apply to the Russell Group, because it might not be the right decision for them. We decided that the best message was to urge these 16-year-olds to look further afield and not just assume they should go to their local university. Travel costs may be a factor, but for whatever reason the richer you are the more likely you are to go to a university a long way from home. Forty-two per cent of university entrants from more disadvantaged backgrounds attend an institution within half an hour of their home as against 26 per cent of the more affluent. Of those going to an institution more than six hours' drive away, 45 per cent are from the richest backgrounds as against 4 per cent from the poorest.[44] After lots of discussions we had ended up just endorsing that distinctive English tradition of moving away from home for university with which this chapter opened.

Some employers say they do not have the time to visit and recruit directly from a hundred different universities and one simple way of winnowing out applications from a range of universities is to recruit only from a sub-set. One social enterprise (Performance in Context or PIC) has a smart high-tech solution. Imagine you are an employer keen to recruit a diverse talented workforce. You understand that looking at absolute measures of performance is inefficient and instead you want to look at students' performance in context. You may want to know if someone with apparently lower grades actually did very well in a non-academic school in a poor area. You could run your own version of the California scheme and say you would interview potential recruits who had been in the top 10 per cent of their school rather than focusing on their A level grades. You can use the charity's software to identify precisely such people out of those applying to you. It is a classic example of digital technology driving disintermediation—the employer can bypass the political arguments and find the talent for themselves. This may be a better solution than just relying on the political process—after all, one of the great attributes of capitalism is supposed to be that the hunger for talent and profit overcomes the sheer wastefulness of discrimination.

The future is for more of this data to be available for universities, policy makers, employers, and of course prospective students. This is where the US is already far ahead of us. American analysts of social mobility such as Professor Raj Chetty at Harvard can track individuals in the US through school and on to university and out into the jobs market. They have far more granular data than we have and can compare the performance of individual schools and colleges using millions of data points. By contrast the widespread and probably erroneous belief that social mobility in England has declined is based on a comparison of 17,000 people born in 1958 and in 1970. The American revolution in data is now coming to the UK—data linking legislation, access to HMRC earnings data, and new secure social policy data-sets.

I chaired a Committee with the very boring title of the Social Mobility Transparency Board but what it actually did was really rather important—we got different Whitehall Departments and agencies to share data so that we could track young people through school and university and out into work and find out what helped deliver social mobility. We are starting to get useful findings from the Labour Force Survey question on which university you went to and what you studied so we can link that up to the job you do. Eventually we should be able to use data to see, for example, that one school or one university provides an unusually high proportion of the country's black lawyers or which town is best for upward social mobility for its citizens. We may even be able to track the impact of individual school or university teachers if we see a pattern for their students to do particularly well. We are at the early days of the data revolution transforming not just the social mobility debate but also our ability to measure the individual performance of schools and universities.

What we can do about access: OFFA

The Blair Government set up the Office of Fair Access to tackle a genuine concern that low-income students would be put off when fees and loans were brought in. Universities have to submit to OFFA an agreement on how they will spend some of their fee income on broadening access—and ultimately if they are not doing enough OFFA can refuse them permission to set high fees. The 2017 legislation renames it the Directorate of Fair Access and Participation and incorporates it in the Office for Students but still with a distinct responsibility to ensure everything is being done to promote disadvantaged students getting to university and then fully participating while they are there. We kept the system for every university wishing to charge fees above £6,000. English universities obtain about £3bn of income from fees above that level and about £1bn of that goes on access spend. It is tempting to see this as a pot of public money which can be used as ministers want, but the income belongs to the university. And it is a long-term cost for individual students because it comes out of their fee loans which they will be repaying—we are on the limit of how much cost can be imposed on them to fund activities which go beyond their own education.

On top of this there is a peculiar confusion about which universities should have extra resources. The Coalition was very proud of the pupil premium because it was harder work educating disadvantaged kids in Tower Hamlets compared with a prosperous county town. But when it came to universities the argument was often reversed and it was assumed that the elite universities should be able to charge higher fees which would bring in more funding for teaching, a kind of reverse pupil premium. They certainly benefited from higher research funding (as we saw in Chapter Four), but when it comes to teaching there is a strong case for more funding for universities with more students who find it harder and need more support—a student premium. As this public spending was cut back the universities with most disadvantaged students could argue for higher fees. Successive Governments have judged that these rival claims broadly balance out.

In 2014/15 universities and colleges spent £725m of their own fee income on access measures under their access agreements (excluding the National Scholarship Programme). This was 28 per cent of their income from fees over £6,000 p.a. The spending broke down as follows: £480m on bursaries, scholarships, and fee waivers, with the vast majority of this money (81 per cent) going to the poorest students, i.e. those with a household income under £25,000; £105m on outreach activities for people with the potential to succeed in higher education; £100m on student success and progression activities to help students stay on course; £30m on disadvantaged students to support progression from higher education into work or further study. Total spend should rise to about £750m by 2019/20, with a particular boost for outreach spending, which rises to £150m.[45] Low-income students understandably particularly like programmes which give them more cash to spend while they are at university. But it is hard for them to work out in advance how much help they will receive, so it is not clear how much it really boosts applications. Outreach activity is more effective at broadening access for those who are not sure about applying. But here the problem is overlapping disparate initiatives from individual universities with some secondary schools covered by several universities and others missed out entirely. And the measures of university performance contributed to the problem. Birmingham University have not failed if they run programmes in tough local comprehensives as a result of which more apply for Warwick, but it does not show up as a success in their metrics—hence the need for co-ordination of activity, which is now being developed.

OFFA has to operate within a legal framework which protects university autonomy and forbids the Government from attaching conditions to grants regarding the admission of students.[46] Despite this tight constraint on its powers OFFA is viewed with suspicion by some commentators, and for a long time the Conservative party was committed to its abolition, though I reversed that policy. The appointment of Les Ebdon as Director of OFFA in 2012 unleashed a media storm. Les Ebdon is a thoroughly decent man—a Baptist lay preacher and a graduate of Imperial College. Behind all the unfair personal comment there was a real issue—how far could or should the Government go in requiring universities to broaden their access? What can it expect universities to pledge to do as part of their access agreements with it?

The fear is that the academic standards of our leading universities would be compromised. The purists oppose universities exercising a judgement on any other basis than actual A level grades. They argue the problem is poor prior attainment and universities should not be required to solve a problem that lies in our schools. A low-income student with decent grades is supposed to have as good a chance of getting in as anyone else. However, it is not quite true that everyone with the same grades has an equal chance. On average a state school student would need one A level grade higher (AAA not AAB, for example) than a privately educated student to be admitted to a Russell Group university.[47] This is because of the subtle ways the well-advised can work the system. So, for example, the more disadvantaged students tend to apply for big name popular courses, which are the most competitive, whereas a school that knows the ropes will urge some candidates to try for less well-known subjects—anthropology not history, or biological sciences not medicine. Students might not appreciate the significance of getting a 'facilitating A level', as universities used just to specify tariff points but not reveal that some A levels count for more than others.

I experienced at first hand both how admirable are the aspirations of many teenagers and how lack of information advice and guidance can make it harder to fulfil them. A teenager on a council estate in my former constituency had become very interested in politics and decided she wanted to be a politician. She had googled information about politicians and found a lot of us—including me as her own MP—had studied PPE at university, so she wanted to study that too. She thought, therefore, that she should do Politics, Philosophy, and Economics as her three A levels. It looks obvious, but those A levels are actually a poor route in to PPE at university. That is the kind of knowledge easily available to advantaged students but not to kids from modest backgrounds—setting a trap which the well-advised do not even think of as a barrier to entry.

Moreover, it is not the case that the only way to tackle the problem of access to university is by improving prior attainment at school. It is a widespread but misconceived approach to public policy to think the only way to tackle a problem is to address its original cause. In my experience this is often an excuse for inaction. What if a town were suffering from severe flooding and the minister turned up and said storms were now more intense because of global warming so we must tackle carbon emissions? That may be true but it is still worth improving the flood defences. I want to see improved academic standards in 'bog standard comprehensives', but sadly it may be a long wait for a comprehensive in Hull to match the academic standards of one of London's elite academic schools. Meanwhile we have to offer something to a 17-year-old in Hull today. And getting away to university is the best single thing we can do to boost their life chances. We have had endless political and media agonizing about social mobility but very little support for practical measures which would actually do anything about it. Instead we have a largely erroneous belief that spending large amounts of public money on early years programmes could do the trick, combined with an ambition for all schools to be of an equally high standard—an admirable goal, though distant and hard to achieve. Investment in early years and ambitious school reform shared one key feature—they do nothing for a real 17-year-old now emerging from a poorly performing secondary school but with the potential really to achieve something for herself and her country. They only have one life and for them delay means betrayal. That is why it is right to focus on access to university.

This was caricatured as a bunch of liberal progressives trying to force universities to admit students who weren't up to it. The argument was that we tolerate school failure if we adjust for it. Instead of challenging weak schools it lets them get away with poor standards. But the trouble is that it is not the students' fault that their schools are poor. Moreover I found there were limits to anyone's purism on this. Some of the same education ministers who disapproved of Les Ebdon then asked me to press universities to do more to admit care-leavers, who are very badly served at every stage of their education. But I could have objected that this rewarded poor-quality children's homes and instead we should get to the source of the problem and improve these homes. Of course bad schools and children's homes must do better, but meanwhile we have to decide what we do with a 17-year-old today whose childhood is not coming back. The disadvantage need not be permanent unless we make it so. Magnifying the effect of a weak school by not allowing for youngsters to bounce back from it seems particularly harsh. The question was whether the evidence showed they could bounce back.

As I listened to opponents arguing that we were ignoring merit in the interest of fighting a class war I had in front of me evidence of the sort which an IFS researcher crisply summarized as follows: 'when comparing pupils with the same background characteristics and prior attainment, studying at the same universities in the same subjects, those from selective independent schools are 2.6 percentage points more likely to drop out, 6.4 percentage points less likely to complete their degree and 10.3 percentage points less likely to graduate with a first or a 2:1 than pupils from non-selective community schools'.[48] So who were the real meritocrats? It must be legitimate to apply the Vaizey test and allow in disadvantaged students with lower grades when we can reasonably expect that, with help, they can perform at university. One decision rule is for a university to recruit so as to equalize the chances of students from different backgrounds getting a good degree, say a First or 2:1. If you can show that students from tougher backgrounds outperform at university then you could allow them in with lower A level grades.

The really tricky question is how to apply such a rule in practice. When judging an applicant's potential should the university look at the individual or the school or the neighbourhood? One way to escape these issues is to say universities should look at the individual not the group. But this just pushes the issue back a stage because you need to know what factors are relevant when assessing the individual. Some universities look out for specific features of candidates—from having been eligible for free school meals or ethnic background or disability—and flag them up for special consideration.

The explosive issue is the treatment of privately educated versus state educated students. Here, frustratingly, on this most fraught of issues, the evidence is hard to pin down. Parents who have worked hard to earn the money to pay for a private education for their children see this as unfair social engineering. But research for HEFCE did suggest that the crucial gap in performance is state vs private schools.[49] In fact this particular evidence is tricky for everyone, as it says that it is state pupils as a group who outperform, not disadvantaged as against advantaged pupils. State school pupils also do better than private, according to studies at Cardiff and at Oxford Brookes.[50]

After a lot of fraught discussion David Cameron drafted the key sentence for our White Paper in his own handwriting, that procedures should be 'fair, transparent and evidence-based'.[51] It was a masterful summary. It rightly leaves open for universities what it is in a person's life story they should adjust for and why. And the Prime Minister's formulation was in a way a reminder of the importance, following on from the Schwartz Review a decade earlier, of professionalism in admissions.[52]

This gets to the heart of the argument. What is background context you adjust for and what is foreground information you accept as a fact about a person for direct comparison with others? One approach is to adjust for disadvantages which have held people back and can be overcome, but not for permanent cognitive barriers. It is where we think the university can make a difference that we can look at context. Any such adjustment to A level requirements would have a narrowly meritocratic purpose—to maximize the academic talent in the university. Universities can judge potential. Admission is not just a reward for good grades—that is the Soviet/Chinese system.

This cautiously meritocratic approach is still far short of the American system. It is not about identifying future business leaders or players for the university football team or ensuring ethnic mix. Nobody in England would dare contemplate 'molding the class' the way they do at Harvard, but it is hard to object on the grounds that Harvard's standards and status have suffered. The trickiest question, rarely spoken, is whether there could there be more to university admission than academic merit? One university Vice Chancellor with a prominent medical school did quietly ask me if he was supposed to be recruiting the most academically gifted medical and veterinary students or the people they thought would make the best doctors and vets. This is again where the power of academic departments over admission really matters. They are focused above all on academic excellence and thinking of potential future academics.

English education is riddled with selection not only to identify the candidates with greatest potential but to ensure the producers get the most prestige with least effort to add value. That is why it is right to put them under pressure to broaden access. We are trying to create an open, fair, national higher education

system on top of a deeply divided school system. We saw at the beginning of
this chapter that universities may make schools more socially selective. But they
also have the power to reverse the effect of this on children's futures by providing
opportunities to disadvantaged students.[53] Compared with school before it and
the jobs market after it, higher education is a model of meritocracy, in which
students from the most disadvantaged parts of the country out-perform. Now
we must investigate what happens when student and university meet: what is
the student academic experience?

EIGHT

The Student Academic Experience

What students do with their time

I can still remember going to my first economics lecture when I arrived at Oxford to study Politics, Philosophy, and Economics. It was a rather plodding account of the main British industries of the 1970s—manufacturing, mining, etc. The only vivid moment came when we were breaking up at the end and a student sitting nearby turned to me with a question: 'What', he asked, 'is coal?' International students really do bring different perspectives. Looking back now I can see that the economics faculty could have done so much more with that first lecture. They should have fielded Oxford's most eminent professor to give us a powerful account of the shape and significance of economics. That first lecture was always going to stick in the memory: it was a missed opportunity. Oxford subsequently reformed their lectures for new students and deploy their most prestigious academics. Other universities have done this too. One academic told me, with just a hint of cynicism, the first lecture to new students was like empty skips appearing in your street—you need to fill them with your rubbish before anyone else can put their rubbish in.

The teaching of economics has been caught up in swirling controversy. It involves big arguments about the role of the state and how the global financial crisis should change the discipline. But it is also about what constitutes good teaching. Here is an account of how the subject was taught at one university: 'Tutorials consist of copying problem sets off the board rather than discussing economic ideas, and 18 out of 48 modules have 50% or more marks given by multiple choice.'[1] Proper teaching involves keeping a subject fresh by endlessly updating it as some contested issues are resolved or just become moribund whilst new areas of exploration and dispute emerge. Einstein is supposed to have set students the same physics questions two years in succession, but when he was challenged he replied that although the question was the same the answer had changed.

The quality of teaching is the biggest problem facing our universities. I have heard too many horror stories of students not getting serious personal academic contact and desperate for more academic input and challenge. When I met with student union representatives at individual universities they were not demanding Marxist revolution or the nationalization of the banks: they were asking for smaller seminars and for their work to be returned promptly. Indeed, the lack of prompt academic feedback is students' biggest single source of frustration—its effectiveness has been clearly shown, across the whole ability range.[2] Throughout my time as minister my colleagues would come up to me at the end of Cabinet meetings or while we were voting in the Lobbies with reports of a son sitting at the back of lectures with little academic contact or a daughter who seemed to be able to do all the academic study that was required whilst working two days a week in a vintage clothes shop. Universities were slow to cotton on to how much dissatisfaction there was about the quality of teaching—perhaps more intense amongst parents than their children. But universities had a good excuse—the decline in the unit of resource. The shift from an elite to a mass higher education system had brought with it a significant decline in the quality of the academic experience. Arresting the decline in the funding of students was essential, and a precondition of raising standards.

Let's start with estimates of how much time is actually being spent studying in English universities. Average academic contact time is 12.2 hours—as against 13.5 hours scheduled by their institutions. Private study hours are about 14.3 hours. Adding in time on courses outside the university or studying with friends gives a total weekly workload of just over 30 hours for most subjects but 40 hours or more in medicine and education courses.[3]

In the annual survey of the student academic experience, 28 per cent of students said their experience had been better than they expected and 12 per cent worse. Forty-nine per cent said it was better in some ways and worse in others. Of the 61 per cent for whom at least in some respects their experience was worse, their top reason was 36 per cent saying they had not put in enough effort themselves—an honest recognition that what you put in determines how much you get out. But next was 32 per cent saying the course was poorly organized and 30 per cent saying there were fewer contact hours than they had expected.[4] An earlier survey showed that of those students with under eight hours of contact, 45 per cent were dissatisfied as against only 15 per cent of students with over 25 contact hours.[5] Moreover, 'while contact hours are an incomplete measure of teaching and learning, students with fewer scheduled hours: are more likely to say they would have chosen another course if they had their time again; often think they are receiving poor value for money; and find their lives less worthwhile.'[6] Contact hours ('quantity of teaching time') is the largest source of dissatisfaction for students according to UUK's Student Funding Panel Survey: over 20 per cent were dissatisfied with these—twice the number dissatisfied with the *quality* of teaching.[7] Also, students' perceptions of value for money correlate with contact hours, as Table 8.1 shows.

There is only one conclusion from all this evidence: contact time matters. It matters particularly for students, whereas if we look at educational outcomes, what they do in those hours and the quality of their engagement matters more. We will return to this later in the chapter.

We saw in Chapter One that Europe has agreed a common currency for education: it is rather more successful than the Euro and outside the EU structure. The Bologna agreement between governments makes it easier for students to move between different national systems. That common currency is based on hours of study, which yield credits. A Bachelor's degree is supposed to be based on 1,500–1,800 hours of study a year: 4,500 to 5,400 over three years. Our own Quality Assurance Agency expects ten hours per credit and 360 credits over three years for an honours degree or 1,200 hours per year. (Most degrees in the UK are honours degrees and require 360 or more credits, whereas you can be issued a degree without honours on the basis of 300 credits.) This is less than the official Bologna measure and leads to raised eyebrows at international meetings—which we get through by sheer self-confidence and

Table 8.1. Perceptions of value for money of students from England, by scheduled contact hours

Contact hours	University is poor value for money (%)
0–9 hours	44
10–19 hours	32
20–9 hours	24
More than 30 hours	22
All	34

Source: The HEPI-HEA Student Academic Experience Survey 2015, figure 13, p. 18.

because other countries have their problems too. But if our students are on average doing 30 hours per week in an academic year of 30 teaching weeks that comes in at just 900 hours a year. Some are doing 20 hours per week, which is 600 hours in an academic year, well below half of the Bologna minimum. Total hours of study can be enhanced by work outside term time, where the evidence is weak. But overall we do appear to have a problem of just not enough time studying. There is a paradox here—whilst in higher education we seem to have some of the shortest working hours, when it comes to the labour market Britain has some of the longest working hours in Europe: we need to work longer hours to generate the same amount of output as France or Germany. This is our productivity problem. The two phenomena could be linked. Perhaps one reason we are less productive and have to work harder later is that we spend less time studying when we are at university and so bring less investment in human capital to our work. This in turn might be linked to the hypothesis that selective higher education systems based on prior attainment involve less work by their students because there is less to play for: your future is heavily influenced by which institution you have got to, not what you do when you are there. Following this argument to its logical conclusion, the unusual structure of English higher education, with so much weight attached to which university you went to, may be one reason for our low productivity performance. (Some corroboration is that Japan is one of the few other advanced economies with competitive selective entry to university. Recruitment to elite jobs is mainly from the most prestigious universities. Japan too has relatively low hours of study in higher education and low productivity afterwards.)

There is other evidence that English university students just do not have enough time on task. European exchange students who have studied in more than one country found the UK less demanding. Though the survey was more than a decade ago, 37 per cent found their UK course less demanding than at home as against an average of 31 per cent across all European countries and 22 per cent for students going to Germany.[8] The views of Erasmus students studying in Britain in a later survey suggests that we do organize our learning differently from many Continental countries. Erasmus students found the UK just as intellectually demanding, but had considerably fewer contact hours. The implication is that they felt less well taught. Part of the proffered explanation is cultural: 'all the [Erasmus] participants [in the survey] were used to a large number of taught hours, 22 hours per week being the average and to large group sizes, 35 people being the average. . . . As these students were faced with a very different system in their British University, with a 12 hour teaching week, a heavy bias towards seminars, group work, aural and oral work and independent learning, it can be argued that their costs of adaptation were bound to be high. . . . Erasmus students agreed that whilst overall their workload was similar to their home institutions, with the same intellectual demands, British Universities put much more emphasis on independent learning.'[9]

A different study found that UK students did about 30 hours of study per week compared with 36 hours in Germany and 42 hours in France—the top performer in Europe for study hours and an economy with low but productive working hours. UK students are also unusual in reporting that they are doing more work than is required in order to pass their exams—52 per cent—and a similar proportion said that they were striving for the highest possible marks. This is encouraging evidence that it is not that British students are lazy—if anything it is the opposite and students are asking for more work and more challenge.[10] Perhaps it is evidence that the students want to work hard, don't know how to do so independently (or don't expect to work independently), want direction, and get little of it from teaching staff. Where a system relies heavily on selection and a belief in fixed abilities it may be assumed that anyone who gets through the tests *already* has the right kind of learning habits and so is already a fully formed independent learner. Partly as a result of this it is very focused on exam-based assessment at the end of the year, whereas other countries such as France or the US with continuous assessment also show more hours worked. England's university teaching models may not have fully transitioned from an elite to a mass HE system. It could be that as higher education expands so the marginal students who are admitted need more direct teaching and support, which is sometimes lacking in universities focused on the Oxbridge model of the motivated independent learner. It costs more to provide lots of teaching support, but this need may be concentrated in less prestigious institutions which the conventional wisdom says should have less funding.

The Government has now legislated to enable three years of fees and loans to be compressed into two years provided there is a substantial increase in intensity of study. This flexibility is welcome, though there may be cases where it is too easy to compact courses because the course is too thin to start off with. There is an argument that as well as compressing what is currently done in three years down to two, it should then be possible to add back in a third year. This would help make a broader curriculum possible—an issue I return to in the Chapter Fourteen.

Graham Gibbs, the guru in this area, is relaxed about the balance of class contact hours as against independent study hours as he says that what matters is the nature of class contact and the total amount of time students are on task.[11] His concern is about class size, a crucial measure obscured by the focus on contact hours, which counts as identical an hour sitting in a lecture with 500 other students and in a seminar with five others. He says the smaller the class, the greater the learning. The Oxbridge tutorial model may not show up as long hours of contact, but the hour or two a week when your work is scrutinized rigorously by a serious academic is actually one of the most intense and valuable educational experiences. But it is an expensive and unusual form of university teaching. Two-thirds of 11.89 hours of academic contact was in class sizes of sixteen or more.[12] Only about 3.93 hours of teaching in 2014 was in small groups of 0–15, though it has been on a modest upward trend in the past few years—it was 3.64 hours in 2006. Table 8.2 shows a detailed breakdown of average hours attended by size of teaching group with further breakdowns for some specific disciplines.[13]

There is a further pressure on study time. We have seen that the English model is for students to move away from home to go to university. This presents in particularly acute form the challenge of how to fund their living costs. We have, unusually, a system of maintenance loans to help with these costs. But for many students this is worth only about £8,000 per academic year. For many students this is the biggest pressure point they face—especially with rents for student accommodation rising. They seek more cash to meet their living costs. The student finance system expects many parents to supplement their maintenance loans—though this is not communicated as clearly as it could be. Half of full-time students now also do paid work to top up their income whilst studying.[14] If students do a lot of paid work—20 hours or more—this detracts from their studies.[15] One detects a convergence between the study hours of supposedly full-time students who are also doing paid work while studying and

Table 8.2. Breakdown of student contact hours by group size and subject

Group	0–5	6–15	16–50	51–100	100+	Total Overall
Hours	1.14	2.49	4.05	1.59	2.02	12.09
Medicine	4.46	4.08	3.04	1.49	4.28	18.14
English	1.24	2.35	4.41	3.22	2.49	14.52
Sociology	0.37	2.24	3.08	1.50	1.34	9.34
History	0.36	3.05	2.35	0.59	0.28	7.43

Source: Which/HEPI Student Academic Experience Survey 2013. Overall totals on p. 8; breakdown between disciplines in supplementary analysis.

supposedly part-time students who are studying whilst working. It is rather like the devout Catholic who shocked his priest by asking if he could smoke while he was praying: after this request was refused he asked instead if he could pray while he was smoking. The doctrine is that working whilst studying is bad but studying whilst working is heroic.

What the student gets out of it

University teaching is not assessed very favourably compared with school teaching, especially by privately educated students. Of state school students, 38 per cent thought university teaching better and 42 per cent thought school teaching better, so minus 4 per cent overall—whereas it was minus 44 per cent for independent pupils.[16]

The National Students Survey (the NSS) is largely about what students think of their academic experience—together with added factors such as employment outcomes. Basically it asks, 'How was it for you?', but increasingly fleshes this out with much more specific questions about the academic experience. Overall levels of satisfaction are high: in 2016, 85 per cent of full-time and 87 per cent of part-time students reported being satisfied with their course.[17] Table 8.3 shows the lowest positive responses are for feedback—the only other aspect of university life which students are even more dissatisfied with is student unions.

There are, however, stories of the questions being gamed. One university was caught out blatantly pitching to students that what they said in the survey would affect their university's place in the rankings and hence the value of their own degree. It is a seductive argument: 'Of course we need to know what you

Table 8.3. Student satisfaction with assessment and feedback (%)

Assessment and feedback	f/t	p/t
The criteria used in marking have been clear in advance.	77	84
Assessment arrangements and marking have been fair.	77	85
Feedback on my work has been prompt.	71	82
I have received detailed comments on my work.	71	87
Feedback on my work has helped me clarify things I did not understand.	68	79

Source: National Student Survey results 2016, National Student Survey summary data, Sector results for full-time and part-time students: England Teaching Institutions, HEFCE, 5 October 2016.

think—but this is not the place for that. Instead this is about the value of your degree: it is worth more if you push us up the league tables and that depends on your giving us a good rating here.'[18]

The National Survey of Student Engagement (the NSSE) is rather different. It is trying to get at the quality of educational experience by asking students what they do, not what they think of it. It includes important questions like how difficult they found parts of the course. It is an attempt to assess what the students get out of the course. Even if it is not being gamed the NSS can be addressed by conventional management techniques such as decreeing that academic staff are available two hours per week for students. Student satisfaction can become an end in itself—just please the students—and the underlying quality of the education can be ignored. Doing better at the NSSE is a more distinctive educational task. It raises issues such as what is in the curriculum and the most effective pedagogy. This makes it more uncomfortable and challenging for both staff and students. I required universities to publish more data on student satisfaction—much of it from the NSS—and was very frustrated by the lack of other data which is now becoming available. And the NSS itself is now incorporating more questions around student engagement. Interesting patterns are also emerging—London universities, for example, are doing badly on student satisfaction and to some extent so are universities in other major cities. This is so widespread it may reflect a city effect—issues such as the cost of accommodation, transport issues, and the weaker sense of a distinct campus. NSSE-type surveys are also conducted in the US, which makes some comparisons possible, as Table 8.4 shows.

The classic measure of what students get out of their education is of course their degree. Employers increasingly look only at potential recruits with a 2:1 or better. A 2:2—a Desmond—is bad news. So after three years of advanced education we have ended up with basically a binary pass/fail system. A growing number of complaints to the Office of the Independent Adjudicator are from students who have been placed on just the wrong side of this crucial divide. Some employers even assess graduates on their A level grades, which does seem a waste of later university-based assessment. In response a rather more subtle Grade Point Average has been developed. Marks from every exam and module are converted into an average point score measured to one decimal place between 1 to 4. It is also why the Higher Education Achievement Report was painstakingly developed by Bob Burgess, when he was Vice Chancellor of Leicester University. In July 2015 Jo Johnson, the minister for universities, announced Government support for GPA and that he wanted 'the green paper

Table 8.4. Comparisons of student engagement in US and UK

During the current academic year, how much has your coursework emphasised analysing in depth an idea, experience, or line of reasoning:

US: 22% No, 78% Yes

UK: 20% No, 80% Yes

During the current year, have you combined ideas from different courses when completing assignments?

US: 28% No, 72% Yes

UK: 35% No, 65% Yes

During the current year, have you often examined the strengths and weaknesses of your own view on a topic?

US: 33% No, 67% Yes

UK: 37% No, 63% Yes

Has your experience at this institution contributed to your ability to explore complex real world problems?

US: 36% No, 64% Yes

UK: 31% No, 69% Yes

Source: Alex Buckley, UK Engagement Survey 2015 (UKES 2015 data spreadsheet), 10 December 2015; for US, National Survey of Student Engagement 2015: Summary Frequencies (Senior Year), Center for Postsecondary Research Indiana University School of Education, 20 August 2015.

to examine how the new Teaching Excellence Framework can encourage universities to adopt dual running of the GPA and honours degree system, as recommended in the recent Higher Education Academy report'.[19] There is, however, a lot of institutional inertia to overcome—and that in turn reflects the attitudes of employers.

Universities have responded to these pressures for a good degree, In 2000 55 per cent of students (135,000) graduated with a First or 2:1. By 2015 that had risen to 74 per cent and the raw number had doubled to 275,000.[20] The trend is so strong we can now see it happening year by year in Table 8.5.

This is a striking contrast with GCSEs and A levels where the number of top grades fell steadily after 2010 as part of Michael Gove's pressure for rigorous standards. External examiners are supposed to maintain standards of university degrees and there are legitimate arguments that there have been real improvements in underlying intelligence and effort. Nevertheless an increase on this scale is surprising and worrying. Put alongside the evidence of relatively modest hours worked by students it also suggests there is an implicit contract between academics and students—we'll give you a good grade to get you a decent job if you let us get on with our research. It may also be an effect of competition

Table 8.5. Proportions of students getting a
First or an Upper Second 2011/12 to 2015/16

	First	Upper Second
2011–12	17%	49%
2012–13	18%	49%
2013–14	20%	50%
2014–15	22%	50%
2015–16	24%	50%

Source: Higher education student enrolments and qualifications
obtained at higher education providers in the United
Kingdom 2015/16, HESA, First degree graduates.

between universities so that if one is inflating its grades others are under pressure to follow suit. There is a legitimate role for the Office for Students in ensuring as a minimum that external examiner arrangements are effective.

Our students may just not be learning enough stuff. How do we get away with it? There are two explanations. First, it is disguised by early specialization. We get to the same amount of knowledge in a specific discipline by learning more at A levels but with a narrower base of knowledge overall. An 18-year-old going up to university to study physics already knows more than his or her equivalent at a Continental or American university, who needs to put in more time and effort to catch up—but they have a broader education. Secondly, some educationalists argue that focusing on exactly what you know is rather vulgar and misses the point of education. This is the Oxbridge tradition of the cultivated gentleman, someone with the self assurance to dispense justice as a solitary district commissioner surrounded by natives. But it has been updated a bit—now it is someone with good social skills who knows how to conduct himself at a job interview, deliver a speech or write a column on any subject at two hours' notice, or who can sell assets to foreigners with panache so as to keep the British economy funded. We call them soft skills. It is the courses linked to specific professions where you do indeed need to learn stuff to do the job that also have the longest hours of study. But for the rest perhaps it is just that students are being educated in a way that fits them well for an updated model of British gentlemanly capitalism.

There are deep questions here about whether ultimately education is about knowledge or skills. There is a respectable argument that 'education is what is left after all that has been learnt is forgotten'.[21] Learning stuff is mainly a means for developing skills and we should not confuse the means and the ultimate objective. Universities are not spoon-feeding school pupils but creating an adult learner. Any actual knowledge you need you can look up on Google anyway. Perhaps you can cut out the tiresome intermediary subject altogether and go straight to developing cognitive and interpersonal skills without having to bother with memorizing French irregular verbs or reading Jane Austen. After all, you can take exercises to be physically fit without engaging in any particular sport.

Whilst skills are fundamental, I do not accept these arguments against learning stuff. For a start that may be a good way to develop skills. For most jobs you may not actually have to know why Byzantium fell or how sub-atomic particles interact. But if you have grappled with these you may be better at understanding cause and effect in human affairs and at disentangling complex systems. Moreover the world would be grey and meaningless if we just had skills and no knowledge. We improve our cognitive skills if we have more knowledge sunk in deep memory, so liberating our working memory for more advanced tasks.[22] We could not actually use Google very well if we did not start with a lot of prior knowledge—the more you already know, the more you can get out of a search engine. It is hard to see how you could be an effective scientist or lawyer or historian or almost any sort of professional without mastering your subject at some point, though that could happen at graduate school.

Our anxieties are both about what students know and their cognitive skills. It is not just that we worry they have not read Jane Austen or cannot design a nuclear power station. It is that they do not appear to show much cognitive gain after three years of study at university if you set them a sophisticated comprehension test or some maths challenges. This is the devastating evidence from the College Learning Assessment, a survey of American students in one of the most potent books on universities to have come out of America in the past decade—*Academically Adrift* by Richard Arum and Josipa Roksa.[23] Its findings are disputed because of significant methodological problems which afflict any attempt to monitor cognitive gains by surveying students. If it is a no-stakes test just for research purposes then students may be slapdash. And if you pay them to do it you may select those who are most disadvantaged. But overall this evidence does suggest there is a problem. It is of course an American problem—where the culture of just giving the students what they want is far worse than here—and reinforced by explicit use of student reporting on their professors. But it is a growing issue across the OECD countries, including England. It is not that students are lazy or academic staff are malign—far from it. But they are working within a system with perverse incentives which we must now analyse.

Adam Smith analyses the problem

Weak teaching at university makes sense when we look at the incentives institutions face. One view, classically set out in Newman's lectures on the Idea of a University, sees it as a teaching institution passing on a body of knowledge to the next generation. 'The view taken of a University in these Discourses is ... it is a place of *teaching* universal *knowledge* ... the diffusion and extension of knowledge rather than the advancement. If its object were scientific and philosophical discovery, I do not see why a University should have students.'[24] The view that Newman caricatures—if you focus on research why bother to have students at all—is the unspoken belief of many research-active academics. Any profession can sometimes succumb to this view of the world—hospitals would work so much more smoothly if there were fewer patients and being an MP would be so much more straightforward if only there were not so many constituents with their complicated problems. But few institutions have such strong pressures to act on such a perverse belief. There are detailed metrics of research performance, like citations, whereas there are no equivalent measures of teaching performance. There is intense competition for research funding whereas until recently each university was just allocated a fixed number of student places and fined if it over-recruited. Academic promotion came to depend on research performance with teaching way behind—indeed, one survey put it behind discharge of departmental administrative tasks as a factor in promotion.[25]

   The prestige of a university and its place in the rankings is largely determined by research excellence and the selectiveness of its intake with little weight for teaching. These rankings matter as they influence student choices of where to study and where an education minister on the other side of the world will decide to send students overseas on scholarships. We saw in the previous chapter how the Department for Education reinforced these pressures further by introducing a new measure of school performance—getting their students into the Russell Group of research-intensive universities. It would not be so much of a problem if in turn research and teaching were complementary activities, not substitutes. This is the attractive idea of teaching informed with the latest research—like freshly baked bread. But there is little evidence that what drives the rankings, the research intensiveness of a university or selectivity of its intake contributes to teaching quality—though it is harder to show value is being added when students have high prior attainment.[26] Indeed there is American evidence that the selectivity of a university is negatively associated with some good practice such as teacher feedback—perhaps because teachers are more research active.[27] Overall selectivity seems to have little effect one way or the other, only accounting for 2 per cent of variation in educational practice.[28]

Graham Gibbs observes that 'While league tables in the UK invariably include A level point scores as an indicator of educational quality; if the US is anything to go by, they tell us almost nothing about the quality of the educational process within institutions or the degree of student engagement with their studies.'[29] These perverse incentives mean universities put far more effort into selecting the right entrants than teaching them well when they arrive—as happens so often in English education, the producers compete on who they select not how well they teach.

Compounding these pressures, teaching has also lost out in funding. We saw in Chapter Six that the intellectual climate favours shifting education spending to the early years. Then within higher education there has tended to be much more of a focus on research spend. Science and research spending had a degree of protection under successive governments whereas there has been no such protection for public spending on university teaching. Academics were entitled to say that it was hard for them to deliver a high-quality student experience when there were continuing and severe cuts in resources for teaching. This is one reason it was so important to reverse that trend with the Coalition's funding reforms—it was a necessary precondition for promoting other policies to raise teaching standards.

All this adds up to a host of reasons for university teaching to lose out relative to research. Adam Smith helps us to see the bigger picture. As we saw in Chapter One, Oxford and Cambridge were at their low point during the eighteenth century. Adam Smith had a brief and unhappy experience at Oxford: 'In the university of Oxford the greater part of the public professors have, for these many years, given up altogether even the pretence of teaching.'[30] In *The Wealth of Nations* he turned his forensic intelligence to explain what had gone wrong and why Scotland's universities were so much better. Part of his argument is that universities with endowments do not depend on students for funding and hence have no incentive to offer a high-quality student experience. He advocates the Scottish system, with fees paid directly to the professors:

In some universities the salary makes but a part and frequently but a small part of the emoluments of the teacher, of which the greater part arises from the honoraries or fees of his pupils. The necessity of application, though always more or less diminished, is not in this case entirely taken away. Reputation in his profession is still of some importance to him, and he still has some dependency upon the affection, gratitude, and favourable report of those who have attended upon his instructions; and these favourable sentiments he is likely to gain in no way so well as by deserving them, that is, by the abilities and diligence with which he discharges every part of his duty.[31]

Smith has a second argument too which is even more telling and relevant to us today. Oxford and Cambridge degrees were a secure route to a sinecure in the Church of England. If going to university is an automatic and also exclusive route to jobs, such as in the Church, then the student comes not for the teaching but for the job afterwards: 'Whatever forces a certain number of students to any college or university, independent of the merit or reputation of the teachers, tends more or less to diminish the necessity of that merit or reputation. The privileges of graduates in arts, in law, physick and divinity, when they can be obtained only by residing a certain number of years in certain universities, necessarily force a certain number of students to such universities, independent of the merit or reputation of the teachers.'[32]

Smith brings these two points together when he praises the philosophy schools of Classical Greece: 'no teacher appears to have had any salary from the public, or to have had any other emoluments but what arose from the honoraries or fees of his scholars.... There was nothing equivalent to the privileges of graduation, and to have attended any of those schools was not necessary in order to be permitted to practise any particular trade or profession.'[33]

What Smith is describing is what we now call rent-seeking behaviour (capturing economic gains without adding value). The universities did not have to educate you because they guaranteed you a graduate job in the Church. Back in the bad days of eighteenth-century Oxford the academics did not have to teach, and they had alternative activities, even if they were not research. One student reported: 'We were lectured immediately after chapel, and generally in a very hasty manner, as Parkinson not infrequently was equipped in boots and spurs, which his gown but ill concealed.'[34] The academics were certainly not recruited for their deep learning. Lord Chesterfield wrote to his son: 'What do you think of being a Greek Professor at one of our universities? It is a very pretty sinecure and requires little knowledge.'[35]

The temptations and rewards of research can be a modern and rather more serious-minded version of the same problem in which the student can expect that her CV will be put under the noses of recruiters from Goldman Sachs or McKinsey. They won't care much exactly how much she has studied but they will know she has been selected by a rigorous institution and gained some understanding of how to think. Indeed, the quality of the university's research may matter more to the student than her own educational experience as it is the research which drives the rankings which the prestigious employers focus on to decide who to consider for a job. It is a modern version of Adam Smith, but instead of sinecures in the Church of England it is status in the job market via the quality of your university's research. It is a model in which the university academics get on with their research, the leading employers get their recruits, and meanwhile the student has an enjoyable few years. In fact what impressed me in these circumstances was that individual academics were still dedicated teachers and cared about the quality of their students' education. But we need to get beyond this to robust evidence about what is happening to teaching in our universities.

What to do about teaching?

Governments measure universities' performance in research and access but have had less success in developing reliable metrics for teaching. Universities have a quality regulator, the Quality Assurance Agency, to ensure the university maintains the standards which are key to a quality higher education. It is not an OFSTED for universities. The last Labour Government launched the Teaching Quality Assessment in the late 1990s, which did include inspectors with their clipboards sitting at the back of lectures and seminars monitoring academics' performance, but there were such protests that those exercises were largely abandoned early in the Noughties. The QAA has tended to retreat into ensuring that processes for maintaining quality are in place.

Now teaching is once more back on the agenda. We need better measures of teaching quality at university. The QAA could go beyond mere process to satisfying itself that there is actually real learning gain happening. Onora O'Neill says it is almost as if we wish to avoid measuring the real things—'how many hours the students at a given university work; how competently students speak and write the language of instruction; how many pages of written work a student produces in a year and how many of these pages receive detailed comment and feedback'.[36] Graham Gibbs has identified some intermediate measures which are reliable indicators of teaching quality: class size; extent of close contact with teachers; extent and timing of feedback on assignments; extent of collaborative learning. There is admittedly the risk of falling foul of Goodhart's Law that any indicator which becomes a target ceases to be a reliable measure. Nevertheless it is surely reasonable to expect these key indicators to be measured and published, perhaps matching this with a cull of less significant measures which universities are currently obliged to publish. Indeed, this might have the welcome effect of reducing the significance of graduate earnings, which has become such an important indicator of university performance because as well as being significant in its own right it has been taken as a proxy for quality of teaching when there is little evidence to justify that assumption.

At the moment universities are way behind schools in measuring value added. There is no reliable measure of a student's intellectual advance over three years. We need a reliable survey—not an exam sat by all students—which does just this. It could be, for example, a complex comprehension test administered to a representative sample of students at the start of their degree course and at the end. It might, one hopes, show significant improvements in performance across many universities. The most selective ones, however, do have a legitimate concern that it is harder for them to show cognitive advance by their students, who arrive already working to exceptionally high standards. The OECD tried to design something like this with the Assessment of Higher Education Learning Outcomes or AHELO. It is difficult to capture intellectual progress if the measure is identical across all disciplines as they advance in such different ways. Can one expect music students to make progress in linguistic analysis just like English students? As soon as some maths and logic are included one is favouring another set of disciplines. The assessment was therefore going to have to be divided into several different types which broadly related to the kind of discipline being studied. The OECD were going to start with some defined disciplines such as economics and engineering. However, there was insufficient support for it amongst member states and genuine methodological doubts, so that project has been abandoned. Then there were further questions—should the results be available university by university? Is there an external agency which administers the tests? If they were not sat by all students how could one be confident the sample was representative and not made up of their University Challenge team? These were quite sensitive issues as many universities see the power to set their own exams as fundamental to their character and autonomy. They did not want to see the degree replaced by a new cognitive test.

Meanwhile, back in England, the minister for universities, Jo Johnson, launched an ambitious attempt to measure teaching quality and link it to fee increases. He identified three intermediate measures of teaching quality—student satisfaction, drop-out rates, and employment six months after leaving university—creating a Teaching Excellence Framework or TEF, whose first results were published in June 2017. The Government's Green Paper proposing these measures recognized that they were all subject to strong selection effects. If a university recruits students from affluent families with good A levels they get lower drop-out rates and better employment outcomes. As a result the Government has contextualized performance on all these measures—a complex process. Many universities were unhappy with these flawed metrics. And there is an argument that, even if they capture things which students care about, they are not good proxies for teaching excellence. Nevertheless, 134 universities did apply for the TEF, together with 94 further education colleges.[37] The first results were published in June 2017. A third of the universities, forty-five, achieved gold, sixty-seven got a silver, and twenty-five a bronze. Chris Husbands, the Vice Chancellor of Sheffield Hallam University who chaired the TEF, summarized the results as follows:

> Institutions with a gold rating come from all parts of the sector, with different missions and approaches. Their practices do, however, have some common and compelling characteristics. It is clear that the very best provision genuinely engages students. It takes their interests, needs, aspirations and trajectories seriously and sees them as real partners in the development of teaching, going way beyond instances of student representation.[38]

It was refreshing to see a very different ranking of universities, with Golds for Coventry, De Montfort, Portsmouth, and Huddersfield, for example. There were different reactions from the universities which got Bronze. Southampton, a very effective research-intensive university, challenged the methodology whereas the LSE seemed more willing to recognize that it needed to do more to raise the quality of teaching and the student experience.

The TEF is really the start of a journey in which better metrics of teaching are developed. The measurement of the three current criteria can be improved. For example, employment after six months is a poor measure of long-term performance and can be replaced by much more granular long-term data on employment outcomes as these become available. And the metrics can over time be replaced by others more directly related to teaching quality—one suggestion from the Higher Education Academy is some kind of professional fellowship of university teachers which includes assessment of performance and continuing professional development as a key measure. More intrusively academics could simply be required to hold a teaching qualification, but that could mean that people with worthwhile research or relevant experience— entrepreneurs recruited to a business school, for example—could be excluded, which would be a real loss. There are perhaps subtler ways of achieving this such as going further in providing training in teaching to PhD students or even requiring it for UK PhD accreditation. But PhD students do not necessarily want to be academics and it would be wrong to assume this. More ambitiously HEFCE launched pilots of measures of Learning Gain—the Holy Grail of these measures pursued by Andreas Schleicher of OECD, though without success so far. The need for new and better measures here is now so great that over the next decade these issues are going to have to be addressed.

The Office of the Independent Adjudicator (OIA) says student redress can get universities to improve student experience. And the quality of the redress process is itself part of student experience. OIA complaints were recently rising at 25 per cent per annum. They now publish cases where there is a public interest with the name of the university with a summary of the complaint. OIA send cases causing concern to QAA and HEFCE. Seventy per cent of complaints are academic on issues such as degree grade or whether a student was really guilty of plagiarism.

These are useful interventions but they really get traction when they are reinforced by empowering the student as consumer. This is controversial because education is not the same as consumption. Nevertheless the university fee, even though not paid by the student up-front, is the basis of a contract to supply a service and students are entitled to redress if the contract is not delivered. The applicability of this legal framework was established in a court case involving a further education college, a veteran car repair course, and some rather disgruntled students. Six students successfully sued Rycotewood College in Oxfordshire because their higher national diploma course on historical vehicle restoration had failed to deliver what the prospectus promised. One had brought in an old car, borrowed from his parents, which had been dismantled during the course, but neither he nor his teacher had been able to put it back together.[39] But when do you stop? What if you do a philosophy course which dismantles your religious and moral beliefs, leaving you more confused than ever? What if a course on English literature leaves you unable to enjoy the novels of D. H. Lawrence any more? One hopes the courts would not stray into such deep waters.

There are also opportunities to harness the power of choice and competition. This comes with a lot of ideological baggage and we will try to unpack it in Chapter Eleven. But whatever the theory, there are a range of examples showing other systems benefiting from such competitive pressures. Great medieval universities like Bologna would have had a standard prescribed course and several different teachers teaching the same part of it at the same time, with students free to choose the lecturer who inspired them the most.[40]

The Oxbridge structure of college-based teaching and a university-based assessment means that there is a kind of external exam and the possibility for competition between colleges in educational standards if that matters to them. In American universities students do not commit in advance to a specific course which they are then obliged to stick to. This is closer to the Scottish model and is a consequence of the breadth of study before university. Even if they have chosen a major in advance they can also choose from a range of minor options and in their second year they can change again. This creates competition between different faculties far greater than in English universities, where the specialization forced on 16- year-olds reduces their ability to choose between a range of competitive courses at university and enables English universities to require pre-commitment.

Innovative new providers have also provided competition to incumbents. Professional schools and academies arose as an alternative to university, especially after the decay of the medieval university. And as higher education globalizes there are increasing opportunities to study at competing universities abroad. Universities can of course just take the lead themselves in raising their educational offer. Edward Acton, while Vice Chancellor at the University of East Anglia, was one of the foremost leaders on this. At one point he was proposing to offer humanities students a commitment that during their time at his university they would get to write at least 100,000 words on which they would get academic feedback. Subsequently the offer focused more on teaching infrastructure and careers advice.[41] Technological change could drive transformation of the education experience, as we will see in Chapter Thirteen. The good news is that after years of neglect teaching is now high on the agenda for most universities. A cultural shift is under way in universities, and a good thing too.

III

The Useful University

NINE

Vocational Higher Education

The liberal arts

A beautiful large stained-glass window dominates the end of the Great Hall of Birmingham University. My great-grandfather was one of the glaziers who made it—my family were Birmingham artisans, craftsmen, and engineers. His son, my grandfather, remembered being taken to the opening of Birmingham University in 1902—Joe Chamberlain, the founder of the university, believed that the workers who had built it should be invited, not just the academics. From a distance it looks like the stained-glass window in an ancient cathedral with figures of saints, but close up you see the radicalism of Joe Chamberlain's vision. It is dedicated to the arts and sciences. Instead of saints and bishops the figures represent disciplines like geometry or music, but alongside them, equally prominent, are contemporary trades: there is an electroplater, a rather Michelangelesque miner, and a demure bookkeeper too. It is a celebration of the range of trades and professions of the early twentieth century, 'as practised in the university and in the City', said the local paper.[1] England's first university in one of its great bustling industrial cities was claiming a new role for the university based on its civic commitment. This great window embodies a very different idea of the university from the Oxbridge tradition. It is a vigorous statement in an argument that was raging within Government at the very time that Chamberlain was planning his new university. The question was whether public funds should go to help pay for higher education courses outside Oxbridge on a systematic basis and if so which courses at which institutions. (At this point what would become our Redbrick universities were typically university colleges teaching for the external degree of the University of London and funded locally, though with occasional public grants.) The question came to the Chancellor of the Exchequer in 1895, who replied: 'As an old Oxford man myself I must confess to a feeling, which you may call a prejudice, that

University education, in the full sense of the term, can hardly be obtained except at our old Universities.'[2] The Treasury consulted Oxford and Cambridge on what they should fund. They were advised that these nascent universities should not become mere training colleges and so the Treasury deliberately decided to exclude utilitarian courses such as medicine, technology, and engineering from Exchequer support.

That question about what types of subject you study at university reverberates to this day. There is still a widespread view, mistaken and pernicious in its effects, that the university is not for vocational training: for that students have to look elsewhere. That view has a respectable intellectual pedigree going back to Aristotle's idea of a liberal education. The liberal arts were what a man did freely: they were not what you had to learn to do a job. 'Of possessions, those rather are useful, which bear fruit; those liberal, which tend to enjoyment. By fruitful, I mean, which yield revenue; by enjoyable, where nothing accrues of consequence beyond the using.'[3] That quotation from Aristotle is cited by Newman, who does rather better with his definition of the liberal arts than he managed with the etymology of university: 'first, in its grammatical sense it is opposed to servile . . . bodily labour, mechanical employment and the like, in which the mind has little or no part. . . . Liberal education and liberal pursuits are exercises of mind, of reason, of reflection.'[4] But this is not the end of the matter for Newman: 'we contrast a liberal education with a commercial education or a professional; yet no one can deny that commerce and the professions afford scope for the highest and most diversified powers of the mind.'[5] So it is not solely intellectual demands which make an activity liberal: it also requires that they have no utilitarian purpose. He adds that some sports are liberal. The reason is 'because that alone is liberal knowledge, which stands on its own pretensions, which is independent of sequel, expects no complement, refuses to be *informed* by any end. . . . The most ordinary pursuits have this specific character, if they are self-sufficient and complete; the highest lose it, when they minister to something beyond them.'[6] Hence horse-racing is a liberal pursuit unless used as an occasion for gambling. This links the liberal arts to the idea of a gentleman— and is one reason why to this day Oxbridge has to battle against perceptions that it is socially exclusive. The image of privileged young men still hangs over it, however unfairly (see Figure 7). It is also why so many academics insist that the study of their disciplines should be recognized as inherently worthwhile rather than merely useful. It does, however, make clear that the liberal arts are not restricted to the arts and humanities; they include sciences, though not technology or engineering.

Figure 7. The image of privileged young men still hangs over Oxford.

This idea of the university was neatly caught by defining it as 'A place where nothing useful is taught'.[7] Oxbridge could afford such a definition, as Macaulay pointed out: 'A chartered and endowed college, strong in its wealth and its degrees, does not find it necessary to teach what is useful, because it can pay men to learn what is useless.' But in London, 'To be prosperous it must be useful'.[8] This purist idea of a university had particular power in England because of the 600-year Oxbridge duopoly: they actively used their power to stop the creation of other universities on different models—and that advice to the Treasury was just another example of this exercise of power. Over in the US that was the view of the President of Harvard and there were doubtless grand old Boston Brahmin families who thought the same way but, unlike in England, they could not stop a Midwestern state and its local businesses setting up a local university and funding it to research potatoes or automotive engineering and train the people who could take advantage of their research. When Joe Chamberlain used his political power to bypass Oxbridge, leapfrog the other civics, and create Birmingham University he impudently celebrated his more (though not exclusively) utilitarian view of the university in a form redolent of its own traditions—in stained glass. It was mocked then: 'He gets a degree in making jam, | At Liverpool and Birmingham'.[9] It still is. David Lodge lists, though with more affection, 'the esoteric disciplines in which Rummidge, through the support of local industry, had established an unchallenged supremacy: domestic appliance technology, tyre sciences and the biochemistry of the cocoa bean'.[10]

Joe Chamberlain directly challenged the Oxbridge model and thank heavens he did: we are all in his debt. His vindication came within a few years of his death. Technological competition was an important element in the First World War and even more important in the Second: they say that scientifically World War I was fought in chemistry and World War II in physics. When British military planners looked for the research partnerships between university academics and industry which led to these technological advances, Birmingham was the main university they turned to, though with some of the other leading civics and, after a big change of heart, Oxbridge too. During the Second World War Birmingham was crucial in the development of radar, and its links to local businesses enabled it to make crucial early progress in filtering uranium for use in the atomic bomb.[11] From 1915 until about 1970 the twentieth-century British state put enormous effort into promoting R&D and key industries in order to maintain Britain as a global power: as we saw in Chapter Four, it was not just a welfare state; it was also a 'Warfare state', and sponsoring university research was a key part of this.[12]

The classic liberal idea of a university gets renewed significance when it is applied to the modern research university as it justifies blue skies, curiosity-driven research. An American scientist, asked by a Congressional Committee if a proposed particle accelerator contributed to American security, famously replied: 'It has nothing to do directly with defending our country except to make it worth defending.'[13] These sentiments strike a chord with anyone who cares about research in its broadest sense. Universities certainly need to provide the space for this precious activity. But the experience of two world wars reminds us that there is a different, utilitarian account of the role of the university in which the work it does is directly useful. That is what we will focus on in this chapter and the next. And of the various ways in which a modern university does this, the most important is directly training students for jobs.

Professional education

The hostility of Oxbridge to anything like professional qualifications forced the English professions down a more vocational route outside university.

The issue had already arisen in the Middle Ages with the training of lawyers kept out of universities, unlike in some other European countries. Another battle fought by Oxbridge was to stop the Inns of Court getting university status. By the mid fifteenth century the four Inns of Court had their own collegiate structure; indeed, with 200 students each was actually larger than any Oxbridge college. Medicine also developed on an apprenticeship model in guilds such as the barber-surgeons. Medical education developed in London based in hospitals separate from a university because the Oxbridge duopoly meant there was no university in London until the 1830s. To study medicine in a university you had to travel to Scotland or to Leiden or Padua.[14] Many people within these professions preferred that they were not university-based. They feared that moving into a university would mean their profession becoming 'academic'—a fate to be avoided at all costs. So the university traditionalists and key members of the professions formed an alliance to keep professions and universities apart. These professions can provide a framework for living a life at least as strong as that which comes from an academic community of scholars. Indeed, the moral philosophy of Alasdair MacIntyre or Charles Taylor, the profound dilemma of moving from Is to Ought, is resolved by the requirement that you follow the rules which are implicit in the description of your role within a community, and the most compelling example of such a role is a vocation.[15] University expansion has meant the gradual incorporation of different professions into higher education. Bringing a profession into a university can change its character. If the arguments in Chapters Five and Six on the influence of a university education are correct then we should indeed find that it has an effect: it would be very peculiar if it did not. Is this effect desirable or not?

Is the reflectiveness of academic study in conflict with craft skills? Paradoxically intellectuals based in universities can wax more lyrical about craft skills than about higher education. Instead of deracinated sceptical intellectualism you get the unreflective commitment to vocational skills. Richard Sennett's *The Craftsman* and Matthew Crawford's *Shop Class as Soulcraft* are eloquent examples of the genre which in England goes back to Ruskin.[16] Indeed, Richard Sennett defines craftsmanship as 'doing something well for its own sake' and thus ingeniously incorporates it within the liberal arts tradition.[17] Robert Pirsig's *Zen and the Art of Motorcycle Maintenance*, was the cool version of the argument in my youth.[18] Behind this respect for craft skills are new anxieties, especially about the role of the white working-class male, given the disappearance of the kind of semi-skilled jobs, many of them in manufacturing, which they used to do. Saying they can all go to university does not sound right—tantamount to saying they have to become liberal intellectuals—whereas re-creating apprenticeships seems much better.

This issue can be traced deep into the philosophy of education. John Locke and the English empiricists imagined thought as an intellectual process whereby an idea is imprinted on the tabula rasa of the mind: 'Let us then suppose the mind to have no ideas in it, to be like white paper with nothing written on it.'[19] They saw a sharp distinction between such propositional knowledge and practical knowledge. This is not of course the same as our earlier distinction between liberal and vocational; it is more the difference between intellect and craft. If, however, you superimpose these two distinctions on each other and envisage the university as only for liberal not vocational learning and only for propositional not practical knowledge then you do end up with a particular and narrow conception of a university. And if you think that is what a university must be like then you want to keep a lot of people away from it because it is clearly not for them. But the university need not be so restricted. Rousseau's *Emile* is a different picture of learning, integrating physical and mental, which can be both intellectual and practical.[20] Music is a good example, and Richard Sennett's training as a cellist helps to explain his eloquence on this view of skills—these values are preserved in our excellent conservatoires, an important part of higher education, some of which are now in institutions with university title. Roger Spratt, one of the founders of the Royal Society, envisaged a time 'when either the Mechanick Labourers shall have Philosophical Heads, or the Philosophers shall have Mechanical Hands'.[21] I have met a young man at a work-bench in the University of Surrey physically making sophisticated new technology to enable satellites to communicate with each other in orbit: he had not done A levels but now this work counted towards his university doctorate. It was a vivid example of how the modern university can break down these barriers in just the way that the founder of the Royal Society hoped. David Hume made a powerful connection between these different types of disciplines: 'An advantage of industry and of refinements in the mechanical arts is that they commonly produce some refinements in the liberal; nor can one be carried to perfection without being accompanied, in some degree, with the other. The same age, which produces great philosophers and politicians, renowned generals and poets, usually abounds with skilful weavers and ship-carpenters. We cannot reasonably expect that a piece of woollen cloth will be wrought to perfection in a nation which is ignorant of astronomy or where ethics are neglected.'[22]

If there is this happy interdependence of academic and other skills then the case for a wider range of study at university is stronger. The argument for practical training in universities has carried on ever since, with many traditionalists opposed. Ernest Barker, the leading political theorist and Principal of King's, issued a warning of the 'great mistake of blurring the distinction between university and technical colleges'.[23] The great American thinker on universities and founder of the Princeton Centre for Advanced Study, Abraham Flexner, bemoaned 'such excrescences as the School of Librarianship and course in Journalism at University College, London (for which the university grants diplomas not degrees), the Department of Civic Design at Liverpool, and the work in Automobile Engineering at Bristol'.[24] The argument was particularly intense in Germany, with mockery of *Brotstudium* leading to a belief that universities needed to free themselves for the life of the mind, though this in turn came to be seen like an escape from the moral and political challenges of the day.[25] We saw in Chapter Four that great novels such as Thomas Mann's *Magic Mountain* or Herman Hesse's *Glass Bead Game* convey this ambivalence about disengagement from the world. It was not just an issue in Germany. James Hilton's *Shangri La*, written at the same time, is hidden away in Tibet, but he compares it to somewhere much closer to home: 'it reminds me very slightly of Oxford where I used to lecture. The scenery there is not so good, but the subjects of study are often just as impractical, and though even the oldest of the dons is not quite so old, they appear to age in a somewhat similar way.'[26]

In England these battles were fought out in the new civic universities which, like Birmingham, had often been created by business leaders keen to have more trained professionals in their cities but which were then staffed by academics from Oxbridge with a different picture of a university. Exchequer funding helped to liberate them from the missions envisaged by the local businessmen who had founded them. As we saw in Chapter One, public subsidy for research was not a threat to their autonomy but a means of delivering it. The creation of polytechnics was an attempt by Government to create a new way of protecting vocational higher education outside universities. This competitive challenge actually led universities to engage in 'reverse academic drift' and deliver more vocational education themselves.[27] There are even a few universities which educate both doctors and nurses, straddling deep social and academic divisions which are as deep in universities as in the rest of English society. There are powerful pressures keeping them apart, however, as the leading research-intensive universities have medical schools, but if they offer courses for nursing as well this tends to mean they accept entrants with lower grades, which pulls them down the conventional rankings—so a 'good' university is less 'good' if it educates nurses as well as doctors; such are the perverse effects of the status system in English higher education. There are fifty-six English universities with nursing schools. Twenty-six English universities have medical schools but only twelve of them have a nursing school. So a university is slightly more likely to have a nursing school if it does not have a medical school than if it does.

The argument still rumbles on about what are acceptable university courses. One recent universities minister denounced what she called 'Mickey Mouse' courses. The term was coined by Margaret Hodge, who was referring to courses 'where the content is perhaps not as rigorous as one would expect and where the degree itself may not have huge relevance in the labour market'.[28] (There is actually a Disney Chair at Cambridge—though sadly its founder, John Disney, was no relation to Walt.) In America you can go to the Disney University and get what is literally a Mickey Mouse degree 'complete with gown and... mortar-board adorned with a rather fetching pair of ears'.[29] It is, incidentally, an example of what can happen if there is no control over the use of the title 'university'. But I have seen some excellent 'Mickey Mouse' courses. You need an A and two Bs to do Golf Studies at Birmingham University and, even more demanding, a golf handicap of 4.4. It is essentially a business studies course focused on this particular part of the leisure industry. At Southampton Solent University I have met students doing a course in navigation and marine operations management as training for working as an officer on a cargo ship. In fact those courses which are most vocational have their standards and rigour protected by the requirements of employers, who need graduates qualified and trained to do a particular job: a professional body can maintain standards more effectively than conventional external examiners. So the Royal Institute of Chartered Surveyors accredits courses for surveyors at university and they are not going to allow standards to slip. Indeed, 38 per cent of university courses are accredited by a Professional Statutory and Regulatory Body.[30] To be fair to Margaret Hodge, her 'Mickey Mouse courses' were ones with little relevance to the labour market. It is very frustrating for students if they believe a course is preparing them for a job when it is not—I can remember the bitterness of a student who had embarked on a public health course at one university but then discovered it was not recognized as a validated route to employment as a public health officer.

More and more professional training is heading to university. Over 40 per cent of university students are doing vocational courses, such as over 12 per cent of students on courses in subjects allied to medicine, 7 per cent in education and training, and 6 per cent in engineering (42% on a definition of vocational education as 'designed to offer a pathway to a specific career or profession—by developing specific, technical skills used in that career').[31] Add in the 14 per cent of students doing business studies, and almost 60 per cent of students are doing what one might regard as a 'utilitarian' course. If young people want to go to university for the wider experience and as a transition to adulthood it makes sense for professions to locate their training there too. Like the robber asked why he robbed banks who replied, 'Because that is where the money is', so vocations go to universities because that is where the smart young people are. They may also hope that their occupation will gain from links to deeper reflection on professional practice. And the funding model provides a strong financial inventive too. I always found it peculiar that whilst people think we have made university expensive the truth is the opposite—it has much better quasi-public funding, through loans, than almost any other way of getting a professional qualification with no up-front costs. Why is it that when you sink into your seat on a British Airways plane the captain is called Jeremy and sounds like someone from the local golf club? It is because commercial pilot training is a course you have to pay for and is not available at university.[32] The performing arts are caught in this dilemma. They do not believe that the only route into them should be via a university course—there should be a vocational route to being an actor without going to university. But, like many other vocations, you actually need some training before you get an employer so apprenticeships may not work for them. They are driven down the university route.

It is one of the peculiar accidents of higher education funding that whilst the incentives are for individuals to get their training at university the financial and career incentives for the academics who are supposed to be educating them are instead to focus on research. That in turn affects what they teach and how. The pressures to take professions out of universities can just be the worst sort of anti-intellectualism. We need professionals with the intellectual rigour that comes from higher education. But how can we be confident that this is what they are getting if their professors are all focused on research so there are not strong enough links to the rigour of professional practice? We will investigate these issues in key professions.

Social workers, nurses, and teachers

These arguments about what kind of education and training should happen in university and whether that properly values craft skills are most acute with some key professions concentrated in the public sector such as social workers, nurses, and teachers. Education reformers argue that whilst teachers should have a knowledge of their subject at a university level, teaching itself is a craft which needs to be liberated from the dangerous theorizing of university teacher-training departments. We are told that nurses should be people who care but that since nursing became a university route these values have been eroded. And effective social workers are supposed to be street-wise grannies, not do-gooders who have spent three years at university being told that all social problems are structural and the only way to tackle them is to change the system. As a result, throughout my time as minister I faced persistent attempts to push universities out of their role in training these professions.

The critics had vivid and genuine examples of the problem of poor-quality higher education. Sir Martin Nairey conducted a review of social work and cited this account by a young social worker which is a powerful example of the problem:

> I successfully completed a master's course in social work. The university had a good reputation and any assessor looking down the list of modules that I completed would probably feel confident that I was being trained in the necessary areas. However, the actual content of the courses and its delivery was grossly deficient. The course was too focused on academic ability and essay-writing skills. There was no training for the real nature of social work. I wrote many essays on theoretical viewpoints but I was never once taught how a statutory team in children's services worked.... When I started my first job (in a child protection team) I had never heard of an initial assessment form or ever seen or been schooled in the strategies for questioning parents.... I never had any quality child development training and I never had any session on how to work directly with children.... I can say in all honesty that I started my first day in a child protection team as competent as I would have been never having attended the master's course.[33]

This is what can go wrong with professional training in a university. The example may be from a university with a strong research ethos which might not have seen the practical issues raised by the student as relevant. Perhaps the student might have received more practical training at a university with a more vocational mission. And universities can change and take a broader view of their role. When Sir Martin produced his report on training social workers dealing with children, three years after he cited that example, he did not suggest ending university-based training of social workers: instead he proposed a series of practical reforms aimed at ensuring that social work training in universities improved.

Nursing only became a graduate profession in the late 1990s. The argument was that women increasingly aspired to a degree as their opportunities opened up and nursing would gradually lose out unless it fulfilled that ambition.

Moreover with medicine becoming increasingly complex and technical, nursing needed higher levels of education and training. But ever since then the criticism has been that nurses are too posh to wash and too clever to care. The scandal of poor care and high mortality at Mid-Staffs hospital was supposed to show what had gone wrong with university-based nurse education and training. But only 14 per cent of nursing staff were graduates at Mid-Staffs—half the national average. The Francis Report on Mid-Staffs made some very sensible proposals for creating a career path for nursing assistants to progress on to nursing but could not show that university nursing education was the source of the problem. Indeed Francis specifically identified as one of the problems the wrong staff mix, with too many care assistants and not enough qualified nurses—who tend to be the graduates. The Francis Report does, however, claim that while 'most of those with whom the inquiry had contact agreed that the increasing technical demands of the role required degree-level training and education...they recognised that the progress made in this direction had sometimes been at the expense of exposure to personal experience of the basic tasks that all nurses should be able and willing to do'.[34] But actually a 50 per cent balance between practice and academic study has been maintained for years. A subsequent inquiry into nursing education 'saw no evidence to support the view that graduate nurses are less caring or competent than non-graduates, and indeed heard of evidence to the contrary'.[35] Requiring all trainee nurses to spend months doing nursing assistant work has not been shown to help them become better nurses and might even set some bad habits.[36] Since the Francis Report there has been a rigorous study of nurse education in more than ten European countries. It shows patient mortality 7 per cent lower for every 10 per cent increase in the number of nurses with degrees.[37] Another study showed newly qualified nurses with degrees had the same levels of competence in fundamentals of care as diploma-level colleagues.[38]

Teaching is the most vivid example of the debate about the role of universities in training professionals. Teacher training colleges go back to the nineteenth century, many of them founded by particular Church denominations and training mainly women for their faith schools. Some were already attached to universities as training colleges, but Robbins devoted a chapter to the question of whether or not they should all become integral part of universities and looked forward to the day when they were. He saw this as part of a growing future role for universities in training other professions too: 'In recent years more and more professional bodies have been changing their requirements so as to give certain exemptions to candidates having degrees or other qualifications obtained in institutions of higher education. We have no doubt that this tendency will grow and we welcome it, not only in the interests of liberal education but also because nothing but good can come from a more intimate co-operation between professional bodies and institutions of higher education.'[39] But Robbins recommended against shifting teacher training into universities because he was concerned this would tilt the balance of the argument towards university policy being in the Department of Education, to which he was strongly opposed. Teacher training instead became a key role of the polytechnics, and so the teacher training colleges eventually gained university status in 1992 when the polytechnics did. There are still universities where the ethos of the old teacher training colleges has been transmuted into the mission of training for the public services. We should be proud of these admirable institutions. Yet these rather earnest places with their high-minded Victorian origins are now seen by their critics as hot-beds of dangerous progressivism. (My problem with them was rather different—at one point early in the Coalition we had two universities in what one might regard as special measures because of weak financial management. They had in common a role for the Church of England in appointing representatives to their governing body because they had been Anglican teacher training colleges.)

Within a few years of teacher training becoming a university function it had become a key target for the critics of declining education standards. The narrative was very clear. The last Conservative Government had reformed schools with grant maintained status but we had not reformed teacher training, which was the source of the 'Blob', the dangerous progressives who corrupted young trainee teachers before they had got into the classroom. Soft-headed liberals and ageing Marxists in university departments of education were diverting keen young trainees into the sociology of education. They were not providing useful training in classroom practice. Instead they focused on the structural barriers to personal educational advance. They trained teachers to think that their students could not progress without first overturning the oppressive class structure of society, when really trainee teachers should come out excited by the capacity of a good school to transform young people's lives whatever their background. This problem was increasingly not just attributed to the views of some academics but was seen as an inherent flaw of university-based teacher training. Michael Gove put the argument with typical panache in 2010: 'Teaching is a craft and it is best learnt as an apprentice observing a master craftsman or woman. Watching others, and being rigorously observed yourself as you develop, is the best route to acquiring mastery in the classroom.'[40] The argument was that teachers needed to be graduates who had mastered their subjects at university level, but mastering the craft of teaching was very different and should be classroom-based. Ironically this misses out one of the key features of an apprenticeship—time off for education—a point we will return to.

The craft narrative sounds compelling but the evidence is frustratingly inconclusive: it is surprisingly hard to measure and predict what makes a good teacher.[41] There has undoubtedly been poor-quality teacher training in university, but there is not much evidence of other forms of teacher training performing significantly better. Even quality of subject knowledge does not appear to matter that much. At one point the DfE said teachers should have a 2:1 degree or better, but they abandoned that partly because it did not appear to correlate with teaching quality—apart from in maths, where teachers who are particularly strong at maths do appear to teach it better. And conventional postgraduate teacher training to get your PGCE only takes nine months, with over half that time spent in a classroom setting. The remaining few months are barely sufficient to give a trainee teacher the rudiments of what we know about child development: the philosophy of education and its history have long since gone from most courses. So it is hard to see why those few months in a university should do quite as much damage as the critics claim. This is certainly an area where we need more innovation and experiment to find out what works.

Meanwhile the DfE ploughed ahead with School Direct, which aimed to put schools in charge of teacher training with universities being commissioned by schools to deliver specific educational programmes the school needed. Over the decades I have been involved in a range of attempts to create quasi-markets in public services and this was one of the most inept and ill-conceived of the lot. It cut across everything we were trying to do in higher education. It weakened student choice because, instead of choosing a university to go to for their PGCE, graduates had to choose a school, which in turn decided to which if any university they should send their trainees.[42]

It also deprived universities of their power over admissions as they just had to accept the students sent by schools who contracted with them. The schools collected a fixed payment for each student teacher they took on so they had a strong incentive to keep as much of that money for themselves as possible, and as they had no obligation to take on their trainees as permanent staff they did not have to worry much about the quality of what they produced. The DfE cut places allocated to universities and increased places allocated to schools to try to promote the non-university route. But young university graduates did not want to go down the school-based route, so these places remained empty whilst universities were heavily subscribed. This fed through particularly into a shortage of STEM teachers. And as university income for teacher training was shrinking, some universities were pulling out of provision altogether, reducing the options available to schools that were looking to get their teachers trained. It was a mess which made the teacher recruitment crisis worse.

There is a better way of delivering reform. First, recognize that young people want to choose the university where they do their PGCE. Then focus on the problem that too many starter teachers drop out and those that stay appear to plateau after five years or so, when they stop progressing. They should be able to do some kind of Master's course after they have had the experience of teaching. Our supply-side reforms in higher education make it possible for new providers of such Master's courses to come in and deliver them. That would be an opportunity to improve classroom practice. But they might also find that young teachers were getting more interested in the child psychology or how best to tackle potential extremism in a predominantly Muslim school. And bringing the rigour of higher education to these types of issues could really help these teachers.

Medical education

To challenge one's automatic assumptions about higher education you don't need to look to some far-off country: instead, just consider English medical training, a distinctive enclave within a sprawling empire. About 15 per cent of all undergraduate and postgraduate students are engaged in medicine and sub-jects allied to medicine—340,000 full-time and part-time students.[43] Medical schools bring prestige to a university: it was the common feature linking the members of the Russell Group when it was created. Research in the life sciences is one of the great strengths of British science. And for many of us our most important experience of the benefits of education is when we are treated by a doctor or nurse, applying what they have learnt at university. Put all this together and medical education matters. It is also very different from the rest of higher education with a much more significant role for the public sector. Until 2017 nurses used to get special bursaries whilst they were studying at university but now that has been replaced by the standard fees and loans model. The main recipient of high-cost subject funding is medicine, receiving about 40 per cent of the HEFCE funding for high-cost subjects—about £250m out of a total of about £660m for 2015–16.[44] Because there is so much public funding per medical student there have always been number controls which continued even as all other controls on the number of students were removed. Partly as a result, medicine is the most competitive of all courses: in 2016, there were twice as many applicants as places.[45] The practicalities of patient care mean that the academic model and the apprenticeship model are intertwined. Although medical schools do have distinctive characters there is no real hierarchy—they enjoy broadly equivalent status. So do medical students—there is no degree ranking, no Firsts or Seconds when they graduate.

The route taken by a medical student is different too. It is a very long training sustained by what is in effect a guarantee of a job in the NHS for a competent medical graduate. That job guarantee is one reason the NHS is always holding down the number of doctors it trains. The training comes in three stages, with first an undergraduate medical degree taking five years, then two years' foundation experience, and after that two years of specialized training leading to a certificate of clinical competence. By the end of medical training a lot will have been spent on educating and training a doctor—£560,000 of public money to educate a consultant, £80,000 of which is in repayable loans, but as a consultant goes on to earn up to £100,000 this can be repaid.[46]

With the public sector spending so much for so long on training a doctor there is a case for controlling the number of medical students who embark on such an expensive and arduous route. But as number controls have been removed from the rest of the system this leaves medical education looking even more unusual. We have the full panoply of manpower planning with Health Education England producing neat charts and tables stretching out into the future. So, for example, the intake target for 2013–14 was 6,071 medical students and 901 dental students, a cut from 6,195 previously planned. Indeed, I had to fight off attempts by the Department of Health to introduce more number controls over, for example, pharmacists when there clearly are alternative jobs available for people with those skills. There are other long and demanding vocational courses which operate without number controls or the assumption of a guaranteed job at the end—law and architecture, for example. And as there was free movement of labour across the EU, the attempt at British manpower planning did look like a doomed attempt at 'socialism in one country'—in fact, as these plans are generated locally with allocations by local population size, it looked more like socialism in one county. These number controls shape the medical profession. It means that the courses are heavily subscribed and you need solid A grades to have any kind of chance of getting in. Meanwhile the NHS saves money by not training enough doctors. The NHS is like a classic bad British employer always saving money by cutting back on training and depending on trained workers from abroad. Of 107,000 doctors working in the NHS in England, 70,000 qualified in the UK, 8,000 in the rest of the EU, and 28,000 outside the EEA.[47] Because of these restrictions on numbers the NHS ends up as a microcosm of British society as seen by UKIP. It has middle-class British-born doctors who are increasingly female, and brings in overseas doctors, but it has very few white working-class men or women doctors. 71 per cent of students accepted into medical school came from the top three socio-economic classes, while 15 per cent came from the lower four. 38 per cent of students accepted came from socio-economic class I, and only 2 per cent came from class VII.[48] This is despite an explicit statement that the medical workforce should be representative. This is nothing to do with fees but all to do with number controls, early specialization, and recruitment arrangements. The radicals want to tear up this extraordinary structure. They argue that medical pay is artificially inflated by these limits and would like to see more doctors in training to change the balance of power in medical pay negotiations. We have been an importer of doctors when we could be an exporter of training. And there are doubts about the quality and breadth of medical education too.

The lack of competition has led to the classic public sector problem of restricted access to very expensive medical courses. Now at last alternative private models are emerging, outside the number controls, showing medical education can be delivered at lower cost. Aston University and the University of Buckingham are both developing new medical schools outside conventional number controls. We could combine the HEFCE grant and placement fee (the medical Service Increment for Teaching or SIFT) into a single grant package per student to the institution. It could even be a voucher to a medical student. This would be a shift of some budget from the Department of Health to student support which would take some negotiating. As part of this one could give lower-cost support to a wider range of university medical education providers. Much of the current regulation is based on time served and is too rigid. Instead Sir David Greenaway recommended a four- to six-year training programme, after a Foundation Course, depending on specialism and progress.[49] And trainers say postgraduate training has become too bureaucratic, with box ticking and limited relationships between trainers and doctors in training. Trainee doctors are moved around the country from post to post with little say in the matter. It is possible that this deeply unsatisfactory postgraduate training experience is one reason for the radicalism of the junior doctors displayed during the dispute over their contract in 2016.[50] Trainee doctors need longer times in placement and a more apprenticeship-based relationship in this period. We also need more flexibility so that if a discipline changes the training can still be useful—it can take ten years to train someone, in which time disciplines change. Reforms along these lines have regularly been proposed in a series of reports from Sir John Tooke in 2008 to Sir David Greenaway in 2014.[51] The Council for Science and Technology also wrote a powerful letter to the Prime Minister about it in 2012.[52] But, as with teacher training, Whitehall Departments consistently fail to tackle manifest defects in the training for which they are ultimately responsible.

At the same time the NHS is missing out on the opportunity of earning extra revenues by training overseas doctors: this is because they only get a valid registration with the General Medical Council (GMC) as a trainee doctor after they have practised in the NHS for a year and this limits the capacity of the system. Currently medical schools are limited to only recruiting up to 7.5 per cent of their intake target internationally, which works out at around 500 per year (and with a 5 per cent limit for dental schools). Instead registration should be brought forward by a year and aligned with graduation so that overseas medical students do not need limited foundation year places. However, the British Medical Association (BMA) has opposed the removal of the 7.5 per cent cap and an attempt by the Coalition to reform it was stymied. It is, however, back on the agenda.

The current restrictions are so tight and do such damage to the supply of doctors that new alternative private provision is beginning to appear outside the publicly funded and controlled medical schools. The current model is both too restrictive and too expensive: it cannot be sustained. The future is for more of medical education to be funded via the established mechanisms of loans and graduate repayment, together with a significant improvement in the quality of postgraduate training and an easing of number controls. The Government responded with an important first step to liberalize the system. In October 2016 Jeremy Hunt announced plans to expand the cap on numbers of medical students by 1,500 a year (it's currently a little over 6,000 a year). To ensure that the value of this publicly funded training was not lost to the UK he also proposed to put in place a requirement that doctors trained by NHS England remain in the UK and work here for four years. The BMA welcomed the expansion but said it would do little and take too long to have an impact on current doctor shortages.

Entrepreneurship and business schools

So we have seen that the public sector does not do a very good job of harnessing universities to provide the highly qualified staff they need. The structures for both teacher training and for medical training need reform so that they better meet the needs of young people. In particular the recent clumsy systems for allocating teaching trainees and medical postgraduates show insufficient respect to these new recruits to important professions. Perhaps universities do better when it comes to business? Business studies should be an example of how universities can bring intellectual rigour to a modern vocational subject. Almost every English university now has a business school: there are 136 and they have about a fifth of the student population, around 80,000 per year. They might be expected to focus on training people in business skills and advancing knowledge relevant to business. But if academics want promotion and the business schools want funding and prestige they need to do highly ranked research. This means research published in the most prestigious journals, which in turn tend to be based in America. You get into these by developing innovative research techniques, and these are often best deployed on large data-sets which are probably American and are often historic. So using novel statistical techniques to analyse a big American business sector is how to get on in an academic career. That can take the academic staff at the business school some way from the needs of their local engineering firms. But it is a rational response to the incentives created by the system of promotion reinforced by the Research Excellence Framework (REF). The rankings compound the problem because the prestige and status of being a 'good' university goes to the institutions which follow these incentives. A university taking students with lower A level grades, educating them well in its business school, and working closely with local firms successfully to train them as effective managers would conventionally be placed by a newspaper columnist or a politician low down the rankings and dismissed as a 'bad' university, whereas the 'good' one they wanted their own children to go to would have a business school producing novel research for elite journals on how electrification changed the structure of the American steel industry in the early twentieth century.

Business schools face another problem, however—academicism in universities is matched by anti-intellectualism in business. There is a belief in the special gifts of the self-made entrepreneur unencumbered by excessive education. The university and its graduates are seen not as a driver of enterprise but an enemy of it. The entrepreneur is supposed to live on his or her wits, having built up a business after selling stuff from a barrow aged 15. That is why a Conservative minister advised, 'Young people should think about starting their own business instead of university.'[53] Or, as Premier Berlusconi of Italy put it: 'Why do we need to pay scientists when we make the best shoes in the world?'[54] But the evidence, mainly from the US, is that the more educated you are the more likely you are to set up a business. When as ministers in BIS we looked at Britain's deep-seated economic problems, from exports to innovation to productivity, it was clear that the businesses which lagged behind the international competition were the ones which had low numbers of graduates. A study of America's high-growth businesses showed 95 per cent of their employees were graduates and 45 per cent had advanced degrees.[55] Even in Silicon Valley there is the seductive myth of the garage start-up when actually the new company is more likely to trace its origins to a doctoral research project. You can visit Dave Packard's garage at 367 Addison Avenue, Palo Alto where Hewlett Packard's first product, an audio oscillator, was manufactured in 1939. It is celebrated as the origin of Silicon Valley but it can actually be traced back to Hewlett's earlier Master's thesis at Stanford University.[56]

There are, however, two important qualifications which may help explain the anti-intellectual folk wisdom. First, people who have very little education do appear to be more likely to set up as self-employed than those with some education. Perhaps they have lower chances of getting into a conventional career and necessity drives them. It looks as if entrepreneurship is concentrated at the two extremes—the ill-educated and the highly educated. One researcher summarized the evidence: 'there is a U-shaped relationship between entrepreneurship and ability: Self-employment rates are highest for people with relatively high or low levels of education, and lower for people with intermediate levels of education.'[57] Figure 8 shows the phenomenon in the US.

Secondly, there is a high correlation between entrepreneurship and dyslexia, and dyslexia in turn is a barrier to conventional educational achievement. Behind the anecdotes of dyslexic entrepreneurs like Sir Richard Branson there is a real and rather intriguing phenomenon. One survey of entrepreneurs found that 35 per cent identified themselves as dyslexic. It looks as if the skills you develop to deal with dyslexia are great training for entrepreneurship: 'One reason that dyslexics are drawn to entrepreneurship is that strategies they have used since childhood to offset their weaknesses in written communication and organizational ability—identifying trustworthy people and handing over major responsibilities to them—can be applied to businesses.' Dyslexics

Figure 8. Who becomes an entrepreneur?

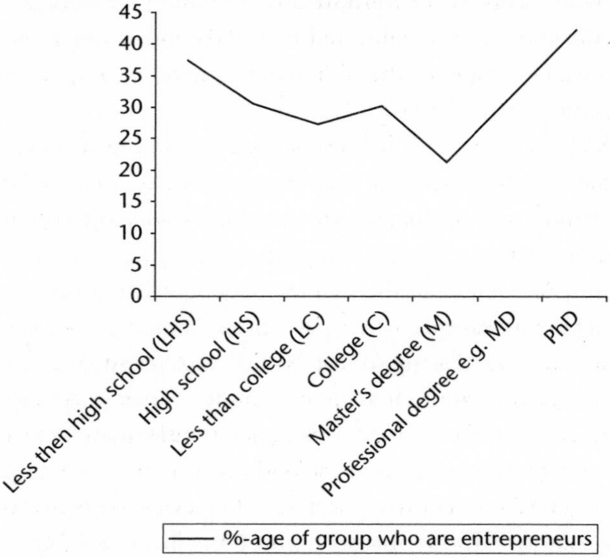

──── %-age of group who are entrepreneurs

are 'more likely than non-dyslexics to delegate authority and to excel in oral communication and problem solving and were twice as likely to own two or more businesses'.[58] Dyslexia is a real barrier to completing a university education. Indeed, it may first be diagnosed at university because of the sheer volume of the reading and writing and the extended vocabulary required—one estimate is that a student needs to grasp 800 new words in her first year at university.[59] It is harder to get away with the usual evasion strategies than at school. (One study suggested that 40 per cent of dyslexia cases are first diagnosed at university. This, incidentally, is more evidence that university is a real educational experience.) It suggests one way universities could become more business friendly would be by providing more support for dyslexic students.

After that initial blip of the least educated being self-employed, thereafter the more educated you are the more likely you are to set up a company. Increasing numbers of students want to set up and run their own businesses.[60] There are ways we can make this easier for them. At the moment an entrepreneur needs not just a distinctive set of skills but a great business idea too. They may not have that as well. This is where an excellent charity, the Alacrity Foundation, comes in. They talk to bigger businesses about the gaps in the services or products they are receiving to identify possible business ideas, which they then provide to student entrepreneurs. There are worthwhile initiatives helping students start up their first companies with, for example, competition for start-up loans. This whole third stream of funding for student start-ups and enterprise education is now allocated to UKRI and is not under the Office for Students—an example of the difficulties of dividing responsibilities neatly between teaching and research.

Graduates also possess the qualities needed to run big successful businesses. And again there is clear evidence that education helps. One of Britain's problems is the weakness of our management, which is linked to the relatively low education level of our managers. Companies with graduates are far more likely to be exporters. As a report by the London School of Economics and McKinsey put it: 'Governments can play their part in encouraging the take-up of good management behaviour. Doing so may be the single most cost-effective way of improving the performance of their economies... better educated managers will be a key component of the performance transformation that both established and emerging economies must undertake if they are to maintain and improve their global competitive position.'[61] The evidence is that our managers are less well educated than in many of our competitors, as Table 9.1 shows.

Small and medium sized businesses do seem to find it difficult to recruit graduates, however. This may be because of the way the milk round works. It is well-designed for big companies who can go from university to university. It is less well suited to a small business looking to recruit one or two staff. We need more imaginative ways of linking universities and local employers. One of these mechanisms is the innovation voucher. This puts some money directly in the hands of a small business for them to spend at a local university on a problem

Table 9.1. Average share of managers with degrees

	Percentage of managers with degrees
UK	43
Sweden	46
Italy	51
France	60
US	60
Germany	65
Japan	70

Source: Nick Bloom, Stephen Dorgan, John Dowdy, and John Van Reenen, *Management Practice and Productivity: Why they Matter*, McKinsey and LSE report (July 2007), 10.

they face. They may need to use a powerful computer for some specific modelling. Perhaps there is an expensive piece of equipment they need for one specific operation which it would never be economic to buy outright. They may want to research a new overseas market. The innovation voucher is a reason for them to step over the threshold into their local university.

Apprenticeships and higher education

There is a widespread belief in the value of apprenticeships as an alternative to going to university and the best way to tackle the problem of training people who are not academic. We think we know what we mean by an apprenticeship. We mean an older experienced guy with a pencil behind his ear and a biro clipped in the breast pocket of one of those brown coats which Ronnie Barker wears in the 'Four Candles' sketch, passing on his craft skills to youngsters in a factory making something useful. I do not mock—it is part of my own family history. There are still a few real live examples and they do work. I have seen tattooed, skinheaded 17-year-olds who are not going to sit behind a desk and concentrate on a geometry lesson but who are working out how to calculate lengths and angles because they are physically assembling the rafters to make a roof. That was the educational part of an apprenticeship course delivered at a further education college, the Cinderella of post-16 education. Apprenticeships thrived in big stable companies often linked to local colleges. Cohesive small business sectors can also sponsor them through Group Training Associations. The trade you master is then supposed to be with you for life. It gives you security and the means of keeping a family.

Traditionally you used to leave home to go and live with a master as his apprentice to learn his trade. You might then move from job to job on various short-term contracts as a journeyman until you set up and became a master in your own right. This feature of the apprenticeship, the managed transition to adulthood, has been taken over by the experience of travelling away to university. Indeed, a traditional Oxbridge MA, secured several years after graduating, which baffles graduates now because it requires no extra study, is a vestigial trace of the origins of the Oxbridge model as an apprenticeship to a corporation, followed by time away, after which you become a master. There are still a few residential apprenticeships, and as new national centres for specific skills are created there is a new need for them. That move away from home is important in enhancing their status.

When politicians talk about creating millions of apprenticeships they are appealing to a picture of this kind of world of big stable employers and well-established trades. But it is a world we have largely lost. And we lost it in the 1980s when we took a decisive route to a far more flexible labour market and saw apprenticeships as a barrier to that. They tied people to particular industries and trades, leaving them vulnerable to structural changes in industry. I remember the meetings in Downing Street when we said they aren't really unemployed miners or unemployed steelworkers; they are unemployed ex-miners and ex-steelworkers. But those workers were understandably proud of their skills and their traditions and reluctant to move on. It is called the problem of stranded skills, and apprenticeships leave people vulnerable to it. That is why economies with liberal labour markets such as the US and the UK tend to have fewer apprenticeships and more graduates, ensuring greater flexibility during their working lives.

Apprenticeships survive in Germany because access to many more jobs depends on securing a licence to practise, which means that you have to complete an apprenticeship training before you can do a job. At the same time these industries are sustained by Government intervention, including through influencing global technical standards to support them. They are also protected from takeover by family shareholdings and holding by subsidized regional banks which have been largely left untouched by the Single Market. Germany has ended up as a Western economy with an unusually high proportion of GDP coming from manufacturing (23 per cent as against 12 per cent in the US and 11 per cent in the UK and France).[62] This model also operates with an unusually low number of university graduates—30 per cent of 25–34 year olds as against 45 per cent in France, 47 per cent in the US, and 49 per cent in the UK.[63] That is the German model and it works for them: I admire them for it. But it is an outlier: in fact it is more of an outlier than we are. It is very different from most other Western countries and a world apart from Anglo-Saxon capitalism in the US and the UK with its more flexible labour markets. The German model relies on protections for jobs and industries which would not be acceptable in Britain any more—and indeed which we never succeeded in making work even when we were trying to emulate the Germans.

There are some excellent apprenticeships, but apprenticeships of that quality are never going to come back as a large-scale alternative to higher education because there are not enough big employers in stable industries. Their historic origins in time served mean they do not always yield nationally recognized qualifications. Work-based learning is not easily accredited by colleges and

Table 9.2. Average lifetime earnings and annual earnings for different types of qualifications

Qualification	Average lifetime earnings	Annual earnings
Oxbridge degree:	£1.8m	£46,000
Russell Group degree:	£1.6m	£41,000
Non-Russell Group degree:	£1.4m	£36,000
Higher apprenticeship—Level 5:	£1.4m	£34,000
Advanced apprenticeship—Level 3:	£1m	£23,000
A levels:	£970k	£23,000
No qualifications:	£700k	£16,000

Source: Dr Philip Kirby, *Levels of Success: The Potential of UK Apprenticeships*, Sutton Trust (October 2015), 14–15.

universities. Some of it is a nostalgic appeal for a return to regulated labour markets and industries which have largely disappeared—it is the acceptable way of saying we want to be a different type of country with a different type of labour market and a different industrial structure. If we are to have more apprenticeships we need a very different approach. One way to encourage more young people into apprenticeships would be to recruit them as they leave university. As well as all the advantages of university education there is another feature which appeals to employers—the recruitment process is easier when there are big agglomerations of young people. Their major complaint about university graduates is that they do not always have enough practical job experience, and recruiting them on to apprenticeships helps tackle that problem. Universities themselves are now being encouraged to deliver higher-level apprenticeships where the educational element is of university level. This is an excellent initiative, but so far only 5 per cent of all apprenticeships are at this level.[64] These high-level apprenticeships do provide a substantial premium in the labour market, unlike most apprenticeships. Indeed, there is a strong correlation between educational level and earnings as Table 9.2 shows, so it is only those apprenticeships which approach the educational level of a degree which command a high premium in the labour market.

The case for universities having the option of buying their own student loans

With more and more young people going to university, the focus of attention rightly has to be on improving their employability still further. We saw earlier how the incentives for young people to go to university are stronger than the incentives for universities to focus on making them highly employable—instead universities focus on research. We need more powerful incentives for universities to focus on their students' employability. Here is a specific proposal which would do just that.

As more students at English universities take out student loans, the Government is looking to sell this growing asset to reduce its debt. This reduces Government debt because of the way student loans are treated in the National Accounts. Assume the Government has to borrow money now to make the loans to students. This is not regarded as adding to the flow of net public borrowing as it is matched by an obligation on the graduate to repay the loan. (And, for the same reason, it does not count as public spending, as we saw in Chapter Three.) However, it does add to the stock of net Government debt because the asset which the Government acquires, the loan, is not regarded as sufficiently liquid to count as a financial asset to balance the extra Government debt to finance the student loans. The money raised by selling student loans raises cash, a new financial asset which therefore reduces net Government debt.[65]

Successive Governments, which have the aim of reducing their net debt, have therefore looked at selling the student loan book, starting with older loans from the Blair Government. This is currently seen as just a financial transaction, though at one point the Coalition did say the proceeds would pay for the increase in student numbers. But it becomes much more than financial engineering if it gives universities the opportunity to buy and become owners of their own graduate debt. It completes the circle of our reforms because a university which improves the prospects of its graduates gets an improvement in its returns through greater debt repayments. It would actually be most exciting for some of the universities with high RAB charges because their graduates earn less and so repay less of their loans. They would have the biggest incentive to track their graduates down and offer them continuing assistance with getting better-paid jobs. The impact is much greater with our larger post-Browne loans where the potential increase in the amount of debt to be repaid is greater. It would not, of course, be compulsory. However, some universities would be seriously interested in taking up the option. For the first time they would have a real financial incentive to raise their game because they would get more repayments on their debt. It could also enhance university autonomy if they had this solid stream of income.

There are objections to the idea. First, our universities are very diverse and some have poorer employment outcomes and lower graduate repayments.

This may not mean they are bad universities—they might be taking students from more disadvantaged backgrounds with weaker entry qualifications. Would universities just want to recruit the type of students who go into well-paid jobs? English education is already bedevilled with selection effects which make it hard to judge where there really is excellent performance, and the last thing we should do is intensify the incentives for such behaviour. But my proposal addresses this problem because the market value of the outstanding loans when the universities buy them will vary according to these factors. The type of students the university has recruited and their graduate incomes will be reflected in the price the university pays for the debt of its graduates. Oxbridge graduates might be expected to pay back most of their debt, so if those universities want to buy £100m of graduate debt they probably have to pay close to the full face value of £100m. But if you are a university with less advantaged students and with lower graduate earnings the cost for that university of buying its debt would be much lower. Such a university might find it could buy £100m of its graduate debt for, say, £50m, and if it really put an effort into boosting the earnings of its graduates it could perhaps gain an extra £25m and recover £75m. Its potential gains would be greater than for universities whose graduates already do well. If a university changes strategy for the future and stops recruiting future theologians and instead recruits prospective lawyers, that does nothing to improve the repayment of the debt it has already bought, and when it comes to buying that new debt in future it will find it is paying the price of law graduate debt, which could well be higher. Graduate debt becomes a ready-made social impact bond with higher returns to universities the more they improve graduate job performance. It would be not just an asset sale—however useful—but a real improvement to our education system as well.

The second concern is whether universities have strong enough balance sheets to take on this amount of risk. A university with 10,000 undergraduates will now be accumulating over £100m of extra student loans each year, which would soon dwarf all their other assets. But it would be possible for a bank to take on the asset and then offer the university a share in the gains if their graduates perform better in the jobs market. Another possibility would be to set aside a proportion of the graduate debt for universities to obtain at a discount to the market price if they wished, sharing their extra revenues with Government if graduate earnings were indeed boosted.

When I looked at this idea in government I concluded it was not deliverable at the time. It was frustrating, but the IT systems of the HMRC and the Student

Loans Company could not cope yet—but they should be able to do so in future. And the size of the graduate debt was so small that there was not a big incentive for universities to gain from an improved employment performance by their graduates. There was another obstacle too—the need for universities to get information about their graduates from the Student Loans Company.

They say in the US that if Osama bin Laden had been a graduate of Harvard Business School the Americans would have found him within twenty-four hours. That witticism conveys the energy American universities put into keeping in touch with their graduates. By contrast this is how David Lodge describes our system: 'Under the British system, competition begins and ends much earlier. Four times, under our educational rules, the human pack is shuffled and cut—at eleven-plus, sixteen plus, eighteen plus and twenty plus—and happy is he who comes top of the deck on each occasion, but especially the last. This is called Finals, the very name of which implies that nothing of importance can happen after it.'[66] It captures the traditional attitude of universities to their graduates. It is reinforced by regulatory barriers which we should remove. At the moment the Student Loans Company is not permitted to communicate with universities about their own graduates. The law would have to be amended so that universities could get basic information about their graduates' names, addresses, and perhaps employment, provided the graduate consented. Universities could then track the performance of their graduates and see far more clearly what routes they take and where they end up. Removing this barrier to communication between a university and its graduates would strengthen the connection between universities and their graduates, which is currently far too weak. It would make it possible, for example, for universities to approach graduates when their repayments were about to end, asking them if they would like to carry on voluntarily funding their university—a nudge policy. The Student Loan Company does not do this, and would be condemned if it tried to, but if a university invited its graduates to carry on contributing that might be more acceptable. Graduates who go abroad might be more likely to keep in touch with their university than with the Student Loans Company.

I believe one of the biggest transformations of the way universities function in the future will be for universities to do much more to sustain their graduates after they leave than they do now. It would not just be conventional alumni relations, which are far more professional than they were a decade ago. Instead universities might offer refresher courses. They would want to monitor if a graduate was unemployed or poorly paid and if so they would have a reason to offer them a bit more training or careers guidance to boost their prospects. They might want particularly to help groups such as women returners after time out with young children, where there is still a potential hit to long-term earnings which can be addressed by help with, for example, new software or updating on new regulations affecting their profession. The university would at last be doing more to nurture its graduates and to live up to the wonderful image of what an alma mater should be.

TEN

Driver of Innovation

Scholasticism, utilitarianism, and the usefulness of useless knowledge

We saw in Chapter Four that the UK can be proud of the quality of the research conducted in its universities. But we need to be clear what this success is. Success means relentless pressure on academics to produce papers that are going to be assessed by fellow academics as of the highest quality and frequently cited. For most academics today that means getting published in the most prestigious peer-reviewed journals which is what matters for promotion, even though the assessment of their research excellence in the REF is supposed to be independent of the status of the journal in which their work appears. That drives competition in research performance whose logic is as obvious as rewarding a football team for scoring goals. The sure way for a university to move up the rankings and boost its prestige is to promote or hire hot-shot academics with strong publishing records. In science as in football we run the most open and most competitive league in the world—and hope to continue to do so even outside the EU. It has projected our universities high up the rankings, alongside the US. (There is one important difference from football—under the rules of the REF, academics could take their publications with them when they moved. It as if when you buy a star striker you get the goals he scored in the previous season as well. The logic is that it is part of their personal research performance that is being assessed. It has driven up the pay of the academic stars but also provided opportunities to younger post-docs after they get something published. Nicholas Stern's review of the REF in 2016 proposed that such portability should end.[1])

The high rankings of our research-intensive universities are a real achievement. But that is not the same as having the best national R&D system or contributing to tackling big global challenges or successfully commercializing new technologies or making a region a lively innovation cluster. We might hope that our research strengths contribute to these wider goals. But we may have been forced to make trade-offs to achieve research excellence which can actually make it harder to achieve other objectives. A great Formula One racing car is not good for rally-driving; a fine thoroughbred cannot do the work of a carthorse. The very features of the system which give us our excellent academic performance might weaken our performance in other ways. Researchers, for example, stake their claim to having discovered new knowledge by making it openly available—a powerful incentive for the production of this public good.[2] The race to publish findings in peer-reviewed journal means that academics are not thinking that there is something in their discovery which is commercially valuable and should be kept confidential for a while until they have protected the IP (Intellectual Property). Academics may regard a five-year stint in a company R&D lab without publishing anything as professional death, and indeed doctoral projects with industrial collaboration tend to result in fewer journal publications. Promotion that depends on research performance may not reward success in commercialization.[3] America's advantage is that it is so big and operating at the frontier of new knowledge in so many fields that it has a reasonable chance of capturing the gains from the new knowledge it generates. It is harder for a medium-sized economy like Britain's to be so confident. Graphene was discovered in Manchester, but the big companies which might use it are mostly in Asia. At least we may hope to be the European R&D centre for understanding it. For us the stronger argument may be that it is only operating at the intellectual frontier that enables us to absorb new ideas and technologies from elsewhere.

There is also a risk that the most reliable way to keep on getting highly cited papers is to work within an established line of research rather than take the risk of embarking on a completely new one which might prove to be a cul-de-sac. Then one starts to see the classic weakness of academic research, which is scholasticism—looking inwards not outwards. Sydney Smith was caustic on the decline of Oxbridge into scholasticism before the great Victorian reforms. In a powerful essay in the *Edinburgh Review* he asked to whom Oxford would give the epithets of scholar and learned man:

> Are they given to men acquainted with the science of government? Thoroughly masters of the geographical and commercial relations of Europe? To men who know the properties of bodies and their action upon each other? No; this is not learning; it is chemistry, or political economy—not learning...the epithet of scholar is reserved for him who writes on the Aeolic reduplication and is familiar

with Sylburgius.... His object is not to reason, to imagine, or to invent; but to conjugate, decline and derive.... Would he ever dream that such men as Adam Smith and Lavoisier were equal in dignity or understanding to, or of the same utility as, Bentley and Heyne?[4]

Sydney Smith's essay was vigorously attacked by Newman in *The Idea of a University*, who argued that Smith and Oxford's other critics were trying to reduce the pursuit of knowledge to mere utility—though that was his stock criticism of just about everyone he disagreed with, and it is still deployed against any argument which appeals to the consequences of something.[5] Kingsley Amis provides a mordant critique of modern scholasticism, drawing on his experience as a junior lecturer in English at Swansea. In *Lucky Jim* he gives Jim Dixon a research project on the 'strangely neglected topic' of *The Economic Influence of the Developments in English Shipbuilding Techniques, 1450 to 1485*. 'It was a perfect title in that it crystallised the article's niggling mindlessness, its funereal parade of yawn-enforcing facts, the pseudo-light it threw upon non-problems...'. Tudor maritime history was the speciality of the history professor at Swansea in Amis's time, so there is a personal edge to the satire.[6]

Universities can end up trapped between the twin perils of scholasticism and utilitarianism. Outsiders accuse them of ivory-tower scholasticism and press for their work to be relevant and useful. But academics may resent pressure to place impact and immediate utility above the advancement of knowledge through curiosity-driven research. They may fear that focusing on short-term relevance may sacrifice long-term advance: I remember a Professor of Geology regretting the pressure on his doctoral students to research topics directly relevant to the North Sea Oil industry at the expense of investing in greater fundamental understanding at the start of their careers. There is an undercurrent of anxiety from some university academics that ministers do not back blue skies curiosity-driven research. But I did not complain, nor did my Coalition colleagues, that if only we could stop university academics putting so much effort into researching sub-atomic particles or the decline of the Holy Roman Empire then instead they could focus on designing a better widget.

There are classic replies to this challenge to be more immediately relevant. Faced with a group of sceptical American Congressmen, John Bahcall, the American astrophysicist, made the case for the Hubble telescope boldly: 'I believe that the most important discoveries will provide answers to questions that we do not yet know how to ask and will concern objects that we cannot yet imagine.'[7] Moreover, even the most recherché blue skies research can be justified on utilitarian grounds, if that is what you care about, provided you

allow long enough. Martin Rees quotes Babbage: 'in mathematical science...
truths which are at one period the most abstract, and apparently the most
remote from all useful application, become in the next age the bases of profound physical inquiries, and in the succeeding one...furnish their ready and
daily aid to the artist and the sailor...'.[8] Discoveries which add to the body of
scientific knowledge may well have practical benefits out in the future but we
cannot know in advance what they will be. Nobel Prize winner Robert Aumann
published a paper in 1955 on the asphericity of alternating knots. I attended an
event with him when he explained that he had tackled this puzzle out of pure
intellectual curiosity and was perversely proud that he had managed to do a piece
of research of no practical use whatever. However, decades later, his grandson
phoned him from university to say that they were using that maths in modelling DNA. Professor Aumann had tried his absolute best to come up with
research of no practical significance but had failed. It is a vivid example of what
Abraham Flexner pithily called the 'The Usefulness of Useless Knowledge'.[9]

It is hard to define what constitutes blue skies research. It can mean curiosity-
driven research. That in turn can be taken as Research Council funding made
available to scientists in responsive mode—the researcher comes up with the
idea and applies for funding—as distinct from challenge-led research where the
funding agency identifies the issue. But each step of this argument is tenuous.
Funding shaped around big national or global priorities may itself promote
fundamental 'blue skies' research. Research can be both a quest for fundamental
understanding and directly prompted by a real human need. Donald Stokes has
defined research along two axes—one is whether or not there is a quest for
fundamental understanding and the other is whether it is driven by considerations
of usefulness. Research which is both a quest for fundamental understanding
and inspired by its potential use is placed in what Donald Stokes calls Pasteur's
Quadrant, named after Louis Pasteur's fundamental research in microbiology
that yielded vaccination.[10] Francis Narin's important work, drawing on Eugene
Garfield before him, has shown that research which is more highly cited by
academics is also more likely to be cited in patent applications, and in turn the
patents which cite important fundamental research have more commercial
value and significance.[11] Indeed, by a neat irony the very work which Eugene
Garfield, Francis Narin, and others did in developing indices to measure citations
and to weight them was in turn used by Larry Page and Sergey Brin to create
Google's PageRank. The intellectual origin of Google in citation rankings of
research papers is itself a vivid example of the powerful but unanticipated consequences of research projects.[12]

These satisfying reconciliations of apparently conflicting types of enquiry in Pasteur's Quadrant were confirmed in my own practical experience. I opened a sophisticated new wind tunnel at Imperial College which had been funded by the Engineering and Physical Sciences Research Council. There were three distinct accounts of what it was doing. First, it was collecting more readings of the actual flow of air than previously possible and using powerful new software to analyse the information—so it was a big data project. Secondly, turbulence was described by Richard Feynman as 'the most important unresolved question of classical physics', so the project was of value to physicists trying to improve their theoretical model of turbulence. Thirdly, the aerospace and automotive industries were going to use it for designing better engines and wings for planes and more aerodynamic cars and it is hard to do this without a better understanding of turbulence. These three complementary accounts show how theory and practice, science and technology, curiosity and use are often intermingled.

These tensions are particularly vivid in the humanities, where there is perhaps the greatest anxiety about threats from a preoccupation with usefulness. These disciplines in particular wish to assert the inherent value of what they do. That of course is true, though it is also true of other disciplines. Moreover work in the humanities may change the world, and may be aiming to do so. The Western novel does not just reflect our sensibilities, it changes them. And as soon as you start trying to apply science through technology it becomes essential to understand human behaviour—the driverless car is not just a technological challenge but also raises difficult and deep ethical questions about who is responsible for what and they need to be addressed to construct an effective legal and regulatory regime. The humanities are of enormous public value and can embrace that without sacrificing their claims to be inherently worthwhile.[13]

The need for publicly funded R&D
outside the science budget

There are pressures in the British system working against applied research. It just seems obvious that you should only fund the best research—just as obvious as that a 'top' university must be best. But actually there is a complete ecosystem here, and higher education can no more just comprise the elite than the army can just comprise the SAS. We devote a higher proportion of our total research spend to the very highest performers than most other systems, as we saw in

Chapter Four. During my time as minister we went further in that direction and decided the REF should only fund three-star or four-star research.[14] We did it under public spending pressures, but it was pushing the star system too far and narrowed the type of research which was rewarded as a result.

Imagine that an academic has produced a good solid assessment of welfare to work policies in Scotland or an analysis of some important properties of an alloy or updated estimates of fish stocks in the North Sea. The academic uses state of the art analytical methods but does not actually push the boundaries and develop new ways of reaching his or her results. The researcher draws on current economic theory or materials science in analysing these effects but does not propose any innovative new theory. That research is unlikely to be published in one of the leading journals and unlikely to get one of the highest scores in the REF. But it is really rather useful. However, if a researcher had historic data from Jimmy Carter's welfare to work initiatives (using America's bigger data set because it lends itself to more advanced statistical techniques) and analysed them in a novel way it might have been ranked higher because it would have been more 'innovative'.

I remember talking to a group of business leaders about the universities they dealt with. They were in awe of our leading research universities, but sometimes they did not want novelty and brilliance: instead they were after good reliable use of existing knowledge, but they felt that was not enough to command the attention of an academic at one of our most prestigious universities. One businessman ruefully observed that he just could not get our top university researchers interested in the viscosity of hair shampoo so instead he had gone to a less prestigious university, which had got stuck into the project with gusto. (By contrast in the US MIT research is behind the success of Jennifer Aniston's hair care company Living Proof, and indeed one of the products is named Perfect hair Day or PhD as a tribute to the research on which it rests.[15]) Another academic, who was doing cutting-edge research, told me that she relied on a really competent computer scientist who wrote the software for her experiments and was acknowledged as a co-author, but his computer science department did not score many stars so the university was tempted to close it down as it did not generate public funding through the REF—but if they did so her own work would suffer. It would be like raising a cricket team's batting average by removing the wicket-keeper because he wasn't good at batting. That is why the university group Million Plus argues: 'Currently much of the government's funding is allocated to research that is judged to be excellent and of world leading or international significance. This means that there is much research which is judged to be excellent but of regional or national significance that misses out on government funding. This does not create a balanced base of research funding.'[16] It might be that an excellent eco-system is not quite the same as every individual scoring a world-class ranking.

Academics who are not getting research grants from Government are more likely to describe their research as applied compared to those who are grant recipients (46 per cent to 29 per cent), which is presumably the result of a delib-erate policy of publicly funding the research which scores most highly on these academic criteria of pushing out the boundaries of a discipline.[17] An economist based at a local university who studies the regional economy is not a bad economist, and indeed may be a real local asset, but there is virtually nothing in the British model of funding university research which recognizes this.

Nicholas Stern's Review of the REF proposed that all researchers on a university staff should be submitted to the REF.[18] This seriously exacerbates the problem because it means that all university researchers would have to be subject to assessment under the REF criteria. But some research staff of the university may be receiving funding from other sources to do useful applied work—it does not need to be assessed for the REF. At best submitting is a waste of everyone's time; at worst it will further narrow our idea of what is 'good' research, rather like what has happened to our idea of a 'good' university. Occasionally one sees why the modern university could be seen as the agent of a destructive kind of globalization because useful research into local cultural or economic issues is not rated and all that counts is the kind of research needed to get into the leading, usually American, journals which count in the citation scores. That may not be an issue in particle physics but it may be in many other disciplines.

One way for the UK to offset this problem is to ensure there are ways of publicly funding research for a specific practical purpose outside the pure Haldane principle. The science budget is protected by the Haldane Principle that ministers do not decide on specific research projects, but the principle need not apply fully to departmental budgets. They could fund research that is useful to them with departmental science advisers maintaining scientific standards. That brings us to one of the most acute problems in British research policy—funding research outside the science budget. Out of all the official reports on science and research since the war the most striking and penetrating was produced by Victor Rothschild in 1971 for the then Secretary of State for Education and Science, Margaret Thatcher.[19] It got to the heart of the issue of the pressure on the science budget to yield practical results and proposed a kind of dual system. On the one hand there would be a science budget focused on blue skies research and academic excellence and protected behind the bulwarks of the Haldane Principle. But this on its own was not enough. Governments needed to be able to commission applied research to meet public requirements and objectives:

> However distinguished, intelligent and practical scientists may be, they cannot be so well qualified to decide what the needs of the nation are, and their priorities, as those responsible for ensuring that those needs are met. This is why applied R & D must have a customer.... Basic, fundamental or pure research, called basic research in this report, has no analogous customer–contractor basis...[20]

Whitehall Departments were those customers and they should have budgets which they could spend on the applied research they needed. This was very much the model Haldane had envisaged in his original report back in 1918. He too had proposed that, separate from a general science budget, Departments should become contractors, buying the research that was needed for their priorities. They might even use the funds to run their own research institutes. Rothschild proposed that these substantial departmental R&D budgets would be financed by a transfer to them of significant funds from the science budget.[21]

Rothschild's model has its limitations. It fails to recognize that the interplay between theory and application often drives the most creative research—theoretical advances may improve our capacity for practical problem-solving and the need to solve practical problems may drive advances in underlying theory. Nor does he recognize the importance scientific advice to ministers: he is focused on Departments sponsoring key sectors such as agriculture. But, despite these flaws, it remains the case that British research would benefit from greater diversity of public funding, with Whitehall Departments directly contracting for research projects and maintaining research institutes to help tackle the problems they are concerned about. So DEFRA (the Department of the Environment, Food and Rural Affairs) should fund that research on North Sea fish stocks and the DWP (the Department for Work and Pensions) the Scottish welfare to work study which I referred to earlier. Departments behave, however, like the worst of British industry, always cutting the R&D budget, so after an initial transfer of science funding to Departments they then failed to deliver Rothschild's model. Departmental funding for research and research institutes dried up whereas the block funding to universities for research out of the science budget carried on. During the 2010 spending review I wrote, together with the then Chief Scientist, asking Departments not to cut their R&D spend without letting us know. But it was like trying to get attention with a polite cough during a brutal fist fight. We have ended up with only two significant departmental R&D budgets—in Defence and Health. This is a crucial gap in Britain's public support for applied R&D. The Department for Education should be funding substantial social science research on social mobility and the Department with responsibility for energy policy should be funding applied nuclear research. Instead the Research Councils find themselves expected to plug these gaps, which can be at the expense of more profound long-term research. It is not just that the money is tight: contracting with Government is not easy, with slow decision-taking, very long documents, unlimited warranty and liability clauses.[22]

There is a further twist to the story. The Secretary of State for Education and Science who received Rothschild's report in 1971 was Margaret Thatcher. When she came to office as Prime Minister at the end of the decade she drew on Rothschild's distinction between pure and applied research. But this time round her interpretation of his model had shifted: the customers who were supposed to be purchasing the applied research were businesses. The job of Government was limited to funding the pure research. She puts it very clearly in her memoir:

> It was only years later, when I was Prime Minister, that I was able to formulate my own answer to the problem, which was that Government should concentrate on funding basic science and leave its application and development to the private sector. But I already felt deeply uneasy about any policy that threatened to starve pure science of funds.[23]

So the network of public sector research establishments which had survived to the 1980s were regarded as 'near market' and therefore to be cut or privatized.

Rothschild himself had been the head of the Agricultural Research Council for a decade so one can understand why he envisaged the Ministry of Agriculture promoting research of direct use to British farmers. But it is a case study of what has gone wrong since his report. The Agricultural Research Service was created after the Second World War, with over thirty research institutes, which were the responsibility of the Ministry of Agriculture, Fisheries and Food (MAFF). There was an Agricultural Development Advisory Service (ADAS), also funded by MAFF, whose job was to transmit the results of research to thousands of farmers. Historically one of Britain's strengths had been highly efficient and innovative agriculture and these arrangements maintained that lead. The implementation of Rothschild meant a cut in the upstream scientific research budget and a shift to MAFF. But over subsequent years MAFF and then DEFRA cut its R&D spend further, as research was not a priority alongside all the other claims on its budget—this was, after all, the period of European food surpluses. There was an added ideological push in the 1980s with the belief that Government's job was just to fund pure research. ADAS became a commercial consultancy. Many of the institutes were closed or merged. The Plant Breeding Institute was privatized, so the only way to get applied R&D funded was via big agrichemical and plant and seed companies who got their returns through the price of their seeds. Just a few research institutions survived, usually because they had independent charitable status, but this meant they were excluded from access to public funding for science capital, which made it harder for them to maintain their facilities—something I tried to reverse when I negotiated with the Treasury a substantial boost to our science capital budget. In the US, however, large-scale agricultural R&D continued to be publicly supported right through the Reagan revolution—the emergence of the Californian wine industry, for example, was based on close R&D links between commercial wineries and publicly funded universities such as the University of California at Davis. In the UK our Biology and Biological Sciences Research Council kept up its funding of research through world-class institutes but it did not have the mechanisms to apply this research by communicating it to farmers. The effects of these changes started to show up in a decline in the rate of productivity improvement in British agriculture so that by the first decade of this century this rate had fallen to zero and our agriculture was no longer seen as a global leader.[24]

There was some public funding for genetically modified crops but there was a public backlash against them which largely halted progress. The debate was between hostile NGOs and large commercial agrichemical companies who wanted to go ahead, making their returns by the price they would charge farmers for their seeds. There were not many trusted independent experts in the debate because of the loss of non-commercial institutes such as the Plant Breeding Institute. It is not the only example. Publicly funded R&D in agricultural engineering, complementing the private sector, has led advances in technologies for crop-picking in places such as California and Israel. But in the UK our historic R&D capacity in these technologies was largely abandoned and areas such as East Anglia became heavily dependent on low-paid transient migrant labour, which created social and political tensions. Meanwhile commercial food manufacturers advertised their products with images of rubicund peasant farmers carrying baskets through sun-dappled fields, downplaying the role of science in agriculture. But, with thousands of research papers on its development and genetic enhancement, a modern tomato is as much an achievement of modern science as an Apple (computer). So British agriculture is a case study in inadequate applied research and its consequence in low productivity. I tried to reverse that pernicious process, assisted by my adviser, George Freeman MP. Working with colleagues at DEFRA and Innovate UK we brought together representatives of the agricultural sector in a new agri-tech strategy which George Osborne as Chancellor funded to the tune of £180m. The funding was allocated through BIS to the Technology Strategy Board (now Innovate UK) not DEFRA so we could be confident it would be spent on applied R&D.

This is just one example of how over a generation a sector can lose its technological cutting edge even if upstream research remains world-class. This process was repeated in other key sectors. One could tell a similar story about nuclear power, for example, as the Department of Energy failed to maintain any core competence in nuclear research. The National Nuclear Laboratory only got project funding: it had no core funding to retain a capability in nuclear research. Our Pressurized Water Reactors lost out to Advanced Gas Cooled Reactors but are well suited to new small modular reactors—however, we were not in a position to take advantage of this fantastic market opportunity without investing a lot of funding to catch up.

Stefan Collini claims that large amounts of research have to go on 'national priorities', but he is wrong.[25] Compared with almost every other country Britain has renounced the funding streams which would enable us to invest in national priorities and—as we saw in Chapter 4—also the R&D institutes where this kind of research might have happened. If anything the striking feature of the British system is how nobody takes a view about anything: it is all about peer-review and academic excellence. This then leads to the misplaced belief that our academics and our universities are unworldly and stuck in an ivory tower when really the problem is elsewhere—the failure to support research labs or departmental R&D budgets outside the scope of the Haldane Principle. That the one serious attempt to tackle it, Victor Rothschild's proposals, led to a cut in the science budget to fund a transfer of funding to departments which were then cut, left the science community wary of any repeat of that risky manoeuvre. But when other public sources of funding for R&D fall away you are just left with the science budget protected behind the ramparts of the Haldane Principle. In reality the Research Councils were realistic enough to see that they had a responsibility to deploy their funds across the range from curiosity-driven basic research through to the big global challenges and they have increasingly been working with Innovate UK on applications. Creating

UKRI (UK Research and Innovation) is the latest attempt to tackle this, though it does not directly tackle Rothschild's challenge of getting the rest of Whitehall to contract for the research need.

The unusual role of universities and what that means for innovation policy

We saw in the opening chapters how the mantle of Oxbridge autonomy has fallen on more and more universities. So a university founded by the local business community to meet their needs becomes increasingly detached from these origins. It operates in an environment where there is only one way of being 'good' and that means becoming a prestigious research-intensive university. Universities compete on research performance, which is measured by academic standards such as citation rates. Applied research does not score so well in the university rankings which matter to attract students. Other types of university activity and streams of funding which provide for engagement in local or national priorities lose out and the model of the research-intensive university dominates, allocating its research budget to move up the rankings of research quality. Public research institutes seek the safe haven of a university and research becomes predominantly a university activity. So there is a limited range of funding streams and a limited range of types of institution doing the research— notably the research-intensive university. Diversity is lost.

The UK appears incapable of doing what other major Western countries do and operating public research institutes and using departmental budgets to procure R&D—as Rothschild envisaged. The Whitehall Departments that have cut their own budgets want the science budget to be used for their priorities. There is increasing pressure on the Haldane Principle and the science budget to achieve national objectives such as promoting R&D in key business sectors or boosting the regions, when really what is needed is parallel additional research budgets which are outside the science budget. If one forgets there ever was supposed to be departmental R&D and just thinks of the science budget as everything which the Government spends on science then Haldane appears to be a tiresome anachronism which needs to be curtailed.

We end up with a single model of excellence in higher education, and most public funding for research allocated via the science and research budget and going to universities. This environment enables us, even with a relatively limited budget, to get our research-intensive universities high up the global rankings.

But it leaves us weaker on innovation and translational research. We are, for example, a poor performer when it comes to patenting new inventions. We are sixteenth in the world for national patent filing relative to GDP and eighteenth between Singapore and New Zealand for patents filed internationally.[26] There is some consolation that we do seem to be good at generating wider intangible assets such as the value in brand names. But there are few British companies in the lists of the world's innovative businesses.[27] However, the argument that the role of Government is to focus on the pure research means that there is an alibi: any weakness in applied research can be blamed on business. Left and Right agree that the problem is that gentlemanly British capitalism lacks an entrepreneurial culture of risk-taking. My explanation of what has gone wrong is rather different. We saw in Chapter Four that there are specific design flaws in the regime for public funding of R&D. There is no reliable core funding for public sector research establishments which matches that for universities. The status of our universities in the private sector gives them a considerable advantage over public sector institutions, which face a penal regime and want to escape to a university environment. And although from Haldane to Rothschild there have been high hopes of Whitehall Departments as commissioners of applied research, they have been singularly poor at discharging these responsibilities.

We fear that somehow we are less entrepreneurial or more risk averse when the reality is that in the US there is far more Federal and state support for technology and innovation than in Britain. Agencies like the National Science Foundation (NSF) and the National Institute for Health (NIH) fund research and technology closer to market than our Research Councils, which tend to stop further upstream.[28] Innovation agencies such as DARPA (Defense Advanced Research Projects Agency) and specific state programmes also support new technologies and new businesses without diluting the stakes of the company founders by smart procurement and by grant aid—partly because they are not constrained by the EU's state aid rules, which may not constrain the UK either post-Brexit. Despite America's free market rhetoric there is significant public spending to support new technologies—all justified by America's fundamental strategic aim of ensuring it is global leader in all major technologies so that it never faces a technological surprise threatening its security. Our weakness is not in research but in the long and risky process of taking new technologies out into the market.[29] That is why David Sainsbury, when he was science minister, created a separate funding agency, the Technology Strategy Board, since renamed Innovate UK, to fund this more intermediate research. I then tried to link some of its budget more closely to Research Council funding by creating Catalyst

Funds with the aim of funding projects all the way from the university lab through to the market. I can still remember the phone call with the excellent John Savill, chief executive of the Medical Research Council, in which, with typical foresight, he agreed to contribute £90m of his budget if I could get an extra £90m out of the Treasury for the Technology Strategy Board so that between them we could create a £180m fund for biomedical projects all the way from the lab to the market. Evaluations suggest that initiative has been strikingly successful: by 2016 £120m of public investment in commercial projects had triggered at least as much follow-on commercial investment. The Chancellor announced a further £100m investment in this Fund in October 2016.[30] That in turn suggests that the analysis outlined above is valid.

As well as funding stopping sooner, Britain also lacks intermediate R&D institutions between the university and the market. Germany has 22,000 scientists working in sixty Fraunhofer Institutes jointly funded by Government and business to conduct R&D and product development across a range of technologies. By contrast successive UK Governments have, as we have seen, repeatedly thinned out or removed entirely networks of intermediate R&D centres: we are unusually dependent on universities for the commercialization of our research. But our universities do not have the firepower or the skills to bridge the valley of death from research to proper commercialization. That requires getting an idea scaled up sufficiently to demonstrate it really can be a commercial proposition. University academics tend to overestimate the initial value of their idea and underestimate the value that is added by scaling up. Our universities complain that there are not enough major companies at the top of supply chains, primes, to do this in the UK, and this is part of the problem, but even the primes need big intermediate labs first. The recent creation of Catapult centres roughly modelled on Germany's Fraunhofers is a conspicuous attempt to plug this gap. So, for example, our scientists can grow heart muscle from stem cells on a Petri dish: it is amazing to look through a microscope and see them beating rhythmically just like a heart. But then they have to be grown to scale and regularly and safely injected into patients with diseased hearts. That is a massive challenge and is where the Cell Therapy Catapult comes in. The funding of these centres is broadly one-third public money, one-third private, and one-third project-related. These Catapult centres are also a source of solid sustained research expertise in big areas. We would have done better in commercializing technology and sustaining high tech businesses if we had a stronger network of these labs alongside our research-intensive universities. I wished to see the Catapult network growing and becoming an umbrella body which other public sector research establishments could join as an alternative to universities. It could even include a few former research associations which have survived because of their charitable status. Another successful initiative is the Office of Strategic Co-ordination of Research, which provides an overview of Medical Research Council and NHS funding of health R&D—this model could have been applied to other key research areas. These are all welcome attempts to create a far richer and more effective network of institutions and funding to bridge the divide between research and commercialization.

There is a complementary approach which we will focus on in the rest of this chapter. It recognizes the obvious—British universities are where most of our publicly funded research happens. It would be risky to deprive them of funding, so any rebalancing is going to require significant extra public spending to bring us closer to the performance of other Western countries. So as well as promoting new funding flows and new institutions we should make the most of what we have got. That means the university takes on a broader role as the driver of innovation. The sceptics are wary of another example of attempts to make the modern university useful. But it is an unavoidable result of their success in taking such a dominant role in research: such power brings responsibility.

The third mission: universities and clusters

Cambridge or Göttingen or Princeton have long been important universities generating big ideas. But they were small towns and very pleasant in a gentle kind of way. The centres of economic activity were elsewhere—near the coal-mines or the ports or the river crossings. The distribution of natural resources determined where economic activity was. Now instead of physical capital it is human capital that matters: that is what drives innovation. They don't cluster in Silicon Valley for the silicon. Economic activity clusters around places where there are concentrations of well-educated, productive, and innovative people, and the university is at the heart of these clusters. As the old anchors of economic activity—the steelworks or the coal-mine—prove to be vulnerable so the university becomes the most reliable anchor attaching economic activity to a place. Those localists who understand the importance of place and roots should appreciate that they have in the university one of the few modern institutions which normally has a place name in its title. Universities have often been active in an area for a very long time and hardly any have moved location. That gives them an added advantage when most other institutions seem more mobile. They become the key place-shaping institution of a modern economy.

The world's most dynamic clusters are centred on Stanford and CalTech, Harvard and MIT, and the Golden Triangle of Oxford/Cambridge/London. Britain has other significant clusters, such as Digital/IT around Bristol and Cheltenham, both in life sciences and in robotics/IT on the Glasgow/Edinburgh/Dundee axis, and around Manchester/Daresbury. These are highly effective innovation ecosystems. US patents cite previous inventions that tend to be in the same area. The likelihood of being cited for research rises if the research was conducted within one kilometre and is even higher where researchers are in the same building and share the same elevator.[31] Clusters work for modern two-earner families as you and your partner can move jobs without having to uproot the family. Indeed, my definition of a cluster was where you could move jobs without taking your child out of school: it was trumped by a friend in Palo Alto who said it was moving firms without changing where you parked your car at work. This easy mobility in Silicon Valley has been reinforced by the California Supreme Court striking down non-compete clauses in labour contracts, so making it easier to move from job to job. Concentrations of similar jobs together with easy mobility and smart funders make these clusters lower-risk environments for high-risk activities. Whilst in Britain we think we lack a culture of risk-taking, America realized that it is the good safety net provided by a cluster which enables acrobats to be bolder.

The diversity of higher education institutions within them is another one of the assets of these clusters. As well as elite research-intensive universities they have a range of complementary higher and further education institutions that are more focused on vocational skills or on serving wider business needs. Less research-intensive universities get funding for non-research business needs such as professional development work.[32] These different roles can complement each other. We have for example a centre of expertise in nuclear power in the North-West. The University of Central Lancashire, UCLan, in Preston is not far from the nuclear facilities of Sellafield. Manchester University focuses on the nuclear physics but UCLan is strong on public health. One of the main issues when planning a new nuclear power station is popular concern about health risks. Nuclear facilities have been operating at Sellafield for decades: thanks to the NHS there are reliable complete health records for people in the area. So UCLan has researched long-term patterns of illness in the area surrounding the nuclear facility and developed a valuable and remunerative role as expert consultants to nuclear enquiries across the world. This is academic entrepreneurship and a useful public service. To take another example, Oxford Brookes University may not do medical research like the other university in Oxford but it has a global reputation for organizing effective drug trials.[33] These distinctive roles are easily overlooked and undervalued in the conventional rankings of universities but they are an important part of a modern cluster. A university will have a substantial impact even if it is not one of those at the top of everyone's list of great universities. The presence of an American land grant college in a metropolitan area results in 25 per cent more college graduates and significantly higher wages compared with similar places that did not get one. They boost demand for college graduates because of companies created directly out of universities and the high-quality jobs associated with university medical schools as well as general spillover effects.[34]

The university may not have sought economic greatness but finds greatness is thrust upon it. The role of the university is brought into every discussion of growth, innovation, and productivity. As well as teaching and researching they take on what is called a 'third mission' of promoting economic growth. One formulation of this is that modern economic policy comprises a triple helix linking Government, industry, and university in which universities themselves take on an entrepreneurial role of promoting new technologies.[35] This new role is a source of discomfort for some within the university. They may see it as a Mephistophelean pact in which the university sells its soul, promising to the politicians that it will unlock growth and prosperity in return for public funding. We will investigate some of these concerns in the next chapter. As well as doubters within the universities, there are sceptics outside them too. Townspeople may be unhappy as, for example, house prices are pushed up for locals and 'studentification' changes the character of neighbourhoods. They may doubt whether there really are local benefits from having a big successful university in their midst. These are the modern form of ancient tensions between town and gown.

The evidence is that these universities can bring benefits to the whole area— but the scale and the nature of these gains vary. We have already seen that the more educated you are the more likely you are to set up a business. And these are the high-tech companies of the future with the potential to become very big indeed, companies like ARM, founded by holders of Cambridge doctorates. But where will these graduates create the businesses and then employ others as they grow? Will it be where they went to university? The university is a crucial weapon in the low-profile but intense demographic competition between city regions. There is some stickiness of graduates at the place where they studied but the evidence is that it is really postgraduates that matter for high-tech growth and they are more mobile. In America these trends are analysed very carefully as different states work out how best to generate economic development in their own areas: the American evidence is that undergraduates tend to stay put whereas postgraduates are more likely to migrate out of state to America's high-tech centres.[36] So if you are a low-income low-tech state, then invest in undergraduates as they will stay there and boost your performance but you may not get back so much from your postgraduates. If you are a high-tech state like California or Massachusetts then you invest in postgraduates as they are very likely to stay and you will capture the benefits from the investment. Postgraduates educated elsewhere will also migrate to your state. There is a massive difference in the returns to postgraduates in an affluent versus a poor state of 26 per cent vs 9 per cent.[37] Clusters work because they raise the gains from key investments, notably in human capital. There are also spillover effects boosting the wages of everyone, as Enrico Moretti shows. We can now see the underpinning for the claims in Chapter Five that going to university brings a wider economic benefit. American high-school graduates earn more in areas with more college graduates—indeed, high-school graduates in high-tech areas earn more than college graduates in low-tech areas.[38] Analysis conducted for the Resolution Foundation found that for the period 2004–9, there were 0.7 new jobs created for each tech job.[39] UK data shows that increasing the share of high-paid occupation workers in a travel-to-work-area increases the hourly wages of least-paid quintile occupation workers.[40]

In the UK we are fortunate in that we have attracted undergraduates and many postgraduates from abroad so we have had a great opportunity to capture in Britain the gains from higher education from around the world. If Brexit and anxieties about immigration should deter these flows then we will instead find we export our graduates to clusters where their skills earn them more and we will be back to the days of the brain drain. It need not be so. The Golden Triangle of Oxford/Cambridge/London has a strong claim to be one of the world's great innovation clusters. There is, however, growing competition from hot areas of Europe, around, for example, Switzerland's excellent universities, and increasingly in China around Peking and Tsinghua Universities in Beijing and also Shanghai. To gain the greatest benefit from them, Oxford and Cambridge should already be much bigger cities than they are: it is a responsibility they cannot escape, especially as we saw in Chapter One that their prestige and status comes partly from centuries of blocking universities elsewhere.

The biggest single constraint is planning—especially in Oxford. There is an outrageous agreement between Oxford University and the city council which limits the number of students who will be placed in private rented accommodation, and so if the university or a college wishes to expand they have to build their own new accommodation first. This is a major constraint on growth. Oxford University is also at last embracing its wider research network, including Culham and Harwell (the site for Oxford's nuclear research after it was decided that perhaps doing it in the middle of town was a bit risky). Cambridge has got its act together and invested in significant new buildings, though only a few years ago I attended a meeting of local high-tech businesses whose main worry was the planning objections to installing new electricity sub-stations which they needed to keep their labs working. If planning and other constraints are too tight then instead of economic development you get a zero sum game in which public investment in more research capacity actually squeezes out private commercial activity—and there is some evidence of this problem in Oxford. At the time of the last census the public sector employment rate in Oxford was 28 per cent (against a UK average of 17.8 per cent) and private sector employment was 41 per cent (compared with a UK average of 53.4 per cent).[41]

Spin-outs and other ways of promoting innovation

There is already a lot happening to promote university–business links. Most of our academics are not squeamish about working with industry or other outside bodies and creating successful businesses—most universities now rather like having a Porsche or two in the staff car-park. A recent survey showed that 30 per cent of academics interact with private businesses; 35 per cent with the public sector; 41 per cent with the third sector.[42] There is, however, one form of commercial activity which tends to get disproportionate attention—the university spin-out. It is great when a successful enterprise is spun out from a university. Indeed, I sit on the Board of one of our most successful university spin-outs, Surrey Satellites, which originated in Surrey University and was sold by them to Airbus. However, there are dangers in focusing too much on the spin-outs. It can be counterproductive if universities become preoccupied with generating lots of start-ups, many of them too small and vulnerable to survive. Despite America's dazzling innovation record, the UK actually produces more than twice as many spin-outs per million dollars spent on R&D than the US. We create a spin-out for every £23.7 million spent, whereas in the US it is one for every £55.9 million.[43] I increasingly came to suspect we were actually generating too many spin-outs. Measuring a university's performance by counting its spin-outs created incentives to spin out too many too soon when instead they should have been funded as research projects for longer. They needed to stay in the womb for their natural term, whereas too often they were born prematurely. They also need a strong supportive environment, a nursery, where they can grow before they become fully commercial. Our science parks do not make the same kind of commercial return as a retail park but we have no systematic arrangements to support them.

Universities can enjoy economic returns from their activities in many more ways than taking a stake in a company that is spun out. Indeed, our universities were under too much pressure to take big stakes in these spin-outs, which reduced the rewards for the academics and other commercial partners. They say that MIT makes more money from sales of its T-shirts than from its stake in spin-outs. But actually it has a powerful social contract with its alumni which is quite simply that if they make a lot of money they will give some of it back to MIT. This is a matter of manners and morals, not legally enforced contracts, and it works. There are signs of such an attitude growing in Britain—even without the alumni and donor preference schemes discussed in Chapter Seven.

There are other ways in which universities can work with business to promote innovation which are very different from the preoccupation with counting their start-ups. I introduced a scheme—the Research Partnership Innovation Fund or RPIF—in which universities could bid competitively for capital funding for new R&D facilities on their campus. But they had to have external partners who would provide at least twice the amount of public money they were after. We launched it with a modest investment of £100m and were soon overwhelmed with proposals. George Osborne could see the case for this and we immediately increased the public funding to £300m, and that first round alone secured a total of over £1bn of new investment on our campuses. Many of the partners were companies but there were also links to charities. It showed that there is a real appetite for co-location of research facilities on university campuses and for doing research with them.

It is not always easy for firms to find out what relevant research is happening on university campuses. About 17 per cent of larger UK firms have co-operation agreements with some other partner on innovation activities—and it appears to be rising. Only about 6 per cent have formal agreements with the public science base, but about 23 per cent are co-operating informally, using universities and/or public research institutes as a source of information for their innovation activity. Many more could access what universities have to offer.[44] A small- or medium-sized company that perhaps finds itself using a new alloy finds it very helpful to identify a university conducting research on its properties or even one which has expertise on a part of the world to which they would like to export. That is why the National Council for Universities and Business created a new portal giving information about all publicly funded research projects—Konfer. It is also a useful tool to help identify clusters of research strengths as one can see where the grants are going.

Conclusion

So we have seen that universities have a higher proportion of public research spend than anywhere else and more of it is covered by the non-interventionist Haldane Principle than anywhere else. This explains why our universities are so good at generating so much high-quality academic research for a given budget. It also explains why we have a problem commercializing research. There are vague explanations that somehow we lack a culture of risk-taking, but these are unsatisfactory: it is an entirely rational response to the institutions and incentives within which our researchers work. As minister I set out the arguments for this wider role for Government in supporting innovative new technologies on the long journey to market. We thought they might be controversial within my own Party but they were not. They are widely accepted. We introduced initiatives such as Catapult Centres, the Research Partnership Innovation Fund, and Catalyst Funds, which all came from a recognition that Government should help bridge the 'Valley of Death' between the research lab and the marketplace. They are performing well and the Government's Industrial Strategy and the creation of UKRI is an opportunity to build on this success. But whilst many in Government are embracing the economic role of universities this causes anxieties within academia about what it means for the character of the university. We will try to understand and address these fears in the next chapter.

ELEVEN

The University in the Marketplace

Markets and consumers

The opening chapters of this book were a story of expansion, in which more and more universities were created after progressive reformers finally broke the Oxbridge duopoly. And, just as important, in the second part of the book we have seen it is also a story of personal growth and advance as more people have their lives transformed by higher education. In the previous two chapters we have then seen how useful this institution has become—broadening its role in professional training and promoting growth and innovation by working with business and government. The university is one of the key institutions of the twenty-first century and finds itself deeply embedded in the market economy. But there are doubters who are wary of this very success because it is changing the character of the university.

One of my main objectives as universities minister was to create a more open and diverse higher education system which would work better for students. That meant more choice and competition between universities and easier entry for new providers as well as removing the number controls which limited the scope for universities to grow in response to student demand. I believed these changes would ensure students were better served and make British universities stronger in a higher education market which is increasingly global. In effect our funding reforms gave students an education voucher to be spent at the university of their choice if they met its admission requirements, to be repaid when they were graduates if they could afford to. We replaced funding via a Government agency providing grants to universities with funding via the fees (funded by loans) which students brought with them. Many people in higher education are suspicious of this wider agenda. They worry about 'marketization' and, just as bad, 'consumerism'.[1] Those market values pervade the wider environment within which Western universities operate.

All these changes open up a key question: to what extent should universities themselves absorb these values or should they deliberately hold themselves apart? There are sceptics who fear that as universities grow bigger and more economically significant they betray their distinctive values. It is the latest form of the dilemma which universities have faced throughout their history—how open should they be to the wider world within which they operate? Universities are distinctive institutions with distinctive values—preserving knowledge, passing it on from generation to generation, and also adding to it. To protect their ability to do that they need to be strong, proud of their ethos, and with boundaries beyond which they will not go. But how permeable are these boundaries? If they are too open they can compromise their ability to pursue what is intellectually significant and challenging, however uncomfortable. They sell out. Michael Oakeshott was clear about the importance of keeping the university unsullied by the outside world: 'The doctrine that the university should move step for step with the world, at the same speed and partaking of every eccentricity of the world's fashion, refusing nothing that is offered, responsive to every suggestion, is a piece of progressive superstition and not to be tolerated by any sane man...the contemporary world offers no desirable model for a university.'[2] Malcolm Bradbury captures this view too through one of his battered and bewildered humanities professors: 'The world, in Treece's view, was an ominous organisation; he had been fighting it for years now. The world was a cheap commercial project, run by profiteers, which disseminated bad taste, poor values, shoddy goods, and cowboy films on television among a society held up to permanent ransom by these active rogues. Against this in his vision he was inclined to set the academic world, which seemed to him, though decreasingly so, the one stronghold of values, the one centre from which the world was resisted.'[3] But there is an equal and opposite problem if universities become inward-looking and lose contact with the wider community which sustains and funds them: it is not a virtue to refuse to serve society's needs.

Conventional politics may still be largely divided between believers in the market and believers in the power of Government, but many within universities see both of these forces as equally malign and indeed in an unholy alliance. Market values are thought to erode academic values by turning students into consumers. Government is thought not to understand the distinctive value of the university and instead just to expect universities to train professionals, research what is relevant, and promote economic growth. And the willing instrument of these hostile forces is university management, getting in the way of the academics who desperately want time to think, research—and just possibly teach. So universities feel under pressure from markets, ministers, and managers. Many of these anxieties are particularly strongly felt in the humanities.[4] Howard Jacobson vividly captures the feeling of some academics about how they are treated:'Mindful of its obligations to a technological society and anxious not to be confused with Oxford or Cambridge, the Polytechnic aspired to that ideal system of relations which obtained in the best engineering factories and machine shops. It would have been pleasing had all the staff consented to wear overalls.'[5]

The inevitable focus of public policy is on issues like funding and regulation. That means Governments can appear to miss the point of the university—only ever talking about the plumbing of a building and failing to appreciate the beauty of its architecture. Ministers can sound utilitarian and reductionist and unsympathetic because even when we love universities we do not express it. The White Paper I was responsible for in 2011 had some pretty dreadful bureaucratic prose and the tone of its successor in 2016 was if anything worse—appearing not to appreciate the autonomy of the university and just treating higher education as another failing public service which should spend taxpayers' money better. That is partly because of the peculiar dynamics of modern British politics in which, as David Hare shrewdly observed, 'If there were a Ministry of Fruit Picking the only way an ambitious Tory minister could advance his career would be by launching a blistering attack on fruit-pickers.'[6] But there are other pressures too. Paradoxically, restricting oneself to talking about the mechanisms of higher education can arise out of respect for universities. Ministers should be sticking to their responsibilities and not trespassing on those of universities themselves. I did plan a chapter for the 2011 White Paper on the value of the university. It could have been a fruity, claret-soaked Oakeshottian prose poem to these great institutions and might just have softened the criticism that we were only capable of seeing them as economic engines. But the only significant comment from No. 10 on the draft was to remove that chapter—they wanted a crisp and action-oriented document. There is no place for belles-lettres in modern Government. And they had a point. Government has to do its job. Higher education policy is about providing an environment where student and academic can work creatively; not prescribing what they should do. Universities function within a framework of regulations, contracts, and financial arrangements. We have to try to get these right even though they do not capture the ultimate value of the institution.

I and my successors Greg Clark and Jo Johnson pressed for these arrangements increasingly to resemble the operation of a market. The critics see 'marketization' as an alien hostile force imported from America and rashly introduced into our ecosystem, like skunks in an English woodland. But the incumbents are in a very strong position in British higher education so we need to promote more challenge, competition, and choice. That is not an attack on the values of the university: it is the opposite because there is a crucial difference between the individual institution and the wider higher education system. Universities as individual institutions can stand for their own distinctive educational values and also thrive in an overall higher education system which itself rests on competition and choice. I believe that greater market competition leads universities to focus more on the classic quality of the academic experience. If we were bringing in the New World it was in order to redress the balance in the Old. But 'marketization' does not mean Americanization. Whilst I admire features of the American system—the breadth of its courses, the idea of 'molding the class', and its diversity of institutions—we cannot and should not copy them. In particular our nationwide taxpayer funding of undergraduates so they do not pay up front is fundamentally different from the American model.

Our universities would say that there is already intense competition between different universities—much greater than in most other systems, as we have seen. So are they really such powerful incumbents? It might not feel like that if you are a Vice Chancellor competing for students both domestically and internationally and competing as well for research grants and hot-shot researchers, whilst all the time having to balance the books. But when one looks at the system as a whole the story is one of remarkable stability in which the 'top' universities are unchanged over decades, except for one or two bold moves such as the rise of the University of Warwick since its creation fifty years ago and more broadly the rise of London institutions. And Vice Chancellors themselves may find it hard to change things within their institutions as they rarely have anything like the power of a chief executive. They may feel as if they are presiding over a network of self-employed sole traders who oppose any exercise of power over them. The irony which Clark Kerr identified is that sometimes the very academics who were radical about everything else are intensely conservative about their own institution: 'The faculty member who gets arrested as a freedom rider in the South is a flaming supporter of unanimous prior faculty consent to any change whatsoever on his campus in the North.'[7] External competitive challenge may be the best way to get anything done differently within one of these institutions.

The market I was after was essentially the English model, which, as we saw in Chapter Two, was created in the early 1960s, though with roots deep in our distinctive educational history. The structure that was created then did, however, suffer from certain flaws. We have seen how the Robbins structure had not properly answered the question of how to pay for higher education as it expanded. And because universities depended on a fixed amount of grant distributed by HEFCE there was no mechanism for matching supply to demand from prospective students. As public spending pressures intensified, specific student number controls were imposed on each university. This in turn meant that prospective students were being turned away from a university they had chosen and which was willing and able to admit them, just because of a limit imposed by government. They might end up at their fourth- or fifth-choice university. Some prospective students who wanted to be educated and that a university wanted to admit were deprived of higher education altogether. This was a serious defect in the old system we inherited and our funding reforms mean it has now largely been fixed.

Universities still have their academic standards and there are of course limits to their capacity, so students are not guaranteed a place at the university of their choice. But our reforms have removed artificial limits set by Government. They have resulted in quite high rates of expansion—and in some cases contraction—as individual universities respond to the pattern of demand. So just between 2013/14 and 2014/15 Aston, Exeter, Bristol, and UCL increased their enrolment by around 8 per cent whereas London Met, Bedfordshire, Cumbria, and Middlesex saw theirs decrease by at least as much. These shifts are part of a longer-term trend: those universities losing students actually lost 16 per cent between 2010/11 and 2014/15 and those gaining received 31 per cent more in the same period.[8] More students are now getting their first choice of university. At last we are closer to the model envisaged by the reformers of the late 1950s and early 1960s based on our tradition of individual choice and admission. The idea of a market in higher education is not new and American, it is old and English.

There are objections to student choice driving the system, with some academics arguing that 18-year-olds don't really know what is best for them and their choices should not shape the pattern of English higher education. They argue that prestigious universities expand by taking students with lower grades but don't then provide the teaching support that these students need. With so many affluent middle-class students, it might be a tough environment for students from more modest backgrounds who have not got the spending power to join in the expensive social activities of their peers. But I reply that there is no moral superiority in students failing to get their first choice because

Government has limited the number that university can take and so instead having to settle for their second or third choice. Prospective students will of course choose universities for a host of different reasons—as happens whenever we exercise choice in a marketplace. But the evidence is that they do care about things like the quality of student experience and employability. The top five factors affecting student choice are: course content; overall academic reputation; graduate employment rates; the quality of the academic facilities; links between the university and employers.[9] It is leading a cultural shift in our universities towards teaching.

This is what I mean by a market in higher education and led me to claim we were unleashing the forces of consumerism, provoking another round of controversy. One of my saddest experiences during my time as universities minister was when I tried to deliver a lecture on some of these issues in Cambridge but was shouted down by students chanting that they were not consumers. They are not just consumers: the relationship between student and university is a special one which goes beyond just consumption. But there are elements to the relationship which are those of a consumer and are regulated as such. For a start we have seen that the student's role in choosing their university is greater in the UK than in many other systems. As a result prospective students need more and better information before they choose. Ironically the NUS, who challenged the very idea of the student as consumer, linked up with none other than the Consumers' Association in an excellent initiative to provide prospective students with more information. In HEPI/HEA surveys of 2014 and 2015 10 per cent of students said there had been misrepresentation by universities in prospectuses of what was on offer—this is exactly the sort of area where they are entitled to all the usual consumer protections.

Moreover we saw in Chapter Eight that there is a contract to supply services, established in a court case over a decade ago. A more recent investigation by the Office of Fair Trading (OFT) was actually prompted by the NUS, who argued that universities were not entitled under contract law to withhold a degree from a student who had not paid their rent for university accommodation. Universities objected that this failed to recognize the nature of the educational community. The OFT got to the heart of the issue: 'We have been told that going to university is not akin to buying any other service and of the specific importance of maintaining an effective relationship between the student and the university. It has been emphasised to the OFT that, for many institutions being a student is about being part of a community in which staff and students each have rights and responsibilities.' If this communitarian model holds, then the withholding of the degree is 'a sanction placed on students who have failed to fulfil their obligations to the community'.[10] The OFT, however, rejected this communitarian defence and stated plainly: 'It is the OFT's view that a university's rules and regulations that purport to govern the relationship between university and undergraduate students are likely to form part of a contract for the provision of educational services. The terms set out in the rules and regulations are likely to be subject to the test of fairness under the Unfair Terms in Consumer Contracts Regulations 1999.'[11] That is the basis on which they said a university could not withhold a degree if a student owed rent—just as the NUS had argued. The NUS should embrace this role as the voice of the student as consumer.

Key features of the relationship do therefore place the student in the position of the consumer: exercising choice between institutions; the need for information before making the choice; and a financial transaction subject to contract law. They are part of the fabric of contemporary higher education and should be welcomed as forces which push up academic standards and get more of a focus on teaching quality. The student is not simply a consumer, however. One could also think of the university as acting in loco parentis. 'Alma mater', after all, means a nourishing mother and is the motto of the University of Bologna, Europe's oldest university. One of Newman's more poetic remarks was that a university is 'an Alma Mater, knowing her children one by one, not a foundry, or a mint, or a treadmill'.[12] But students now have all the rights of adults and so there is little legal base for the idea of the university acting in loco parentis, though it can be expected to take on a duty of pastoral care. It is a complex relationship, but there is no doubt that it now operates within a legal framework in which the student is a consumer.[13]

Alternative providers

One of most controversial parts of the 'marketization' agenda was my drive to create space for insurgent new providers to challenge incumbents. We have already seen how the story of English higher education in the past two centuries is of successive waves of new entrants. Every English university was an alternative provider once: Oxford was an alternative to the Sorbonne; Cambridge an alternative to Oxford; UCL an alternative to Oxbridge; King's an alternative to UCL; the Redbricks an alternative to Oxbridge and London—and so it goes on.

The criticisms of alternative providers today are remarkably similar to those denunciations of UCL back in the 1820s or Birmingham at the beginning of the twentieth century.

The incumbents now are the institutions which were receiving public funding as grants from HEFCE. HEFCE was their funder, their regulator, and their patron. They are not, strictly speaking, part of the public sector but you can see why someone might think they were. They have specific additional duties imposed on them, such as being covered by the Freedom of Information Act, which are usually associated with being in the public sector. But they are private bodies whose spending and borrowing are outside the public sector. And although there are many who argue they are public institutions they rarely follow that argument to its conclusion and propose that our universities should be brought within the public sector, subject to all the constraints that follow.

When I arrived at BIS it thought higher education in our country was just those institutions funded by HEFCE. But there are a host of other entities delivering higher education in England whilst receiving no public funding. The only one which had a high profile was the University of Buckingham, which was strongly supported by Margaret Thatcher as a heroic alternative to the university consensus. Nobody knew much about the rest so I commissioned a piece of research to find out what there was. It reported that there were 674 private providers of higher education with 160,000 students.[14] This other non-HEFCE-funded part of the sector was largely unknown to Government and was barely regulated at all because the regulator was the public funder, HEFCE, and these institutions had no link to HEFCE. The main regulatory power over them was that they could not call themselves a university without the consent of the Privy Council. If we can protect the name of Cheddar cheese we can protect the right to call oneself a university. The term 'college' is not protected, however—you could set up something called a college tomorrow if you wished.

These alternative providers come in many shapes and sizes. They are particularly concentrated in London where many overseas institutions set up so as to provide their students with the opportunity of studying here, though they may also be open to domestic students as well. Some had a vocational role—the College of Law belonged to the Law Society; the London School of Finance was sponsored by the banking industry to deliver training for banking exams. Others survived by historical accident or as the emanation of ancient charities. Entrepreneurs might spot a gap in the market for training which mainstream providers did not meet—such as the modern music industry with the Institute of Contemporary Music Performance and BIMM (the British and Irish Modern Music Institute). They deliver HNCs/HNDs and degrees validated by universities. Robbins himself had envisaged that these vocational institutes would join the universities, which do after all provide a lot of vocational training, as we saw in Chapter Nine. I wanted to make it easier for these alternative providers to get student loans for their students, easier for them to get full higher education and university status, and make it easier to establish new providers as well. Insurgents drive innovation. The desire for educational experiment was indeed one of the reasons for the creation of new universities in the 1960s, not just the expansion of old ones. The then UGC (University Grants Committee) explained: 'there is a need for constant experimentation in the organization of university teaching and the design of university curricula. New institutions, starting without traditions with which the innovator must come to terms, might well be more favourably situated for such experimentation than established universities.'[15] That argument is just as true today, but unlike the 1960s we were not going to create new institutions by Government plan.

Many alternative providers were delivering sub-degree-level qualifications. HNCs and HNDs had missed out because Foundation Degrees had been promoted as an alternative but they were well known and trusted by employers. However, some new colleges expanded their provision of these qualifications on a scale that meant standards suffered and we tightened up on their designation. There were abuses and some courses received loans which should not have done. But equally there was worthwhile innovation. New courses were often focused on practical training for jobs. My policy, taken further by Jo Johnson, provoked a lot of opposition and controversy from those who feared it was Americanization of higher education. But we did not repeat elementary American mistakes such as providing a year's fee loans up front so institutions could collect all the money regardless of whether their students dropped out. Even so, one independent review of the American experience delivered the following judgement: 'For-profit higher education is more likely to flourish in providing vocational programs that lead to certification and early job placement—programs that have clear short-run outcomes and that can serve to build institutional reputation in the labor market...For-profits also have been successful at designing programs to attract non-traditional students who may not be well-served by public institutions.'[16] That could stand as a fair assessment for England as well.

Alternative providers challenge the conventional way of doing things. One man's innovation is another's betrayal of academic values. Is the academic year sacrosanct, for example, or can you recruit through the year and design courses in modules so this can work? Can you employ academic staff just to teach on conventional employment contracts and with clear lines of responsibility to a chief executive? Does a higher education institution have to have a library—which used to be a HEFCE requirement? This, incidentally, is a good example of the tensions prompted by such challenges. The innovators say libraries are over-rated nowadays when so much material is available on-line, but the mainstream London universities complain that students at alternative providers come in to use their libraries without paying for them through fees.

The previous Labour Government had taken a modest step to recognizing some of these alternative providers by accepting that their students could be entitled to fee loans of £3,000 as it was then. I was keen to use this as a bridge-head and to extend this loan scheme to more students in more of these entities. They did not need to get into HEFCE's inner circle and receive public grants—the main thing was to be designated so your students were eligible for fee loans to fund their education. I pushed the maximum fee loan up to £6,000. OFFA (Office for Fair Access) requirements to fund access programmes kicked in if fees were over £6,000 and this avoided tricky issues about whether we could require them to be part of OFFA. Students at mainstream providers could get fees of up to £9,000. Mainstream providers were not allowed to set a fee higher than the £9,000 loan for UK and EU students whereas alternative providers could charge a higher fee than £6,000, which was the limit for their loans. However, their fee had to be the same for all students—whereas HEFCE-funded universities were exempt from this requirement so they could charge higher fees to non-EU students. Students at alternative providers were also entitled to maintenance loans and grants on the same conditions as other higher education students.

One reason why we could do this was that not much public spending was involved—other than if any part of these loans had to be written off in the future. One fear was that the RAB charge for these loans was going to be higher than average. But that was a result of the type of students some of these providers were attracting—the safest way to hold down the RAB charge is to recruit well-brought-up young people from academic schools whose parental background means they are very likely to go into good jobs. A lone parent wanting to become a lawyer or a Polish builder doing a business studies course are going to be riskier propositions. But there was some abuse of the system. EU students were eligible for fee loans but they were also eligible for mainten-ance loans if they had been living here for three years, and I had to suspend these payments to alternative providers whilst we double-checked that this residency requirement was being met.

Our White Paper had proposed legislation which would have set up a proper regulatory framework for all this, but there was political reluctance to deliver on this commitment partly because it could provide an opportunity for another Parliamentary vote on fees. Therefore we had to improvise instead, using existing powers in ways that had never been originally envisaged. So we developed a system for assessing and then designating courses for approval as eligible for fee loans. Usually we designated courses at alternative providers, not whole institutions.[17] This opens up the possibility that in the future a mainstream provider might only get some specific courses designated as eligible for student loan support. This would be a bad idea because it would involve Government choosing some courses over others—but there was a precedent in the alternative regulatory framework.

At the same time as acting on student funding we were also trying to act on the institutional side by giving better academic recognition to these alternative providers. That meant improving the process for getting degree awarding powers and, beyond that, university status. Again, we really needed legislation to create a new regime which treated institutions equitably regardless of whether or not they received an HEFCE grant. The College of Law was the crucial case in breaking down the barriers and the taboos. It had been created by the Law Society to fulfil their charitable purpose of providing legal education to people regardless of their personal financial circumstances. The College had grown and become very valuable. The Law Society thought that they could best fulfil their charitable purpose not by running a law college themselves but by selling it and using the proceeds for a charitable endowment to help fund legal education for low-income students. The sale was a fantastic opportunity, and the College was bought by a venture capital company which shared the vision of its management that legal education was an area where we excelled and aimed to create a big new for-profit enterprise providing legal education to the world. But the potential new owners wanted assurances that they would meet regulatory requirements and would be on a path to university status. Nobody had done this for a private profit-making institution before, and in the absence of legislation there was no clear framework—the rules of the Privy Council for university status did not apply to such cases. BIS officials and my excellent special adviser Nick Hillman worked hard to steer the project through. We found an ingenious route to do this—by using separate legislation on trade names to give it university title. It was a necessary piece of improvisation and a peculiar way to establish new universities, made necessary by the absence of a legal framework. Today we have the University of Law, as our first private profit-making university (though the venture capital fund subsequently sold it to another alternative provider).

Two for-profit institutions gained university title during my time as minister—BPP University (a 'university for the professions') was the other one. (Then in 2015 Arden University, specializing in on-line education, became our third for-profit university after it secured degree awarding power during my time as minister.) Regent's College, a private not-for-profit liberal arts college, also got university status as Regent's University. Buckingham had been the great Thatcherite vision of a challenger university but had not grown to be as big a player as was hoped. I believed this was because it was constituted as a charity and had not gone the whole hog of becoming a profit-making body. They had been approached by a for-profit enterprise wanting to take them over and expand but had turned the approach down as they wished to keep charitable status—much to my disappointment. I was personally proud that we had broken a log-jam that had built up since the Buckingham case and that three alternative providers of good quality were able to secure university status during my time as minister. It was not easy. We also liberalized the process for taught degree awarding powers, which were gained by another four institutions. These seven institutions that have gained degree awarding powers or university title or both match the number of new universities created at the time of the Robbins expansion. I believe that they will be recognized as the next wave of creation of new universities in the great English tradition. We liberalized in other ways too. There was a rule that you had to have 4,000 students to enjoy university status. It was unnecessarily tough on specialist colleges which were already delivering good-quality higher education. And again it was a higher limit than had been applied during the Robbins expansion. So I reduced the limit to 1,000, and ten smaller institutions gained university title as a result. That minimum 1,000 requirement for university title has now been removed as well, though the requirement that more than 55 per cent of total students must be studying at higher education level has been kept.

Next I hope we will see new universities emerging in some of the cold spots which do not have one at the moment—like Hereford, Shrewsbury, and Yeovil. We need to remove barriers to entry and communicate the message that innovative new provision is welcome in English higher education—which Jo Johnson has been doing with vigour. Innovative new ways of teaching engineering or medicine are being developed. So, for example, Herefordshire may get its first higher education institution, introducing here the very well regarded Olin method of teaching engineering which has been developed in the US. We are beginning to see new private medical schools as well.

Sometimes one would think from the comments of the sceptics that there was a direct link between such alternative providers and the decline of Western civilization. Then I would go to a BPP college and meet earnest young people working hard for an accountancy qualification and wonder quite what all the fuss was about. The underlying issue was what you think a university is. Traditionally in England we think of a university as having a trusteeship role. A crucial part of their *raison d'être* is to pass on a growing body of knowledge from one generation to the next. Universities stand for the permanent things.[18] Some of these new types of university, however, see themselves instead as enterprises. They are more willing to take risks and they are devoid of the same assumption that they should still be around a century from now—that all depends on the market. There are reasons for this aspiration to permanence—a university degree stays with you through your working life, and you might prefer the institution which gave it to continue to place its reputation behind it. For these kind of reasons I did not wish to force any existing conventional university to change its status and, for example, literally become an enterprise quoted on the Stock Exchange. But it would be an enormous advantage to Britain if we did have some serious commercial university enterprises which could expand abroad as well. Other countries have created them but we have not.

One issue is how long it should take for an institution to get degree awarding powers and with what safeguards. The 2017 Act provides for probationary degree awarding powers immediately, though with rigorous assessment of the proposals, and opens up the prospect of gaining university title within a few years. Some fear this could mean a flurry of poor-quality institutions gaining university title and damaging the reputation of British universities as a whole. But there are still checks in the process and these institutions will take a while to get university title, whereas the new institutions of the Robbins expansion got university title straight away, as did the Open University. A rather different critique is that entry by these innovative new providers won't just happen and the Government and its associated bodies should take on more responsibility for promoting them in, for example, cold spots across the country.

There are other models for alternative providers as well. I greatly admire the Victorian model of the University of London external degree programme, taught by free-standing teaching institutions. It was thriving internationally—indeed it has far more of an international presence than the Open University—but it had lost any real presence domestically. I wanted to see it revived in the UK, but I was disappointed we did not achieve that—though it could still happen. It would be a great way for new institutions to establish strong academic credentials or for individuals to get a distinctive and well-regarded qualification, as they did in the nineteenth century. But there were barriers. There were persistent reports that existing colleges of London University did not want new providers competing with them by offering a London University degree within the M25. Courses for the external degree at some colleges were potentially liable to VAT. And the higher education regulatory regime required the University of London to exercise a close supervisory relationship with any body offering its degrees.

The case of the New College of the Humanities (NCH) was particularly frustrating. It should be just what our higher education system needs—a new liberal arts college of the highest standard, challenging our elite research intensive universities by focusing on teaching. I always liked the idea and still do. I would have steered it through the regulatory process, but I discovered that one of its backers had also provided some financial support to help run my office in Opposition, so the Permanent Secretary rightly advised I should not take any decisions about it. And, most frustrating, it had got off to a bad start with the University of London, whose degrees it wanted to teach, and neither side seemed able to reach an agreement. The policy issue was whether BIS should designate University of London International Programmes as eligible for student loans where the course was taught at an alternative provider such as NCH even without a validation agreement with a parent university, which is a requirement of the current process. That would release the University of London from its overall responsibility for courses leading to a University of London qualification. This responsibility is a key feature of quality assurance regime. The BIS view was that for a degree course to be designated for student loans it must be validated by a degree awarding body. But the University of London will not validate other institutions to teach its degrees unless they fit into its own Teaching Institution Recognition Framework, which NCH did not wish to apply for (though individual students could get a University of London degree at NCH). NCH could try instead for their own degree awarding powers, but for this they ought to have been teaching someone else's validated degree first and they found this arrangement hard to secure—though they did eventually link to Southampton Solent University.

A. C. Grayling, the creator of NCH, argued that this showed that the incumbents would not validate the degrees of a new competitor and this barrier to entry needed to be removed by legislation. His persuasive powers were one of the reasons this was a prominent feature of the 2017 Act. This was not, however, a new issue, and in the days of the Polytechnics the old Council of National Academic Awards carried out the role of being the degree validator of last resort. This responsibility then passed to the Open University, but there was a dispute with the QAA about the rigour of their procedures which meant that for a time they were reluctant to carry out this role. Had I been involved in the NCH case during my time as minister I believe I could have got them, the QAA, and the Open University round a table and sorted this out so that the NCH could have started life with a degree validated by the Open University if not by the University of London.[19] The 2017 Act provides for the Office for Students to act as validator of last resort—an odd extra role for the regulator to take on. But the Government cannot oblige the Open University or any other university to take on this responsibility and so they needed this fall-back power.

The 2017 Higher Education and Research Act

It used to be so straightforward. Our universities were funded by the Higher Education Funding Council, the successor to the University Grants Committee which dated right back to 1919. HEFCE was not just the funder but also the regulator by virtue of its power to attach conditions to the grants it gave out. But now we have increasing numbers of universities which do not depend on HEFCE for their grant. If they receive taxpayer funding at all it is via student loans provided by the Student Loans Company. There was a clear need for a new legal framework. I thought the sensible way forward would be to set out a model in a draft Bill and then consult. There was political nervousness about legislating when the wounds from the student fees controversy had not healed, especially for the Lib Dems. However, we could at least produce a draft Bill with a view to legislating in the future. But for reasons that I never fully understood No. 10 and the Cabinet Office always blocked this, even after the Lib Dems had come to see the case for consulting on draft legislation. It was very peculiar: it was as if we had privatized an industry but without a regulator in place and were expected to use the legal framework of the old nationalized industry. I knew that we would need a Bill and my fear was that we would end up with a rushed exercise without adequate preparation which intruded too much into the internal affairs of universities.[20] Preparing draft legislation and then consulting universities was the best way to avoid this. Jo Johnson, much to his credit, finally persuaded colleagues of the need for legislation and it was introduced in 2016. It provoked some anxieties about, for example, protecting university autonomy and was amended as a result. That was not the fault of my successors—it was the consequence of the earlier hostility of No. 10 and the Cabinet Office to proper preparation and consultation in advance.

The old system certainly looked simple—it rested on ten crucial words in the legislation giving HEFCE the power to fund universities 'subject to such terms and conditions as they think fit'.[21] It worked because there was trust in HEFCE. I had hoped that we would create a 'son of HEFCE' which kept its ethos but replace regulation via the power of the purse with something far more rule-based and transparent—just as has happened in many other areas of public policy. Meanwhile the Home Office became the regulator by default, as they determine highly trusted status for the purpose of the student visa regime. This was not a role they sought, and their ministers were as frustrated as I was that there seemed to be no willingness to grasp the issue at the centre of Government; and they themselves pressed for a new legal framework.

The new regulatory framework in the 2017 Act separates out the regulation of teaching and support for research. The Office for Students covers teaching whilst research assessment and funding goes into UK Research and Innovation. We have had a single funder/regulator for universities since the creation of the University Grants Committee in 1919, and the loss of such a body looking at universities as a whole may create problems. Not all the activities of a university divide neatly into teaching or research—from Muslim extremism to the finances of the university pension scheme and the overall financial health of the institution. Universities are big, sprawling bodies, and HEFCE told me they had dealings with ten different Government departments covering everything from the impact on local housing pressures through to security issues. The role of HEFCE as the intermediate body is to act as a single point of contact which both makes communication more efficient and protects universities from direct Whitehall intervention. One danger with the new model is that it will be harder for Whitehall Departments to deal with universities as they have to work out if it is a research or a teaching matter. The two roles are now split between two departments of state as well, though a shared minister can bridge this divide. The most likely long-term outcome is that the Office for Students will become in practice the Office for Universities and Students and take on overall responsibility for university issues. The new legislation does also require collaboration between the two agencies.

Successive waves of university creation also left behind them different types of university each with a different legal status. There were ancient institutions with Royal Charters—and some so ancient they have papal bulls, as we saw in Chapter One. There were charities and not-for-profit limited companies. The legislation converting polytechnics to universities left them with another legal status and specific rules on their governance. We ended up with at least four different legal forms of the university. Just to merge all these is tidy-mindedness for its own sake and not necessary. However, it is important to ease the heavy handed regulation of universities created as higher education corporations in 1992—they should be allowed to govern themselves like other universities and the 2017 Act accomplished this.[22]

The 2017 Act establishes a regulator responsible for higher education whatever the type of institution and whatever its financial relationship with the Government. There are three categories of higher education institution.[23]

First there are those several hundred independent entities which Whitehall had not even been aware of before. It is hoped that they will become 'registered' with the Office for Students, though this is not compulsory. (There is still therefore a group outside these categories who do not register at all—perhaps five hundred of them.[24]) Those who register will be officially recognized as HE providers but they cannot access Government funding, student support, or a Tier 4 licence. They must meet basic academic standards (set out in the Framework for Higher Education Qualifications or FHEQ) and subscribe to the Office of the Independent Adjudicator (OIA). This minimum requirement should give their students some confidence in them.

Second, there are 'approved' higher education providers. Their students can access a tuition fee loan up to a maximum of £6,000 and, if they do well in the TEF, £6,000 plus inflation. They will need to pass checks on Competition and Markets Authority requirements and adhere to the OIA framework and will be subject to a quality assessment and meet financial sustainability, management, and governance requirements.

The third category is 'approved (fee cap)'. They charge up to £9,000 (plus inflation, according to their TEF rating) with an Access Agreement; they can receive Government grant funding (including research funding) and their students can receive full tuition fee loans. In addition to the requirements for 'approved' providers, they will have more stringent financial sustainability, management, and governance requirements, comparable to those faced by institutions currently funded by HEFCE.

This third category actually covers all of our established universities, who themselves have a range of funding relationships with Government. Some of them still receive substantial public expenditure as well as from fees and loans. They teach high-cost subjects such as medicine or engineering, whose extra costs are still covered by public grants, and they also get public funding for their research. Then there are universities which don't do much research and don't have a medical school: they stick to teaching low-cost subjects. Perhaps they were originally a teacher training college and still specialize in academic training for people in public services. They used to get an HEFCE grant but it has dwindled to virtually nothing, apart for some modest funding for disabled and disadvantaged students. Instead they get most if not all of their taxpayer funding via the Student Loans Company, which provides the loans to cover their full fees. There are now about thirty to forty mainstream universities which also fall in this group, which used to be funded by HEFCE but now receive very little direct public funding other than via student loans for fees.

One issue is how easy it will be in future to move from one of the three categories to another. So, for example, what if an alternative provider in the second 'approved' category wanted to teach a high-cost subject? Historically only universities funded by HEFCE could get public subsidy for these costs, which is a barrier to entry. Indeed, part of the STEM problem is not enough innovation and competition. It should be possible for alternative providers to deliver these STEM courses, receiving the funding to make it possible. We saw in the previous chapter that examples are already emerging in medicine. Then we would also see more subject-specific specialist higher education institutions, such as a software university or university of engineering: these could be created by alternative providers.

There also needs to be a more open regime for applying for research funding. I tried to exercise a bit of flexibility in the science capital budget so as to help, for example, the network of science and discovery centres and independent charitable research institutes. That was only possible because the capital budget was going up substantially. But we should be able to do the same as and when research spending is increasing so at least there is access for new universities and intermediate institutions.

The legislation plugs some other gaps in the legal framework. The Government finally delivers on its pledge of a legal regime for Sharia-compliant student loans, for example. A serious gap which needed to be addressed is a failure regime for a university going bankrupt. There is rightly no Government guarantee behind our universities, though whilst that has to be the official doctrine to ensure prudent behaviour the reality is more complex. I was working in No. 10 when University College Cardiff nearly went bankrupt in 1986, with a lively and destabilizing public debate about whether it should be allowed to go bust before it was eventually rescued, even when Margaret Thatcher was at the height of her power—it shows how hard it is to let a university go bust. Now Cardiff University is a prominent, successful, research-intensive university. In the past HEFCE had the funds and the power over the sector to organize a rescue—and it did from time to time organize shotgun marriages to sort out these sort of problems—indeed, Cardiff was rescued through an enforced merger with the University of Wales Institute of Science and Technology. These mergers did not always work well—sending a weak swimmer to rescue a drowning man can make things worse. But they avoided collapse of an institution.

As a minister I did my best to prepare confidentially and informally for such a scenario by approaching the big international chains to take over a university in these circumstances, and for an institution in the South-East there would probably have been a taker. The charitable purpose behind the institution would have been protected by a payment for the assets in the event of a takeover—not unlike what happened with the College of Law. The likeliest scenario for this kind of crisis would be a Home Office crackdown on overseas students withdrawing a university's right to issue visas for them and hence wiping out a significant proportion of an institution's revenues and its export market. The Home Office did this to London Metropolitan University in the summer of 2012 but before HEFCE's funds had shrunk as much as they have now. The excellent Alan Langlands of HEFCE played a crucial role in sorting out the mess when the Home Office were not interested in the wider ramifications of pushing a university over the brink. It was not tenable to leave this whole issue unresolved any longer and the legislation makes useful progress.

The 2017 Act does give the Office for Students the power to require universities to have a Student Protection Plan to show how students could be helped in such circumstances. However, the new responsibility on the OfS to promote competition could lead it to try to stop mergers in these circumstances—as seen with Monitor, the health regulator, which opposed some hospital mergers because of its interpretation of its duty to promote competition. It would be very hard on students halfway through a course to turn up to find the university build-ings closed and a notice saying 'in receivership'. The University Superannuation

Scheme is a last-man-standing scheme in which the survivors pick up the bill for those who go bust and this too is a reason for trying to keep a university going. Closing a university with a padlock at the gates, tumbleweed blowing across the campus, and students unable to complete their degree, including overseas students with concerned governments behind them, would be very difficult indeed. The loss of the important local and regional role played by universities would be a big problem too. There would be powerful pressures for ministers to intervene and help find a solution. I was assured by BEIS that the legislation ensured OfS would have the power to make loans in these circumstances and would not be constrained by its duty to promote competition as its overriding duty was to protect the interests of students.

The changing character of the university: autonomy and academic freedom

One reason for opposition to legislation was that it might be seen as a threat to universities' autonomy. Ministers are always itching to intervene, especially when they fear money is being spent badly: it was ever thus. When the Board of Education asked for information on staff teaching hours, one Vice Chancellor complained, perhaps tongue-in-cheek, that 'nothing so ungentlemanly has been done by the Government since they actually insisted on knowing at what time Foreign Office clerks arrive at Whitehall'.[25] Regius Professorships were originally created by King Henry VIII to get direct power over professorial appointments. When we marked the Queen's Jubilee by creating a dozen more, it would have been inconceivable that ministers would try to intervene in such issues. During the post-war period, however, the UGC did try to impose a limit on the proportion of senior academic posts at universities to save money.[26] That too would be inconceivable now. The European University Association recently found that English universities have substantially more autonomy than those on the Continent.[27] In the United States, state governments have considerable power over their universities. A heavy-handed and intrusive Bill would indeed raise such anxieties, which were vigorously expressed when the legislation reached the Lords in January 2017. But the post-war path of English universities has been towards greater autonomy, and legislation has hitherto been part of the process for protecting that, even if that was not what the Government of the day intended. It was, for example, a rebellion in the Lords led by Pauline Perry that led to an explicit ban on Government intervention in admission and courses of study in the 1992 legislation. The Government did indeed amend its 2017 legislation to provide a much clearer obligation on the Office for Students to respect university autonomy.[28]

In the 1980s policies denying a platform to controversial speakers were depriving some right-wingers of their right to speak on university campuses, so the Government included in 1986 legislation a clear right to freedom of speech on university campuses. This provision now stands in the way of the most intrusive attempts to limit Islamist speakers at university and the wilder attempts by student groups to deny a platform to speakers with controversial views.[29]

University autonomy and academic freedom are linked. The ability of the individual to publish uncomfortable and heretical ideas is protected by a strong institution which supports him or her. That is one reason why any change in how universities work is scrutinized as a possible threat to freedom. One anxiety about open access, in which universities pay for the publication of articles so that they can then be freely accessible, is that it gives a new power to university managers to decide which publication costs to pay for. That fear betrays how bad trust is between academics and administrators in some universities. Nevertheless it is a good example of the truth of the observation that the price of freedom is eternal vigilance.

University autonomy has been protected and indeed grown because of the prestige of the Oxbridge model. The mantle of Oxbridge autonomy now covers the whole sector. Those Fellows of Magdalen College, Oxford who opposed King James II's attempt to impose Catholic Fellows on the College have led us to the position where there is no Government power to tell an ex-poly to expand its computer science department—even if it was originally set up by some local magnate to provide engineers for his textile business. Whitehall's arrangements have reflected this too. Universities are great British institutions which feel more like the British Museum or the BBC than either a company or a school. Some universities thought that being moved out of the DfE to BIS was barbarism, though actually I believe it was good for their autonomy. Sir David Bell, when he became Vice Chancellor of Reading, having previously been Permanent Secretary at the DfE, told me he was pleasantly surprised at how little interference there was from Whitehall and described it as 'probably the least regulated part of the education system'.[30] That is why Robbins did not want universities in the DfE: he wanted them in a department which dealt with autonomous bodies—he envisaged a kind of Department of Culture, Media and Sport (DCMS), and that was the culture of BIS, given the inhibitions on detailed intrusion in business. The return of universities to the Department of Education must not jeopardize this.

There is a final irony to all this. Many academics even with impeccably progressive views and a faith in benign rational Government do sound, when it comes to their own affairs, just like a small businessman complaining about Government red tape. Immanuel Kant remarked on this parallel: 'A minister of the French government summoned a few of the most eminent merchants and asked them for suggestions on how to stimulate trade ... an old merchant ... said "Build good roads, mint sound money, give us laws for exchanging money readily etc.; but as for the rest, leave us alone!" If the government were to consult the Philosophy Faculty about what teachings to prescribe for scholars in general, it would get a similar reply: just don't interfere with the progress of understanding and science.'[31]

Many academics, however, see Government not as standing for autonomy but just imposing absurd bureaucratic burdens. It is a standing rebuke to all of us who have had responsibility for policy—we should aim to lift these unnecessary burdens and to respect their autonomy. My aim was not to try to tell the sector what to do but to serve it—though you could deliver uncomfortable truths and identify challenges they needed to try to address, especially if you were fundamentally trusted to have their best interests at heart.

Sometimes when a particularly egregious bit of administrative nonsense was brought to my attention I would find that it had nothing to do with Government at all—it emerged from a university's own management. I could see how it happened. A medium-sized university might well have a total budget of £400m and a larger one £600m or more. They have to discharge all the obligations of any large organization—a policy on disability, on sexual harassment, on respect for religious beliefs. They have students and staff from across the world with very diverse cultural assumptions. And to make this even trickier, most of their academic staff are temperamentally sole-traders with their own market stalls who hate being treated as if they are middle managers in Marks and Spencers. (Newman indeed feared the modern university was 'a sort of bazaar or pantechnicon, in which wares of all kinds are heaped together for sale in stalls independent of each other'.[32])

The question of how universities should run themselves now they are big, significant, complex organizations is a genuinely difficult one. These issues are difficult and strongly felt, so it is understandable displacement activity for all the participants to attribute changes in the character of the university to Government when they are not the consequence of Government policy but arise from deeper changes in the role of the university in a modern economy. The growing economic significance of the university is not some plot by free-market Governments to undermine their academic ethos: it is a global trend driven by changes in the structure of the economy and a growth in importance of R&D, much of which is located in universities. The shift from elite to mass higher education has happened in some form or another across most developed countries. It does change universities in the same way as mass holidays have changed Majorca from the place that Robert Graves knew. These lead to real changes in the inner life of the university and are largely independent of Government, whether it be malign or enlightened. Paradoxically I sometimes felt that academics believed Government had more power over them than we actually had or indeed wished to have. Universities may not be the only example of this phenomenon.

The purists may concede this change is happening and that there is a wide range of types of higher education as a result but insist these other types of institution should not be called universities and that, for example, for-profit higher education cannot be a university. Definitions of university can be broad or narrow. We saw in the opening chapter that the classic requirement is autonomy, exemplified above all by the power to award their own degrees. This does not solve our problem but pushes it on a stage—should these new institutions have this power? That was a decision of Popes and is now a decision for Governments. Many Western countries, notably the US, have gone for a broader definition than our purists would accept. That is a legitimate public policy decision as part of defining the framework for higher education. On balance it is the English historical experience of successive waves of new institutions becoming universities, often with controversy at the time, which leads me to back the broader approach.

These wider forces increasing the economic role of the university and affecting its character are not going to abate: they will intensify. Moreover the university has not yet experienced the full force of powerful contemporary trends—globalization and the digital revolution. What it teaches will also change. In the final three chapters we will look at the future of the university as it faces these pressures.

IV

The Future

TWELVE

Where: Globalization

Academic mobility

'High, high above the North Pole, on the first day of 1969, two professors of English Literature approached each other at a combined velocity of 1200 miles per hour.'[1] That vivid opening to David Lodge's *Changing Places* captures how globalization has reached the modern university. We saw in Chapter Four that only 28 per cent of British academics are defined as 'sedentary' having never worked abroad. 50 per cent have worked abroad for up to two years. The rest have migrated, moving away for more than two years or coming back after such a long stay abroad. We have fewer sedentary academics than any comparable country, apart from Canada which has an open border with the US. Thirty-six per cent of German researchers are sedentary—and 52 per cent of Italians.[2] Half of research papers by British academics are now co-authored with someone overseas and they are more likely to be cited.[3] David Lodge's two professors were travelling back to the future: in the Middle Ages Europe's universities formed a highly integrated international system. The structure of the medieval disciplines was the same across Europe and so were the key texts. There was a common language of scholarship—Latin. Degrees were recognized across Christendom, entitling a teacher to teach anywhere (the '*Licentiate ubique docendi*'). Scholars and students such as Thomas Aquinas or Erasmus moved between Rome, Paris, and Cologne. Now Europe's Bologna and Erasmus programmes are gradually re-creating levels of integration which our universities achieved in the Middle Ages: we must hope that Brexit does not cut Britain off from this.

The Bologna process is not an EU programme: it is an intergovernmental declaration agreed in 1999 which sets a common structure of university study to make it easy for students to move between European countries. Heavily influenced by the English model, it specifies that a Bachelor's degree takes 3–4 years, a Master's degree 1–2 years, and a doctorate 3–4 years. Erasmus, by contrast, is

Table 12.1. Student movement under the Erasmus Programme

	Spain	Germany	France	UK
Outbound 2000/01 to 2012/13	570,000	276,000	285,000	107,000
Inbound 2000/01 to 2012/13	340,000	230,000	270,000	222,000
Difference (out–in)	230,000	43,000	13,000	−115,000

Source: *Erasmus Programme, Statistical Overview for Years 2007/08, 2009/10 and 2012/13,* Directorate-General for Education and Culture, European Commission, Brussels.

the EU programme for promoting student and academic exchanges. It has proved particularly fruitful: over a million babies have now been born to students who met a partner from a different EU country as a result of the Erasmus programme.[4] Erasmus is supposed to promote matching two-way student exchanges but it does not quite work like that. The UK has received more Erasmus students than we have sent out whereas all the other major European countries operate with varying levels of net outflow, as Table 12.1 shows.

This imbalance costs us. EU Erasmus funding has been for information and for travel costs but not for the cost of educating the exchange students, because the idea was that for each country the flows would broadly balance. Erasmus students have also been exempt from normal fees. The unusual imbalance of flows into Britain and the prohibition of fees has meant Erasmus has been a cost for British universities. I wanted to see it reformed so that there was EU help with education costs: then we could have supported further expansion. How we might participate in Erasmus is part of the Brexit negotiations.

The mobility of students and academics between universities extends way beyond Europe. The university, originating in a few cities of medieval Europe, is now one of the great global institutions. The distinctive programmes of study, degree classifications, academic hierarchies, and even graduation robes and ceremonies of the European university are found across the world. In 1945 there were around 500 universities of which most were in Europe and North America. Now there are around 10,000 universities across almost 200 countries.[5] The university is one of Europe's great gifts to the world and now most students and the bulk of universities are outside the West as Table 12.2 shows.

There are approximately 165 million tertiary-level students.[6] A rough rule of thumb is that almost 2.5 per cent of these students go to study abroad. That is not very much for a supposedly globalized world and a lot lower than the 20 per cent of students from abroad at medieval Bologna, but even so it adds up to about 4 million overseas students and is growing fast: it could be 5 million

Table 12.2. The location of the world's students by continent (millions), 2015

Asia	91
Europe	27
N America	19
S America	16
Africa	11
Oceania	1
Total	**165**

Source: UNESCO Institute for Statistics, Enrolment by Level, Levels 6–8. Total student numbers, Bachelor's and higher, latest year usually 2015.

Table 12.3. Where the students go to and where they come from, 2015

	Inbound students		Outbound students
1. United States	907,000	1. China	791,000
2. United Kingdom	429,000	2. India	234,000
3. Australia	266,000	3. Germany	116,000
4. France	235,000	4. Republic of Korea	108,000
5. Germany	229,000	5. Saudi Arabia	85,000
6. Russian Federation	213,000	6. France	79,000
7. Canada	151,000	7. Nigeria	71,000
8. Japan	133,000	8. United States	67,000
9. China	123,000	9. Kazakhstan	67,000
10. Italy	88,000	10. Malaysia	65,000

Source: UNESCO Institute for Statistics, Enrolment by Level, Levels 6–8; Inbound and Outbound Internationally Mobile Students by Country of Origin, 2015.

within a few years even if one just assumes a broadly stable proportion of total students.[7] A lot of them travel to a country where they will be taught in English. So most of them go to the US, then the UK, with Australia a strong third. Table 12.3 shows that the bulk of students travel from a small range of countries and go to another small group.

Others countries are now entering the market. Germany is teaching increasingly in English. Malaysia provides a distinctive combination of the English language and a Muslim culture which attracts students from the Middle East and Asia. So far these global student flows have taken two main forms—more movement across borders in Europe and an appetite for Western higher education in the emerging economies of Asia.

Export industry or migration loophole

At the moment Britain attracts around half a million students from abroad, making up about a quarter of our student body. During one Cabinet discussion I suggested that we should set ourselves the ambition of doubling this and attracting a million overseas students. It met with a certain *froideur*. Whilst our other major competitors are aiming to boost their numbers there is currently no appetite for this in British Government. It has all got caught up in the fraught national debate about migration and this in turn has raised the question of whether these overseas students should be regarded as migrants at all. But there is more to the debate than the definitions used in international statistics. It gets to the heart of what you think a university is and its role in the world.

Italy's medieval universities had so many students from abroad that they divided themselves up into 'nations'. (At Bologna the Ultramontane students were divided up into fourteen groups including Gauls, Catalans, Picards, Germans, and English. At the Sorbonne it was Gauls, Normans, Picards, and English.) These organizations of foreign students were crucial to the emergence of the modern university as an institution. There were clumsy attempts by some Italian cities to penalize foreign students, who reacted by organizing themselves in these groups. Whereas previously individual students had paid individual teachers, these 'nations' organized collectively to commission their teaching and in turn linked to other 'nations' to become the core of the modern university. This is one of the earliest examples of the concept of the nation in European history—nationalism and universities were entangled together from the very beginning, and indeed some claim that the medieval university is the origin of the concept of the nation.[8] Foreign students were an important source of revenue and this in turn gave them considerable bargaining power. It was the universities they shaped which were therefore the universities of students we analysed in Chapter One. Oxford's nations were North (including Scotland) and South (including Wales and Ireland) with the River Trent roughly as the dividing line, and serious fights occurred between the two groups.[9] Oxford and Cambridge had smaller revenues from international students and so their exclusive access to domestic students mattered more. This is one reason they were so keen to preserve their duopoly. Now the position is reversed: the revenues from overseas students are particularly valued by British universities and help to ensure they are insulated from the vagaries of public spending pressures and contribute to protecting their autonomy. The £1billion revenues English universities receive from educating Chinese students are not now much below their total public funding for teaching.

The EU principle of free movement of people requires that students from the rest of the EU should pay the same fees as English students and should be entitled to fee loans. (However, there can be diverse regimes within member states: hence the Scots can charge fees to English students though they are not allowed to do so for students from elsewhere in the EU.) Brexit means that British universities will no longer be obliged to set £9,000 fees for EU students and they will not be entitled to student loans—though this might be asked for by the EU as part of the negotiation. A pessimist might see this as leading to a fall in EU students, depriving our universities of revenues and our students of the opportunity to mix with them. At the other extreme is a more optimistic picture in which EU students will continue to come but now we can charge them the full overseas price. We may receive fewer students from the EU but charge each of them more, though as there is little culture of paying directly for higher education on the Continent the number coming could fall a lot. However, the fall in the value of the pound after the Referendum lowered our university fees in terms of other currencies, so we may hope for an increase in overall overseas students because of this improvement to our competitiveness in the international market.[10] There are of course many other ways in which Brexit may impact our universities, such as a loss of European freedom of movement, reducing their ability to recruit researchers and academic staff.

Whilst student fees and the loans to cover them have had to be set at the same level for students across the EU, when it comes to fees for students from outside the EU there is a global market. A crude rule of thumb is that every overseas student pays an average fee of something over £10,000 and their rent and personal spending are about the same amount. Even on these cautious underestimates about 450,000 overseas students bring in export revenues of £9bn a year. Table 12.4 shows the biggest group is almost 100,000 Chinese students in Britain on courses over a year. Together with Chinese students on shorter courses, and adding in their personal spending here, that means we earn around £3bn a year from them, making our university exports to China second only to motor-cars. As well as the direct economic effect there is an indirect

Table 12.4. International students in the UK by home domicile, 2015/16

International students by home domicile	
China	91,000
Malaysia	17,000
United States	17,000
India	17,000
Hong Kong (Special Administrative Region of China)	17,000
Nigeria	16,000
Germany	13,000
France	13,000
Italy	12,000
Ireland	10,000
Greece	10,000
Cyprus (European Union)	9,000
Saudi Arabia	9,000
Spain	8,000
Singapore	8,000
Romania	7,000
Bulgaria	6,000
Thailand	6,000
Canada	6,000
Poland	6,000
All others	140,000
Total	440,000

Source: Higher education student enrolments and qualifications obtained at higher education providers in the United Kingdom 2015/16, Statistical First Release 242, Higher Education Statistics Agency, tables 8 and 9.

one—many Chinese investors first come to Britain because they have a child studying here. Indeed, one reason so many powerful and significant international figures come through Britain is that they have children at university here.[11]

Many overseas students come for a postgraduate Master's qualification, with England's unusually short one-year course a particular attraction. Indeed, 70 per cent of full-time Master's students are from abroad.[12] There are protectionist pressures, with some countries refusing to recognize the shorter English Master's qualification as valid for employment in public services back home—an issue with India and also Spain. Education is rife with these sort of non-tariff barriers to trade, which I tried to reduce through negotiation. They are the sort of issue which should now be pursued as part of our post-Brexit trade negotiations.

Opponents of these large inflows of foreign students argue we should only recruit the best and the brightest who will contribute most as migrants. But that confuses selling a service with migration. Overseas students have to be suitably qualified to participate properly in high-quality university education, but we do not have to go beyond that because after they have finished the course they go back home. Would we impose a quota on how many motor-cars we would sell overseas? Or only sell prestigious products—Bentleys not Minis? Or only sell to people who have an advanced motoring qualification? I think not. However, equivalent proposals are put forward for overseas students because of the misconception that we are not just selling a service but also accepting migrants.

International education is a service sold to legitimate students who come here to buy it and then return home. It is a great British export opportunity. Professor John Van Reenen of the LSE put it very well: 'In the 1990s universities were seen as factories for raising skills and in the 2000s they were seen as the source of growth-boosting innovation. Both views are right but partial—universities are also significant export industries.'[13] They are now the leading export industry of towns and cities from Exeter to Bradford. One study showed that Sheffield enjoyed a net benefit of £140m from its overseas students.[14] They are rather special exports which bring many other benefits too. Postgraduate students from abroad promote innovation, boosting patent activity for example.[15] Our own students prefer being educated alongside overseas students—76 per cent agree that studying alongside students from other countries when you reach university is useful preparation for working in a global environment.[16] Their main worry—from 29 per cent—is that learning alongside people for whom English is not their first language could slow down a class: that is why it is right to set decent standards of basic English. The demand of overseas students for subjects like science and engineering helps to ensure the viability of university departments which would otherwise not be run for English students on their own. They help make England, especially London, a centre for international visitors, as parents and others come to visit them. And we create lasting friends abroad—with fifty-five foreign leaders in fifty-one countries educated in British universities.[17] We will soon have a million Chinese graduates of British universities back in China, who should be a source of advice on accessing the Chinese market and understanding that key country.

The trouble is that this has got caught up in an argument about reducing net migration into the UK to the 'tens of thousands'. David Cameron announced that commitment on the BBC's Andrew Marr programme in January 2010. His main arguments were that he did not want the population to grow over 70 million and that migrants placed a burden on public services like education and health. These arguments do not apply to students who leave the country at the end of their studies and tend to be healthy young people who are not a burden on public services and anyway are now paying a levy to the NHS. There was no collective discussion in the Shadow Cabinet at the time of how the tens of thousands should be measured and I still do not know how or why we went for the UN definition.[18] I personally doubt that anyone in the Conservative policy group who set the tens of thousands of migrants target ever deliberately intended to cover overseas students. The UN definition might well have been offered by a harassed Conservative special adviser in answer to a question from the media. We might just have easily used the OECD definition of 'permanent migrants', which explicitly excludes students.

The UN definition is not used for migration policy by any other major country. Our major competitors for international students all provide statistics on the UN measure but none of them uses it for policy purposes. They present their migration figures in their own way to meet their own domestic priorities. Australia has a very tough approach to migration yet it includes students in 'net temporary arrivals' along with tourists and separate from 'net permanent arrivals'. Canada puts overseas students in the 'net non permanent residents' category. In the US they are 'non-immigrant admissions' as distinct from legal permanent residents. All these countries are trying to manage migration but they are also trying to attract overseas students and deliberately separate them out from their domestic targets. They set their policy according to their own national needs, not according to the UN definition. I never understood why the British Government should contract out our migration policy to an international body like the UN when this is not a conspicuous feature of Conservative policy-making in any other area. We should 'take back control' and set our own migration policy, based on a measure that reflects our priorities—just like other major countries. Voters are not worried about overseas students: they rightly think that immigration is about people coming to settle here. Ceasing to use the UN definition would move domestic policy closer to what voters are worried about. That is why it has even been UKIP policy to take overseas students out of the definition. This is how Enoch Powell put it in his notorious 'Rivers of Blood' speech: 'nothing will suffice but that the total inflow for settlement should be reduced at once to negligible proportions, and that the necessary legislative and administrative measure be taken without delay. I stress the words "for settlement". This has nothing to do with entry of Commonwealth citizens, any more than of aliens, into this country, for the purposes of study or improving their qualifications.... They are not, and never have been, immigrants.'[19] If even Enoch Powell could have excluded students from his measure of migration then the Conservative Government ought to be able to.

The Home Office response was to claim that overseas students were a problem because many of them, 90,000 or more per year, abuse the system and do not go home even when they should.[20] These claims were widely believed by policy-makers across Whitehall but were not supported by the evidence. The data on departures are unreliable, but a survey of overseas students in the UK showed that the opportunity of staying permanently was not significant for them.[21] Overseas students wanted and expected to return home; though they did want opportunities for post-study work. If as many students were overstaying as the Home Office claim, then I would regularly have been challenged by the Chinese and others Governments as to why so few of their students were returning home, but it was never raised as an issue. It would mean that after years of large-scale student movements we should have a million or more overseas students still here—but they do not show up in labour force statistics, or other population surveys, or indeed any reports on migration pressures. A Government study to get to the bottom of all this was reported to have found that only 1 per cent of international students break the terms of their visa by failing to leave after their course ended.[22] The Institute of Public Policy Research found that five years on 40,000 overseas students were still in the UK and they had valid reasons to remain.[23] The ONS statistics were rightly down-graded to 'experimental' in July 2017.

Meanwhile there have been years of sustained hostility from the Home Office to overseas students. Instead of taking a growing share of a growing global market or at least grown with the market, we have instead seen overseas student numbers in the UK broadly flat, which means we have been losing market share—and largely as a result of deliberate Government policies. There was abuse which needed to be stamped out. People should not come here ostensibly as students when their real purpose is to work as a taxi driver or in their uncle's kebab shop. But the measures have gone way beyond that. Some private providers were abusing the system, but the crackdown was so tough that at least one training provider which had won the Queen's Award for Exports was put out of business. The Home Office played a cat and mouse game with universities—frequently changing the rules and catching them out. One Vice

Chancellor recruited someone from the UK Border Agency to join his staff so he could ensure he complied with all their requirements. His new recruit suggested a simple way of ensuring compliance—just attach electronic tags to every overseas student. Another university had a visit from the Border Agency to check their records were all being kept properly. The official asked to see a particular certificate. The university clerk recognized that this was very important and said he therefore kept those certificates in a specific filing cabinet where they all were to be found. But the official said the regulations referred to that certificate being kept with each student's file and so marked them down as in breach of the regulations. The Home Office regarded a high rate of visa refusals as evidence a university was slack, but these decisions, taken locally, were often unreliable and harsh—an Indian student who wanted to come to Britain to do an MBA and then return to help run her family business was told that no MBA was needed for a family firm and so her application was refused. Some countries have high rates of visa refusal—Nigeria, for example. But it seems unfair to punish universities running courses which happen to be relevant to students from those countries and therefore have higher rates of refusal—Scottish universities running courses training for the oil industry, for example. One Home Office minister bravely came with me to the LSE to discuss the issue with students and staff. He asked if there was anything he could do. They explained that a student from Korea had had to go home early because she was ill and had then flown back to sit her Finals but had been detained at Heathrow despite the LSE having highly trusted status. Could the minister perhaps secure her release so she could sit her Finals? He did. But there were far too many incidents like that. Despite—indeed because of—the reluctance to create a new regulatory framework for universities, the Home Office became in effect the main regulatory body for universities. The real obstacle affecting insurgent new providers like the New College of the Humanities was whether the Home Office would grant them highly trusted status so they could take overseas students.

One of the most egregious crackdowns was to make it much harder to stay on for post-study work here compared to our competitors. The number of overseas students staying on to work fell from 40,000 to 6,000 between 2011 and 2013. One Australian minister took me aside at one of our meetings to say mischievously: 'On my country's behalf, thank you for abolishing post study work rights.'[24] To stay on to work, the overseas student has to have a job earning graduate pay. This is fixed nationally and so is a much higher benchmark relative to average earnings in the Midlands and the North than in London. It is an anti-regional policy, driving overseas students to work in London. In Germany they actually encourage overseas students to stay and work for a time, arguing that the economic return from this is one of the main benefits to Germany of educating overseas students. The same goes for the US. We educate keen young Chinese graduates who could stay on for a year or so to help a local company get into the Chinese market but who instead have to leave straightaway. Getting a job defined as a graduate job means going through a complex Home Office registration procedure which puts most small companies off. We should not try to define graduate jobs but instead set a simple pay threshold lower than the present one, but of course continue to require graduates to leave after that, unless they have a legitimate reason for staying on. Nor should we require them to have a 'permanent job' when many employers and sectors offer short-term contracts.

The Home Office could argue that universities were making money out of selling the chance a graduate might be able to get to stay here legitimately. It is true that some students from overseas do end up staying here—their study is prolonged, they marry an English partner, or they can do such a special job that we want to keep them. Indeed, the American approach to overseas students has been called the world's longest job interview. It could be argued that if we did not have universities attracting so many students from abroad then we would not have every year up to 40,000 overseas students legitimately staying on with valid visas after five years. That is a legitimate national policy decision. I believe that if we tried to stop this then Britain would be the poorer, and not just in the financial sense. The overseas student who settles here legitimately is a national gain not a loss.

A two-way process

The migration mindset does not just infect our approach to attracting students from abroad to study here. It also constrains our approach to British students abroad. Whilst half a million overseas students come to Britain every year, the number of British students going abroad to study is far lower—about 30,000. This is the lowest rate of any major Western country. It is far too low. But the media regularly describe students going abroad as a brain drain as if it is the same as emigration—the Home Office fallacy again but in reverse. Globalization means that you spend some of your life in another country—it does not mean that the ties of nationality and belonging are all severed. It is, however, rather peculiar that England has more of its graduates living abroad than most other

OECD countries whilst we also have such low numbers studying abroad.[25] This is an interesting paradox and one might speculate that the two phenomena are linked—perhaps because our young people do not study abroad they then take other opportunities to go abroad afterwards. One might hope that these low rates of study abroad are a ringing endorsement of the quality of our universities. But actually we are the losers when so few young British students get the experience of living in a different culture. It would be good if they also learned a foreign language—one of the biggest frustrations of our employers. Our poor export record is partly because of the failure of our young people to get to know other countries. I also found that the best way to encourage an overseas education minister to remove barriers so that more of their students could come to Britain was to say it should be a two-way process and that I wanted more British students coming to his country.

Our media regularly reported any increase in the number of British students going to the US, for example, as evidence of a shocking brain drain.[26] But actually the number of Americans coming to study in Britain is also going up and we are still a net recipient of American students. In 1999 7,100 British students went to the US and 11,700 American students came to study in the UK. By 2014 9,700 Brits were going to America but 15,000 American students were coming to Britain.[27] It is hard to get excited about these figures. The reporting can also suggest that the increase in our students going to the US is all to do with fees in England. The scholarships offered by America's elite universities do make them very attractive. But there are a small number of places at these Ivy League universities, which are really postgraduate research institutes. And when you look at what the students actually say about their reasons for studying in the US, it is often the opportunity of studying in greater breadth than in England which appealed to them. Here is a typical quote: 'I liked the breadth of academic study in the US. Reading economics at Cambridge is a very restrictive programme but here I'm doing eight subjects of my choice each year, including French, psychology and philosophy which is a great preparation for life.'[28] Ironically the very newspapers which see this flow to the US as a rebuke would probably denounce any minister who actually tried to reform English education so it matched the breadth which makes American universities so attractive. But there are just the first straws in the wind that this appeal of travelling abroad to get a better broader education is beginning to become significant. The most important single reason for opening up overseas study to British students is the competitive challenge to our universities. They might have an incentive to broaden their courses if they see they are losing out in the international marketplace to other universities. Meanwhile UCAS took an important step in 2015 by opening itself up to universities from the EU. This could be another significant boost to British students going abroad, though their terms oblige member universities to do all their recruitment via this route, which is a high barrier protecting our universities and could come under pressure in post-Brexit trade negotiations.

English universities are still sheltered behind too many non-tariff barriers to trade which make it harder for British students to go to university abroad. The most significant of these is the restricted coverage of our fee loans. Norway is perhaps the most enlightened and open country—young Norwegians can take their public funding to go to universities across the world.[29] Most countries don't go quite as far as Norway but nevertheless they do much more than us. Many have schemes for sending students to study in Britain with public funding. America, for example, provides loans to their students coming here when we have no equivalent provision for ours. There is one obvious step which we should take—we should extend entitlement to fee and maintenance loans to English students going to study abroad. I extended fee loans to alternative providers as a competitive alternative to the incumbents and I wish I could have extended loans for overseas study in the same way. As we enter trade negotiations post-Brexit we may well find that open access to each other's universities becomes an issue. We could offer to extend fee loans to our students going to study abroad as part of a wider trade agreement. I inserted a reference to this in our international education strategy. It would really help my successors if they had such a substantial negotiating mandate when they are trying to persuade an overseas education minister to send more students to us. We could also ask for easier access to overseas courts to recover unpaid student loans, usually from British graduates—New Zealand is vigorous in recovering them from their students who stay abroad.[30] This would work well in Australia, where there are quite a few British graduates but they repay little of their student loans—attention tended to be on EU students, who actually repay rather well, when the trickier issue was getting British students to repay if they moved abroad.

There is another advantage of the proposed policy. British universities are making global alliances with leading universities, such as in Australia, which should enable a single degree course to be delivered across universities in two or more different countries. This is a great way of getting an English student to acquire precious overseas experience. The biggest single obstacle to such arrangements is that it is hard to finance a British student for any time when she is studying abroad, unless perhaps it is as part of the Erasmus programme.

Warwick University, for example, have an alliance with Monash University in Australia, but it is hard to fund English students from Warwick to do a year there. Extending fee loans to them would help.

As soon as Governments are providing funding for their students to go abroad one confronts the question of how to define the universities which are eligible for this funding. Overseas education ministers with scholarship schemes for study abroad would have official lists of approved overseas universities. The US list excluded our small conservatoires because it said that to be eligible for funding an institution had to award its own degrees. It took careful negotiation to get round this problem. Overseas ministers with scholarship schemes would start by proposing that their students should go to Oxbridge, and perhaps if they were feeling expansive Imperial as well. My position was that we had the QAA, so all our universities were of a reliable quality but with distinctive missions. If they wanted engineers for their growing automotive industry they would be wrong to miss out on Sunderland or Coventry or Oxford Brookes just because they did not do research which put them at the top of a conventional league table. These emerging economies are often going through massive social change, and as well as STEM students they also need social scientists who can help them understand what is happening to their society and help them design the basics of a modern welfare state—so I would point to universities like Essex or Bath with a strong social science tradition. Then there is training people as healthcare professionals, where, for example, the University of Salford delivers excellent programmes for India. These are just illustrations of a wider point—as soon as you are thinking of how our higher education system can meet the diverse needs of another country you are forced to go beyond the conventional assumptions of excellence and come to appreciate the strength of the system as a whole and the significance of the reputation of British universities as a whole.[31]

In December 2016 the College of Policing announced that policing would shift to a graduate profession and that they would be identifying twelve universities to take the lead in police education.[32] It was another example of the spread of graduate employment. I doubt that these will be classic research-intensive universities and none the worse for that. But how would the Home Office react if these universities also decided to recruit overseas police cadets so that they would increase the variety and the funding for these courses—and spread the influence of British policing techniques internationally? Would they be sensible and see that as an excellent initiative, or would they try to stop it on the grounds that the very universities that were chosen for police students were not prestigious enough to recruit the 'brightest and best'? It is also important that when focusing on issues like teaching excellence or school destination measures we do not promote the very misconceptions which can be a barrier to success in overseas markets. One of the risks of the TEF (Teaching Excellence Framework) is that overseas Governments decide not to provide scholarships or loans for their students going to British universities which get a mere Bronze—thus hitting our overseas market.

Education and development: helping other countries with their Robbins moment

We have seen that there are around 200 million tertiary-level students across the world, of which over 4 million are studying outside their home country. So far we have focused on the ones who travel abroad to study. But there is another and bigger challenge—contributing to the education of the other 195 million who are not moving, many of whom are in middle-income countries where student numbers are growing fast. They are facing a massive demovgraphic challenge. As they become more prosperous living conditions improve, and many more babies make it past childhood. They say the demographic transition is when first we stop dying like flies and then we stop breeding like rabbits. During this transition there is a massive increase in the number of young adults, which is very disruptive, socially and economically. It is the moment when these countries are perilously poised between triumph and disaster. If surging numbers of young people are left without opportunity and employment then you get a revolution—that is the story of the Arab Spring. But if you invest in the education of these young people, reinforced with a liberal labour market and promotion of business investment so that education is put to good use, then your country is on a path to becoming a prosperous modern society. Helping countries in that transition is one of the most important things we can do.

Many of the leaders of these countries have extraordinary ambitions for growing education. Brazil aims to increase graduation rates tenfold. The former minister of education in Indonesia told me he wanted to increase the number of students in higher education by 250,000 a year, year after year. That meant they were aiming to match each year the growth in English student numbers over the entire twenty years after the Robbins Report. In 2014 the then Indian government set the target of boosting tertiary participation rates to 30 per cent by 2020, which would require an additional 14 million places in six years, over and above the 2 million places created between 2009 and 2014.[33] By contrast the British Government's excellent Chevening Scholar programme helps perhaps fifty Indian students per year. These countries look to us as world leaders in tertiary education. There are opportunities to sell education services to them, which we will turn to. But above all we can and should help them through our substantial aid programme. That means breaking with the doctrines which shaped the old aid consensus.

The overseas aid community succumbed to early years determinism. All the effort was on getting every child into primary education. This is admirable, but pursuing it to the exclusion of other educational goals has massively distorted education programmes. I can still remember the powerful anger of Naledi Pandor, the experienced and shrewd South African education minister, as she told me how the West had failed to support universities across Africa. I remember as well the Afghan minister who could not understand why Britain would not help educate Afghan geologists and mining engineers so that they would know what mineral resources they had and could use their own experts to negotiate with the mining companies. It is not just science and engineering. These countries want their own novelists and historians who can help to make sense of what is happening to them. Instead the doctrine of the World Bank and the British Government, shaped by powerful figures such as Gordon Brown, was that primary education was what really mattered. The original Millennium Development Goal was 'to achieve universal primary education' but it said nothing about tertiary education. Imagine what Britain's economic development would have been like if we had not had any universities until we had achieved 100 per cent literacy. The World Bank has at last shifted its view in the past decade, not least because of evidence from its own economists that in these developing countries higher education yields higher returns than any other stage of education. The World Bank now states that

> By level of schooling, the returns are highest at the tertiary level, on average at 16.8 percent, followed by primary at 10.3 percent and secondary at 6.9 percent. Returns to schooling are highest for all levels in Sub-Saharan Africa, reflecting the scarcity of human capital in this region. High returns to tertiary show that high skills are also in scarce supply, presenting considerable challenges for many countries in the region. Low returns throughout in the Middle East/North Africa are puzzling, yet relatively high returns to primary schooling signal this as a priority. There are very high returns to tertiary schooling in South Asia. In East Asia and the Pacific there are high returns at the primary and tertiary levels.[34]

The West actually left behind some quite good universities when Africa was decolonized but then, tragically, we abandoned them. The Western consensus from the 1960s was that universities just trained people to emigrate, reinforced with active hostility to elite institutions like the University of Khartoum. The external degree model collapsed with decolonization. As a result many of Africa's universities went backwards. This failure by the West is one reason why 60 per cent of engineers in Africa are now supposed to be Chinese. More higher education could have provided those countries with an educated middle class—and that perhaps was why local rulers did not like them either. Freedom and human rights might have been better protected if the West had done more for the universities in these places. The focus on schools was harder to deliver because of the lack of well-educated teachers—a reminder of the mutual dependence of the different stages of education. This error is compounded by a second doctrine which particularly afflicts British policy-makers— that aid should be concentrated on the poorest members of the poorest countries. This means that we abandon countries just when they are reaching the stage when we could really help them with the next steps of their development. The Coalition Government, despite its admirable commitment to spending 0.7 per cent of GDP on aid, withdrew its aid from India and South Africa just as the French and Germans moved in. I introduced the Newton Fund, which counted as Overseas Development Assistance, to provide real funding for university links in research—having to overcome considerable hostility from the Department for International Development (DFID) to do it.

The contrast between German and British education aid spend brings out the effect of these two doctrines. Six per cent of our bilateral education aid went on tertiary education. It was 66 per cent of German education aid—mainly in the form of scholarships to study in German universities. And far more of the German spend goes to emerging countries as well.[35] Now the international doctrine is changing, and in my last year as minister I had far more promising discussions with the then Secretary of State and the then Permanent Secretary at the DFID. The Sustainable Development Goals 2015 replaced Millennium Development Goals, and 'achieving quality education for all' is Goal 4, within which there is a specific target which includes tertiary education for the first time. The UNESCO Education 2030 Framework for Action, Incheon Declaration 2015 is linked to Sustainable Development 4 and has this specific aim: 'By 2030, ensure equal access for all women and men to affordable and quality technical, vocational and tertiary education, including university.'

This specific reference to the university—after decades when these crucial institutions were ignored—is very good news indeed. One way Britain could show it grasped this important shift in thinking would be to introduce a far more ambitious scholarship scheme for students from developing countries to come to study here—it could be a useful element of trade negotiations with them.

Transnational education

We cannot meet this enormous demand for education just through aid programmes any more than we could do it just by educating their young people in Britain. The challenge and the opportunity are even greater. Many of these developing countries have an emerging middle class for whom investing in education matters even more than in the West, and if it can't be done collectively they will do it individually. Many of them look to British institutions to deliver it. And if they can't afford to travel to us we must bring British education to them. This is the true transnational education opportunity and it comes in many forms, adding up to a comprehensive educational offer.

It starts with schools. It is one of the many paradoxes of Whitehall that although the DFID was preoccupied with focusing the aid effort on schools, the DfE was actively hostile to efforts to promote British schools abroad, seeing that as a distraction from raising standards at home, and evinced no interest in playing a role in this international effort. There are estimated to be about 530 British schools abroad.[36] We have probably the world's most prestigious education brand at the school level, but we do not invest in it and benefit from it as much as we could. We can't require a connection to Britain in these cases, but we should make it more worthwhile to have a connection to the UK. For a start we should offer a special form of OFSTED inspection for British schools abroad, for which OFSTED could charge full cost, after which they would get a British overseas school kitemark. They should then be able to provide eligible teacher training and apply for training school status. We should continue to support British exams which are taught abroad. These yield good revenues for our exam boards. They also put students onto a route leading to a British university as they are doing exams which are easily recognized here. It was therefore a great pity that the DfE and Ofqual removed the iGCSE as part of school performance tables when many overseas students sit it. Schooling should be part of an ambitious British plan placing education at the heart of new international trade negotiations.

We tend to assume that higher education is becoming international but that vocational training is not. However, there is a lot we can do here as well. Many developing countries lack vocational qualifications which are recognized by employers. That means their young people cannot signal the skills they possess to, for example, international companies active in their countries. Our HNCs and HNDs and City and Guilds and BTECs are recognized the world over and can contribute to development and recognition of skills. They can even be turned to recognize indigenous traditional craft skills and so help ensure they are valued and not lost in the headlong rush to globalization. Currently the QAA assesses HE courses delivered abroad, but FE courses are only assessed domestically as OFSTED is not allowed to do so abroad even when it charges full costs—this is another missed opportunity.

One way we can help provide higher education in these countries is through overseas campuses of British universities. The University of Nottingham has led the way with excellent campuses in China and in Malaysia. Liverpool University has also got a well-regarded campus in China and a few other universities have also done this, though it does require a lot of work. There are other ways in which we can promote higher education overseas. Our universities can offer links with researchers, joint degrees, and access to university programmes to prepare overseas students for coming to the UK. There are many other services as well: computer programmes to manage the complex timetable of a modern university; design and build of university buildings; training for Vice Chancellors, etc. When the autonomous Iraqi region of Kurdistan created a new university they downloaded the articles of association of an English university off the web because they regarded that as the model to apply in their own country, but no commercial English law firm was available to help them do this. There is an extraordinary range of opportunities here which we are well placed to take.

There is, however, one big opportunity, the biggest of the lot, which, sadly, we could miss. When you look at the volume of investment required and the management capacity to deliver this rapid growth in higher education it is clear that there is an enormous opportunity for global higher education businesses. One reason why I was so keen on promoting alternative providers was that I hoped at least one big British-based global higher education chain would emerge. But there is no sign of this. The world now has fifty mega-universities, several with around a million students. But there is only one British institution on the list—the Open University with around 200,000 students.[37] Approximately 30 per cent of all the world's university enrolments are in private institutions, but virtually none of them are British. There are global university chains such as Amity, Phoenix, Laureate, Manipal, and Kaplan but none of these are British. A major investment bank came to see me as minister to say that if we could create a commercial model of British higher education they could immediately raise $1bn to invest in it because the global brand was so strong and the international opportunities were so great. I had hopes that at least one leading British university would create a vehicle to list on the Stock Exchange, and the structure to go global, but none has yet done so. That would give it access to private capital and the capacity to create the broader management structures needed for a big international organization. The Open University does not have as big a presence abroad as one might expect, with only around 8,000 overseas students, because its model involves physical access to tutors at study centres which they have not established internationally. Pearson is our biggest educational company and has created Pearson College but has not so far tried to create a chain delivering higher education across the world. Even the University of Buckingham, supposedly our first private university, decided to stick to its charitable status rather than accept a takeover bid which would have converted it into a for-profit commercial entity.

This tells us something important about our idea of a university. It is a trusteeship model which means: 'Higher education has been provided in this specific place for decades or even centuries. Our job is to preserve it here and pass it on to the next generation in at least as good a shape as we found it.' There is nothing ignoble about that. Our universities are tied to places and are reluctant to move beyond them and so limit their growth. It is indeed true of many of the world's most prestigious universities. That is a choice they can make and we never could or should force a university to abandon it. Their rootedness is what makes them anchor institutions in places where almost every other activity is potentially mobile. But there is also a very different enterprise model of the university which goes like this: 'The world is hungry for higher education. Our task is to mobilise all available resources using the power of modern commerce to deliver higher education of good quality at scale to hundreds of thousands of students across the world. The need is urgent so we aim to grow fast. The only way to attract sufficient resources to the task is to reward it through the profit motive.' That in its way is admirable too. But nobody in Britain has seen that as a challenge to which we should rise. As in so many other sectors we prefer the cottage industry to mass production. The future of large-scale higher education is therefore likely to be with American, Indian, Chinese, and Hispanic global higher education enterprises. I suspect it is also an industry in which we will see sub-Saharan Africa emerge too as a key market, perhaps with new higher education organizations of its own, because that is where the next surge of young people hungry for education is coming from. Britain, with our historic ties and our record on development aid, has a real African educational opportunity but so far we are failing to take it.

Conclusion

There is a risk that the combined effect of Brexit, the TEF, and tough new controls on 'migration' could see us deliberately strangling one of our great international success stories. But it need not be like that. There is an opportunity too. To pay our way in the world post-Brexit we should promote key service industries for which there is a global demand, and education is one of them. If that becomes a priority in trade negotiations with mutual recognition of qualifications and removal of other non-tariff barriers then we could see our whole education system become a significant force in the world. This would be good for our exports and it could also enable more British people to learn from a spell studying abroad. It is a crucial test case of whether Britain turns outwards or inwards post-Brexit. We can set ourselves a very big ambition—of helping to educate the world, drawing on the prestige of our education institutions and exams and the global role of our language. It would involve creating an ambitious education strategy covering not just universities but also schools, colleges, language schools, vocational training, teacher training, textbooks, qualifications, and assessment. There is even a role for the financial services industry in promoting savings instruments which enable families across the world to save to get a British education. Indeed, as part of our Industrial Strategy I launched a report which estimated that already by 2011 the total value of our education exports totalled £17.5bn and showed how we could grow these, so we set the aim of increasing them to £30bn by 2020.[38] Promoting this ambition should be one of the high priorities for our Trade Department and our Industrial Strategy.

THIRTEEN
How: EdTech

Education: ancient and modern: three key trends

I have attended the launch of an education programme. It was blasted into orbit. I was in French Guyana for the launch of an Ariane rocket carrying a telecommunications satellite which would deliver broadband access to educational services for parts of Africa not reached by fibre or mobile phone masts. Many education programmes and teaching materials are available on-line but schools and colleges in parts of Ethiopia or Kenya or Rwanda do not have the broadband connections to access them. A small and affordable satellite dish at a local school or college opens up higher education to them.

For centuries our picture of education has been very different. A wonderful image in a medieval illuminated manuscript shows a professor lecturing a class (Figure 9). It is a scene we recognize today: students at the front who are keen and attentive and others at the back who aren't. The place is Bologna and the lecturer is Henry of Germany so the university is international. Some of the most profound features of university life are not very different from what those students experienced centuries ago, even whilst at the same time a student may be learning about the latest intellectual advances. This mix of ancient and modern is part of the particular appeal of the university—graduates dressed up in medieval robes and perhaps with some Latin thrown in are awarded doctorates for research out at the frontiers of knowledge.

We are now at the moment when the technological revolution which has changed so much else in our lives is going to transform education. It won't be the first time innovation has had this effect—the Victorian Penny Post made the correspondence course and the University of London external degree possible. There are sceptics who doubt the balance of ancient and modern is about to change radically. They argue that even whilst technology has changed the classic forms of academic study—the lecture, the printed book, the essay—are

Figure 9. Henry of Germany lecturing to his students in mid-fourteenth-century Bologna.

going to continue to be impervious to innovation because they meet deep human needs. Moreover there have been bold claims for the impact of technology on education which now sound pretty silly. Thomas Edison thought that motion pictures would replace ordinary lectures, but it is still the sage on the stage. Then it was going to be radio and after that TV as new tools of learning.[1] This led to the extraordinary achievement of the Open University, created by Harold Wilson and protected in its vulnerable youth by Margaret Thatcher but very much focused on mature students.[2]

Three powerful forces are converging to change education, especially higher education. First is the sheer scale of the prospective increases in university students. We tend to think the expansion of higher education is behind us: it isn't; it is ahead of us. This is obviously the case for big emerging economies such as India or Vietnam or Mexico, as we saw in the previous chapter. But it is also true of mature advanced economies, where the number of students keeps surging past whatever limits—30 per cent or 40 per cent or 50 per cent—we think might bring growth to a halt. Korea is a model for transforming a poor country into a successful, innovative, rich one and now has almost 70 per cent of its young people going to university. In the West we may need to turn our attention to better access to higher education for older people who lost out on the opportunity of going to university first time round. The need to educate so many more students leads educationalists to look for innovative ways of doing so. It is hard to see how traditional bricks and mortar buildings can be put up fast enough to meet the demand from societies aiming to educate surging numbers of students, young or old.

Just when the world faces this massive growth of student numbers digital technologies are at last becoming available to deliver education in a different way. These new technologies are the second factor driving education innovation. They replace the conventional economics of rising marginal costs of output with a new model in which the marginal costs of an extra student on a course are close to zero. Education has been a classic example of the Baumol cost disease in which personal services can't match the improvements in productivity achieved in manufacturing but nevertheless need to match their pay and so find their costs rising. Universities are under pressure to boost their productivity but argue it cannot be done.[3] Baumol's example is 'a half hour horn quintet calls for the expenditure of 2.5 man hours, and any attempt to increase productivity here is likely to be viewed with concern by critics and audiences alike'.[4] But education technologies offer the prospect of transforming productivity even in education. (Already the broadband connections between universities on the JISC network are so powerful that the quintet can perform together on-line when they are in five different places, which is a kind of productivity gain.) It is like the shift from theatre to cinema. There will be more students and new ways of educating them.

Technological advances are not always benign. There is a danger that the quality of our education deteriorates as we come to depend on technology rather than on what is in our own heads. That is often the fear with new technologies. Plato's *Phaedrus* attributes to Socrates the objection that the replacement of the oral tradition by writing was destroying true learning, which depended on memorizing not reading: 'anyone who leaves behind him a written manual . . . on the supposition that such writing will provide something reliable and permanent, must be exceedingly simple-minded . . . written words . . . seem to talk to you as though they were intelligent, but if you ask them anything about what they say, from a desire to be instructed, they go on telling you the same thing forever.'[5] Einstein was more astute when he observed, 'My pencil and I are smarter than I am.'[6]

This is where the third trend comes in. The empirical foundations for education practices today are not much better than they were for medicine a century ago. But new evidence about what works and why is beginning to surge through education. Advances in neuroscience and educational psychology mean that we are beginning at last to understand how we learn and how memory and comprehension work. The explosion in our capacity to collect and analyse data is also transforming our knowledge of how each of us is learning. As a textbook goes on-line and becomes interactive so every key-stroke can be analysed and educators can find patterns in our personal learning which would previously have been impossible to spot. There are many specific questions about effective education practice on-line which can at last be answered empirically—multicoloured or black/white presentations; female vs male voices; single or multiple presenters. And rigorous empiricism is challenging conventional schooling too: we remember better if we review a subject after a while, whereas cramming is a less effective way of storing material in our long-term memory—but conventional exam design incentivizes cramming.[7]

One of the early assessments of MIT's on-line course, *Circuits and Electronics*, analysed 230 million interactions just from that one course.[8] We can also harness Big Data to track students through their education and out into the jobs market. Imagine that we found that one university department, despite having lower entry requirements, produced more top lawyers than anywhere else. That would enable us to spot real strength in teaching without intrusive classroom inspection. This kind of analysis of big data is a powerful force to open up social mobility and improve teaching quality.

This happy convergence of greater demand, new ways to supply, and more evidence about what works means education is going to change more in the next fifty years than in the previous five hundred years. The old ways will not all be abandoned—we can expect education to continue to be that mix of ancient and modern—but the balance of the mix will change. Personal contact with a teacher will continue to matter: just as easy ubiquitous access to music has if anything raised the significance and value of the live performance as a very special way of listening to music. But that will be part of a hybrid education blended with other ways of learning, and for some types of learner those alternative ways of learning will dominate.

MOOCs and beyond

The Massive Open On-Line Course or MOOC epitomizes these technological changes. MOOCs have already ridden the cycle from being hot (the *New York Times* called 2012 'The year of the MOOC') to has-beens (was 2014 'the year the media stopped caring about MOOCs?' asked the *Chronicle of Higher Education*).[9] Now we can reach a more balanced assessment. MOOCs, like so many technologies emerging from the American West Coast, are a potent amalgam of techno-utopianism and commercial calculation. Their origins lie in the admirable ambition of making educational resources freely available.[10] In 2002 MIT became the first major university to commit to Open Course Ware, making openly available on the web all the teaching materials associated with its courses. As there was no further educational interaction this was really an opportunity for teachers in other universities rather than for students. (There is now a lively on-line market in which teachers put course materials they have developed on the web for sale for a small fee. The *Times Educational Supplement* does this in the UK and there is a much larger market in the US.) Even Open Course Ware was not straightforward. Some educators hope that their lecture notes are their pension fund because they will become a best-selling textbook, so there are delicate issues of who owns what IP. Moreover teachers at less prestigious universities may resent the implication that they should teach using materials from a more highly ranked institution because of the presumption that it was the quality of their teaching materials that gave these institutions their superiority, when this was not necessarily the case: indeed, an open trade in such materials might reveal that true excellence is not always reflected in the conventional rankings.

This model also assumed there was still a classic didactic role for the teacher. Indeed, MOOCs themselves were criticized by radicals such as Nicholas Negroponte for this very weakness:

> Today, programmes such as Khan Academy, Coursera and MIT's own edX are, in my opinion, blindly focussed on teaching, not learning. Course correction is needed. Pun intended...computer programming is a way for children to learn about thinking...the iterative process of debugging [a computer program] is the closest approximation a child will get to understand and see his or her own learning. This view of education, so-called constructionism...call it learning by doing, fell off the table over the past quarter century of educational technology, while people and companies made more and more applications to be 'consumed' by children and teachers alike.[11]

The next step was more radical—using the web to end the hierarchical model of education as the teacher instructing the student in a body of knowledge, already organized in a neat structure. Instead the web would create networks of learners in which such distinctions and structures broke down. There is a seductive analogy between the neural networks of the brain, the digital economy's networks of servers and laptops, and the physical networks of people in a modern innovation cluster. It is all about connections. Education is thought of as another form of network and hence this movement calls itself connectivism and draws on Ivan Illich's hopes of 'De-schooling society' with its vision of an end to hierarchies in education. Very neatly, the first so-called MOOC, in 2008, was an open on-line course developed by George Siemens and Stephen Downes at the University of Manitoba on 'Connectivism and Connectivist Knowledge.' The first undergraduate credit-bearing MOOC at a mainstream British university sounds much more interesting: 'Vampire Fiction', delivered by the entrepreneurial Dr Ben Brabon of Liverpool Edge Hill University.[12] The web may make it easier for students to learn from each other by transferring feedback from academics to peers: these are cMOOCs.[13] The radicals also argue that the traditional canon depends on the sheer physicality of books, paintings, and other stuff—they have to be organized in physical space on bookshelves and in museums and galleries, which means they are ordered in subjects, schools, and chronologies. But there are no such requirements on-line, where 'everything is miscellaneous'.[14] Everyone becomes their own editor, shaping their own body of knowledge and understanding. This promotes a post-modernist view of the world in which there are just competing narratives and a diminishing shared body of knowledge or understanding. However, one way I advanced my study of philosophy at university was by looking through the bound journals in the library and reading the articles with the worn pages which indicated that they were the significant papers everyone was reading. Sad but true. It was a more reliable indicator than my tutor's very limited range. Looking back I can see it was a primitive example of how, even if left to our own devices, a canon need not be constructed but can instead be discerned. And the digital revolution may paradoxically make this easier.

This post-modern narrative is moreover challenged by a new problem— there is so much unfiltered information available of variable quality. As well as knowing what and knowing how, there is if anything greater importance than ever to knowing where to find the information you seek and in a place where it is more likely to be reliable. Prior knowledge is crucial for this. We can discover far more if we start with a sense of the shape of a discipline and can absorb new ideas into a receptive and adaptable framework whilst avoiding the bogus and the fake. Educationalists drawing from neuroscience would also say that if more information is already held in our long-term memory then we free our working memory to hold new ideas whilst we learn—we have a memory to enable us to have new thoughts.[15]

The radicals see the teacher as the latest middle-man to be dis-intermediated in the digital revolution. The assessment of an essay by five students is supposed to result in an evaluation very similar to that of one educator, though that may be a disproportionate effort to get the right result through more background noise. Radically egalitarian peer learning also begins to look like a suspiciously neat way to save money on educators. The sensible and cautious British QAA allows peer assessment provided there is academic supervision. If assessment is not to be by fellow students we can expect machine learning to be harnessed for increasingly sophisticated educational assessment. One evaluation has already shown that automated essay scoring is actually superior to human marking because it is more consistent.[16]

It looked as if the biggest commercial opportunity was to become a new form of educational middle-man—the world's dominant on-line education platform, delivering the menu from which students can choose whatever they wish. These platforms are the natural monopolies which emerge in the digital economy. So West Coast venture capital piled into on-line education at the beginning of the decade, hoping that they had found the equivalent of an Amazon or a Google for educational programmes. Charitable foundations like the Gates Foundation also promoted them early on as a bold way of removing barriers to education. There was an arms race of investment to try to get there first. Several different groups—some commercial like Coursera and Udacity and others set up by universities themselves like edX—delivered extraordinary growth in numbers of students. During 2016, 58 million people signed up for at least one MOOC; there were over 700 universities providing them and approximately 6,850 courses. The top providers, by registered student numbers, were Coursera (23m), edX (10m), XuetangX (6m), Futurelearn (5.3m), and Udacity (4m).[17] This is already a substantial and significant education movement.

A visit to the West Coast for a Goldman Sachs education conference at Stanford in 2011 (that very combination reveals what was going on) gave me an opportunity to observe this close up. Britain had some of the world's most prestigious universities, but I thought there was a real risk that they would end up with their on-line courses accessed via an American website. I did not wish to see an American education platform extracting monopoly profits from global access to education material, much of which was British in origin. So I strongly encouraged our universities down a distinctive route with the Open University at its core—FutureLearn. Ironically, global MOOCS are now being promoted by national champions—France, for example, has FUN (France Université Numérique). India is developing its ambitious national MOOC platform, Swayam, and aims for credits earned on it to be recognized across higher education. That tells us of the cultural significance of education and also the anxiety that American entrepreneurs should not get to dominate yet another web platform, and profit massively as a result. It now looks less likely that we will have a dominant platform. Students do not need to go to a single website, as the distinctive branding for specific types of education is strong. The value continues to lie in the specific education brands, not the website that brings them together.

One of the many barriers to the ambitious visions of global access to higher education is a recognition that teaching materials are more culturally rooted than had been recognized. Early on the World Bank funded the African Virtual University, which was then handed over to African Governments to run: it has graduated over 40,000 students, which is useful but nothing like the scale that was expected. One reason was that Western teaching materials were not as accessible as hoped: instead it has the challenge of creating new educational material of its own.[18] Brazil was another country which might have hoped for a boom in on-line learning, but English was not widespread and not enough of the materials were available in Portuguese. But there are some cultures where on-line learning may be particularly effective—for example, where deference to the teacher is so great it may inhibit learning whereas challenge and dispute may be easier on-line.

The poor quality of MOOCS is another problem. 2013 was the key year when attitudes to MOOCs started to deteriorate. It began with a bold experiment by the Governor of California to fund MOOCS as an alternative and cost-effective way of delivering education across the state. (Governor Brown observed: 'Whatever it costs, it'll be cheaper than a high-speed rail.'[19]) Sebastian Thrun of Udacity, who got the contract, said in January 2013 that his work with San José State could 'change the life of Californians'. But 74 per cent of the students in traditional classes passed as against 51 per cent of Udacity on-line students—though it is possible that there were differences between the two groups. By October Thrun was saying, 'We were on the front pages...and at the same time, I was realising we don't educate people as others wished, or I wished. We have a lousy product.'[20] It was on-line education's Ratner moment.[21]

Attention shifted to the problems with MOOCs. Just putting a lecture up on-line does not add much educational value if you do not have access to an educator to help you and if it has not been designed specifically for on-line learning. There are also very high drop-out rates. This is not necessarily anyone's fault—people might want to browse through some education materials and taste them rather than pursue them to a suitably moderated and credentialized result. Those who do successfully complete tend to be older people, many of them already with a degree: thirty-one of the 1,000 students enrolled on that first British MOOC in its first year completed—and they were mostly mature students who already had a degree. That is hardly opening up education to those who were previously excluded, though the bigger, more vocational courses may do better. A recent evaluation of Coursera does confirm that just 4 per cent of those who watched at least one Coursera lecture then completed the course with a credential. However, given that now a small MOOC may have 100,000 hits this can still be a big absolute number. Moreover, of those who completed the courses, 72 per cent report career benefits and 61 per cent report educational benefits and these are more likely to be for students in less developed countries or low-income backgrounds in developed countries.[22]

FutureLearn is not a website open to education materials of varying quality. Instead of just putting videos of lectures on-line the participants have to invest in creating new educational materials specifically for on-line learning with high production values. They estimate it costs £55,000 per annum to maintain a MOOC of reasonable quality, including academic time. (Seventy universities participate in FutureLearn, of which thirty are in the UK and forty outside. They comprise a quarter of the global top 200. FutureLearn's partners also include the British Museum, the British Council, and the British Library as well as overseas and international institutions such as the European Space Agency and UNESCO.) This investment in specific on-line teaching materials slowed up the process of getting courses launched but also meant that there was higher quality and more student satisfaction when they were available. Initially there was a rather random selection of courses, and the first courses on display at the launch had rather too much dental photography for my taste. But now it has begun to come together with coherent large-scale courses. It can also move rapidly. During the ebola crisis FutureLearn rushed out a course on how to handle it as a public health emergency. 20,000 students signed up, many of them health professionals and 600 of whom were based in Sierra Leone. It is hard to see how conventional training courses could have responded so rapidly and at such scale. A key feature, reflecting the influence of the Open University, is synchronous learning: a peer group of learners is created by a framework of weekly courses. This sacrifices some flexibility in order to promote commitment and mutual support with others. One of the crucial indicators of whether a MOOC is trying to create a shared community of learners is whether it is synchronized or not.

To sustain investment in quality on-line education some real financial return is needed. Indeed, unless on-line courses can be monetized they cannot be kept up to date and will be abandoned—one suggestion is that we will see a reduction in the total number of active on-line courses as ones created in the first flush of excitement are discontinued. Accreditation after a course is one source of revenue. That requires a proctored final exam which can be taken at a conventional exam centre. FutureLearn have now introduced a credentialized MOOC which gains exemption from one of the accountancy exams. The University of Leeds is accrediting the completion of some of its FutureLearn courses, breaking down the barriers between MOOCs and conventional course credits. The student has to purchase an accreditation certificate.[23] Other sources of revenue are employers paying for references and institutions paying if they recruit students via a MOOC. ALISON is a strong on-line presence delivering vocational training paid for by adverts. It has 8 million learners taking 750 different courses with revenues from advertising and certification. The MOOC platforms such as Coursera and Udacity are now shifting their business model and focusing on specific programmes tailored for vocational and management training, for which they can charge companies. There are three business models here. One is B to C—in which an individual student pays for a certificate. Then there is B to B—corporate training. 85 per cent of company training budgets go on hotel and travel, so delivering these on-line can be very efficient. Third, there is B to U—student recruitment and learning design for universities with established brands.[24]

Some on-line courses go even further than FutureLearn in delivering a tailored and quality educational experience. They may be specifically managed by a host university which provides direct academic advice and feedback. It can then involve getting a degree from the host university with the same status as a degree earned on a residential course. There can be substantial fees for these courses to cover the costs of recruiting extra academics to run the programme. One of the strengths of on-line learning when it is closely managed is that every student can be monitored. That image of the lecture in medieval Bologna did reveal one of the weaknesses of traditional education—lack of engagement from the students at the back. Well-managed on-line education with a video image of each on-line student during the class can tackle this by putting the teacher in a direct and equal relationship with each student. That is why 'No back row' is the educational motto of 2U, the leading American provider of this service to universities. (I should declare an interest as senior adviser to 2U.) It is not really a MOOC at all—instead it is a SPOC, a Small Private On-line Course.[25] These tend to be postgrad Master's courses in which you get a vocational qualification that is required for career progression—from MBAs to social work or nursing qualifications. These courses include arranging the job placements which are required as part of the training. This adds up to a worthwhile service.

I expect that in the future 18-year-olds in prosperous countries will still be going off to university for an undergraduate course. They will not want to miss out on mixing with new people, meeting academics, and all the serendipitous ways in which a campus life educates. Their learning will be enhanced by technology—as we will see next—but they will not want to lose the stimulus of the university campus experience. For 18-year-olds the simple requirement of having to get out of bed to attend a seminar or lecture may help give a useful pattern to their learning. There will be many other students, however, for whom this traditional model does not apply. They may be rooted in areas which are geographically remote or in poorer countries. Members of the military serving abroad are a key market—a few years ago I tried an on-line course run by Kaplan and was joined on-line by a British soldier in Camp Bastion in Afghanistan. Going away to university for three years is fantastic if you are young and mobile: it makes much less sense if you are older with a partner, a child, and a mortgage and need a Master's degree to boost your promotion prospects. On-line courses are well-suited to older learners who need to get a qualification to move on and up in their job, or just want to broaden their horizons. They may be more focused on professional and vocational Master's courses. Half of FutureLearn learners are working full time. Only a third are aged under 35. Three-quarters are already graduates. So on-line education is a useful tool for boosting the education and training of graduates who are already in work—one of FutureLearn's successful courses is 'How to Teach Computing', which is designed to help teachers bring coding to younger children. It is key to the revival of part-time higher education. These are useful functions—and add up to a significant positive impact on higher education. They do not mean the demise of the classic university on its campus. However, technological advances are transforming that education experience as well—we will first look at how the activity of learning is changing and then at how advances in learning analytics enable us to measure how the individual student is doing.

Technology-enhanced learning

On-line material can be a useful tool to enhance conventional learning for younger undergraduates. Sometimes these changes are described as 'flipping the class' so that students first study on-line and then check their understanding and get advice from a real live academic. This may not be quite as radical as it claims—homework is still called prep in some schools as it is preparation for subsequent lessons. But perhaps the balance is shifting and the role of the lecture is changing. Already 50 per cent of students who do not turn up for lectures say lectures are not very useful and 40 per cent say it is because lecture notes are available on-line.[26] Many students are now studying course materials on-line and then quite possibly discussing them with friends. University libraries look and sound very different from a generation ago. Indeed, universities have had to respond to rising student demand for the 24-hour library and for more shared spaces within them. This is hybrid learning and may also be highly social. One American academic found that his African-American students did less well at maths than his Asian-American students because the latter studied in groups. So he encouraged more peer working and saw their test scores rise— a good example, incidentally, of empiricism applied to educational techniques.[27] A quick check during a lecture using clickers or other audience response systems can enable a teacher to establish what has been understood so far. At Strathclyde University students get more out of practicals by participating in a mandatory on-line programme first.[28] It is not always clear to older observers what exactly is happening when a group of students are sitting together each with their laptop open, so here is an example: 'The University of Greenwich's Virtual Law Clinic enables teams of students to work together in a secure online environment to draft legal advice collaboratively in response to live queries from the public. The students are supported by staff and legal professionals and are given feedback until their legal advice reaches an acceptable standard when it is signed off and emailed to the client.'[29] That is not a bad way to develop professional skills and knowledge.

One of the early controlled trials of how people learned compared a group in a conventional real-time lecture, with PowerPoint slides and a notebook, with a second group which had access to that lecture on-line. These did better a week later in a simple test of what they understood.[30] It looked as if the key reason was that they could control their own speed of learning. The paradox of on-line learning is that it aggregates in order to disaggregate so we learn at our own pace. Manchester University implemented lecture capture systematically in 2015 and recorded 42,000 lectures, 80 per cent of the total. Students are still turning up at lectures, but they find it helpful to have access to this resource and it is very useful for revision. Ninety-five per cent of students wanted to see it used even more widely.[31] A study of that original MIT MOOC found that a student using on-line learning together with off-line access to a classmate or a teacher or someone with expertise ended up, after adjusting for all other factors, with a predicted score three points higher than someone solely working on-line on their own.[32]

The trouble is that fundamental features of the design of education fail to reward such improvements in productivity. The US is the home of that ubiquitous concept, the credit hour—or the Carnegie unit, after its origins in work by the Carnegie endowment a century ago.[33] This measure of education by time spent means there are weak rewards for improving productivity, so America faces an education cost explosion even though it is the nation which has pioneered the digital revolution.

One area where I expect we can make most progress in technology-enhanced learning is maths at all levels. The arrival of powerful computing both changes some of the maths skills we need and offers us new ways of mastering maths—especially maths for non-mathematicians. Conrad Wolfram of computerbasedmath.org is a powerful advocate of this transformation of maths. He argues, 'We have confused rigour at hand-calculating with rigour for the wider problem-solving subject of maths—the necessary hand mechanics of past moments with the enduring essence of maths...it's the mechanisation of calculating that's powered maths to be applicable to so wide a swath of society.[34] However, these advances should not be seen as a threat to the humanities, which will as ever be sustained by the genuine interest of students. One of the biggest courses on Coursera is philosophy from Duke University. Philosophy is also Edinburgh University's most popular MOOC on Coursera.[35] Availability of digitized primary sources is transforming the humanities. So, for example, students can compare and analyse a wider range of primary material, broadening access to materials for history projects. This educational revolution is not a threat to the humanities—it may well open up new possibilities for both teaching and research as the humanities go digital.

It all becomes even more significant when on-line learning is 'gamified'.[36] Gaming technologies are brilliantly designed to command and sustain attention and their techniques can be applied to that great challenge for every teacher of keeping the student on task. The critics fear that it means learning comes to depend on continuous artificial sugar rushes of excitement. They say it is not real pedagogy. But a computer game absorbs people, sets them challenges, and enables them to measure their progress. Immediate feedback is good for motivation. Students who see, for example, their marks rising during an assignment gain a growing sense of mastery which is deeply satisfying. Gaming sets tougher tasks as one's performance improves—and it all happens in real time. That is what adaptive learning is all about—when a student's performance influences the learning materials presented to her. 'When they excel on formative assessments integrated into the curricula, they are served up more challenging learning objects. And when students struggle, adaptive systems throttle back until they're ready for more. Adaptivity helps students build and maintain confidence which leads to flow.'[37] At its best education and study achieves that extraordinary sense of flow, of focusing on something bigger than oneself and being completely absorbed by it.[38] That sounds like good pedagogy too.

Powerful software also enables intense visualization and new ways of presenting data. This is a particularly good way of training people for a range of difficult scenarios. There are exciting developments in simulating 'real life' for those who can't easily experience it or afford it, such as virtual labs, virtual field trip experiences, and simulators to learn on.[39] Vocational training such as nursing or veterinary science is also being transformed by haptic technologies. Dummies are getting smarter. Doctors and nurses can train with a dummy patient that gives birth. Vets can learn by interacting with a dummy cow—I heard one academic vet waxing lyrical on the quality of a dummy cow's uterus. Dentistry training is changing too. (If you are of a sensitive disposition look away now.) I have used a real drill on dummy teeth whilst observing the jaw on a screen and feeling marked changes in pressure as the drill moves from cavity to healthy tooth to gum.[40] Practice matters and these technologies make practice easier. Imagine having national centres with key simulators such as planes, ships, through to complex building systems and oil refineries to enable a wider population of learners to learn more effectively. It could be a way of transforming access to learning and training. Universities could become the location for these.

The virtual lab need not just replicate a physical experience—it can replicate ethical and professional challenges too. Professional training incorporates role-playing in certain environments. This can even enhance understanding of the standards of a profession by putting people in ethical dilemmas seen from several different perspectives. Professional training for bankers is now incorporating these devices—as well as learning the regulations on insider-trading, for example, candidates for banking exams are put in lifelike situations in which inside information comes their way and they follow through the implications. As co-operative behaviour emerges from repeated interactions, repeated experience of scenario-based role playing may be one way of internalizing people's commitment to professional standards in on-line vocational courses.[41]

Put together all of this and one begins to see a new curriculum—with on-line preparation for a richer classroom discussion, technology simulating experiments and field trips, and redesigned assessment. Manchester Metropolitan University, for example, redesigned its curriculum after a fall in student satisfaction. 'Students wanted a clear view of what they needed to do and by when, where they were meant to be and which books and past exam papers they needed to consult. Further exploration revealed that the curriculum had grown organically with more assessments than necessary. They reformed it with more technology supported learning and better links to assessment. The university got improved NSS scores for teaching, organization and management, assessment.'[42]

Learning analytics

Think of how coaches monitor the performance and fitness of their cyclists or athletes—and now imagine a university could do the same for each one of its students. That is the aim of investigating links between education activity and outcomes, to advance beyond our current primitive understanding of what works and why. We can use data from the many ways students interact with electronic systems to do this. There is already a lot of data—from student satisfaction scores to patterns in assignment marks, etc. But there is much more—the student digital footprint from going to the library, card swipes logging into their virtual learning, the frequency of attendance at seminars. Such evidence can help provide evidence of disengagement and reduce drop-out rates. Monitoring the activities of students means they cannot just coast through unobserved. Loughborough University has developed www.co-tutor.co.uk to record interactions between tutors and students, track down student engagement in learning, support pastoral care, and identify at-risk students.

A range of technologies can help track student learning. The camera in a laptop enables sophisticated micro-imaging of tiny movements of the facial muscles whilst a student is working on-line to reveal how her emotions and concentration change as the education material she is working on changes. Interactive virtual textbooks can help us learn—and big data can show how well we are learning so at last we have rigorous education analytics. They will discover that, as an illustration, 21 per cent of students make the same mistake at the same point in the on-line course so they can design a line of questioning to help students reverse out of an intellectual cul-de-sac. They can spot which stage of the course has the most drop-outs and redesign it so the students stick with it. One option is a kind of educational Fitbit so the students themselves know how they are doing. Nottingham Trent University won the *Times Higher* award for outstanding student support for piloting a student dashboard. Students got their own engagement data compared with others and 27 per cent of students surveyed reported changing their learning activity after using learning analytics.

There are ethical questions here around student consent, which is why JISC published their Code of Practice for Learning analytics in June 2015.[43] Is it acceptable, for example, to link data showing a student is not attending early classes with use of their swipe card in the student bar late into the night?[44] One survey showed 71 per cent of students were happy for their university to use information about their learning activities if it improved their grades. The NUS have been broadly supportive as well.[45] Indeed, instead of worries about privacy the student may be frustrated if data being collected by their university is not used in the way Amazon or Spotify would to offer them a personalized service. We saw in an earlier chapter that the US has more subject choices for students: as a result it makes more investment in information systems so students can plan course credits and access to modules. We can look forward to the day when British students, especially those from disadvantaged backgrounds with less family knowledge to draw on, get good data-based guidance—'You have taken these specific modules so next you might want to consider the following suggested ones and if you do this combination you have an x% chance of earning more than £y,000 in the job you say you are aiming at.' Whilst university researchers are harnessing big data to investigate so many other areas it is not yet being used to generate these kind of issues for their own university students. The UK is not the world leader in learner analytics, when it could be.[46] The next step is to use the JISC infrastructure to create an integrated nationwide learner analytics service. This would be a powerful tool to assess the educational performance—rather as the unique NHS patient database is a more powerful tool for medical research than America's more fragmented medical data. We saw in Chapter Eight how hard it has proved to get any reliable metrics for the quality of the academic experience and for learning gain. These kind of developments give us our best chance of cracking the problem.

They say big data has volume, velocity, and variety. British higher education has a lot of data but we are not using it as well as we could. The 2011 White Paper agenda proposed Key Information Sets for students and expected JISC, HESA, and UUK to work together to provide more and better data. There is a deal here in which the burden of historic data collection is eased in return for more flexible real-time data. Collecting historic data is a heavy burden, with 525 separate HE data collections and 93 separate organizations collecting it. So there is a need to rationalize between HESA, SLC, UCAS, and UKVI, and PSRBs.[47] In return we should see the development of useful fluid real-time data such as swipe cards showing which buildings are most used when, how long students spend watching a video of a lecture, and how many books are borrowed.

The radicals think the development of these tools will enable us to cut out the subject and develop cognitive skills directly. One analysis showed a university degree was less good at predicting job performance than a combination of three cognitive skills tests—applied maths, reading for information, and locating information.[48] Moreover, cognitive skills can be developed quite quickly 'Utilising specific curricula designed to improve cognitive skills in ten hours of training in each of the three key cognitive skills can yield gains of two to three years of full-time education.'[49] On-line learning can identify when students are at the right age to develop these cognitive skills by direct training, and it is not always a matter of getting in young: 'Our findings suggest that for certain cognitive skills, training during late adolescence and adulthood yields greater improvement than training earlier in adolescence, which highlights the relevance of this late developmental stage for education.'[50] This has some other very significant implications too, if we can learn skills which were thought to be part of one's innate cognitive ability. The researchers also state that 'relational reasoning can be trained in all the age groups tested here . . . it does not support the notion that matrix reasoning gives an indication of some kind of innate, fixed ability'.[51] This could be a prelude to the biggest disintermediation of them all—cutting out the subject and moving straight to the cognitive skills. I spent a term studying the philosophy of Immanuel Kant but have a very hazy recollection of much of it now. However, I hope it helped me recognize there are deep metaphysical questions out there even if I was not going to devote my life to understanding them and also to develop some rough idea of what makes an argument hold together. Maybe I could have learned all this by a course in critical thinking but I personally would not have found it so satisfying. It is rather like those pills on a bare plate which James Burke used to present on *Tomorrow's World* as the future of nutrition. But that is not really what eating is all about—we enjoy real meals and resist simply seeing them as a time-consuming means of obtaining nutrition. Real subjects are the same. But what about the institutions which deliver these real subjects? Are universities themselves going to be rendered obsolescent by the digital revolution?

Disintermediation

The digital revolution usually drives disintermediation—from the local shop to the national newspaper, the middle man is forced out as the consumer gets what they want directly. At present these processes show little sign of weakening the position of the traditional university. Indeed, they may even strengthen it by opening up its recruitment of international students further. Imagine that you are a smart teenager with an extraordinary gift for maths living in a Mongolian yurt or an Ethiopian village. You do some on-line courses and score very highly. You sample different university courses—using their on-line presence to get a sense of their character—and then apply for some. One of them may see your potential and offer you a place. This replaces the current laborious process in which universities pay agents overseas to help them recruit students. In this case the middle man who will be disintermediated is the student recruiter, especially the agent abroad, not the university which is the disintermediator. The university might even pay the organization running an educational website for each overseas student recruited from it.

The process of disintermediation may not end there however. The next stage could be for the conventional higher education institution and the examining bodies to be disintermediated themselves. The digital revolution exposes universities to these risks as it lowers barriers to entry. 'Everyone is a rookie in the new economy', says Chip Paucek, the CEO of 2U. That makes it inherently disruptive. It also makes it easier to unbundle the different functions of the university and pick off specific ones. But so far this unbundling has been more of back-office functions and has not affected the core academic functions which students most value: the university has not yet been dismantled in front of our eyes.

The university's power rests on the position its qualifications command in the labour market—we may not agree with the claim that all that universities do is credentialize but it is a key role and it could be challenged by on-line alternatives. A student successfully completes an on-line course and then gets a recognition of this achievement which an employer trusts sufficiently to offer her a job. Indeed, the employer might pay the on-line course for providing the recruit. Google are advising companies and professional bodies together on how to create a MOOC which meets their needs without going via an educational institution. University accreditation could be eroded as the student records on LinkedIn or using a blockchain distributed ledger the MOOCs she has completed for companies to use for recruitment. The challenge is to ensure the on-line qualification is valid. The student might pay for a secure and trusted certificate at the completion of a course. That could mean that at the end of the course the student has to sit among serried ranks in a big hall for an invigilated assessment—another ancient image. But other ways are being developed to ensure security: an on-line test can use, for example, an individual's distinctive pattern of key-strokes or iris recognition software linked to an identity card. It will make the rent-seeking of conventional universities identified by Adam Smith and Alison Wolf harder to sustain as they will lose their dominant position in credentializing. We can already see some of this happening—a Microsoft qualification is widely trusted in the IT world. Government rules for funding training are, however, a barrier as they will not fund specific company qualifications. They will, however, fund specific university qualifications—a crucial advantage for universities. Moreover, universities should be able to respond to the competitive challenge with extra features, such as the option to double-click on the degree so it is accompanied by a transcript to enable the employer to learn a lot more about the course and the competencies the student has demonstrated.[52]

Several different forces are at work here which could lead to the 'unbundling' of the different services provided by a university. One is the provision of a specific qualification where another trusted organization such as Microsoft is vouching for an education which might have been provided by a university or could be somewhere else. This takes us back to the days of the University of London external degree. This is the start of the unbundling envisaged by Ryan Craig.[53] Then the actual education function could be taken away as well— Dyson offers to educate students for its degree in engineering. The Condé Nast College of Fashion and Design already has its own degree-awarding powers and offers a BA in fashion communication and the Vogue Fashion Foundation diploma in fashion studies. These are examples of a non-university brand delivering not just certification but education as well in its area. However, a Condé Nast engineering degree or a Dyson degree in fashion journalism might not have such kudos. A general non-educational brand—Virgin for example—might not be constrained in the same way. This might well happen but it has not yet—perhaps because it is not rooted in a place or at least an institution with a wider educational purpose.

Conclusion

So in the future there will be more students and new ways of educating them. It will not be the death of live education any more than on-line music has killed live concerts or cinema has killed live theatre. There will still be students gathering on campuses to be educated by their peers and by academics. But even for them there will be changes in how they are educated and there will be more for whom education takes a very different form. We can already see that the quality of teaching is becoming the most important single issue in higher education. The digital revolution should make it possible both to measure what is happening and create opportunities for new providers to do things differently. Beyond this there is a far more ambitious vision of pervasive and ubiquitous education—for any person, any time, any place, any level, any course, any speed. The danger for the university is if they do not understand this or do not support it. Their opportunity is to be the single body which does more than anyone else to make it happen. The student's ties to her faculty, her university, her fellow students and alumni are strong and do not change even if the technologies for delivering her education do. That is why I expect the university will adapt to the new technology—if not then it will be destroyed by it. Now we must turn to one last challenge. This is not global: it faces English universities in particular. Can England's unusual model of early specialization survive, and indeed does it deserve to?

FOURTEEN

What: A Broader Education

The problem and the explanation

The value of universities is not simply their contribution to human capital and economic growth, welcome though these are. Universities should enable a graduate to lead a flourishing, fulfilled life. That must mean the capacity to engage with the wide range of extraordinary intellectual and cultural achievements to which we are heirs and to which we should add for the next generation. It is the most important single responsibility of our universities and it is where the most significant reform is required. English education requires 16-year-olds to take life-changing decisions to specialize in just three subjects, and indeed allows students to drop a range of subjects at the age of 14. No other major Western country does this. It is the source of many of the other problems which we worry about. Fewer girls do STEM subjects after the age of 16 than in most other countries because in England they are presented with irreversible decisions to give them up when they are much too young. We suffer particularly acutely from C. P. Snow's two cultures because our teenagers can join one of two apparently deeply hostile gangs—the humanities or the sciences, the Montagues and the Capulets of intellectual life—when most other countries avoid promoting such divisions. When employers complain about employability they often mean that young people have been force-fed for a narrow academic curriculum without a wider range of subjects and skills. Above all, as I look back on my education, my greatest regret—and that of many friends and contemporaries as we get older—is that we missed out on great scientific or cultural achievements of our age because of early decisions whose long-term significance we completely failed to recognize. I greatly enjoyed studying History, English, and German for my A levels but now I am shocked at the barbarism of a system which restricted my studies to those three subjects at the age of 16. This is the intellectual and cultural damage inflicted by our educational system when above all it should broaden our horizons and enlighten us. That this system is preserved on the claim it is necessary for high academic standards is even more scandalous.

The gap between the sciences and the humanities and the deep ignorance amongst so many British adults of what lies on the other side of the divide is not some vague cultural problem. It arises from specific institutional arrangements which could be changed. Attempts at reform have failed because they do not grasp the crucial role that universities play in driving the pressure to specialize. This arises from the way academics exercise their exceptional power to decide who to admit to their university. Our narrow structure of A levels and our unusual pattern of higher education are directly connected. It all begins with the power of English universities to decide who to admit. As part of the great Victorian reforms Oxbridge set their own scholarship exams, with applicants having to choose which subject to offer. Our leading civic universities emerged as autonomous institutions during the first half of the twentieth century. They needed a mechanism to decide who to admit and developed their own university entrance exams, the origins of the A level. The old exam boards were emanations of universities like Oxford, Cambridge, Durham, Birmingham, and Bristol. They shaped school key exams and hence had a big influence on the curriculum. The precursor of the A level, the higher school certificate, was introduced in 1918: it was run by these university exam boards, though it was actually rather broader than today's A levels and its purpose was not assessing people for university entrance—that was for separate university entrance exams. The key influence though was the Oxbridge exams, which could secure a scholarship—the only way to fund yourself if you were not from a rich family, and hence a key mechanism shaping the academic curriculum of state grammar schools. Grammar school boys (and girls) dreamed of an Oxbridge scholarship, as did their schools. And you sat the Oxbridge scholarship exam in a particular subject. Redbrick universities did not have the funds to dangle scholarships in front of these teenagers, so an Oxbridge scholarship might be the only way they could afford to get to university—it was that or bust. The curriculum in the school sixth form was shaped around this objective—just as darts matches focus on the triple twenty. In *Technology and the Academics,* Eric Ashby refers to the 'narrow scope and high specialisation demanded for open scholarships by the Universities of Oxford and Cambridge'.[1]

As more teenagers started staying on in secondary education after the Butler Act, A levels were introduced in 1953, again emerging from university

entrance exams. There was a key review of them in the Crowther Report of
1959 on the education of 15–18 year olds which endorsed specialization at
A level.[2] However, Crowther did so expecting this to be for a small elite going
to university. It is another example of the importance of the order in which
decisions are taken: if it had come after Robbins, not before, it might have
been different. Even so, Crowther envisages between one-third and one-quarter
of the school week set aside for non-specialist subjects, and explicitly this is
arts for scientists and science for humanities students.[3] Then the system of grades
at A level was introduced in 1963 in parallel with the creation of UCCA. It
seems to have been part of a deal envisaged by Crowther in which individual
university entrance exams on top of A levels were abolished in return for
nationwide A level exams sufficiently calibrated to enable growing numbers of
applicants to be selected for specific universities.[4]

Once again what we think of as key features of English education can be
traced back to this crucial period in the late 1950s and early 1960s. And now we
are in the peculiar position where the law expects young people to be in education to the age of 18 but we do not have a general school-leaving exam ready
and waiting for them because we have already got A levels, even though they
were specifically designed for university recruitment. That in turn has had a
massive impact on the secondary school curriculum for the majority of English
teenagers despite having been designed with very different intentions.

We saw in Chapter Seven that in many European countries there is a right
for students to go to their local university—usually depending on their having
achieved some school-leaving standard. Many American states operate a similar
system. In England there is no such entitlement. Instead individuals apply anywhere across the country and universities decide who to admit, mainly though
not solely on the basis of A level performance. (Individuals may find themselves
living in the vicinity of a recruiting university which will take them even with
modest qualifications, but this is largely a matter of luck.) This gives English
universities a particularly powerful influence over what is taught and how in
our secondary schools. Our secondary schools do not aim for the breadth of
knowledge which you need to be an effective well-educated citizen as embodied
in a set of nationwide school-leaving exams. Instead their purpose is success in
the competition for university entrance. So schools become a means to an end,
and it is the A level grades and hence the place at university which are the end.
In the wise words of Peter Swinnerton-Dyer: 'Each stage of English education
is designed for the benefit of those who will go on to the next stage, however
unsuitable it may be for the rest.'[5] I believe this key feature goes back to the

unusual way our university recruitment is conducted, and nowhere do we see its effect as visibly as in specialization.

There is a further twist. Some other countries also have our selective entry to university, but none have exams which are so subject-specific and require such detailed knowledge of a particular subject that teenagers have to choose them two years in advance and study them in depth. This unique model arises from a distinctive feature of English university admissions. American Ivy league universities operate highly selective admissions—but power over admissions is separate from the individual academic departments of their universities. England has a very different arrangement in which individual academic departments have much greater power to decide who to admit to their own courses. You are not recruited to a university—you are recruited to a course at a university. There is usually now a separate admissions function, and the balance of power is shifting to them, notably because of the access agenda, so final decisions may not be in the hands of departments. But academics in particular departments still set the criteria in their own subjects, which admissions offices have to adhere to—so the physicists will set the criteria for who is admitted to study physics and the historians for history.

Funding drives this as well—through the way research funding is allocated to universities based on the performance of individual academics. This weakens the power of the university as an institution. Instead there is a star system and a transfer market rather like in the football league. Academics who can bring in big research grants and REF funding are worth a lot to a university. Our highly competitive system for allocating research funding significantly affects the power structure within research-intensive universities and is another reason why their departments still have a big say in admissions rules. It may be one reason why less prestigious universities doing less research have more centralized recruitment practices and broader, more generic courses.

The English idea that you come to university to study a subject you have already decided on in advance and to which you are committed is not the usual Western model. In many other countries those decisions will be taken during your first year or later as the student chooses between different subjects and combinations. They assume you do a wide range of subjects until you finish school and go to university for continuing broad education and then try out several in more depth until you specialize, quite possibly when you apply for graduate school. The ultimate example of this is the American liberal arts degree, which includes maths and science as well as humanities. England requires greater pre-commitment with much less flexibility for the student when she arrives at university—she is a captive customer of a particular academic discipline which makes moving between subjects far harder than elsewhere. After Nabokov fled to the US he tried his hand as an academic at Wellesley and Cornell, the basis for *Pnin*, one of the greatest and funniest of all campus novels. He is supposed to have started a lecture in the wrong lecture-room to the wrong class. Before he left the room he turned to the class and said, 'You have just seen the "Coming Attraction" for literature 325. If you are interested you may register next Fall.'[6] That story only really makes sense in an environment where you could make that offer to a group of baffled students regardless of what they were studying that term.

All this means that individual subject disciplines in English universities have a power over admissions which is exceptional by international standards. They use this power in an entirely understandable way—to identify young people who already know a lot about or at least have displayed a real aptitude for the subject the academics will be teaching them at university. This is what the A level helps them assess. And it means that schools focus on getting good A level grades in the subjects which each student will be hoping to study at university. A student's A-level grade in a particular subject may not be a particularly good predictor of how you will do in that subject at university. (The best predictor of your performance in history at Oxford was supposed to be your mark in GCSE chemistry; they claimed it was the best indicator of whether you worked hard even when you were bored.) England has a unique amount of specialization at the age of 16 because of the exceptional power of university departments over admissions. This argument can be summarized in the following empirical proposition about education systems across the OECD: the greater the control university departments have over their own admissions the greater the subject specialization in secondary school.

Universities were consulted about the future of A levels, with the predictable conclusions whenever you ask subject specialists—physicists pronounce themselves shocked by the low level of understanding of physics in today's university applicants and call for standards to be raised. Meanwhile the historians say they are deeply disappointed that young people come to university to study history without a basic knowledge of the shape of British or world history. These criticisms will be strongly supported across the media as evidence of the failings of English education, and each discipline gets its A level made 'harder'. Anyone who dares to point out that those 18-year-olds turning up at university already know more physics or history than in almost any other advanced Western country will be dismissed as a soggy progressive. But imagine what would have happened if the academic community were asked a different question. What if we asked the physicists to set out the minimum basic physics they would expect a graduate who has studied history or English to know as part of being a functioning well-educated citizen in the twenty-first century? And what if we asked the historians for the basic grasp of the shape of world history and the issues prompted by it that they think a well-educated physicist or vet should have in their heads? That challenge is much more relevant to tackling England's educational failure. It would be hard to enforce any such programmes on students in universities organized as they are now. But—taking a leaf from America's book—what if each discipline agreed to clear, say, 25 per cent of the time for studying their disciplines so that the students could choose these kind of options? (Incidentally, as the evidence suggests that student hours worked in English universities are relatively low, it might be possible just to add these options with no offsetting cuts.)

What would it do for the quality of their teaching if the university academics all knew that they had to compete with each other to get the student's attention for these broader options? Incentives to focus on teaching would improve if they knew that if they attracted some of these students they could then opt at the end of their first or second year to major in this discipline as an alternative to what they had started with. That internal competition and choice is what is possible in most higher education systems but is very unusual in England. Subject specialization and prior commitment reduces competitive pressures within universities—the English model is very unusual in making the competition external, between universities, and not within the university, between courses.

There are people in universities who understand the problem of hyper-specialization and we have had a series of unsuccessful attempts at tackling it. After the First World War Sir A. D. Lindsay, the Master of Balliol, designed PPE (Philosophy, Politics, and Economics) to overcome these barriers—ironically, many politicians benefit from this unusually broad course, as I did. It depends on a self-denying ordnance within Oxford making it impossible for students just to study any one of those subjects, notably economics, on its own. Natural Sciences at Cambridge depends on a similar restriction on the opportunity for undergraduates to study physics on its own. Robbins wanted broader courses and less specialization: it was a key theme of his Report and his subsequent writings: 'We do not believe . . . that it is in the public interest that a student of natural science or technology is frequently not competent in even one foreign language . . . and a student of history or literature may be unaware of the significance of science and the scientific method.'[7] When the new universities such as Sussex were set up post-Robbins they experimented with exciting new broad curricula. A. D. Lindsay himself became the first Vice Chancellor of Keele and introduced a bold experiment with broader courses and a four-year degree there. But those experiments collapsed. A major reason was that they involved the expense of studying for four years rather than three and were therefore discouraged by the funding agencies which had to pay for them. There is also a problem because this requires a collective decision. Some universities might relax the specialized A levels they require for entry, but if a 16-year-old wants to keep her option of going to a university which has not liberalized she still has to specialize.

The Tomlinson report to the Blair Government in 2004 proposed a reform of A levels, but the Prime Minster, despite his massive majority and a genuine passion for education, ran scared of the obvious and predictable media narrative and buried it. Blair's advisers also believed that they had found a different way forward with a commitment that every area should have a secondary school providing the International Baccalaureate (IB). This is often cited as the model of broadly based study for university and is assumed to be the exam of the future. But the numbers of teenagers studying for the IB and of schools offering it are now falling. English participation peaked in 2010 at about 230 schools and since then has declined to 140.[8] One reason is that it is really only suitable for the top 20 per cent of students, so either the school has to be academically selective or it faces the complex and expensive logistics of running the IB alongside A levels. There is another reason too. Universities are asking for very high marks in the IB to count as the equal of good grades at A level. It is hard to get in to do maths at Cambridge with the IB—you need specialized maths. This high exchange rate is often seen as a tiresome technical problem but it actually gets to the heart of the issue. It means that the physicists, for example, are saying that if an IB student is to join their physics course they need to have done as much physics as well as a student with a good A level grade in that subject and they will attribute little or no value to their foreign language or their essay writing skills. Many university courses are constructed on the basis of a certain amount of assumed prior knowledge and they do not want to change them. This requirement for high-level accomplishment in the subject you choose for university combined with the breadth of the IB is why schools see it as requiring particularly high standards in England. It is why, most unusually, it is in decline in England, while it is growing in most other advanced Western countries—this regrettable trend can be explained by our unusual university admission arrangements.

The treatment of the IB is not the only evidence for the argument set out here. Personal statements were introduced as an innovation in recruitment and are widely used in the US too. In the US they are indeed about the student as a person. They are about your community service or how you play the violin in an orchestra. In England the advice to the prospective students in the schools which understand how the system works is to make your personal statement a passionate pledge of your love of the subject you are applying to university to study—and as one statement has to be used for all applications this also means students tend to apply for one course alone.

One reply to all this is that the system is actually becoming more flexible in subtle ways. So teenagers are more likely to do a wider mix of A levels than before. However, the reality is that to get in to the prestigious universities you still need a narrowly targeted set of A levels. The Russell Group now publish their advice on A level choices—an excellent initiative which I called for in Opposition—and it is very revealing. Here is what they say: 'If you are a very talented scientist/mathematician, it is very important that out of the four available sciences—Biology, Chemistry, Maths . . . and Physics—you should choose three. If you know you are inclined towards the Life Sciences then you should choose Chemistry and Biology. If you know you are on the Engineering side you should choose Mathematics (and possibly Further Mathematics) and Physics.'[9] That is an accurate account of the reality of specialization in our schools. It is also a reminder of the importance of good information, advice, and guidance (IAG) to which we now turn.

Better advice, and more flexibility

Adam Smith spotted the problem that young people were expected to take decisions about their future when they were least able to take the decision. 'The contempt of risk and the presumptuous hope of success are in no period of life more active than at the age at which young people choose their professions.'[10] You might think that there would be a pretty obvious social contract here. In England we expect 16-year-olds to take decisions most countries don't expect until you are about 20 years old at least. We do it for our university academics so they can educate students who know more about their subject than in most other countries. We also do it to save money by getting education over with earlier than our competitors. We expect these big decisions of you at a time when your brain is rebooting and hormones are surging through your body. In return for this rather peculiar system we know we owe young people proper advice and guidance. But far from it—this is one of the disaster areas of public policy.

We sometimes say the problem with deprived youngsters is that they lack aspiration. But the evidence is the opposite—they have conventional aspirations but they lack the information and knowledge of how to get there from where they are. They lack the route map. One study of NEETS (young people aged 16–24 Not in Education, Employment, or Training) showed that they wanted to be a soldier or a chef or a lawyer but they did not know how to fulfil their ambitions.[11] In particular many young people do not appear to know what academic qualifications they need to achieve their ambitions. So, for example, almost 40 per cent of young people underestimate the education required for achieving their desired goal.[12] This is a missed opportunity to motivate young people to study. The media narrative of overqualified, underemployed youngsters is untrue and unhelpful—the truth, for many occupations, is the opposite.

Even if you do get to university you do not escape from the consequences of poor advice because you are in a system so rigid you are trapped with the choices you have made. Nearly a third of students say that if they had known then what they know now they would have chosen a different course.[13] The issue is the course specifically—most of them are pleased they went to university. Perhaps you go to university to study accountancy and finance or pharmacy because that is what your parents think is a safe route to a good job. (And we know that, in the absence of good advice and guidance, families have enormous influence on the decisions of young people, especially those from disadvantaged backgrounds.) But really you love novels or you want to act or be a research scientist. That first time away from home is an opportunity for you to change to what you really love. Or you want to experience life abroad. Many countries see the university as precisely such an opportunity to change the direction of your life. But in England the combination of narrow A level choices and internal university restrictions makes such a shift very difficult.

In some English universities moving from one course to another means resigning and starting all over again. I met a young man who wanted to go to China to study for a year, but it was not recognized as a credit to his course at an English university so he ended up having to abandon his degree course to go. Harvard and MIT are twinned so students can move between them, unlike London, where moving between UCL, King's, and Imperial is not easy despite their all being part of the University of London. You used to be able to do a two-year PPE course at New College after transfer from Ruskin—but that kind of transfer is much less common today. The Higher Education and Research Act includes a remit for the Office for Students to investigate and promote credit transfer arrangements: this is an opportunity to try to address this problem within as well as between universities.

It is very different—and far more flexible—in the USA. About 1.4m students entered American higher education in 2004, of which 240,000 selected a science/engineering field to major in. By 2009 80,000 of them had shifted out to non-science. But at the same time 100,000 who had arrived with a very different major had opted in to science/engineering, giving a net inflow to those subjects of 20,000.[14] And the subject most frequently identified by American university applicants for their future study is on neither the science nor the arts side. It is 'undeclared'. They turn up at university and then they sample different courses and decide what they might focus on. Just think how radically English universities would be changed if that were our system too. That is many more round pegs in round holes than we permit in England—though offset by some butterflies who never really settle with any subject long enough to do it in any depth. But for many young people that early specialization does not really reflect what they come to be interested in and they do not really follow it with passion and commitment. As they discover what they want to do as a career, those decisions at the age of 16 seem irrelevant. Hence the paradox that we specialize early and often end up often with ill-educated generalists.[15] This suggests another feature of the social contract on education in a system with early specialization. It increases the risks of people studying what they come to see as the wrong courses for them. So adult education and good options for mature learners are particularly important. But, as we have seen, that is not where we spend our limited educational resource. This is where the sciences miss out in particular—it is easier to move from chemistry to law than the other way round. The specialization is so early and the required body of knowledge so great that the English education system can be seen as offering a one-way street out of the sciences with no traffic the other way.

Case studies of the problem: engineering and medicine

So far we have focused on the structural features of English higher education which lie behind our specialization problem. But early specialization is not some abstract issue. It blights people's lives as, looking back, they realize that they took the wrong decision at 16. It affects the shape of our economy too, as the decisions of 16-year-olds determines and limits the numbers of skilled recruits flowing into key sectors. Here is a practical example of the problems created by our bizarre system. We will look at higher education for engineers. I am not convinced that there is an overall shortage of STEM graduates—if there were we would see a much stronger signal in wages for graduates in these disciplines. But companies and employers do regularly complain that they are desperately short specifically of graduate engineers. Of 37,000 engineering graduates aged over 65, 38 per cent are still employed. This suggests there could be a problem and it is a case study in what is wrong with our system.

The two key A levels required for engineering courses at most of our universities are maths and physics. There are about 700,000 pupils per year in English schools. After they have done their GCSEs about 28,000 of them opt for those two A levels together. So by the age of 16 our potential cadre of young graduate engineers is down to 4 per cent of young people—in almost every other advanced Western country it is much higher and in some it is 100 per cent. Of those A level students around a half, about 14,000, go on to do engineering at university. Some of them go on to work in the City and consultancy, so that leaves about 9,000 graduate engineers per year to go into actual engineerin—an extremely small number. The pipeline is sealed early on and then gets very narrow very fast. (If anything this understates the pressure for specialization. Engineering comes in many different forms— mechanical or civil or electrical or aero-engineering, for example. Some universities expect young people to choose these specific courses in advance and it is not always easy to move between different subdivisions of engineering.)

There is one source of talent which engineering really ought to tap. Only 9 per cent of engineering professionals in the UK are female, much lower than in most other Western countries.[16] This tells us again that we are dealing with some specific feature of the English system which reduces the flow of women into engineering—if our account of specialization can explain this, it is further evidence we are on to something. We have seen how engineering courses at university tend to require A level physics. Only 25 per cent of girls with A★ at GCSE physics convert to A level physics. This is because they are thinking instead of doing medicine, which is the preferred science of middle-class teenage girls. Fifty-six per cent of girls with an A★ at GCSE biology stay with it to A level. For boys the ratios are the other way round. Fifty-two per cent of boys with A★ at GCSE physics go on to do it at A level but only 41 per cent of boys with A★ at GCSE biology.[17] The key early moment for girls is the progression

Table 14.1. Percentages of girls and boys with
GCSE A★ doing that subject at A level

	Girls	Boys
Physics	25%	52%
Biology	56%	41%
Maths	67%	80%

Source: Tom Sutch, *Progression from GCSE to AS and A Level*,
Cambridge Assessment, December 2013, table A2, p. 29.

from GCSE to A levels. Table 14.1 shows the different percentages going on to
A level having got A★ in that subject at GCSE.

So the girls who are interested in science do the A levels that lead to medicine. They follow that advice from the Russell Group (which represents universities with medical schools) and opt for A levels in maths, biology, and chemistry.
That is what the girls and their parents want and that is what the schools offer.
Of 16,000 girls with three As at A level about 1,900 or 12 per cent went on to
study medicine whereas 4 per cent did physical sciences and 3 per cent did a
combination of physical sciences and other science. So medicine is by far the
most popular of the science options.

But now comes the next twist. Medicine is one of the few subjects where
there is still a direct cap on student numbers—because it costs so much public money to train a doctor. So many of these girls get turned down for
medicine at university even with good A level grades. UCAS shows that in
2012 there were 11,700 female applicants for pre-clinical medicine with 4,000
accepted. Boys had 9,470 applications with 3,500 getting a place. Many of
these girls have advanced up what may seem to them like a blind alley,
though the A levels themselves are of wider value. And the girls' parents and
the media think the barrier they have encountered is all to do with class
discrimination—in two very different forms. Sometimes they say that Emily
has got three good A grades and did voluntary service in a South African
hospital so she can only have been turned down because she went to a private
school and therefore it is all the fault of Les Ebdon, director of Fair Access to
Higher Education. Or they say Tiffany should have got a place because her
A and two Bs were a heroic achievement at her mediocre comprehensive and
she can only have been turned down because of Oxbridge-style snobbery.
(This was the backdrop to the Laura Spence controversy.[18]) I was regularly on
the receiving end of both complaints. The truth was that under our system
both were losing out. We end up with a lot of disappointed 18-year-old girls

who might have done medicine—and of course some boys as well, though there are fewer of them. At this point they might think of another scientific subject and that could include engineering. But they have not got A level physics, and this massively reduces the options open to them. Indeed, the biggest single group of 18-year-olds with good A levels who do not go to university straightaway are those applying for medicine who do not get a place. If you have watched the misery and the waste caused by this system year after year you begin to think something needs to be done about it. There are a range of policy options.

The first option is to do better at the PR for science in general and engineering in particular—try to persuade girls early on of the appeal of engineering by promoting female role models. We can also try to get the girls to see that there are other ways of improving the world than medicine—bio-engineering, for example, does this quite well. All this makes sense within the logic of our system—if youngsters are having to take a key decision at 16 then we do need to get at them young. And of course the narrative we get from great successful individuals appears to confirm the model—they say how excited they got about a subject at age 11. But the evidence is that sadly such initiatives are not having a massive effect and they are of course accepting the system as it is. The real problem is that such a decision has to be taken by 16-year-olds at all.

The second option also goes with the grain of the system. Many universities used to expect A level physics for the study of medicine and one suggestion is that they should do so again. That has a double effect—it narrows the number of eligible candidates for medicine and also gives the ones who are not selected a wider choice of alternatives, including engineering. Some universities are doing this.

Thirdly, you can say engineering should not require physics A level and should broaden the range of 18-year-olds from which it can recruit, including those disappointed 18-year-old girls. The revival of university Classics is a case study in how to rescue a subject confronted with a collapse in relevant A levels. Fewer and fewer students were doing A level Latin or Greek so now you can do Classics at many universities without those prior qualifications. What if teenagers suddenly stopped studying physics at school—would engineering departments close down? I doubt it. Instead they would have to change their admissions rules and provide more support in the first year. Universities which abandon a narrow A level requirement have to revise their first year and that would have to include the basics of physics needed for engineering. This requires an important change of approach—it means a university engineering department has to teach 18-year-olds who know rather less physics when they start. One reason it is possible to study Classics at Oxford without an A level in Greek or Latin is that the course is four years long—an important clue which we will return to later. Economics also does not expect economics A level—though maths is almost essential.

There is an increasing and very welcome trend for universities to introduce some broader courses. Consumer demand from students is beginning to overwhelm the power of the academics in departments. They have to accept that they will be plugging gaps in knowledge because their students have given up so many subjects at age 16 which they then resume as part of their university course. (The paradox of our system of specialization is that as soon as our universities broaden out they are dealing with students who gave up subjects at 16 and are therefore more ignorant than in most other countries, and English university courses have to be even more elementary and remedial as a result.) At this rate we could see the emergence of a very peculiar hourglass structure of English education where after two years of hyper-specialization you then go back to a broader study at university which includes plugging the gaps left by the omissions of late secondary education. It may be a necessary transitional stage before the pressures for reform of A levels become irresistible.

There is a fourth reform which is also about greater breadth. This alone really gets to the heart of the issue—allowing our secondary students to do a broader range of subjects to age 18; then universities would have to work from a broader base of understanding but with rather less detailed prior knowledge. We will revert to that later in the chapter. But first we must look at this issue from the perspective not of engineering or medicine but of the humanities and social sciences.

Humanities and the problem of the two cultures

C. P. Snow's 'Two Cultures' lecture of 1959 still echoes through this debate. Looking back on his experience as a Government scientist and a novelist he observed that 'I felt I was moving among two groups—comparable in intelligence, identical in race, not grossly different in social origin, earning about the same incomes, who had almost ceased to communicate at all, who in intellectual, moral and psychological climate had so little in common that instead of going from Burlington House or South Kensington to Chelsea, one might have crossed an ocean.'[19] He rightly observes that 'this cultural divide is not just an English phenomenon: it exists all over the western world. But it probably seems at its sharpest in England, for two reasons.... One is our fanatical belief in educational specialisation, which is much more deeply ingrained in us than in any country in the world, west or east.... Talk to schoolmasters, and they say that our intense specialisation, like nothing else on earth, is dictated by the Oxford and Cambridge scholarship examinations. At age eighteen our science specialists know more science than their contemporaries anywhere, though they know less of anything else. At twenty-one, when they take their first degree they are probably still a year or so ahead.'[20] So the argument set out earlier in this chapter is very similar to C. P. Snow's.

The passage of time has, however, changed the dynamics behind that lecture. C. P. Snow speaks on behalf of the scientists with a chip on their shoulder about the assumed superiority of the humanities. I do not believe that is any more a problem. Today's mood is captured in that great line in *Ghostbusters*: 'Back off, we're scientists.'[21] Now it is the humanities which have developed a bit of a victim complex.[22] Trying to correct misapprehensions about lack of funding for humanities can then just get the response that all you talk about is money so you don't really get the point of the humanities. The humanities are of course fundamental to the good life and to the quality of our national life. It is important to say this and it has the merit of being true.

Howard Jacobson captures the mood of some academics in the humanities: 'The Department of Twentieth-Century Studies, so called in order to meet the Polytechnic's stringent requirements of relevant contemporaneity, fooled nobody.... He recognised it to be...the same tired collection of sentimental grammar school boys with indifferent degrees and a hostility towards advertising...the same weary campaigners that had once been Humanities and before that Arts and before that Liberal Studies and before that English and History. It seemed that there was no getting rid of them. Deprivation, derision, bribery, had all failed. Back they always came, scorched, flattened and featherless, like the indefatigable victim in the sort of Walt Disney cartoon of which they didn't approve. They had nowhere else to go. So they were kept on, kept busy, and kept apart...'.[23]

Nowadays some of the boldest arguments for precedence come from maths: that kind of symbolic analysis seems to be of particular significance in the modern digital world. When one tries to link qualifications to employment and earnings the clearest single result is that for any given level of educational accomplishment, if it includes maths there is a further 10 per cent boost to earnings.[24] Leading academics, however, are too wise to get caught up in arguments about precedence: they recognize that the big intellectual and global challenges can best be tackled by drawing on the insights from more than one discipline. A study of Nobel Prize winners showed that many of them had experienced a disruption in their intellectual development—migrating to a different country or indeed to a different discipline—which gave them a different perspective and new insights. The structure of DNA, one of the great post-war scientific advances, was discovered not in a biology lab but in the old Cavendish Lab for physics. Instead of thinking of maths and IT as claiming precedence we should think of them as tools which enable other disciplines to advance. Digital recording and analysis of images is transforming the study of the history of art.[25] I urged the humanities to bid more boldly for the substantial capital funding for research with a project like digitizing every word written in English up to 1900. What now happens at our universities is that a politics student who may have exclusively done humanities A levels finds that to study American presidential elections they need to read key academic papers which use large data-sets and regression analysis. Or there are students of social policy who want to understand how to tackle poverty but to do this they need to be able to use advanced statistical techniques to distinguish between correlation and causation. That is why I allocated funding to the Sigma project, which provides emergency maths programmes for humanities students who find they need a set of skills which our educational system said they did not need to study beyond the age of 16.

This remedial role for our universities in plugging gaps in knowledge is a growing part of the value of the higher education experience. It is not just giving humanities students the opportunity to improve their grasp of maths: it is also about enriching the study of the sciences. Many universities will offer some kind of low-cost access to basic courses in a foreign language. If we want entrepreneurs from the sciences they may gain from a business studies programme offered as part of their science degree. Technological advances involve changes in human behaviour and hence insights from the humanities.[26]

Reversing the pressures for specialization matters for education standards. The point is put very well in a report on the US, whose schools have a mediocre score in PISA (Programme for International Student Assessment): 'Each of the nations that consistently outranks the US on the PISA exam provides their students with a comprehensive, content-rich education in the liberal arts and sciences...that is the common ingredient across these varied nations. It is not a delivery mechanism or an accountability system that these high performing nations share: it is a dedication to educating their children deeply in a wide range of subjects.'[27]

Above all there is here an important principle which should shape not just secondary but also tertiary education—that the range of human accomplishment should be available for every child regardless of social background through to the age of 18.

The four-year university course and the taught Master's

So we have to reform our education system and raise standards by reversing the pressures for specialization. We have focused on the underestimated power of English universities to shape what schools do and the peculiar way that influence is exercised in Britain. But that is not the whole story—specialization is driven by an alliance of university departments and Government. Governments are complicit because it saves money by enabling us to get away with a shorter higher education than most other countries. We save money by specializing early and getting our graduates out into the jobs market paying their taxes early too. We have some of the youngest graduates—on average, they graduate aged 23—of any advanced country.[28]

It looks efficient if you just educate people in things they are really focused on—it is much harder work if you have to educate a broader range of abilities across a broader range of subjects. If you are to study a wider range of subjects you will need longer to achieve a given level of knowledge in an area in which eventually you do specialize, if that is necessary for your career. In the US law and medicine are only studied at graduate school. One structure—though not the only one—would be for more graduates to do a Master's. This can also help with the access challenge by enabling a student to move on from one university to another. In the US where you did your undergraduate studies matters less than where you were at graduate school. There have been modest English attempts to move in this direction—though with much more reluctance for students to move on to a different university. The second part of the Cambridge Tripos was introduced as a more specialized stage and earns a student a Master's. It is a traditional and well-respected model for teacher training. Unusually in England our Master's degrees can be secured in one year's study. And, given the thinness of the time actually spent studying in a usually undergraduate course, it should be possible to add significant breadth during the first years and still get useful specialized knowledge in a Master's degree after four years in total. With the continuing growth of education we must expect that more students will stay on for longer and this is the best way of channelling that trend. Increasing numbers of professions expect a Master's, so access to a Master's is becoming a new barrier to social mobility. The academic career itself is an example. If you want to become a researcher or an academic you will wish to do a PhD, and public funding for them is of course available, usually via Research Councils. But first you will need a Master's, and that is the bottleneck. These immediately postgraduate taught courses are not seen as part of the responsibility of research bodies but neither have they had access to public funding.

There is another pressure too. You can teach very efficiently if you have a group of 18-year-olds with good grades in A level maths and physics who have chosen to devote their three years at university to aeronautical engineering. It means that by the age of 21 they have fantastic expertise, long before a young person even in the American Ivy League. But an education system designed for them comes with very high collateral costs and we have to decide if we have got the trade-off right.

The issue, however, has always been how to pay for that extra year. It was above all the public spending constraints which killed previous reform initiatives such as those proposed by Robbins. Sometimes as a minister you look back on a decision you took almost unthinkingly and realize that it mattered and you got it wrong. Early on in our university funding reforms we worried that now there was a loophole in our spending regime. Universities and students could just add an extra year to courses and get loans to cover them and offer the students a Master's. It is actually what the Cambridge Tripos already does, and there was no reason why universities across the country should not follow them. As we wanted to control total outlays on loans I remember agreeing pretty much unreflectively to insert a stern warning into our annual university grant letter to HEFCE discouraging such arrangements. Since then policy has advanced in a much more enlightened way and the Treasury and BIS are now significantly extending entitlement to postgraduate loans. This is the right thing to do. After decades when reform of university courses was held up by public spending pressures we now have this unprecedented opportunity provided by our fees and loans system and yet we do not have a coherent programme of education reform to take advantage of it. But actually this opportunity alone—setting aside all the other arguments we analysed in Chapter Three—makes our changes to higher education financing worthwhile. Indeed, Jo Johnson has been steadily increasing the scope of student loans so they help students fund Master's courses and also doctorates—this wise approach is gradually easing the financial pressures for early specialization.

The trouble is that we were not able to align these changes in higher education with reforms at the school level where, much to my frustration, the trend was in the opposite direction. The years 16 to 18 were not covered by any pledge to protect education spending and—as we saw in Chapter Six—never attracted much sympathy. So the DfE restricted funding at secondary schools and colleges to three A levels to try to stop the tendency for a further subject to be added. The abolition of AS levels was a further narrowing of education for this age group—where some might, for example, at least have kept up their maths for one more year. The counter-argument was that it stopped a summer term being wasted on yet more exams. Michael Gove was himself by temperament a reformer and had personally benefited from the much broader Scottish educational system—though his very familiarity with it perhaps made him more sceptical of its merits. However, he very much focused on restoring the traditional three-A-level model. He argued that this specialization was also driven by competition between exam boards for the favour of universities, which was the way to get schools to adopt them, and his idea of a single exam board would have been a useful precondition for a broader curriculum. Sir David Bell, the former permanent secretary at the DfE, described where we are now as follows: 'five years of permanent revolution has seen us come full circle to a decades old system which culminates in sixth formers still specialising in three or four "gold-standard" A levels, with two years of study ending in a pass–and–fail exam'.[29]

We now have a very unusual model indeed. Now that taught Master's courses are going to be funded out of fees and loans the funding barrier on a broader undergraduate course plus a more specialized year has been removed. It is also what students want—indeed it is a powerful example of how consumer pressures can drive up standards and promote reform. And we have also seen the competitive challenge from English universities losing students to overseas universities with broader courses. So universities like UCL and King's are introducing broader courses. At last the liberal arts degree is going to flourish in English universities, and a good thing too. The enhanced power of students and competition for them is going to break down the barriers between disciplines by weakening the power of individual departments and to move us closer to the idea of a university as place where different disciplines are linked not separated. But this powerful university reform movement comes after 16- to 18-year-olds have specialized in three subjects. It means, as we saw earlier, that universities have to provide remedial education to plug gaps in their students' education left by their giving up on subjects at the age of 16 only then to resume them. That is why the pressure for reform of the education of 16- to 18-year-olds will become irresistible: it should be the next big education reform.

Conclusion

The university

Universities are important, sophisticated institutions but they are not well understood even by academics themselves who are busy researching gravitational waves or the rise of populism. They may, very reasonably, find their discipline much more interesting than their institution. Instead the campus novel, from Kingsley Amis's *Lucky Jim* to Malcolm Bradbury's *The History Man*, David Lodge's Brummidge, and Howard Jacobson's Sefton Goldberg, is the main way people working in universities investigate what they are like and communicate it to the wider world. But they can't tell the whole story. There are also academics in British universities researching universities but not many of them—most of the books about the university are American. Meanwhile crude conspiracy theories claim to explain what is happening to a complex institution. One such narrative is 'the university is under attack from managers/ministers/markets threatening my/your/all disciplines'. Another narrative is 'Universities are ivory towers: there are too many of them and too many people go.' That is why I have tried to convey what I have learnt from my university education over the past decade and assembled the evidence to explain why both of those narratives are wrong. Such is my respect for the values of academia that, even if one might suspect this is just a heavily disguised ministerial memoir, it is at least the first example which has been subject to academic peer review.

The behaviour of our universities is influenced by their environment and the incentives they face. That environment is very unusual and took its modern form as a result of a series of haphazard decisions taken in the late 1950s and early 1960s. Competitive nationwide entry gives our universities exceptional power to decide who they admit. That in turn has driven an intense educational arms race in our secondary schools which in turn has led to very early subject specialization. The behaviour of schools is shaped by the competition to get into the 'best' universities. However, we have seen that there are different types of universities, each well adapted to a distinctive role. Recognizing this makes one wary of the idea that universities can be ranked in a single neat hierarchy stretching from good to bad with Oxbridge at the top and an ex-poly at the bottom. But that is how most people think about universities most of the time.[1] Oxford and Cambridge are wonderful but their cultural dominance has limited our understanding of what a university can be. Moreover they achieved this dominance by obstructing the creation of other universities for six hundred years.

We are fortunate to have great universities with world-class research—not just Oxbridge but other leading research-intensive universities. They are exceptional institutions and rightly enjoy great prestige and authority. This is in many ways a good thing for the sector as a whole. The influence of their model is one reason why the entire English higher education system is structured the way it is with institutional autonomy and nationwide mobility of students—Oxbridge writ large. The respect commanded by our leading universities is important for protecting the freedoms of every university and more widely the freedoms we all enjoy. Edmund Burke had an image of a nation's historic institutions and its corporations as sturdy oaks providing shelter and protection for individuals.[2] Nowadays we think of rights as accruing to individuals but it is often strong civic institutions such as universities which help preserve these rights. However, the very status which protects the freedoms of academics and students can also enable prestigious universities to escape some of the competitive pressures which institutions in many other walks of life have to deal with. Their reputation means they can become an example of what economists, going back to Adam Smith, see as rent-seeking behaviour. The status of their degrees in the modern labour market gives them enormous power as incumbents and is why a certain ambivalence about their prestige runs through this book. Moreover their status can lead us to ignore the many other types of university within the system which are essential to its overall functioning—not least because of the flows of students and academics between different types of institutions.

Our distinctive types of universities are often the results of previous movements of university expansion, like the pattern of tree rings telling us about the environment many years ago. Dating back around a century or so there are big sprawling research-intensive universities at the heart of major cities such as Liverpool or Leeds, Bristol or Sheffield, Birmingham, Manchester, Nottingham, and Cardiff. They are known around the world and their alumni lead companies and ministries. We are right to be proud of them. But there are other types of university which are also world class in their way and deserve more appreciation and recognition as we saw in Chapter Seven when we considered which universities students might apply to and why. For example, one can sense the distinctive ethos of our former Colleges of Advanced Technology where sandwich courses linked to industry still thrive and which do very well on graduate employment and which also do excellent applied research. Some universities specialize in training students for public services such as teaching, nursing, and social work—places like Liverpool Edge Hill or the University of Roehampton. There are the cathedral city universities such as Gloucestershire, Worcester, Winchester, Chester, and Chichester, which often have an Anglican ethos going back to their origins as teacher training colleges. Some universities have strong links to business sectors in their region—I doubt that we would have seen the revival of the motor industry in the West Midlands without Warwick University's Manufacturing Group and the work of Coventry University. The University of Sunderland has similar links to the Japanese car-makers in the North-East. Some universities are centres of the performing arts. Nottingham Trent is a leader in education technologies, Bournemouth in media and film production, and Royal Holloway in cyber security. Leicester is strong in space exploration with close links to the space industry. London is one of the world's great concentrations of higher education with its own wide mix including leading research-intensive university institutions such as UCL, Imperial, and LSE. King's and Queen Mary's both achieve the exceptional combination of being prestigious research-intensive universities whilst also recruiting broadly and imaginatively with a much more socially mixed intake. There are universities which do a particularly good job of including students from ethnic minorities—such as London Met and the University of Bedfordshire.

Over the years I have gradually come to recognize and value this diversity and become ever more doubtful of confident judgements of 'bad' or 'good' universities usually made by people who have set foot in very few of them. Too often politicians and commentators press universities to work more closely with industry or recruit more students from poor backgrounds and from ethnic minorities but then treat with disdain the very universities which do those things. Or they wrongly assume that they must look elsewhere for vocational and technical education when delivering it is now one of the main roles of the university.

This diversity of roles played by universities is matched by the diversity of the academics within them. There are great thinkers and winners of Nobel Prizes. But I also visited a university in the North-East where the researchers were trying to help a major multinational develop better dishwasher detergents: their recognition that they needed an accurate measure of the cloudiness of glasses emerging from a dishwasher in order to progress made them true heirs to

Francis Bacon's empiricism. This diversity is threatened if we believe we can rank all our universities on one scale based on academic citations of research performance and the prior attainment of the students they admit.

The student

There is a popular narrative that too many students go to university. But lives are transformed by going to university even if the graduates do not end up in the best-paid jobs. I think of the young Muslim woman so devout that she would not shake my hand at a graduation ceremony but whose degree in pharmacy will take her on as much of a personal journey as the supremely self-confident public school boy on his way to an investment bank via a more prestigious university. Chapter Five provided the evidence from Britain and around the world which shows that universities change people—and by and large for the better. One of the best ways we can pass on something to the next generation is for more of them to be better educated than we are. It is a thought captured by Alfred Marshall in his essay on 'The future of the working classes': 'just as a man who has borrowed money is bound to pay it back with interest, so a man is bound to give to his children an education better, and more thorough than he has himself received.'[3] That is one of the first formulations of an argument which is as true today as it was then.[4] We ourselves may also hope to benefit from this investment as we age and depend on the young generation. So we should welcome the widespread aspiration to go to university and expect more people to go to university. We should also expect the continuing creation of new universities—the alternative is for universities to get bigger and bigger. There are few better indicators of a country's optimism in its future than that it should want more people to go to more universities. Universities are one of the great forces shaping the modern world and driving human progress.

The competition to get in to the prestigious universities is now so intense that there is a danger that school-based education becomes joyless. I had to judge an essay competition organized by the formidable Mary Curnock-Cook of UCAS. It was for first-year students to describe their initial experience of university. Overwhelmingly there was a sense of liberation and excitement that at last they could study and reflect deeply rather than gaming tedious exams largely testing their capacity to memorize and deploy key words and facts the examiners were looking for. This different university experience is particularly transformational for students from poorer backgrounds. Indeed there is some encouraging evidence that students from poorer areas—schools with lots of pupils on free school meals—actually do better at university than students from the most advantaged schools with the fewest on free school meals. That would make university the only stage of education where disadvantaged students catch up rather than fall further behind.[5]

The future

Universities now face the pressures of globalization and new technology. Just as in other industries both are a very significant challenge to the incumbents. I look forward to a new tranche of providers aiming to become global chains and innovative in their use of EdTech. But, unlike in many industries, the old incumbents are not going to disappear. Universities, when they work, prove extraordinarily long-lived and resilient. Many Oxbridge colleges were originally funded as chantries for singing prayers for their benefactor's soul in perpetuity. The average foundation date of a university in the THES world top 200 is 1803.[6] That average age matches the famous advice of the late Senator Daniel Patrick Moynihan when he was asked how to create a great city and replied, 'create a great university and wait 200 years' and as those universities grew they shaped the city and the economy around them. Even some of our newer universities are much older than they appear—winning university title and degree awarding powers long after they were first created as a mechanics' institute or an Anglican teacher training college.

This longevity is a clue to the special character of a university. For a start their graduates will take their degree with them through a long career. They will care about the continuing reputation of their alma mater and their own subsequent achievements may contribute to its reputation for decades. There is an inter-generational exchange as knowledge and understanding are transmitted from one generation to the next and the beneficiaries then contribute to their own university to help the generations coming after them. By contrast a consumer having purchased a car does not feel a need to make further periodic donations to Jaguar or BMW.[7] So, yes, I recognize that the relationship between the university and student is not simply producer and consumer. But we should be willing to accept that it is possible to belong to a profit making multinational corporation whose product is higher education and to be a university—provided that such an institution meets our regulatory standards for university title. This might confirm the fears of the critics who think that recent policies emerge from a neo-liberal agenda, imposed because of ideological predilections rather than any real educational need. I do find the insights from market economics very important in understanding the behaviour of universities. But it is not a matter of ideology: I argued in Chapter Twelve that Britain loses out by not having generated any large commercial chains of universities delivering higher education across the world. Nor was our shift to a graduate repayment scheme driven by ideology: it was a response to universities themselves recognizing they were losing resources to other stages of education and needed sources of funding which were not defined and controlled as public spending. There would be a real risk of diminished funding per student if those reforms were reversed. Enabling a student to take funding to the university of her choice if it has decided to admit her is finally to fulfil the promise of student choice implicit in the UCCA/UCAS system from the beginning.

The idea of the university

Behind the university as an institution there is the idea of the university. It is so significant that academics reflect on the idea of the idea of a university.[8] What comes first—the institution or the idea? T. S. Eliot contrasted two ways of thinking in an account of political parties which I have amended into an account of universities:

> At the beginning may be a body of doctrine, perhaps a canonical work, and a band of devoted people set out to disseminate and popularize this doctrine . . . and then a *university* endeavour to realize a programme based on the doctrine. But . . . ideas may come into being by an opposite process. A *university* may find that it has had a history before it is fully aware of or agrees upon its own permanent tenets; it may have arrived at its actual formation through a succession of metamorphoses and adaptations. What its fundamental tenets are, will probably be found only by careful examination of its behaviour throughout its history.[9]

Higher education has not always taken the pragmatic route: we have seen that many universities were founded as embodiments of an idea of higher education. Humboldt's research university was the culmination of a German debate about the role of the university in research and sustaining a national culture. American universities from Johns Hopkins to Colombia were founded in pursuit of that German idea of the research-oriented university. Even in pragmatic Britain many universities were founded to fulfil an idea of higher education. UCL embodied an idea, new for England, of secular accessible higher education.

Newman's idea of a university was a prospectus for a new institution based on the Oxford model and with the aim of creating a certain type of character. Joe Chamberlain had a plan for a new type of civic university. One purpose of the Robbins expansion was a modernization and broadening of the subjects studied by creating new institutions free from old departmental structures. Alternatively, however, an idea may gradually emerge, heavily influenced by an institution's history and romanticized by it—such as Matthew Arnold's account of Oxford: 'steeped in sentiment as she lies, spreading her gardens to the moonlight, whispering from her towers the last enchantments of the Middle Ages'.[10] More recently the conversion of the former polytechnics into universities was a broadening of England's Oxbridge-style model of a university which was done so suddenly that it took some time for our idea of the university to catch up with the reality.

It is very hard to propose an idea of a university which is broad enough to capture the many distinct types of university but also has real meaning. We saw the legal starting point back in Chapter One: what makes a higher education institution a university is the power to award its own degrees. (Even this, however, is not straightforward as in England it is possible to have taught degree awarding powers before gaining university title.) Oxbridge traditions left us with one historic idea of a university—a place for the study of the liberal arts free from any concern with usefulness. But Oxbridge itself is now much more diverse than that. The university can be useful too, right back to medieval universities training priests and lawyers to work in papal and state bureaucracies. America's state universities set up in the nineteenth century with Morrill Land-Grant Acts are the most successful modern examples of this model.

These diverse missions can either be reconciled within the specific university or within the higher education system as a whole. Clark Kerr identified what he called the 'multi-versity' fulfilling these different roles. But actually the California State Universities over which he presided did not deliver these different roles in a single institution—they were instead allocated to different institutions within the overall system. Arizona State University gets so much attention at the moment because it is the most ambitious attempt to combine these roles within one university—though as a visiting professor at King's I would say that together with Queen Mary's we are ambitious English attempts at combining wide and diverse access, research excellence, and commercial application of research.

What holds such big diverse institutions or systems together? Clark Kerr's witticisms about universities being held together by a shared grievance about parking suggests a nervousness about anything more substantial which would constitute a shared mission. One very English account is that universities act as the bearer of the national culture—studying its history, its literature, and its political institutions and indeed being the respected interpreter of all of them. The later structuralists and post-modernists, however—such as Derrida and Lyotard—argue that there is such deep divergence about the values underpinning modern society that this role is no longer open to them.[11] On this view the anxieties of academics in the Humanities are not really attributable to crass management, tiresome though that is, and instead are a displacement exercise to hide the loss of a shared national history and culture of which they were the respected custodians.

One elegant solution, reconciling the useless or useful, is the case for the modern research-intensive university. This argues that research should be pursued freely, driven by intellectual curiosity and regardless of considerations of usefulness. However, this research might well turn out to be useful—we cannot know in advance how it will be useful but we can know in advance that this will happen. This is an attractive and plausible argument but it leaves open the question of whether this is a happy accident or a fundamental feature of the world. To identify the best way to answer this question we must turn to the most important and productive investigation of the idea of the university which was conducted in Germany at the end of the eighteenth century. The crucial early contribution was Kant's essay on the *Conflict of the Faculties*. It develops through the work of Fichte and Schelling and culminates in Humboldt's creation of the University of Berlin.[12] Kant begins with the medieval faculties—law, medicine, and theology—which trained students for the key professions. These are the higher faculties. Philosophy is the lower faculty: it is the general intellectual training a student needs before moving on to specific professional training. Towards the end of his career Kant encountered censorship by the Prussian authorities who regarded some of his writing as irreligious. Kant's essay is a carefully argued reply. He concedes there is a role for the state in the higher faculties—how future clergymen are trained is, he accepts, an issue of legitimate interest for the public authorities. However, he argues that the 'lower' faculty of philosophy has to be free.

One might see this as an egregious example of aggrandizement by one faculty claiming to be the authentic heart of the university. Leavis's essay placing English at the centre of the university is another example of the genre, making the university the custodian of the national culture.[13] But Kant's argument is more sophisticated than that. By philosophy he really means critical thinking—taking a step outside the internal conventions of a discipline and reflecting upon them. This requires freedom of thought. Kant thought it was the centrality of this critical reasoning capacity which was distinctive of a university: 'It is absolutely essential that the learned community at the university also contain a faculty that is independent of the government's command with regard to its teachings; one that, having no commands to give, is free to evaluate everything, and concerns itself with the interests of the sciences, that is, with truth; one in which reason is authorized to speak out publicly.'[14] Kant's case for the core discipline of philosophy was to become the case for the whole programme of a modern university. His 'lower faculty' became the model for all the critical disciplines in the university as the underpinning of professional graduate schools. Critical reasoning becomes the principle which drives the university. Bill Readings puts it very well: 'The life of the Kantian university is a perpetual conflict between established tradition and rational inquiry.... Each particular discipline develops itself by interrogating itself with the assistance of philosophy.... Inquiry passes from mere empirical practice to theoretical self-knowledge by means of self-criticism.... This is what differentiates it from either a technical training school or a specialized academy.'[15] This argument had a big influence on the design of the university in Germany and then around the world, notably in the US. The modern university is essentially that Kantian idea.

These German universities also developed the classic academic apparatus of the written recording of a research programme presented as a dissertation and discussed at the seminar.[16] This is a profound shift from the medieval role of the university as the place for skilled oral disputation on ancient hallowed texts. Now a university will advance knowledge by the use of reason and evidence. That is what the academic apparatus secures. The footnote, for example, says that there is evidence which connects to or supports what one says. This scholarly apparatus can descend into pettifogging detail. It was not just Kingsley Amis who mocked it. Nietzsche was much more powerful, denouncing 'the whole molish business, the full cheek pouches and blind eyes, the delight at having caught a worm, and indifference toward the true and urgent problems of life'.[17] But behind it there is the noble principle that academic study is to make sense of the world. That in turn rests on one of the most important principles on which the university rests—that there is an order to the world and, if we study it, it can make sense. There is a fundamental human urge to make sense of things and academic enquiry is one of our most powerful ways of fulfilling this need without falling into superstition and unreason. Every little bit of evidence about the world which we accumulate should be consistent with every other bit of evidence. It is not as neat as that, of course, but that is what spurs us on to try to understand better. Writing for an academic publisher such as Oxford University Press with its requirements that every claim be footnoted and subject to peer review has been my own experience of the disciplines of this world. It is how we protect and extend rational enquiry.

The German concept of *Wissenschaft* reflects the belief that there is a unity to what we know about the world. There is not just a unity to all knowledge but also for the individual who is formed by pursuit of this knowledge—*Bildung*. (English early specialization is inimical to this view of education.) We can see how the idea of the interconnectedness of all knowledge lends itself to a certain kind of Germanic Idealism. The university is a place which is supposed to embody this unity through the community of scholars. The tragedy for Germany and for the world was that the pursuit of this unity came to be perverted, with the state coming to be a ghastly totalitarian embodiment of unity under the Nazis. Heidegger's notorious Rectorial address at Freiburg in May 1933 marks the point when Germany lost its moral authority as the home of the modern university, with academics themselves complicit in the perversion of the academic enterprise.[18]

More recently Jacques Derrida has linked the writings of Kant and his own experience of conflict between university and authority in the Événements of 1968 to reflect on the university in *Mochlos* and other essays. François Lyotard's *The Postmodern Condition* originated as a report on universities for the Government of Quebec. Derrida and Lyotard put the university at the heart of contemporary arguments about whether a commitment to truth is viable in a world where we are all supposed to shape our personal narratives and everything is contested. Even the campus novel may hint at the problem: 'The professor in the throes of a midlife crisis, realizing that he will never write his great book, that he has lost touch with his field, that he no longer reaches his students, and that his personal life is just as hollow, is actually an emblem of the academic institution as a whole. It too, cannot fulfil its academic mission and cannot govern itself.'[19] There has been a lot of bleak analysis of the university like that. It is not just worries about funding or intrusive university administration. It is a deeper anxiety that the university is 'in ruins' because there is no longer any coherent account of it in our post-modern world.[20]

I do not share such pessimism. I believe the university can still be committed to the project of making sense of the world, both through research and teaching. Every day academics try scrupulously to apply the tests of empirical evidence and logical consistency. The challenge for universities is how to provide the best environment for this. The conservative option is to trust to the traditional canonical structure of disciplines to keep academic rigour and rely on intellectual free spirits within them to make their discoveries. Another way is to focus more on grand challenges which straddle conventional boundaries—but then it is harder to distinguish between mediocrity and genuine advance. One Vice Chancellor put this very shrewdly. '"Does your university have a Physics Department?" is a supply-side question about structures. "Does your university deal with climate change?" is a demand-side question about functionality. In academia these two questions, and what they represent, do not yet enjoy parity of esteem.'[21] For truly creative research in particular we need to do more to break free from these disciplinary boundaries and if it cannot be done within universities it will happen in research institutes outside them.

Right back in Chapter One we saw that Cardinal Newman made an etymological mistake when he claimed that 'university' meant devoted to the teaching of universal knowledge. But perhaps that mistake contained a deeper truth and there is something universal about the university. John Rawls argued that the social contract which holds a modern liberal society together brings an obligation on us to appeal to public reason—arguments which are of universal validity and do not depend on prior cultural or religious assumptions. That is surely a test we can apply to teaching and research within a university. If we are as rootless as the post-modernists fear then the appeal to reason formulated by Kant and Rawls matters even more because it becomes one of the few things which enables us to communicate with other distinct communities: it is the decision rule for a diverse society. Nowhere is the capacity to reason exercised more fully and thoroughly than in the university with its requirements that arguments have to be logical and statements have to be supported by citing empirical evidence. Those are the values which pervade the research enterprise and which are conveyed in university teaching as well. Every day university teachers ask their students: Is there evidence for that assertion? Does the conclusion follow from the premises? Is that judgement well-founded? Our modern condition is not so troubled that we are incapable of living by that standard. Such an intellectual training is what those increasing numbers of young people wishing to go to university are after. Newman quoted with approval the statement that a university education promoted the 'faculty . . . of speaking good sense in English, without fee or reward, in common conversation'.[22] There is much more to it than that, but it is not a bad place to start. We might hope that many graduates emerge able to fulfil Newman's ambition for them. The modern university in Britain and around the world is providing more such opportunities for more people from a wider range of backgrounds than ever before and most of them leave university imbued with some of these values of pursuing truth through reason and evidence. Indeed, the university matters because it is above all the place where we show that it is still possible to live by such beliefs. That is the value of a university education.

Notes

INTRODUCTION

1. Clark Kerr observed that 'about 85 institutions in the Western world established by 1520 still exist in recognisable forms, with similar functions and with unbroken histories, including the Catholic Church, the Parliaments of the Isle of Man, of Iceland and of Great Britain, several Swiss cantons, and 70 universities...These 70 universities are still in the same locations with some of the same buildings, with professors and students doing much the same things.' See Clark Kerr, *Uses of the University* (Harvard University Press, 2001), 115.

2. 10,476 higher education institutions have 'university' in their title according to the World Higher Education Data Base maintained by UNESCO.

3. Gibbons and Machin find that parents pay between 3.1 and 8.8 per cent on property prices for each 10 percentage point increase in primary school test scores. See Stephen Gibbons and Stephen Machin, *Valuing Primary Schools*, CEEDP, 15 (Centre for the Economics of Education, London School of Economics and Political Science, London, 2001). A later finding was that a primary school getting its children on average into the top 10 per cent of achievement scores would raise house prices by an average of £26,000 in 2006 prices. See Stephen Gibbons, *Valuing Schools through House Prices*, Centrepiece, LSE (Autumn 2012), 2–5.

4. *Higher Education in England: Provision Skills and Graduates*, Universities UK (September 2016), 12.

CHAPTER ONE. THE RISE OF THE UNIVERSITY

1. Alan Cobban, *English University Life in the Middle Ages* (UCL Press, 1999), 8.

2. *Samuel Johnson's Dictionary*, ed. Jack Lynch (Levenger Press, New York, 2003), 522.

3. John Henry Newman, *The Idea of a University*, ed. Frank Turner (Yale University Press, 1996), 3, with Newman's italics, which fail to highlight the error.

4. I draw here on the Classical education of Nicola Dandridge, former Chief Executive of Universities UK. She points out that this makes the university a place of shared endeavour between staff and students.

5. Cobban, *English University Life in the Middle Ages,* 219.

6. 'Eighty-eight leaders of the Lutheran, Calvinist, and Swiss Reformations were university professors in the century from 1517 through the Synod of Dordrecht of 1618 and 1619' (Paul Grendler, 'The universities of the Renaissance and Reformation', *Renaissance Quarterly* 57 (2004), 1–42; p. 19).

7. Quoted in V. H. H. Green, *The Universities* (Penguin, 1969), 25.

8. Figures from Grendler, 'The universities of the Renaissance and Reformation', 2.

9. I am grateful to Dean Machin for these estimates drawing on *A History of the University in Europe*, Vol. 1: *Universities in the Middle Ages* ed. Hilde De Ridder-Symoens (Cambridge University Press, 1992), 62–51; *A History of the University in Europe*, Vol. II: *Universities in Early Modern Europe (1500–1800)*, ed. Hilde De Ridder-Symoens (Cambridge University Press, 1996), 78; and Colin McEvedy and Richard Jones, *Atlas of World Population History* (Penguin, 1978), part 1.

10. See Alan Macfarlane, *The Origins of English Individualism* (Blackwell, 1978).

11. Francis Bacon, *Great Instauration* of 1620, quoted in W. H. G. Armytage, *Civic Universities: Aspects of a British Tradition* (Benn, 1955), 95.

12. Armytage, *Civic Universities*, 118.

13. Lawrence Stone, 'The educational revolution in England', *Past and Present* 28 (1964), 41–80; p. 57.

14. Armytage, *Civic Universities*, 110.

15. Robert Anderson, *British Universities Past and Present* (Hambledon Continuum, 2006), 10.

16. 'In 1931 male university entrants formed 2.3% of the age-group, which is about the same percentage as that achieved 300 years earlier. In quantitative terms English higher education did not get back to the level of the 1630s until after the first World War; did not surpass it until after the second' (Stone, 'The Educational Revolution in England', 69).

17. James Axtell, *Wisdom's Workshop: The Rise of the Modern University* (Princeton University Press 2016), 122.

18. Edward Gibbon, *Memoirs of my Life*, ed. Betty Radice (1796; Penguin, 1964), Chapter III: Oxford (1752–3), 76, and *Miscellaneous Works of Edward Gibbon with Memoirs of his Life and Writings, Composed by Himself*, ed. John Baker Holdroyd, Vol. I (1796; reproduced Cambridge University Press, 2004), 76.

19. Gibbon, *Memoirs of my Life*, 83.

20. Grendler, 'The universities of the Renaissance and Reformation', 26.

21. Adam Smith, *Wealth of Nations*, Book V, Chapter I, Part III, Article II: 'Of the Expence of the Institutions for the Education of Youth' (Oxford University Press, 1979), 761.

22. Ibid. 722–3.

23. Gibbon, *Memoirs of my Life*, 77.

24. Quoted in Anderson, *British Universities Past and Present*, 29.

25. Peter Watson, *The German Genius* (Simon and Schuster, 2010), 232.

26. I am grateful to Terence Kealey for first drawing this case to my attention.

27. Thomas Arnold quoted in Anderson, *British Universities Past and Present*, 101.

28. Green, *The Universities*, 105.

29. Armytage, *Civic Universities*, 172.

30. 'It was, to all intents and purposes, a government department, with the chancellor, vice-chancellor, and thirty-seven members of the governing senate all appointed by the Crown.... Even the curriculum was overseen by the state, with the Home Secretary amending courses and awarding scholarships apparently at will' (William Whyte, *Redbrick: A Social and Architectural History of Britain's Civic Universities* (Oxford University Press, 2015), 48–9).

31. *Yes, Prime Minister*, Series 2, Episode 5: 'Power to the People'.

32. Newman, *The Idea of a University*, 3.

33. The quotation is cited in Sheldon Rothblatt, *The Modern University and its Discontents: The Fate of Newman's Legacies in Britain and America* (Cambridge University Press, 1997), 20.

34. This account of nineteenth-century Oxford draws on several chapters in M. G. Brock and M. C. Curthoys (eds), *The History of the University of Oxford*, Vol. VI: *Nineteenth Century Oxford, Part I* (Oxford University Press, 1997), notably Asa Briggs, chapter 3: 'Oxford and its critics 1800–1835', W. R. Ward, chapter 10: 'From the Tractarians to the Executive Commission 1845–1854'; Christopher Harvie, chapter 23: 'Reform and expansion 1854–1871'.

35. Briggs, 'Oxford and its critics 1800–1835', 145.

36. Frederick Temple's evidence to the Commission. Armytage, *Civic Universities*, 201.

37. Ibid. 191.

38. Ibid. 178.

39. House of Commons, Oxford University Bill, HC Deb 27 April 1854 Hansard Vol. 132 cc921–93, at 975.

40. House of Commons, Oxford University Bill, HC Deb 07 April 1854 Hansard Vol. 132 cc672–779, at 766–7.

41. W. H. G. Armytage, 'The conflict of ideas in English university education 1850–1867', *Educational Theory* 3/4 (1953), 327–43; p. 329.

42. John Sparrow, *Mark Pattison and the Idea of a University* (Cambridge University Press, 1967), 119 and 93. Sparrow paints a subtle and fascinating portrait of Pattison and convincingly argues that he is the model for Casaubon.

43. Stefan Collini, *What are Universities for?* (Penguin, 2012), 28.

44. The Acts were as follows:

    1854: The Oxford University Act
    1856: Cambridge University Act
    1857: Oxford University Act 1857
    1859: Universities of Oxford and Cambridge Act 1859
    1860: Oxford University Act 1860
    1862: Oxford University Act 1862
    1865: Oxford University, Vinerian Foundation, Act 1865
    1871: Universities Tests Act 1871
    1877: Universities of Oxford and Cambridge Act
    1880: Universities of Oxford and Cambridge (Limited Tenures) Act.

45. Armytage, 'The conflict of ideas in English university education'.

46. Quoted by Malcolm Tight, 'Institutional churn: institutional change in UK higher education', *Journal of Higher Education Policy and Management* 35/1 (2013), 11–20.

47. Bruce Truscot, *Red Brick University* (Faber and Faber, 1943), 17.

48. Ibid. 22, 37.

49. Ibid. 61.

50. Sir Walter Moberly *The Crisis in the University* (SCM Press, 1949), 234.

51. A. H. Halsey, *Decline of Donnish Dominion: The British Academic Professions in the Twentieth Century* (Oxford University Press, 1992), 15.

52. George Eliot, *Middlemarch*, Book II, Chapter XXI (1871–2; Oxford University Press, 2008), 221–2.

53. An amended version of Jonathan Wolf's claim, 'All six universities in the American Ivy league have fewer undergraduates than Manchester University' (*Guardian*, 21 January 2014).

54. Axtell, *Wisdom's Workshop*, 279.

55. Armytage, *Civic Universities*, 247.

56. Vladimir Nabokov, *Pnim* (Heinemann, 1957).

57. Suzanne Mettler, *Soldiers to Citizens: The G.I. Bill and the Making of the Greatest Generation* (Oxford University Press, 2005), 7.

58. Claudia Goldin and Lawrence Katz, *The Race Between Education and Technology* (Harvard University Press, 2008), chapter 6, p. 199.

59. Kingsley Amis, *Lucky Jim* (Gollancz 1954), 27.

60. Hansard House of Commons 25 March 1943 vol. 387 cc1738–40.

61. Goldin and Katz, *The Race Between Education and Technology*.

62. Clark Kerr, *The Uses of the University,* 5th edn (Harvard University Press, 2001).

63. Ibid. 138.

64. Clark Kerr Obituary: 'Clark Kerr, leading public educator, dies at 92', *New York Times*, 2 December 2003.

65. See Michael Crow and William Dabars, *Designing the New American University* (Johns Hopkins University Press, 2015) for an account of Arizona State University.

66. For the decline of the California model of higher education see Simon Marginson, *The Dream is Over: The Crisis of Clark Kerr's California Idea of Higher Education* (University of California Press, 2016).

67. Martin Rees, *University Diversity Freedom, Excellence and Funding for a Global Future* (Politeia, 2012), 14.

68. Herbert Butterfield, *The Whig Interpretation of History* (Norton and Co., 1965), 12.

69. 2,305 universities generate more than 1,000 research outputs per year and 3,289 universities generate 200+. See *SIR World Report 2012: Global Ranking*, SCImago Research Group (Copyright 2012), 66 and 95.

70. Speech by Enoch Powell at Magdalene College, Cambridge, 12 June 1991. I am grateful to Richard Ritchie for drawing it to my attention.

71. Collini, *What are Universities for?* Chapter 8 is entitled HiEdBizUK.

72. Britain signed the Sorbonne Declaration of 1999 together with France, Italy, and Germany, leading to the Bologna Declaration of 2000 signed by 29 countries.

73. Bologna Working Group Report on Qualifications Framework, *A Framework for Qualifications of the European Higher Education Area*, 2005.

74. Clause 77 of the 2017 Higher Education and Research Act has a kind of surreal lawyerly logic to it: 'higher education provider' means an institution which provides higher education; 'higher education' means education provided by means of a higher education course; 'higher education course' means a course of any description mentioned in Schedule 6 to the Education Reform Act 1988. One then goes back to this previous legislation, which states that 'a course is to be regarded as providing education at a higher level if its standard is higher than the standard of examinations at advanced level for the GCSE or the examination of the National Certificate or the National Diploma'. So, at the end of all this, the law says higher education means higher than A level.

75. In 2014/15 2.27m students were registered at 162 higher education providers which get public funding. Of these 127 have a university or university college title (this includes the University of London, which is comprised of 9 specialist institutes and 18 colleges, 15 of which have degree-awarding powers). There are a further five institutions with university/university college title that are not publicly funded, bringing the total number of universities in the UK to 132 (HEFCE Register of Providers; HEFCW, Higher Education Institutions; Universities Scotland, Scotland's Universities, 2012). Expenditure across these 162 publicly funded providers totalled £31bn during 2014/15. This ranged from £8.06m (Rose Bruford College) to £1.6bn (Cambridge); the median was £129m (HESA Finance Plus 2014/15, table 1). This analysis excludes alternative providers with HEFCE designated courses which entitle their students to access loans and further education colleges that provide HE-level courses.

76. Jean-François Lyotard, *The Postmodern Condition: A Report on Knowledge* (University of Minnesota Press, 1984). A good guide to these debates is Bill Readings, *The University in Ruins* (Harvard University Press, 1996). Its title is an indication of the pessimism of many of the theorists—a striking contrast with the vigour of the actual institutions.

CHAPTER TWO. ROBBINS AND AFTER

1. This account draws heavily on Nicholas Hillman, 'From Grants for All to Loans for All: Undergraduate Finance from the Implementation of the Anderson Report (1962) to the Implementation of the Browne Report (2012)', *Contemporary British History* 27/3 (2013), 249–70.

2. Robbins breaks the universities down into historical categories on pp. 22–4 of his Report, *Higher Education: Report of the Committee appointed by the Prime Minister under the Chairmanship of Lord Robbins 1961–63* October 1963 Cmnd 2154 (hereafter Robbins Report).

3. V. Bowden, 'Britain's Backwardness in Higher Education', *New Scientist* 216 (5 January 1961), 23.

4. Robbins Report, 15.

5. David Edgerton, *Warfare State: Britain, 1920–1970* (Cambridge University Press, 2006), 70, and see also Richard Vinen, *National Service: Conscription in Britain 1945–1963* (Allen Lane, 2014).

6. Anderson Report, *Grants to Students*, Ministry of Education Cmnd 1051 (HMSO 1960), 13.

7. Hansard, 26 July 1954, cols 127–8.

8. K. O. Morgan, *Labour in Power 1945–1951* (Oxford University Press, 1985), 179.

9. Anderson Report, *Grants to Students*.

10. David Malcolm, 'Anderson appreciated', Wonkhe Blog, 2 June 2014.

11. Robert Anderson, *British Universities Past and Present* (Hambledon Continuum, 2006), 139.

12. Sir James Mountford as paraphrased in Ronald Kay, *UCCA: Its Origins and Development 1950–85* (1985), 12. I am grateful to Ronald Kay, the founding Secretary of the University Central Council on Admissions, UCCA as it then was, for sparing the time to meet me to give his personal account of these events and also to Mary Curnock-Cook of UCAS for putting us in touch.

13. Ibid. 5.

14. I am grateful to Anne-Marie Watson of UCAS for providing these figures.

15. Robbins Report, 101.

16. The Barlow Report, *Scientific Manpower*, Report of a Committee appointed by the Lord President of the Council, Cmd 6824 (May 1946), paragraph 55.

17. Robbins Report, 24. Stirling University in Scotland, Scotland's first new university for four hundred years, was created after Robbins and indeed had him as its first Chancellor.

18. Michael Shattock, *Making Policy in British Higher Education 1945–2011* (Open University Press 2012), 43.

19. Robbins Report, 1.

20. Ibid. 6–7.

21. Ibid. 8.

22. Shattock, *Making Policy in British Higher Education*, 4.

23. Conservative Manifesto 2015, p. 35 As it was edited down in the Manifesto process any reference to aptitude or being subject to universities' own power over admissions was removed.

24. Robbins Report, 48.

25. Ibid. 70.

26. Richard Layard, John King, and Claus Moser *The Impact of Robbins* (Penguin, 1969), 14–21.

27. The exact figures were 216,000 full-time students in higher education when Robbins reported, projected to grow to 558,000 by 1980–1, including 346,000 in universities. See Robbins Report, table 44 on p. 160.

28. Lionel Robbins, *Higher Education Revisited* (Macmillan 1980), 25.

29. As calculated by John Carswell, *Government and the Universities in Britain* (Cambridge University Press 1985), 172.

30. Letter from John Adams to Abigail Adams, 12 May 1780.
31. Michael Young, *The Rise of the Meritocracy* (Transaction Publishing, 1994), 24–5. David Edgerton has however shown that British universities in the 1950s were unusually male, with many of their students studying science and technology: 'By international standards the post-war British university was a very scientific and technical place' (David Edgerton, *Warfare State: Britain, 1920–1970* (Cambridge University Press 2006), 179.
32. Michael Teitelbaum, *Falling Behind: Boom, Bust and the Global Race for Scientific Talent* (Princeton University Press, 2014).
33. K. J. Arrow and W. M. Capron, 'Dynamic shortages and price rises: the engineer-scientist case', *Quarterly Journal of Economics* (1959). Cited in Teitelbaum: *Falling Behind*, 121.
34. *Women and Medicine: The Future*, a report prepared on behalf of the Royal College of Physicians by Mary Ann Elston (June 2009), 24.
35. Harold Perkin, 'Dream, myth and reality: new universities in England, 1960–1990', *Higher Education Quarterly* 45/4 (Autumn 1991), 296.
36. Ibid.
37. Ibid.
38. Robbins Report, 210–12.
39. Ibid. 210–11.
40. Susan Howson, *Lionel Robbins* (Cambridge University Press, 2011), 889.
41. Committee on Higher Education, *Higher Education: Evidence* (1963), Part 2, pp. 139–52, later republished in a slightly different form by the Institute of Economic Affairs as A. R. Prest, *Financing University Education* (IEA, 1966).
42. Lionel Robbins, *The University in the Modern World* (Macmillan, 1966), 41.
43. Robbins, *Higher Education Revisited*, 33.
44. Quoted in Shattock, *Making Policy in British Higher Education*, 172.
45. Anthony Crosland, speech to Woolwich Polytechnic, 27 April 1965.
46. Robbins Report, 155.
47. 'Expansion and the Binary System', speech by Lord Robbins included in his *The University in the Modern World*, 156–7.
48. Vince Cable made a powerful speech on this point on 23 April 2014.
49. Innovation, Universities, Science and Skills Select Committee, Monday, 30 March 2009, Examination of Witnesses, Questions 169–79.
50. *A Framework for Expansion*, Cmnd 5174 (December 1972).
51. Written Statement for Education White Paper, 6 December 1972.
52. 'Higher Education: The Next 25 Years', speech by the Rt Hon Kenneth Baker MP, Secretary of State for Education and Science, at a conference at Lancaster University on 5 January 1989, issued by the Department of Education and Science. Baker talked of participation rising from 'nearly 15% at present' to 'something approaching 20%' in the mid-nineties just by holding numbers as the cohort shrank and then envisaged a world in 25 years' time 'when participation rises to 30%'.
53. See Nick Hillman, 'Why do students study so far from home?', *THES* 23 July 2015.
54. A. H. Halsey, *Decline of Donnish Dominion: The British Academic Professions in the Twentieth Century* (Oxford University Press, 1992), 11.

CHAPTER THREE. HOW TO PAY FOR IT

1. Blair secured a majority of five in 2004: 72 Government MPs rebelled, the largest rebellion on any second reading of a Government Bill since the war. The Coalition's majority fell to 21 in the fees vote of 9 December 2010, the largest Lib Dem rebellion of the Coalition.

2. David Willetts, *The Pinch: How the Baby Boomers took their Children's Future—and Why they should Give it Back* (Atlantic Books, 2010).

3. *The Dearing Report, Higher Education in the Learning Society: Report of the National Committee of Inquiry into Higher Education* (HMSO, 1997), 45.

4. *Long-Run Trends in School Spending in England*, IFS Report R11 (April 2016), 2.

5. The NUS pledge in the 2010 General Election was 'I pledge to vote against any increase in fees in the next parliament and to pressure the government to introduce a fairer alternative.'

6. I wrote to parliamentary colleagues and candidates on 14 December 2009 advising that 'it would be wrong to pre-empt [the review's] results or to bind the hands of the review team just as they are starting work by pledging ourselves to a predetermined result. The review should take evidence from, and value, the student voice. So, it would not be right to sign the pledge at this stage.'

7. See Steven Fisher and Nick Hillman, *Do Students Swing Elections? Registration, Turn-Out and Voting Behaviour among Full-Time Students* (HEPI, 2014).

8. 'If the response of the government to Lord Browne's report is one that Liberal Democrats cannot accept, then arrangements will be made to enable Liberal Democrat MPs to abstain in any vote' (Coalition Agreement, May 2015).

9. *Securing a Sustainable Future for Higher Education. An Independent Review of Higher Education Funding and Student Finance* (October 2010).

10. Higher Education Funding Council for England (HEFCE), Annual Funding Allocations (Final), 2010–11 to 2015–16; Student Loans Company, Student Support for Higher Education in England 2016: 2015/16 payments, 2016/17 awards, 30 November 2016, tables 3A(i) and 4B(i). Fee income figures are for all providers in England, including alternative providers, full-time EU and UK students.

11. 'Fees at British public universities more expensive than US', *Financial Times*, 24 November 2015.

12. £786,000 according to I. Walker and Y. Zhu, *The Impact of University Degrees on the Lifecycle of Earnings: Some Further Analysis*, BIS Research Paper no. 112 (August 2013), 53, table 12.

13. Martin Lewis, *Guardian Education*, 20 September 2012.

14. The switch from maintenance grants to loans put as much as £550 extra cash in the poorest students' pockets. See Jack Britton, Claire Crawford, and Lorraine Dearden, *Analysis of the Higher Education Funding Reforms Announced in Summer Budget 2015* (Institute for Fiscal Studies, July 2015).

15. £10,700 is the maximum maintenance support in 2016 living away from home in high-cost London: it is £8,200 outside London.

16. Higher Education Funding Council for England, Recurrent grants for 2015-16: Final allocations, table 1.

17. *Student Loans—A Guide to Terms and Conditions* (Student Finance England 2013/2014), 2.

18. Milton Friedman, 'The role of government in education', in Robert A. Solow (ed.), *Economics and the Public Interest* (Rutgers University Press, 1955). Friedman distinguishes between public funding for general education which includes some higher education, and separate professional and vocational education, to which he applies the model he sets out in the quotation. He acknowledges the assistance of A. R. Prest in commenting on an earlier draft—so we see the connection to the subsequent British policy debate.

19. Alex Usher, 'Oregon's "Pay it Forward" scheme and the ICR vs graduate tax problem', Higher Education Strategy Associates Blog, 17 March 2014.

20. Willetts, *The Pinch*, chapter 8.

21. I set out this proposal in David Willetts, *Higher Education: Who Benefits? Who Pays?* (King's College London, 2015).

22. House of Commons, Hansard, 3 November 2010, col. 240.

23. The figures are of course imaginary and just to illustrate the point.

24. The problem went back to very tough rules on access to HMRC data. I chaired the inter-departmental group which found a way to make this data available. They agreed on the basis that this project would enable them to understand the long-term shape of the tax base better.

25. Jack Britton, Lorraine Dearden, Neil Shephard, and Anna Vignoles, *How English-Domiciled Graduate Earnings Vary with Gender, Institution Attended, Subject, and Socio-Economic Background* (IFS W16/06).

26. Ibid. 30.

27. The student number control limits list for 2011–12 began with Anglia Ruskin 4,215, Aston University 2,077, and ended with Worcester College of Technology 196, and York College 180. The largest number was University of Central Lancashire 6,711 and the smallest the Courtauld Institute of Art 51. It added up to 364,325 places for first-year undergraduates in English universities.

28. Conservative Manifesto 2015, p. 35.

29. Lucy Hunter Blackburn, Gitit Kadar-Satat, Sheila Riddell, and Elisabet Weedon, *Access in Scotland: Access to Higher Education for People from Less Advantaged Backgrounds in Scotland* (Sutton Trust, May 2016), 43.

30. 'In 2015, offer rates from Scottish universities were highest for students from non-EU countries, at 63 per cent, followed by applicants from England, Wales, and Northern Ireland (between 56 per cent and 58 per cent). Offer rates were lowest for Scottish applicants and applicants from other EU countries, at 50 per cent and 34 per cent respectively, reflecting the fixed number of funded places available for these students....The number of offers made to Scottish and EU students by Scottish universities is mainly influenced by the number of places the SFC has funded at each university for these students. Universities set their own recruitment targets for

students from the rest of the UK and outside the EU…The offer rate for Scottish and EU applicants has fallen over the past five years while offer rates for most other applicant groups have increased. Demand for Scottish university places from Scottish applicants has increased since 2010. Between 2010 and 2015, applications increased by 23 per cent. However, the number of offers made by Scottish universities only increased by nine per cent over the same period. This led to a decline in the offer rate of seven per cent, from 57 per cent in 2010 to 50 per cent in 2015. This means it has become more difficult for Scottish applicants to be offered a place at a Scottish university. In contrast, offer rates for applicants from the rest of the UK and countries outside the EU increased between 2010 and 2015, by, on average, 11 per cent' (Auditor General, *Audit of Higher Education in Scottish Universities* (Audit Scotland, July 2016), 43).

31. Jo Johnson, Minister for Universities, Written Statement HCWS117 of 21 July 2016 extended the exemption from ELQ loans to a wider range of STEM subjects.

32. *The Government's Proposed New Postgraduate Loan Scheme: Will the RAB Charge Really be Zero?*, Institute for Fiscal Studies, 9 December 2014.

33. Department for Education, *Postgraduate Master's Loan Enabling Regulations: Impact Assessment* (July 2016), 12–13.

34. If a student has an undergraduate loan, the PhD loan would be repaid concurrently with it. However, if they also have a Master's loan there would be just one single repayment rate of 6 per cent.

35. Alison Wolf envisages something like this—though she appears to think the student loan scheme is public spending and therefore proposes cuts to it in order to fund vocational loans. Fortunately such a difficult trade-off is not necessary. See Alison Wolf, *Remaking Tertiary Education: Can We Create a System that is Fair and Fit for Purpose?* (Education Policy Institute, November 2016).

36. The sustainability of the UK's higher education system, 6 January 2015, oecdeducationtoday.blogspot.co.uk.

CHAPTER FOUR. THE RESEARCH-INTENSIVE UNIVERSITY

1. Eric Ashby, *Technology and the Academics: An Essay on the Universities and the Scientific Revolution* (Macmillan, 1958), 24.

2. Ibid.

3. Wilhelm von Humboldt, Treatise *On the Internal and External Organization of the Higher Scientific Institutions in Berlin* (1810), in *German History in Documents and Images.* Vol. 2: *From Absolutism to Napoleon, 1648–1815.* See also Thorsten Nybom, 'The Humboldt legacy: reflections on the past, present and future of the European university', *Higher Education Policy* 16 (2003), 141–59.

4. Immanuel Kant, *The Conflict of the Faculties* (Abaris Books, 1979).

5. Renate Simpson, *How the PhD Came to Britain: A Century of Struggle for Postgraduate Education* (Society for Research into Higher Education, 1983), 50.

6. Clark Kerr, *The Uses of the University,* 5th edn (Harvard University Press, 2001), 247 n.

7. German Constitution Article 91b on *Co-operation of Federation and States.*

8. Peter Watson, *The German Genius* (Simon and Schuster, 2010), 324. See also James Axtell, *Wisdom's Workshop: The Rise of the Modern University* (Princeton University Press, 2016), chapter 5: 'The German impress'.

9. Vannevar Bush, Director of the Office of Scientific Research and Development, *Science, The Endless Frontier, A Report to the President on a Program for Postwar Scientific Research*, July 1945; reprinted National Science Foundation, 1960.

10. Bush, quoted in Michael Teitelbaum: *Falling Behind: Boom, Bust and the Global Race for Scientific Talent* (Princeton University Press, 2014), 160.

11. Axtell, *Wisdom's Workshop*, 333.

12. John Henry Newman, *The Idea of a University*, ed. Frank Turner (Yale University Press, 1996), 3.

13. Joel Mokyr, *Gifts of Athena: Historical Origins of the Knowledge Economy* (Princeton University Press 2002).

14. Henry Oldenburg, the first Secretary of the Royal Society, created the *Philosophical Transactions of the Royal Society* in 1665 and asked three of the Society's Fellows with specific expertise to comment on submissions before deciding whether to publish them. See *Science as an Open Enterprise* (The Royal Society, June 2012), 13.

15. *Scheme for the Organisation and Development of Scientific and Industrial Research*, Cd 8005 (July 1915), paragraphs 1 and 5.

16. Simpson, *How the PhD Came to Britain*, 116–17.

17. Ibid. 135–59.

18. Ibid. 149–50. Balfour was Foreign Secretary. 'Mr Fisher' was H. A. L. Fisher, the President of the Board of Education. The key figure through this process was the great J. B. S. Haldane, who was Lord Chancellor, a friend of Balfour, and the key influence behind many of the reforms in science and higher education in the period. The so-called Haldane Principle is named after him.

19. *Report of the Machinery of Government Committee*, The Haldane Report, Cd 9230 (1918).

20. David Edgerton, *Warfare State: Britain, 1920–1970* (Cambridge University Press, 2006).

21. Sir Walter Moberly, *The Crisis in the University* (SCM Press, 1949).

22. The Trend Report: *Committee of Enquiry into the Organisation of Civil Science*. Cmnd 2171 (October 1963), paragraph 43, p. 22.

23. The Research Council structure was updated by William Waldegrave in the early 1990s. See *Realising Our Potential, A Strategy for Science Engineering and Technology*, Cm 2250 (May 1993). The reduction of their individual autonomy was proposed in *Success as a Knowledge Economy: Teaching Excellence, Social Mobility and Student Choice*, Cm 9258 (May 2016), and implemented in the Higher Education and Research Act 2017.

24. HESA Staff Record 2014/15.

25. Eurostat data on R&D personnel which does not include the UK and is not strictly comparable to the HESA data.

26. As of 2017 85 Nobel Prize winners were born in Britain and a further 37 were working in Britain when awarded the prize. I am grateful to Dean Machin and Kathleen Henahan for these calculations based on the Nobel Prize website.

27. *International Comparative Performance of the UK Research Base—2013* (Elsevier, 2013), table 3.1, p. 26.

28. The Vancouver Protocol of 1978 states that substantial contributions to the study are a requirement for being identified as an author. See Bruce Macfarlane, 'Time for a Credit Check', *THES* (10 December 2015), 26, for a discussion of identifying authorship.

29. Chris Pissarides of the LSE, born in Cyprus, won the Nobel Prize in Economics. Andrei Geim and Konstantin Novoselov, born in Russia and working in Manchester, shared the Nobel Prize in Physics. Robert Edwards was awarded the Nobel Prize in Medicine.

30. See David Galenson, *Old Masters and Young Geniuses: The Two Life Cycles of Artistic Creativity* (Princeton University Press, 2006).

31. Alan Hughes et al., *The Dual Funding Structure for Research in the UK: Research Council and Funding Council Allocation Methods and Pathways to Impact of UK Academics*, a report to BIS by the Centre for Business Research, April 2013, showed that the two funding streams promoted research with distinct characteristics.

32. *The Development of Higher Education into the 1990s* (DES, 1985).

33. A. H. Halsey, *Decline of Donnish Dominion: The British Academic Professions in the Twentieth Century* (Oxford University Press, 1992), 188–99.

34. Jonathan Grant, *The Impact of Impact: Lessons from REF2014 and Beyond* (Academy of Social Sciences, January 2016).

35. See *The Metric Tide: Report of the Independent Review of the Role of Metrics in Research Assessment and Management* chaired by James Willsdon (HEFCE, July 2015) and *Building on Success and Learning from Experience: An Independent Review of the REF*, Nick Stern, BEIS IND/16/9 July 2016.

36. 'Policy observations', in Jonathan Grant, *The Nature, Scale and Beneficiaries of Research Impact: An Initial Analysis of Research Excellence Framework (REF) 2014 Impact Case Studies*, King's College London and Digital Science (March 2015), 70.

37. 'In many cases the exercise has been very narrowly interpreted as linking a particular publication to a particular activity or policy decision. We have recommended that impact should be interpreted much more subtly and broadly to link bodies of work and disciplinary or collaborative activity to outcomes understood from a more nuanced and deeper perspective.' *Building on Success and Learning from Experience: An Independent Review of the REF*, paragraph 125.

38. Oxford University, 'A Crick Institute for the Physical Sciences'.

39. The top five—Oxford, UCL, Cambridge, Imperial, and Manchester—received 36% of Research Council funding and HEFCE research funding in 2014/15. The top ten (adding King's, Nottingham, Bristol, Leeds, and Sheffield) received 52%. See HEFCE 2014/15 Adjusted Allocations and HESA 2014/15 Student Finance Record, Table 5b.

40. National Science Foundation, Rankings by Total Federal Obligations, 2014, published 2015. This only covers STEM R&D but this is by far the largest component

of federal public research funds. Universities in both countries get about three-quarters of their R&D funding from the public sector.

41. Written Ministerial Statement, Science and Research Funding, 2011–12 to 2014–15, 20 December 2010, BIS.

42. *The Allocation of Science and Research Funding 2011/12 to 2014/15*, BIS December 2010, Annex A, *Statement of the Haldane Principle*, 57–8.

43. von Humboldt, Treatise *On the Internal and External Organization of the Higher Scientific Institutions in Berlin*, 4.

44. David Edgerton, *The 'Haldane Principle' and Other Invented Traditions in Science Policy*, History and Policy, Policy Papers (2009).

45. This calculation is not as simple as it appears. Nobel Prize winners may have been born in one country, conducted their prize-winning research in a second, and be working in a third when the prize is actually awarded. So, rather like the many fragments of the True Cross in medieval cathedrals, the total of Nobel Prizes claimed by countries and institutions considerably exceeds the total awarded. I arranged for our PM to write to congratulate our Prize winners. There was one who was born in Israel and although he had done his key research in Cambridge had subsequently moved to the USA. We did not wish to be presumptuous and claim him for our own when his loyalties might be elsewhere but we did write and received a very warm reply.

46. A. Hughes and B. R. Martin, *The Impact of UK Publicly Funded Research* (CIHE, 2012).

47. 'The Output rank is 24 places above the Resources rank. This differential is the largest in our 50 countries and is indicative of an efficient higher education sector' (Universitas 21 2015 Rankings of National Higher Education Systems). The later figures are from Universitas 21 2016 Rankings of National Higher Education Systems. The rankings go beyond research performance but the breakdown of the different components of the output measure shows that the UK does particularly well for research output.

48. Paul Nurse, *Ensuring a Successful UK Research Endeavour: A Review of the UK Research Councils* (2015).

49. Source: *International Comparative Performance of the UK Research Base—2013*, figure 4.11, pp. 44–5. The figure title is: 'Field-weighted citation impact for the UK and comparators across ten research fields in 2002 and 2012. For all research fields, a field-weighted citation impact of 1.0 represents world average in that particular research field.' So you want to be as far out as possible and the more circular the shape the better balanced your research base. I am grateful to UUK for an analysis of the data underpinning the report.

50. *Crossing Paths: Interdisciplinary Institutions, Careers, Education, and Applications* (The British Academy, July 2016).

51. Royal Academy of Engineering, quoted ibid. 50.

52. Ibid. 73.

53. Evidence on how international our research community is from *International Comparative Performance of the UK Research Base*.

CHAPTER FIVE. WHY IT'S WORTH GOING TO UNIVERSITY

1. *Futuretrack* follows people who started at university in October 2006. 96% of graduates would choose again to go to university—and this was a cohort who graduated into a jobs market at the bottom of a recession.

2. Javier Espinoza, *The Daily Telegraph*, 25 June 2015.

3. Jeremy Paxman, *Financial Times*, 5 June 2015.

4. Katie Allen, *The Guardian*, 18 August 2015.

5. Alex Proud, *Daily Telegraph*, 29 September 2014.

6. William Bennett and David Wilezol, *Is College Worth It?* (Thomas Nelson, 2013).

7. 98% of mothers with postgraduate qualifications want their child to go to university and an average of 97% overall. Source: Institute of Education, Centre for Longitudinal Studies: Millennium Cohort Study, Fourth Survey: A User's Guide to Initial Findings. Press Release, 15 October 2014, 'Millennium mothers want university education for their children'.

8. John Henry Newman, *The Idea of a University*, ed. Frank Turner (Yale University Press, 1996), 78-9.

9. Ibid. 85.

10. Ibid. 7.

11. This model with UK data was developed by economists within BIS. See *The Benefits of Higher Education Participation for Individuals and for Society: Key Findings and Reports 'The Quadrants'*, BIS Research Paper No. 146 (October 2013).

12. E. Kuntsche, J. Rehm, and G. Gmel, 'Characteristics of binge drinkers in Europe', *Social Science and Medicine* 59/1 (July 2004), 113-27, and J. Bynner et al., *Revisiting the Benefits of Higher Education*, Bedford Group for Lifecourse and Statistical Studies, Institute of Education, University of London (2003), 21-31.

13. Walter McMahon, *Higher Learning, Greater Good: The Private and Social Benefits of Higher Education* (The Johns Hopkins University Press, 2009), 134.

14. OECD, *Education at a Glance 2012*, 209. That measure does not include UK.

15. K. Miyamoto and A. Chevalier, *Education and Health*; OECD, *Improving Health and Social Cohesion through Education* (2010), chapter 4.

16. David M. Cutler and Adriana Lleras-Muney, 'Understanding differences in behaviour by education', *Journal of Health Economics* 29/1 (January 2010), 1-28.

17. J. J. Mandemakers and C. W. S. Monden, 'Does education buffer the impact of disability on psychological distress?', *Social Science and Medicine* 71/2 (2010), 288-97.

18. OECD, *Education at a Glance 2011* and ONS, *Measuring National Well-being Education and Skills* (2011).

19. John Vorhaus, Kathryn Duckworth, David Budge, and Leon Feinstein, *The Social Benefits of Learning: A Summary of Key Research Findings* (Centre for Research on the Wider Benefits of Learning, 2008), 18. See also Bynner et al., *Revisiting the Benefits of Higher Education*, 21-3.

20. John Brennan et al., *The Effect of Higher Education on Graduates' Attitudes: Secondary Analysis of the British Social Attitudes Survey*, BIS Research Paper No. 200 (November 2015).

21. See Alison Wolf, *Does Education Matter? Myths about Education and Economic Growth* (Penguin, 2002).

22. The major British social science cited here tries to allow for selection effects. There is a particularly rich strand of work from the Centre for Research on the Wider Benefits of Learning at the Institute of Education which originated in David Blunkett commissioning more rigorous evidence. However, leading American experts tend not to be so exercised by this problem. Walter McMahon, for example, does not allow for selection effects, which he calls ability bias. He concedes that this may inflate his figures for economic returns by 6–12% by attributing to higher education what is really a return to underlying ability. He argues however that studies of identical twins raised separately and with different levels of education show similar returns for higher education but there should be no ability bias in such cases. He also argues there is an offsetting measurement bias as respondents to surveys exaggerate their educational qualifications and educational institutions and Federal Government agencies exaggerate education participation so that overall levels of education are exaggerated which dampens the measured returns to education. This approach is widely supported by American experts: 'much of the modern literature finds that the upward "ability bias" is of about the same order of magnitude as the downward bias caused by measurement error in educational attainment.' See Alan Krueger and Mikael Lindahl, 'Education for growth: why and for whom?', *Journal of Economic Literature* 39 (December 2001), 1101. See also McMahon, *Higher Learning, Greater Good*, Appendix A: 'Correcting for ability bias in returns to higher education'.

23. David Willetts, *The Pinch: How the Baby Boomers took their Children's Future—and Why they should Give it Back* (Atlantic, 2010), 114.

24. Henry Brougham in *The Edinburgh Review*, 1825, quoted in Asa Briggs, 'Oxford and its Critics 1800–1835', chapter 3 of *The History of the University of Oxford*, Vol. VI: *Nineteenth Century Oxford, Part I*, ed. M. G. Brock and M. C. Curthoys (Oxford University Press, 1997).

25. V. H. H. Green, *The Universities* (Penguin, 1969), 38.

26. Newman, *The Idea of a University*, 3–4.

27. Letter from Keith Flett, *THES*, 15 May 2014.

28. *The Robbins Report* 1963 HMSO Cmnd 2154, p. 6.

29. Robert Anderson, *British Universities Past and Present* (Hambledon Continuum, 2006), 40.

30. Futuretrack 2006.

31. Anna Vignoles, 'Big data shows the graduate pay premium is bigger for women', *The Conversation*, 29 September 2015. The full report is Jack Britton, Neil Shephard, and Anna Vignoles, *Comparing Sample Survey Measures of English Earnings of Graduates with Administrative Data during the Great Recession*, IFS Working Paper W15/28 2015.

32. I. Walker and Y. Zhu, *The Impact of University Degrees on the Lifecycle of Earnings: Some Further Analyses* (BIS, 2013). The key result is table 13, p. 53. Figures for percentage boost to earnings are on p. 6. The researchers compare graduates with those with

two or more A levels who could have gone to university but did not. Parental background does not affect the result.

33. The median earnings of individuals aged 22–30 with at most non-degree higher education or A levels fell 13.4 per cent between 2007–8 and 2012–13. Graduate earnings fell a similar amount but the gap over non-graduate earnings was maintained and graduate earnings tend to rise more steeply with age and experience. See IFS, *Living Standards, Inequality and Poverty in the UK 2014*, chapter 5, 'Young adults and the Recession', pp. 103–7.

34. 'At age 25, the wage differential between graduates and school-leavers is 25% for the 1965–69 cohort and 28% for the 1975–79 cohort. These rise to 45% and 48% for the two cohorts respectively at age 30, and to 58% for both at age 35. Thus, the 1975–79 cohort, which had double the proportion of graduates that the 1965–69 cohort had, had the same or a slightly higher relative graduate wage.' See Richard Blundell, David Green, and Wenchao Jin, *The Puzzle of Graduate Wages*, IFS Briefing Note BN185, Institute for Fiscal Studies, August 2016.

35. Will Abel, Rebecca Burnham, and Matthew Corder, 'Wages, productivity and the changing composition of the UK workforce', *Bank of England Quarterly Bulletin* (2016 Q1), 12–22.

36. Ibid. 18.

37. Blundell, Green, and Jin, *The Puzzle of Graduate Wages*, 3.

38. The IFS report says: 'The Bank report uses wage regressions conditioning on a range of job characteristics, whereas we show the raw data as they are. For example, higher education increases the probability of a higher-paid occupation, therefore conditioning on occupation appears to reduce the return to higher education.' Blundell, Green, and Jin, *The Puzzle of Graduate Wages*, 2.

39. Pew Research Centre, *The Rising Cost of Not Going to College* (2014), 26.

40. David Willetts, *The Pinch: How the Baby Boomers took their Children's Future—and Why they should Give it Back* (Atlantic, 2010).

41. Pew Research Centre, *The Rising Cost of Not Going to College*, 5, 7.

42. Here are the estimates for the graduate premium in the different studies: £125,000, London Economics for BIS 2011; £120,000, PWC for UUK 2007; £129,000, PWC for Royal Society of Chemistry 2005; men £142,000 and women £158,000, Nigel C. O'Leary and Peter J. Sloane, NIESR 2005.

43. 'Our focus is to compare the labour market careers of people who could have accessed a university degree course and did so, with those who could but did not—irrespective of what happens to them after they make this decision.' Walker and Zhu, *The Impact of University Degrees on the Lifecycle of Earnings*, 17.

44. Ibid. 28.

45. Walker and Zhu estimate real earnings growth over time higher for graduates by 0.5% p.a. for men and 0.6% p.a. for women (ibid. 48).

46. Ibid. 7.

47. IFS, *Living Standards, Poverty and Inequality in the UK* (2014), 107.

48. Britton, Shephard, and Vignoles, *Comparing Sample Survey Measures of English Earnings of Graduates with Administrative Data during the Great Recession*, 41.

49. Some recent ONS data suggests a falling graduate premium and it appears to be because of this composition effect. That means it is consistent with Walker and Zhu, who compare people who are more similar and ask what the graduate premium is. I owe this point to Anna Vignoles.

50. 'The participation rate of young people in HE in the UK—having been stable at about 13–14% from 1970 through to the mid–late 1980s—rose rapidly after 1987 to reach 20% in 1990 and 30% in 1995, after which it broadly stabilised at 33%.' Robin Naylor, Jeremy Smith, and Shqiponja Telhaj, *Graduate Returns, Degree Class Premia and Higher Education Expansion in the* UK, CEP Discussion Paper No. 1392 (November 2015).

51. I. Walker and Y. Zhu, 'The college wage premium and the expansion of higher education in the UK', *Scandinavian Journal of Economics* 11/4 (2008), 695–709.

52. Richard Blundell, David A. Green, and Wenchao Jin, *The UK Wage Premium Puzzle: How Did a Large Increase in University Graduates Leave the Education Premium Unchanged?*, Institute for Fiscal Studies Working Paper W16/01 (June 2016).

53. Walker and Zhu also allow for at least some observed differences, like parental background, which we know affect your chances of going to university, so that graduates are compared as closely as possibly with the special subset of non-graduates who did not just have two A levels but other aptitudes which suggest that they could have gone to university but did not. Walker and Zhu, *The Impact of University Degrees on the Lifecycle of Earnings*, 19, 23–4. A different team of researchers take this idea further, using the rich NCDS dataset of children born in 1958 and followed ever since, and taking account of a host of factors apart from parental education, and then comparing the earnings of non-graduates and graduates who scored similarly on the likelihood of being a graduate. There is still a real university effect. See Richard Blundell, Lorraine Dearden, and Barbara Sianesi, 'Evaluating the impact of education on earnings: models, methods and results from the NCDS', *Journal of the Royal Statistical Society* Series A, 168 (2005), 473–512.

54. Dorothe Bonjour, Lynn F. Cherkas, Jonathan E. Haskel, Denise D. Hawkes, and Tim D. Spector, 'Returns to education: evidence from UK twins', *American Economic Review* 93 (2003), 1799–1812.

55. Walker and Zhu, *The Impact of University Degrees on the Lifecycle of Earnings*, 6.

56. Naylor, Smith, and Telhaj, *Graduate Returns*.

57. President Bush's address on returning to Yale University to accept an honorary degree, quoted in *Sunday Times*, 27 May 2001, p. 10.

58. Britton, Shephard, and Vignoles, *Comparing Sample Survey Measures of English Earnings of Graduates with Administrative Data during the Great Recession*, 37.

59. Seth Zimmerman, 'The returns to college admission for academically marginal students', *Journal of Labor Economics*, 32/4 (2014), 711–54.

60. Walker and Zhu, *The Impact of University Degrees on the Lifecycle of Earnings*. table 16, p. 54 shows a graduate premium for medicine of £429k for men and £454k for women.

61. As we saw in Chapter Three, Anna Vignoles and Neil Shephard have for the first time have been able to use confidential HMRC data on earnings and link it to

Student Loans Company information to show the earnings of graduates from different universities and on different courses. They find 'more than 10% of male graduates from LSE, Oxford and Cambridge were earning in excess of £100,000 a year ten years after graduation…a large number of institutions (36 for men and 10 for women) had 10% of their graduates earning more than £60,000 a year ten years on. At the other end of the spectrum there were some institutions (23 for men and 9 for women) where the median graduate earnings were less than those of the median non-graduate ten years on.' Jack Britton, Lorraine Dearden, Neil Shephard, and Anna Vignoles, *How English-Domiciled Graduate Earnings Vary with Gender, Institution Attended, Subject, and Socio-Economic Background*, IFS working paper, April 2016 W16/06. Quotes from IFS press release. This new analysis confirms that most graduates do earn more as a result of going to university—for male graduates median earnings ten years on were £30,000 compared with £22,000 for non-graduates of the same age. The equivalent figures for women were £27,000 and £18,000.

62. See e.g. Philip Brown, Hugh Lauder, and David Ashton, *The Global Auction: The Broken Promises of Education, Jobs, and Incomes* (Oxford University Press, 2011).

63. Walker and Zhu, *The Impact of University Degrees on the Lifecycle of Earnings*, figs. 4, 5, and 6 (p. 29) show distribution of real hourly earnings by gender and whether graduate or not. Figs. 5 and 6 show versions depending on age.

64. An image I owe to Laura Gardiner, Senior Research Analyst at the Resolution Foundation. See L. Gardiner, 'Hollowing out—deeper than it sounds', Resolution Foundation Blog, 23 March 2015.

65. SOC 1–3, which is the top three groups under standard occupational classifications, is one measure of graduate jobs. It includes managers, directors, professional occupations, and associate professional and technical occupations. SOC(HE) 2010 is the new narrower more qualitative measure of a job developed by Peter Elias and Kate Purcell.

66. Universities UK, *Supply and Demand for Higher-Level Skills* (December 2015), 16: 'during the period 2006–12, 40% of the labour force were in graduate jobs, as compared to 32% in the period 1997–2001. Looking at the expansion of graduate jobs, the authors find that approximately 40% of additional graduate employment was due to occupational upskilling rather than the expansion of jobs that have previously been classified as "graduate" or by qualification inflation (sometimes referred to as "credentialism").' The study UUK cite is F. Green and G. Henseke, *The Changing Graduate Labour Market: Analysis Using a New Indication of Graduate Jobs*, LLAKES Research Paper No. 50 (2014). Similarly research by Chevalier and Lindley found that 'whilst post-expansion graduates were less likely to be employed in traditional graduate jobs, most were found to be employed in a range of new jobs which nevertheless used their skills. Additionally, we find no change in the proportion of graduates reporting that a degree was needed to get their job.' Arnauld Chevalier and Joanne Lindley, *Over-Education and the Skills of UK Graduates*, CEEDP, 79 (London School of Economics and Political Science, 2007).

67. 'The proportion [of graduates] that believed their HEI had been an advantage [fell] from 68 per cent to 50 per cent, and the proportion who believed the skills they had developed on their course had made them more employable fell from 78 to 70 per cent.' Kate Purcell et al., *Futuretrack Stage 4 Transitions into Employment, Further Study and Other Outcomes* (HECSU and Warwick Institute for Employment Research, 2012), p. xxvi.

68. J. Bynner and M. Egerton, *The Wider Benefits of HE*, Report by HEFCE and the Smith Institute, HEFCE Report 01/46 (2001).

69. OECD, *Looking to 2060: Long-Term Global Growth Prospects*, OECD Economic Policy Papers No. 3 (November 2012), 18–22.

70. McMahon, *Higher Learning, Greater Good*, 77.

71. Anna Valero and John Van Reenen, *How Universities Boost Economic Growth*, CentrePiece, London School of Economics (Winter 2016), 9–12.

72. McMahon, *Higher Learning, Greater Good*, 106–7.

73. OECD, *Looking to 2060*, 18–22.

74. Craig Holmes, 'Has the expansion of higher education led to greater economic growth?', *National Institute Economic Review* 224 (May 2013), 29–42.

75. Studies include PWC in 2007 and London Economics in 2011. The latest paper which provides these estimates is Walker and Zhu, *The Impact of University Degrees on the Lifecycle of Earnings*.

76. Graduates tend to earn more and have fewer children so you could argue there is a saving on Child Benefit and tax credits though graduates will receive more state pension as they live longer. But family and pensioner benefits are not included in the calculation.

77. D. Holland, I. Liadze, C. Rienzo, and D. Wilkinson, *The Relationship Between Graduates and Economic Growth Across Countries*, BIS Research Paper No. 110 (August 2013).

78. Office for National Statistics (2014), Human Capital Estimates, 2013.

79. See Willetts, *The Pinch*, 50.

80. I am grateful to Dean Machin for these calculations.

81. Timothy Besley, Miguel Coelho, and John Van Reenen, *Investing for Prosperity: Skills, Infrastructure and Innovation*, National Institute for Economic and Social Research, No. 224 (May 2013), pp. R1–R13.

82. See e.g. Richard Blundell, Claire Crawford, and Wenchao Jin, 'What can wages and employment tell us about the UK's productivity puzzle?', *Economic Journal* 124 (May 2014), 377–407.

83. Enrico Moretti, 'Workers' education, spillovers, and productivity: evidence from plant-level production functions', *The American Economic Review* 94/3 (June 2004), 656.

84. S. Machin, A. Vignoles, and F. Galindo-Rueda, *Sectoral and Area Analysis of the Economic Effects of Qualifications and Basic Skills*, Department for Education and Skills (2003), 42–3.

85. Enrico Moretti, 'Estimating the social return to higher education: evidence from longitudinal and repeated cross sectional data', *Journal of Econometrics* 121 (2004), 175–212.

86. Valero and Van Reenen, *How Universities Boost Economic Growth*, 10.

87. Ricardo Sabates, 'Educational attainment and juvenile crime: area-level evidence using three cohorts of young people', *British Journal of Sociology*, 48/3 (December 2007), 395–409.

88. L. Feinstein, D. Budge, and K. Duckworth *The Social and Personal Benefits of Learning: A Summary of Key Research Findings*, Centre for Research on the Wider Benefits of Learning, Institute of Education (2008), 10.

89. Lance Lochner and Enrico Moretti, *The Effect of Education on Crime*, NBER working paper 8605.

90. Bynner et al., *Revisiting the Benefits of Higher Education*, 49.

91. *The Benefits of Higher Education Participation for Individuals and Society*, 18. The original source for the figures is F. Borgonovi and K. Miyamoto, 'Education and civic and social engagement', in *Improving Health and Social Cohesion through Education* (OECD, 2010), 65–110.

92. Bynner et al., *Revisiting the Benefits of Higher Education*, 46–8.

93. *The Benefits of Higher Education Participation for Individuals and Society*, 15.

94. Jim Ogg, 'A brief profile of the new British Establishment', *Political Quarterly* 77 (June 2006), 81–9.

95. *The Benefits of Higher Education Participation for Individuals and Society*, 18, 20.

96. M. Munro et al., *Students as Catalysts for City and Regional Growth* (University of Glasgow, 2010).

97. Valero and Van Reenen, *How Universities Boost Economic Growth*, 12.

98. Stefan Collini, *What are Universities For?* (Penguin, 2012), 99.

99. McMahon, *Higher Learning, Greater Good*, 13, 173. He is concerned that students 'do not value the non-market benefits very highly, presumably because they do not know what they are...A US survey showed that economic motives are listed three and a half times more frequently than non-economic motives for attending college' (pp. 175–6).

100. Kingsley Amis, *Lucky Jim* (Gollancz, 1954), 170.

101. Kingsley Amis, 'Lone voices: views of the 'fifties', *Encounter* (July 1960), 6–11.

102. Ibid. 9.

103. 'By 1958–59...54,000 students were in receipt of means-tested LEA grants (or "county scholarships"), which covered fees and living costs, and a further 12,000 were in receipt of state scholarships.' Nicholas Hillman, 'From grants for all to loans for all: undergraduate finance from the implementation of the Anderson Report (1962) to the implementation of the Browne Report 2012', *Contemporary British History* 27/3 (2013), 249–70; p. 253. That is over a half of all university students.

104. Nelson Goodman, *Fact, Fiction and Forecast* (Harvard University Press, 1983).

105. Alison Wolf, *Does Education Matter? Myths about Education and Economic Growth* (Penguin, 2002).

106. Adam Pritzker, one of the founders of *General Assembly*, quoted in *Financial Times*, 7 November 2011.

107. The paper shows that there are 'positive externalities' from hiring more educated staff. See L. Dearden et al., 'The impact of training on productivity and wages:

evidence from British panel data', *Oxford Bulletin of Economics and Statistics* 68/4 (August 2006), 397–421.

108. C. Harmon and I. Walker, 'Estimates of the economic return to schooling for the United Kingdom', *The American Economic Review* 85/5 (1995), 1278–86 and A. Chevalier, C. Harmon, I. Walker, and Y. Zhu, 'Does education raise productivity or just reflect it?', *Economic Journal* 114 (2004), 49. The idea was to see whether raising the school leaving age increased the education of people beyond the new minimum—if it is relative education that matters for earnings then raising the age should raise the whole distribution of education years—but it didn't. So a prediction of signalling theory was falsified. See also David Card, 'Education matters', *The Milken Institute Review* (Fourth Quarter 2002), 73–7. Also see Krueger and Lindahl, 'Education for growth', 1101–36.

109. C. Harmon and I. Walker, 'The returns to education: microeconomics', *Journal of Economic Surveys* 17/2 (2003), 115–53.

110. $ are 1990 international purchasing power parities. Figures taken from Angus Maddison's historical GDP data: see http://www.worldeconomics.com/Data/MadisonHistoricalGDP/Madison%20Historical%20GDP%20Data.efp (accessed 29 December 2014).

111. *Korea—Country Note—Education at a Glance 2013: OECD Indicators* (OECD, 2013), 3.

112. Boris Johnson, *Daily Telegraph*, 23 December 2012.

113. A. Bellavia et al., 'Fruit and vegetable consumption and all-cause mortality: a dose response analysis', *American Journal of Clinical Nutrition* 98 (2013), 454–9, and *Life expectancy by sex and education level*, Health at a Glance 2013: OECD Indicators, OECD Publishing.

114. Esther M. Friedman and Robert D. Mare, 'The schooling of offspring and the survival of parents', *Demography* 51 (2014), 1271–93.

115. Collini, *What are Universities for?*, 145–6.

CHAPTER SIX. WHICH THREE YEARS?

1. James Heckman, *Policies to Foster Human Capital*, NBER 7288 (August 1999); P. Carneiro and J. Heckman, *Human Capital Policy*, NBER Working Paper 9495 (February 2003); James Heckman and Dimitriy Masterov, *The Productivity Argument for Investing in Young Children*, NBER Working Paper 13016 (April 2007): 'The total rate of return to the Perry preschool program is about 16%' (p. 35).

2. Charles Clarke, speaking at the launch of National Sure Start Month at the Pre-School Learning Alliance conference, quoted by Polly Toynbee, *Guardian*, 6 June 2013.

3. J. J. Heckman, S. H. Moon, R. Pinto, P. Savelyev, A. Yavitz, 'Crime reduction is a major benefit of the Perry Program', *The Rates of Return to the High/Scope Perry Preschool Program*, IZA DP No 4533 (2009). Discussion of criminal activity, pp. 23–9.

4. National Education Association, quoted in 'What shall we be like in 1950?', *Literary Digest*, 10 January 1931, quoted in Christopher Cerf and Victor Navasky, *The Experts Speak* (Villard, 1998), 73.

5. Heckman et al., *The Rates of Return to the High/Scope Perry Preschool Program*, 3.

6. *National Evaluation of Sure Start Local Programmes: An Economic Perspective*, by the National Evaluation of Sure Start Team led by Pam Meadows, DFE Research Report DFE-RR073 (July 2011).

7. See e.g. Jo Blanden, Emilia Del Bono, Sandra McNally, and Birgitta Rabe, *Universal Pre-School Education: The Case of Public Funding With Private Provision*, CEP Discussion Paper, No. 1352 (2015), which shows negligible impact of the programme by the time the children were aged 11 at Level 2.

8. Lorraine Dearden, Leslie McGranahan and Barbara Sianesi, *An In-Depth Analysis of the Returns to National Vocational Qualifications*, Centre for Economics of Education Paper No. 46 (2004). It is cited in Alison Wolf's *Review of Vocational Education* (March 2011); see e.g. p. 32. I myself was also influenced by these findings in earlier policy work of my own and Alison Wolf is right to warn that some vocational qualifications do still have low returns—but it may not be quite as bad as we thought.

9. David Bibby, Franz Buscha, Augusto Cerqua, Dave Thomson, and Peter Urwin, *Estimation of the Labour Market Returns to Qualifications Gained in English Further Education*, Department for Business, Innovation and Skills, Research Paper No. 195 (2014). Augusto Cerqua and Peter Urwin, *Returns to Entry Level, Level 1 and Level 2 Maths/English Learning in English Further Education*, Department for Business, Innovation and Skills (2016).

10. 'Critical' meant that after it the brain was no longer plastic: now neuroscientists would call it a 'sensitive period'.

11. It has sadly not been possible to reproduce this image. The hospital where it originates replied as follows to our request: 'Due to widespread misrepresentation and misattribution, Dr. Perry and The Child Trauma Academy are no longer allowing the use of this image in any publications.' I understand why the unhappy history of misrepresentation of this image should have led them to this conclusion.

12. Victoria Knowland and Michael Thomas, *Educating the Adult Brain: How the Neuroscience of Learning can Inform Educational Policy*, Centre for Educational Neuroscience, Birkbeck College, London (2014). They cite E. E. Birch and D. R. Stager, 'The critical period for surgical treatment of dense congenital unilateral cataract', *Investigative Ophthalmology and Visual Science* 37/8 (1996), 1532–8.

13. John Bruer, *The Myth of the First Three Years: A New Understanding of Early Years Development and Life Long Learning* (Simon and Schuster, 1999), 89 cites J. P. Bourgeois and P. Rakic, 'Distribution, density and ultrastructure of synapses in the visual cortex in monkeys devoid of retinal input from early embryonic stages', *Abstracts of the Society for Neuroscience* 13 (1987), 1044, and J. P. Bourgeois, P. J. Jastreboff, and P. Rakic, 'Synaptogenesis in the visual cortex of normal and preterm monkeys; evidence of the intrinsic regulation of synaptic overproduction', *Proceedings of the National Academy of Science USA* 86 (1989), 4297–4301.

14. Bruer, *The Myth of the First Three Years*, 120.

15. Bruer, *The Myth of the First Three Years*, cites M. Carlson, 'Development of tactile discrimination capacity in Malacca Mulatta', *Developmental Brain Research* 16 (1984), 69–82.

16. *The Simpsons: Secrets of a Successful Marriage*, Episode 1F20, Season 5.

17. Victoria Knowland and Michael Thomas, *Educating the Adult Brain: How the Neuroscience of Learning can Inform Educational Policy*, Centre for Educational Neuroscience, Birkbeck College (2014).

18. Bruer, *The Myth of the First Three Years*, 129.

19. Interview with the author for the BBC recorded in September 2015. A good recent review is K. G. Noble et al., 'Family income, parental education and brain structure in children and adolescents', *Nature Neuroscience*, published online 30 March 2015. It does show some correlation between socio-economic status and brain structure with evidence that a boost of income for poorest families in the early years could boost cognitive capability. But Figure 1 shows the relationship is pretty flat except for the most deprived families. Professor Michael Thomas, who drew the paper to my attention, comments, 'Brains do vary a lot in size, but little of that is explained by SES. Thus the famous photo comparison of the "normal" and "deprived" brain massively over-states the effect.'

20. Patrick Blackett, President of the Royal Society. See David Edgerton, *Warfare State: Britain, 1920–1970* (Cambridge University Press, 2006), 214.

21. Manuel Carreiras, Mohamed L. Seghier, Silvia Baquero, Adelina Estevez, Alfonso Lozano, Joseph T. Devlin, and Cathy J. Price, 'An anatomical signature for literacy', *Nature* 461 (15 October 2009).

22. Sarah Jayne Blakemore and Uta Frith, *The Learning Brain: Lessons for Education* (Blackwell, 2005), 130.

23. See my discussion of Amazonian tribes and patterns of calorie consumption and production in David Willetts, *The Pinch: How the Baby Boomers took their Children's Future—and Why they should Give it Back* (Atlantic, 2010), 155–6.

24. Evidence on balance of spending in IFS *Trends in Education and Schools Spending*, IFS Briefing Note BN 121 (2011), 1998–2009. These estimates of public spending exclude fee loans unlike the figures in Table 3.1 on page 63.

25. Stephen Gibbons and Sandra McNally, *The Effects of Resources Across School Phases: A Summary of Recent Evidence*, CEP Discussion Paper No. 1226 (June 2013), 1.

26. UK HE spend was broadly flat in the period up to 2012, once income from fees consolidated into the figures. Early years spending was going up partly because of high cost structure. Primary school spend per pupil is up about 40% since 2000. By 2016 UK HE spend was up to 1.8% of GDP, ahead of the OECD average of 1.6% if one includes the boost from fees and loans though they are not strictly public spending. Primary school spending is even further ahead of the OECD average: 1.9% for the UK compared to 1.5% across the OECD. See OECD, *Education at a Glance 2012*, table B.2.3, and *2016*, table B.2.1.

27. For example a report by Kathy Sylva for the Sutton Trust, *Sound Foundations: A Review of the Research Evidence on Quality of Early Childhood Education and Care for Children under Three—Implications for Policy and Practice* (Sutton Trust, 2014) proposes all staff

working with funded 2-year-olds should have access to a graduate practitioner. The report also states: 'There is clear evidence for three and four year old children that graduate-led provision is of higher quality, but the evidence is less consistent for younger children' (p. 24).

28. Sue Ramsden et al., 'Verbal and non-verbal intelligence changes in the teenage brain', *Nature Letter*, published on-line 19 October 2011.

29. Matthew Seyd, *Bounce: The Myth of Talent and the Power of Practice* (Harper Collins, 2010).

30. Douglas Kenkel, 'Health behaviour, health knowledge, and schooling', *Journal of Political Economy* 99/2 (1991), 287–305.

31. Gary Becker and Casey B. Mulligan, 'The endogenous determination of time preference', *Quarterly Journal of Economics* 112/3 (1997), 729–58 (pp. 735–6), cited in Francisco Perez-Arce, *The Effect of Education on Time Preferences,* Rand Working Paper WR-844 (March 2011). See also J. Paul Leigh, 'Accounting for tastes: correlates of risk and time preferences', *Journal of Post Keynesian Economics* 9 (Fall 1986), 17–31.

32. Walter Mischel, *The Marshmallow Test: Mastering Self-Control* (Little, Brown & Co., 2014).

33. Perez-Arce, *The Effect of Education on Time Preferences*. Being admitted increased the chance of the seven-day trip by 8 percentage points—on average 57% went for that so the proportionate effect is significant.

34. Suzanne Mettler, *Soldiers to Citizens: The G.I. Bill and the Making of the Greatest Generation* (Oxford University Press, 2005), 10.

35. Robert Frank, *What Price the Moral High Ground? How to Succeed without Selling your Soul* (Princeton University Press, 2004), 156. See also Robert Frank, Tomas Gilovich, and Dennis Regan, 'Does studying economics inhibit cooperation?', *The Journal of Economic Perspectives* 7/2 (Spring 1993): 'We found evidence consistent with the view that differences in co-operativeness are caused in part by training in economics.'

36. Deena Skolnick Weisberg et al., 'The seductive allure of neuroscience', *Journal of Cognitive Neuroscience* 20/3 (2008), 470–7.

37. Joshua D. Angrist and Alan B. Krueger, *Estimating the Pay Off to Schooling using the Vietnam-era Draft Lottery*, NBER Working Paper No. 4067 (May 1992), 18.

38. Carol Dweck, *Mindset: The New Psychology of Success* (Random House, 2006).

39. Seyd, *Bounce*.

40. Strictly speaking we are talking here about the population mean for cognitive skills whereas IQ based on 100 is about one's position in the population relative to that shifting mean. See James Flynn, *Are we Getting Smarter? Rising IQ in the Twenty-First Century* (Cambridge University Press, 2012), 37.

41. Ibid. 27, 15.

42. Ibid. 23.

43. Ibid. 99, 106.

CHAPTER SEVEN. GETTING IN TO UNIVERSITY

1. *American College Testing* and the *Scholastic Aptitude Test* are key criteria for access to university. The latter is not the same as the English Standard Assessment Tests which track a child's progress through stages of schooling.
2. Nick Hillman, 'Why do students study so far from home?', *THES*, 23 July 2015.
3. 'How the land of opportunity can combat inequality', *Financial Times*, 16 July 2012.
4. This American donor-preference scheme is increasingly challenged, however. See e.g. Daniel Golden, *The Price of Admission: How America's Ruling Class Buys its Way into Elite Colleges—and Who Gets Left Outside the Gates* (Random House, 2006).
5. Robin Naylor and Jeremy Smith, *Schooling Effects on Subsequent University Performance: Evidence for the UK University Population*, Department of Economics, University of Warwick Economic Research Paper No. 657 (November 2002), 7.
6. Ibid. 12.
7. '...today I set a target of 50 per cent of young adults going into higher education. in the next century', Tony Blair, Labour Party Conference Speech, 1999.
8. City and Guilds Great Expectations 2015 and Council for Mortgage Lenders 2012.
9. Virginia Woolf, *A Room of One's Own* (Penguin, 1945), 6.
10. In 2014/15 56.3% of all postgraduates were female, 43.7% male. Amongst full-time postgraduates the proportions were 53.8% female, 46.2% male; part-time 59.5% female, 40.5% male. There are, however, still more male than female PhD students: 53% male, 47% female, within which full-time students are 54% male to 46% female, part-time 52% female to 48% male. Source: *HESA Students and Graduates, 2014–15*.
11. HEFCE analysis of participation rates in different local authority areas. Their latest analysis is POLAR3, covering young people who were aged 18 2005–9 and entered higher education between 2005 and 2010. The previous POLAR2 covered young people aged 18 between 2000 and 2004. See HEFCE Issues Paper 2012/26.
12. Mary Curnock Cook of UCAS focused attention on this issue. UCAS report, for example, that 'the average entry rate over recent cycles for state school pupils in the middle quintile 3 in the POLAR classification is 28 per cent. Within that group there are combinations of equality dimensions with much lower entry rates, for example men receiving free school meals in the White ethnic group have an entry rate of 9 per cent—one third the average for the POLAR3 quintile 3 group' (UCAS, End of Cycle Report 2015, published 2016, p. 14).
13. Nick Hillman and Nicholas Robinson, *Boys to Men: The Underachievement of Young Men in Higher Education—and How to Start Tackling it*, HEPI Report 84 (May 2016), 9.
14. 'Analysis by UCAS of higher education participation of 18-year-old state school pupils in the POLAR3 quintile 3 by sex, ethnicity, and free school meal status; and of 18-year-old state school pupils who received free school meals by POLAR3 quintile suggests that, under both measures, white boys from the most disadvantaged groups have the lowest entry rates to higher education (below 10%). In both

cases, however, they are closely followed by disadvantaged white girls (8% and 13% on the different measures) and mixed-race boys (11% and 14% on the different measures), who make up the second and third lowest entry rates. The absolute difference between disadvantaged white boys and girls is also lower than the difference between the sexes for any other ethnic and socio-economic group (the proportional difference is larger, but this is largely because of the very low bases in both cases' (Universities UK, *Working In Partnership: Enabling Social Mobility in Higher Education: The Final Report of the Social Mobility Advisory Group* (2016), 20).

15. POLAR3 data, HEFCE Issues Paper 2012/26.

16. Stephen Machin and Anna Vignoles, 'Educational inequality: the widening socio-economic gap', *Fiscal Studies* 25/2 (2004), 107–28, table 2: 'Percentage with a degree by age 23 by parental income' (p. 116).

17. Thomas Hardy, *Jude the Obscure* (Everyman's Library Classics, 1985), 106.

18. Christopher Wase, quoted in W. H. G. Armytage, *Civic Universities: Aspects of a British Tradition* (Benn, 1955), 120.

19. *British Social Attitudes Survey 28th Report* (2011), chapter on attitudes to HE, by Anna Zimdars, Alice Sullivan, and Anthony Heath (pp. 77, 83, and 85 for the quotation). The *British Social Attitudes Survey 32nd Report* of 2015 showed a slight softening of attitudes but even so three times as many graduates (18%) think that HE opportunities should be reduced than do individuals with no qualifications (6%).

20. A. N. Little, 'Will more mean worse? An inquiry into the effects of university expansion', *The British Journal of Sociology* 12/4 (December 1961), 351–62.

21. This figure has been calculated by taking the number of acceptances by 18-year-olds in England by ethnic group reported in *End of Cycle 2015 Data Resources: Acceptances by Ethnic Group, Age, Sex and Domicile* from UCAS, working out how many applied by using the entry rates for English 18-year-old state school pupils by ethnic group, and then multiplying the resulting figure by 57.6%, the entry rate for Chinese students. I am grateful to Dean Machin for these calculations.

22. Instead of the 368,000 English students who went to university in 2011–12 the figure would have been 570,000. David Willetts, *Robbins Revisited: Bigger and Better Higher Education*, Social Market Foundation (October 2013), 29.

23. Claire Callender, *It's the Finance, Stupid! The Decline of Part-Time Higher Education and What to Do about it*, Higher Education Policy Institute (November 2015), 17–18.

24. Higher Education Statistics Agency, UK Performance Indicators, 2014/15, table T3b: 'Non-continuation following year of entry: UK domiciled young full-time first degree entrants'.

25. *Further Information on Polar Three: An Analysis of Geography, Disadvantage and Entrants to Higher Education*, table 23, HEFCE February 2014/01.

26. 90% vs 88% and for full-time it is 80% vs 74% employment rates). Source: *The Outcomes associated with the BTEC Route of Degree Level Acquisition*, London Economics, Report for Pearson (May 2013).

27. Claudia Goldin and Lawrence Katz, *The Race Between Education and Technology* (Harvard University Press, 2008), 154.

28. Ibid. 155.

29. Rather confusingly the 2017 legislation creating a new Director of Access and Participation uses 'participation' in a different sense—meaning the student continuing to participate fully in higher education after they are admitted and not dropping out or under-achieving.

30. The precise figures from poorest to richest areas by quintile are 3.6%, 5.8%, 8.2%, 23.3%, 21.3%. Source: UCAS, *End of Cycle Report: Analysis and Research* (December 2016), data tables and figure 54.

31. Lord Curzon, *Principles and Methods of University Reform* (Clarendon Press, 1909), chapter 3: 'The Admission of Poor Men' (p. 42).

32. Armytage, *Civic Universities*, 63.

33. NPR, 16 October 2012, report of Gregory Clark, *The Son also Rises: Surnames and the Laws of Social Mobility* (Princeton University Press, 2014).

34. S. Machin and S. Gibbons estimate £26,000 higher houses prices in 2006 for a top 10% primary school as against £80,000 of private primary school fees. A good summary of their research is Steve Gibbons, *Valuing Schools through House Prices*, Centrepiece LSE (Autumn 2012), 2–5.

35. *Further Information on Polar Three: An Analysis of Geography, Disadvantage and Entrants to Higher Education*, tables 29–30.

36. '...there are currently four distinctive clusters of universities in the UK. A stark division is evident between the Old pre-1992 universities on the one hand and the New post-1992 universities on the other hand, with large differences evident in terms of research activity, economic resources, academic selectivity and social mix. The difference between Old and New universities with respect to teaching quality, however, is much more minor' (Vikki Boliver, 'Are there distinctive clusters of higher and lower status universities in the UK?', *Oxford Review of Education* 41/5 (2015)).

37. Malcolm Gladwell, 'The order of things: what college rankings really tell us', *New Yorker* (14 and 21 February 2011), 68–74.

38. Participation of NS-SEC classes 4–7 in higher education in England 2014/15, UK domiciled young full-time first degree entrants. Source: HESA.

39. Stefan Collini, *What are Universities for?* (Penguin, 2012), 155.

40. A letter by Mr John Saunders to the *Guardian*, 27 March 2013, describes the incident. It is not recorded in the minutes of Worcester College Governing Body; however, Mr John Saunders has confirmed that he remembers this being discussed by John Vaizey with Middle Common Room students. I am grateful to him for kindly sharing his recollection of this incident.

41. A. H. Halsey, *Decline of Donnish Dominion: The British Academic Professions in the Twentieth Century* (Oxford University Press, 1992), 157.

42. Graham Gibbs, *Dimensions of Quality*, HEA (September 2010). He was drawing on research such as that 'a student who attended a state school and achieved three A-levels (360 points) was 54% more likely (an odds ratio of 1.54) to be awarded a first than a student with the same A-level score who attended an independent school. And at the lower grade levels, for each category of A-level performance the likelihood of a state school student getting a first was greater than that of one who attended an independent school: with 340 points, for example, the likelihood of a

state school student getting a first was a little less than half relative to an independent school student getting 360 points (0.47), whereas for an independent school alumnus with equivalent points it was less, at 0.40.' Anthony Hoare and Ron Johnston 'Widening participation through admissions policy—a British case study of school and university performance', *Studies in Higher Education* 36/1 (2011), 21–41.

43. I. Walker and Y. Zhu, *The Impact of University Degrees on the Lifecycle of Earnings: Some Further Analysis*, BIS Research Paper No. 112 (August 2013), 44–6.

44. *Further Information on Polar Three: An Analysis of Geography, Disadvantage and Entrants to Higher Education*, tables 33, 34.

45. OFFA website, https://www.offa.org.uk.

46. The Further and Higher Education Act 1992 'states that the Secretary of State may not attach terms and conditions on grants to HEFCE which are framed by reference to: particular courses of study, programmes of research, the criteria for the selection and appointment of academic staff or the admission of students', as cited in BIS, *The Allocation of Science and Research Funding 2011/12 to 2014/15*, 57.

47. Vikki Boliver, 'How fair is access to more prestigious universities?', *British Journal of Sociology* 64/2 (2013), 344–64.

48. Claire Crawford, *The Link between Secondary School Characteristics and University Participation and Outcomes*, CAYT Research Report for the DfE (June 2014), 11.

49. *Difference in Degree Outcomes: Key Findings*, HEFCE Issues Paper (March 2014).

50. 'Comprehensive school pupils do better at university, two new studies confirm', Julie Henry, *Observer* (16 June 2013), referring to unpublished data obtained through FOI. Moreover in Russell Group and Alliance universities more than 20% of state school pupils graduating between 2009 and 2011 got a first as against 18% of independently educated pupils, according to a study by Bristol University: *Access to the Professions for Undergraduates from Less-Privileged Backgrounds: The Issue* (Upreach), 5 and Appendix 2, cited in *Observer* (13 January 2013).

51. The full text was: 'The use of contextual data to identify candidates with the ability and potential to succeed on a potential course or at a particular institution is not a new phenomenon. Many institutions have been using such information on the basis that there is good evidence that for some students, exam grades alone are not the best predictor of potential to succeed at university. The Government believe that this is a valid and appropriate way for institutions to broaden access whilst maintaining excellence, so long as individuals are considered on their merit and institutions' procedures are fair, transparent and evidence-based' (BIS, *Higher Education: Students at the Heart of the System*, Cm 8122 (June 2011), paragraph 5.18, p. 58).

52. The Schwartz Report of 2004 identified five principles for a fair admissions system. It should:

1. be transparent;

2. enable institutions to select students who are able to complete the course, as judged by their achievements and their potential;

3. strive to use assessment methods that are reliable and valid;

4. seek to minimize barriers for applicants;

5. be professional in every aspect and underpinned by appropriate institutional structures and processes.

Fair Admissions to Higher Education: Recommendations for Good Practice 2004, Report of the Admissions to Higher Education Steering Group Chaired by Professor Steven Schwartz.

53. Disadvantaged students do not perform quite as well as students from advantaged backgrounds but compared with other stages of education this gap is smaller. 'Graduates from the highest-participation neighbourhoods have the highest degree classifications compared with graduates from other neighbourhoods. 66 per cent of graduates from the lowest-participation neighbourhoods gained a first or upper second class degree in 2013–14. This is 11 percentage points lower than the highest participation neighbourhoods, where 77 per cent of graduates gained a first or upper second class degree. Taking into account the other factors, the unexplained difference between those from the lowest and highest participation areas is three percentage points.' See HEFCE, *Differences in Degree Outcomes: The Effect of Subject and Student Characteristics*, Issues Paper (September 2015/21), 5.

CHAPTER EIGHT. THE STUDENT ACADEMIC EXPERIENCE

1. Aditya Chakrabortty, *Guardian*, 9 April 2014, citing Manchester's Post Crash Economics Society.

2. Oriana Bandira, Valentino Larcinese, and Imran Rasul, 'Blissful ignorance? Evidence from a natural experiment on the effect of individual feedback on performance', *Labour Economics* 34 (2015), 13–25. The natural experiment occurs within one university where different departments provide different amounts of feedback.

3. Jonathan Neves and Nick Hillman, *The HEPI-HEA Student Academic Experience Survey 2016*, 18–19.

4. Alex Buckley, Ioannis Soilemetzidis, and Nick Hillman, *The HEPI-HEA Student Academic Experience Survey 2015*, 11–12.

5. Bahram Bekhradnia, *The Academic Experience of Students at English Universities 2012* (HEPI), 2. However, the 2016 report noted that 'there appears to be a limit to this, as satisfaction with contact hours tails off above 30 hours per week'. See Neves and Hillman, *The HEPI-HEA Student Academic Experience Survey 2016*, 18.

6. Buckley, Soilemetzidis, and Hillman, *The HEPI-HEA Student Academic Experience Survey 2015*, foreword.

7. *Annex 3: Findings from the Student Funding Panel Survey of Students and Student Focus Groups* (UUK, 2015), figure 11, p. 10.

8. Friedhelm Maiworm and Ulrich Teichler, 'The students' experience', in *Erasmus in the Socrates Programme: Findings of an Evaluation Study*, ACA Papers (2002). For European students studying in another EU country, on average 22% found it more demanding, 47% the same, and 31% less demanding. The UK was about average,

with 22% of students coming to the UK finding it more demanding, 41% the same, and an unusually high 37% finding it less demanding. For Germany the figures are 27% more demanding, 52% the same, and 22% less demanding.

9. Ariane Bogain, 'Erasmus language students in a British university—a case study', *The Language Learning Journal* 40/3 (2012), 359–74; p. 367.

10. John Brennan, Kavita Patel, and Winnie Tang, *Diversity in the Student Learning Experience and Time Devoted to Study: A Comparative Analysis of the UK and European Experience*, Centre for Higher Education Research and Information (HEFCE, 2009), 15, 18–19.

11. Graham Gibbs, *Dimensions of Quality*, The Higher Education Academy (September 2010).

12. Ioannis Soilemetzidis, Paul Bennett, Alex Buckley, Nick Hillman, and Geoff Stoakes, *The HEPI-HEA Student Academic Experience Survey 2014*, 2.

13. Gervas Huxley of Bristol University put in freedom-of-information requests to 103 universities asking about class sizes in physics, history, and economics. On the basis of the responses he received, he disputes the figures in this Table, which his evidence suggests are too favourable. There are two possible explanations of the discrepancy. One is that these figures are means and that median contact hours in small groups is zero. Louisa Darian of *Which* conceded that median time in groups of 0–5 is 0 hours, which is the experience of two-thirds of students. The second possibility is that the wording of the question is unclear and if there are several sub-groups per teacher then working in one of the small sub-groups is counted as small group teaching.

14. 54% of students work and 70% of those say working is essential for living costs, according to UUK 2015 Student Panel Survey Annex 3, p. 14.

15. Students can gain if their work is in placements linked to their studies or boosts their skills in, for example, time management. However, 'students working for financial reasons are considerably less likely to get a first (by 8 percentage points) and more likely to get a lower second (by 9 percentage points)' (S. Jewell, 'The impact of working while studying on educational and labour market outcomes', *Business and Economics Journal* 5/3 (2014), 1–12; p. 6).

16. Populus Poll for HMC, June 2011.

17. National Student Survey results 2016, National Student Survey summary data, Sector results for full-time and part-time students—England Teaching Institutions, HEFCE, 5 October 2016.

18. Daniel Knowles, 'Kingston University students told to cheat on survey', *Kingston Guardian*, 13 May 2008.

19. Speech by Jo Johnson to UUK, 1 July 2015.

20. 1999/2000 Higher education student data published by HESA, Higher Education Statistics Agency, 9 April 2001. Higher education student enrolments and qualifications obtained at higher education providers in the United Kingdom 2015/16, HESA, First degree graduates.

21. James Bryant Conant, diary as a Harvard freshman 1910–11. See James G. Hershberg, *James B. Conant: Harvard to Hiroshima and the Making of the Nuclear Age* (Stanford University Press, 1993), 26.

22. Daniel Willingham, *Why Don't Students Like School? A Cognitive Scientist Answers Questions about how the Mind Works and what it Means for the Classroom* (Jossey-Bass, 2009), and Daisy Christodoulou, *Seven Myths about Education* (Routledge, 2014).

23. Richard Arum and Josipa Roksa, *Academically Adrift: Limited Learning on College Campuses* (University of Chicago Press, 2011).

24. John Henry Newman *The Idea of a University*, ed. Frank Turner (Yale University Press, 1996), 3.

25. Survey carried out by the Centre for Business Research and the UK-Innovation Research Centre reported by Elizabeth Gibney in *THES*, 2 May 2013: 'The factors UK academics consider most important for promotion'.

26. John Hattie and H. W. Marsh, 'The relationship between research and teaching: a meta-analysis', *Review of Educational Research* 66/4 (1996), 507–42.

27. George D. Kuh and Ernest T. Pascarella, 'What does institutional selectivity tell us about educational quality?', *Change* 36/5 (September/October 2004), 52–8.

28. Ernest T. Pascarella et al., 'Institutional selectivity and good practice in undergraduate education: how strong is the link?', *Journal of Higher Education* 77/2 (March/April 2006), 251–85.

29. Gibbs, *Dimensions of Quality*, 18.

30. Adam Smith, *An Inquiry Into the Nature and Causes of the Wealth of Nations*, Book V, Chapter I, Part III, Article II: 'Of the Expense of the Institutions for the Education of Youth' (Oxford University Press, 1979), 761.

31. Ibid. 760.

32. Ibid. 762.

33. Ibid. 778.

34. V. H. H. Green, *The Universities* (Penguin, 1969), 45.

35. Ibid. 50.

36. Onora O'Neill, 'Integrity and quality in universities: accountability, excellence and success', *British Academy Review*, Issue 20 (Summer 2012).

37. '299 universities and colleges take part in Year Two of the Teaching Excellence Framework', HEFCE, 27 January 2017.

38. *THES*, 22–28 June 2017, p. 26.

39. There is an account of the case in *THES*, of 31 March 2006. The key lawyer in the court case was Cherie Blair.

40. Alan Cobban, *English University Life in the Middle Ages* (UCL Press, 1999), 8.

41. *'What do I get?'* Ten essays on student fees, student engagement and student choice, HEPI, 2015, Edward Acton, p. 9.

CHAPTER NINE. VOCATIONAL HIGHER EDUCATION

1. The quotation is from the *Birmingham Daily Post* at the time. See Eric Ives, *The First Civic University: Birmingham 1880–1980 An Introductory History* (The University of Birmingham Press, 2000), 121–2.

2. Keith Vernon, 'Calling the tune: British universities and the state, 1880–1914', *History of Education* 30/3 (2001), 251–71; p. 260.

3. John Henry Newman, *The Idea of a University*, ed. Frank Turner (Yale University Press, 1996), 82.

4. Ibid. 80–1.

5. Ibid. 81.

6. Ibid.

7. Dr Lowell of Harvard, quoted in Bruce Truscot, *Red Brick University* (Faber and Faber, 1943), 47.

8. Quoted ibid. 46.

9. William Whyte, *Redbrick: A Social and Architectural History of Britain's Civic Universities* (Oxford University Press, 2015), 133.

10. David Lodge, *Changing Places* (Secker and Warburg, 1975), 14.

11. Michael Sanderson;, *The Universities and British Industry 1850–1970* (Routledge and Kegan Paul, 1972), 344–50. Edinburgh did not participate in British research in the early 1940s because their leading scientist had objections of conscience: instead they sent one junior researcher and as it was Klaus Fuchs that was even worse.

12. David Edgerton, *Warfare State: Britain, 1920–1970* (Cambridge University Press, 2006).

13. Physicist Robert Wilson before the Congressional Committee on Atomic Energy, 1969.

14. The medical schools all affiliated to the University of London only in 1900 and even then were 'much more closely associated with their parent hospital than to the university'. See Angela Towle, *Undergraduate Medical Education: London and the Future* (King's Fund, 1992), 15.

15. See e.g. Charles Taylor, *Hegel and Modern Society* (Cambridge University Press, 1979), and Alasdair MacIntyre, *A Short History of Ethics* (Macmillan, 1966).

16. Richard Sennett, *The Craftsman* (Penguin, 2008); Matthew Crawford, *Shop Class as Soulcraft*, in the UK entitled *The Case for Working with your Hands: Or why Office Work is Bad for us and Fixing Things Feels Good* (Penguin, 2009).

17. Richard Sennett, *The Culture of the New Capitalism* (Yale University Press, 2006), 104.

18. Robert Pirsig, *Zen and the Art of Motorcycle Maintenance* (William Morrow and Company, 1974).

19. John Locke, *An Essay Concerning Human Understanding*, Book II: 'Of Ideas', Chapter I: 'Of Ideas in general, and their original', §2 (1690; Fontana Library, 1964), 89.

20. Jean-Jacques Rousseau, *Emile or On Education* (Penguin Classics, 1991).

21. W. H. G. Armytage, *Civic Universities: Aspects of a British Tradition* (Benn, 1955), 135.

22. David Hume, *Of Refinement in the Arts*, in *Essays Moral Political and Literary*, Part II, Chapter II (Oxford University Press, 1963), 277–8.

23. Armytage, *Civic Universities*, 267.

24. Abraham Flexner, *Universities: American, German, English* (Oxford University Press, 1930), 255. He is the great advocate of the university as the place for professional training whilst very aware of what types of study are or are not suited for university.

25. *Brotstudium* literally means bread studies: the term was first used by Feuerbach in an anti-Semitic way, referring to Jewish culinary rules, but subsequently came to mean vocational education.

26. James Hilton, *Lost Horizon* (Pansing Hotels for Shangri La Hotels, 1933), 142.

27. David Watson, 'The coming of post-institutional higher education', *Oxford Review of Education* (2015), 5–6 tracks the emergence of what he calls the 'professional formation university'.

28. BBC News, 14 January 2003.

29. Oli Barrett, post *The Alternative University*, 13 October 2010, describing 'An enjoyable six months working at Walt Disney World Florida...The experience culminated with a graduation ceremony from the Disney University, I quite literally have a Mickey Mouse Degree.'

30. Key Information Set Collection 2016/17, HESA.

31. See *Higher Education in England: Provision Skills and Graduates*, Universities UK (19 September 2016), 12.

32. This may be changing. An accredited course as an airline pilot can now be done as a higher level apprenticeship with a degree from Middlesex University.

33. Martin Nairey, 'The Nairey Report: a blueprint for the nation's lost children', *The Times*, 5 July 2011.

34. Report of the Mid Staffordshire NHS Foundation Trust Public Inquiry chaired by Robert Francis QC, p. 1515.

35. The Willis Commission on Nursing Education (2012), 29.

36. S. Robinson and P. Griffiths, *Scoping Review: Moving to an All-Graduate Nursing Profession: Assessing Potential Effects on Workforce Profile and Quality of Care*, National Nursing Research Unit, King's College London (November 2008), 8.

37. Linda Aitken et al., 'Nurse staffing and education and hospital mortality in nine European countries: a retrospective observational study', *Lancet* on-line, 26 February 2014. A separate US study, also by Linda Aiken, showed a 10% increase in the number of nurses with a Bachelor's degree was associated with a 5% reduction in the likelihood of a patient dying within 30 days of admission. See A. Kutney Lee, D. M. Sloane, and L. H. Aiken, 'An increase in the number of nurses with Baccalaureate degrees is linked to lower rates of post-surgery mortality', *Health Affairs* 32/3 (2013), 579–86 and also L. H. Aiken et al., 'Educational levels of hospital nurses and surgical patient mortality', *Journal of the American Medical Association* 290/12 (24 September 2003), 1617–23.

38. Robinson and Griffiths, *Scoping Review*.

39. *Higher Education: Report of the Committee appointed by the Prime Minister under the Chairmanship of Lord Robbins 1961–63* (October 1963), Cmnd 2154, para. 512, p. 167. I am grateful to Gordon Mackenzie for drawing this passage to my attention.

40. Michael Gove, speech to the National College Annual Conference, Birmingham 2010.

41. See e.g. Robert Coe, Cesare Aloisi, Steve Higgins, and Lee Elliot Major, *What Makes Great Teaching? Review of the Underpinning Research* (CEM, Durham University, and The Sutton Trust, October 2014).

42. 'To get a place wannabe teachers are instead encouraged to apply to schools directly. What they offer—how much the training costs, their entry requirements, available bursaries—all differ and can feel bamboozling....Compare the prospect of traipsing

around schools, filling in 53 applications in the hope of landing a poorly paid job, to that of a slick graduate recruiter tempting you down one simple path to a lucrative career' (Laura McInerney, *Observer*, 28 February 2016, p. 34).

43. *Students by Subject of Study, First Year Indicator, Mode of Study and Level of Study 2014/15*, Students, Qualifiers and Staff data tables, HESA.

44. Calculation based on: HESA Student Record, 2014–15; Recurrent grants for 2015–16, HEFCE, March 2015; Guide to funding 2015–16: How HEFCE allocates its funds, HEFCE, March 2015.

45. UCAS reports in 2016 there were 74,860 applications for 7,830 places, a 10.4% acceptance rate (*UCAS Undergraduate End of Cycle Data*, 2016). Most prospective students make five applications.

46. 'How much does it cost to train a doctor in the United Kingdom', BMA Media Note (January 2013), and Marco G. Ercolani et al., 'The lifetime cost to English students of borrowing to invest in a medical degree: a gender comparison using data from the Office for National Statistics', *BMJ Open* 2015; 5. e007335.

47. *NHS Staff by Nationality and HEE, April 2015 and Medical Staff by COQ and HEE, September 2014* (HSCIC).

48. *Equality and Diversity in UK Medical Schools*, British Medical Association, 2009—the remainder did not answer the question about their status on UCAS. See also Kathryn Steven, Jon Dowell, Cathy Jackson, and Bruce Guthrie, 'Fair access to medicine? Retrospective analysis of UK medical schools application data 2009–2012 using three measures of socioeconomic status', *BMC Medical Education* 16/11 (2016). The Extended Medical Degree Programme of King's College London performs well in their evaluation.

49. *Shape of Training: Securing the Future of Excellent Patient Care*, Final report of the independent review led by Professor David Greenaway, recommendation 14, pp. 11, 45, 114.

50. See Simon Wessely, President of the Royal College of Psychiatrists, 'Junior doctors are shuffled around like lost luggage', *The Times*, 31 August 2016.

51. *Aspiring to Excellence: Final Report of the Independent Inquiry in Modernising Medical Careers*, led by Professor Sir John Tooke (MMC Inquiry 2008), and *Shape of Training*.

52. Council of Science and Technology, letter of 26 July 2012, *Transforming the Training and Education of Future Generations of Doctors*.

53. *Daily Mail*, 23 July 2014.

54. Peter Coaldrake and Lawrence Stedman, *Raising the Stakes: Gambling with the Future of Universities* (University of Queensland Press, 2013), 101.

55. Vivek Wadhwa, Raj Aggarwal, Krisztina Holly, and Alex Salkever, *The Anatomy of an Entrepreneur: Making of a Successful Entrepreneur* (Kauffman Foundation, 2009), 5.

56. Mark Dodgson and David Gann, 'Forget the start-up garage myth. We need golden triangles and super clusters', *World Economic Forum*, 3 November 2016.

57. Markus Poschke, *Who Becomes an Entrepreneur? Labor Market Prospects and Occupational Choice*, IZA Discussion Paper No. 3816 (November 2008), and E. P. Lazear, 'Entrepreneurship', *Journal of Labor Economics* 23/4 (2005), 649–80.

58. Julie Logan, a professor at the Cass Business School in London, is cited in Brent Bowers, 'Study shows stronger links between entrepreneurs and dyslexia', *New York Times*, 5 November 2007.

59. The University Word List was developed in the 1980s to help students with the 800 new words they come across at university for the first time. See Konstantina Michail, *Dyslexia: The Experience of University Students with Dyslexia,* PhD Thesis, University of Birmingham, April 2010.

60. Graduate start-ups are defined as companies formed within two years of graduation. The number of start-ups increased by 31.4%, from 3,502 in 2012–13 to 4,603 in 2013–14, and then fell back by 9.6% to 4,160 in 2014–15. The number surviving three or more years rose by 18.4% and then 15.5%. See NCUB, *Higher Education—Business and Community Interaction Survey of 2013/14*, paragraph 72, and *2014/15*, p. 26.

61. Nick Bloom, Stephen Dorgan, John Dowdy, and John Van Reenen, *Management Practice and Productivity: Why they Matter,* McKinsey and LSE report (July 2007), 10.

62. Figures for 2014. Source: House of Commons Briefing Paper 05809, August 2016.

63. *Education at a Glance 2016*, Educational attainment of 25–34-year-olds by programme orientation, Table A1.4, OECD.

64. 27,000 out of 537,000 in 2015/16. Source: House of Commons Library, Apprenticeship Statistics: England, Briefing Paper No. 06113, 21 November 2016, p. 8.

65. These definitions of public spending are not fixed by Government, nor are the decisions on the treatment of individual items such as student loans. The Government complies with international conventions on public accounting and their application to specific cases has to be cleared by the Office of National Statistics and the independent Office of Budget Responsibility. If this leaves you hungry for more detail, the July 2014 OBR Fiscal Sustainability Report has a fuller discussion: see OBR Fiscal Sustainability Report, July 2014, pp. 169–74.

66. Lodge, *Changing Places*, 15–16.

CHAPTER TEN. DRIVER OF INNOVATION

1. 'We recommend that outputs should not be "portable", thereby encouraging a longer-term approach to investment by removing the "market distortion" that comes from excessive uncertainty about loss of staff in whom investments have been made. That could also reduce excess rent-seeking and "transfer activity" in the last period before a REF cut-off date' (*Stern Review*, paragraph 124).

2. This draws on the discussion in Paula Stephan, *How Economics Shapes Science* (Harvard University Press, 2012), 25–6. The insight comes from the sociologist of science Robert Merton.

3. Hsing-Fen Lee and Marcela Miazzo, 'Doctoral students pay the price of industrial collaboration', *Research Fortnight*, 13 May 2015, p. 22.

4. Sydney Smith, quoted in V. H. H. Green, *The Universities* (Penguin, 1969), 50.

5. John Henry Newman, *The Idea of a University*, ed. Frank Turner (Yale University Press, 1996), Discourse VII: 'Knowledge viewed in relation to professional skill'. See also the discussion in William Whyte, *Redbrick: A Social and Architectural History of Britain's Civic Universities* (Oxford University Press, 2015), 80 for another example of Newman taking this approach.

6. Kingsley Amis, *Lucky Jim* (Gollancz, 1954), 14–15. I am grateful to an anonymous OUP external reviewer for pointing out this connection.

7. Hearing Before the Committee on Science, Space, and Technology, US House of Representatives, One Hundred First Congress, Second Session, 13 July 1990.

8. *The London and Paris Observer of Literature, Science and the Fine Arts*, Vol. VI (1830), 72, reviewing Babbage's *Reflections on the Decline of Science in England and some of its Causes*.

9. Abraham Flexner, 'The usefulness of useful knowledge', *Harpers Magazine* 179 (June/November 1939).

10. Donald Stokes, *Pasteur's Quadrant—Basic Science and Technological Innovation* (Brookings Institution, 1997).

11. See e.g. Francis Narin, Kimberly S. Hamilton, and Dominic Olivastro, 'The increasing link between US technology and public science', *Research Policy* 26/3 (October 1997), 317–30.

12. I am grateful to Peter Grus for bringing this point to my attention. See e.g. Stephen Bensman, *Eugene Garfield, Francis Narin, and Pagerank: The Theoretical Bases of the Google Search Engine*, Archives, Cornell University, 2014. http://garfield.library. upenn.edu/bensman/bensmancornellarchives2014.pdf

13. Jonathan Bate (ed.), *The Public Value of the Humanities* (Bloomsbury Academic, 2011).

14. Each academic is allowed to submit a maximum of four papers each one of which is assessed by the REF panels on the basis of originality, significance, and rigour. There are five categories. **Four star**: world-leading. **Three star**: internationally excellent but which falls short of the highest standards of excellence. **Two star**: recognized internationally. **One star**: recognized nationally. **Unclassified:** quality that falls below the standard of nationally recognized work or does not meet the published definition of research for the purposes of this assessment.

15. See MIT News, *Beauty Business Based on MIT Bioengineering*, 7 August 2015. I am grateful to Michael Mire for bringing this to my attention.

16. Million Plus, statement to author, 26 January 2017.

17. Alan Hughes et al., *The Dual Funding Structure for Research in the UK: Research Council and Funding Council Allocation methods and the Pathway to Impact of UK Academics*, UK-IRC and CBR (October 2012), p. xiii.

18. '...exclusion and the associated stigma are being driven by factors that are not wholly related to the quality of an individual's research contributions and potential. Both the literature review and responses to the Call for Evidence suggest that there are long-term consequences to individuals who are not returned in the REF. With these factors in mind we recommend that in future exercises all research active staff are returned in the REF, and allocated to a Unit of Assessment' (Nicholas Stern,

Building on Success and Learning from Experience: An Independent Review of the REF BEIS IND/16 (9 July 2016), 19).

19. *The Organisation and Management of Government Research and Development, 1971* Cmnd 4814. One reason it is so unusually vivid is that it was not written for publication. But there was such anxiety about its proposals in Whitehall that it was agreed they needed to be consulted upon, which in turn led to it being published as a Green Paper alongside a parallel report by Fred Dainton which proposed something like the merger of the research councils implemented in 2017.

20. Rothschild Report, para. 8, p. 4; para. 6, p. 3.

21. See discussion in Miles Parker, *The Rothschild Report (1971) and the Purpose of Government-Funded R&D: A Personal Account* (Palgrave Communications, 2016), 53.

22. A point made, for example, by Praxis Unico—the body representing technology transfer offices.

23. Margaret Thatcher, *The Path to Power* (Harper Collins, 1995), 174–5. John Agar, 'Thatcher scientist', *Notes and Records of the Royal Society* 65 (2011), 215–32, claims that it was her negotiations with Edward Heath on the Rothschild Report which was a crucial stage in making her a Thatcherite.

24. 'Where the UK was once comparable to other western European countries, it now lags significantly behind our major competitors in productivity growth which has stalled' (*A UK Strategy for Agricultural Technologies*, HM Government (July 2013), 15, and see figure 1: 'Total factor productivity in agriculture for selected countries relative to the US'). There was no growth in total factor productivity between 2005 and 2012 though a modest 1.5% increase between 2012 and 2015. See *Total Factor Productivity of the UK Agricultural Industry 2014: 2nd Estimate*, DEFRA (November 2015), figure 1: 'Total factor productivity of the UK agricultural industry', pp. 1–2.

25. Stefan Collini, *What are Universities for?* (Penguin, 2012), 196.

26. Resident patent applications filed at national patent offices per billion PPP$ GDP, 2014. China, Germany, Japan, Korea, and Switzerland are joint 1st, followed by US (6th). We are between France (15th) and Kyrgyzstan (17th). *The Global Innovation Index 2016,* Cornell University, INSEAD, WIPO, table 6.1.1, p. 364. Number of international patents filed by residents at Patent Cooperation Treaty per billion $PPP GDP, table 6.1.2, p. 365.

27. Strategy& PwC, *2016 Global Innovation 1000 Study*, top ten most innovative companies: nine from US, one from South Korea, none UK. Boston Consulting Group, *The Most Innovative Companies 2015 Survey*: Britain has two out of the 50 most innovative companies (Biogen and BT Group); the US has 29.

28. Marianna Mazzucato, *The Entrepreneurial State: Debunking Public vs. Private Sector Myths* (Anthem Press, 2013).

29. A point made, for example, in research reports by Alan Hughes and David Connell at Cambridge University, such as Andrea Mina, David Connell, and Alan Hughes, *Models of Technology Development in Intermediate Research Organisations*, Centre for Business Research, University of Cambridge Working Paper No. 396 (December 2009).

30. *The Biomedical Catalyst: Making the Case to Continue* (Biotech Industry Association, 2015).

31. Enrico Moretti, *The New Economy of Jobs* (Houghton Mifflin Harcourt, 2012), 142.

32. Jonathan Haskel, Alan Hughes, and Elif Bascavusoglu-Moreau, *The Economic Significance of the UK Science Base: A Paper for the Campaign for Science and Engineering* (May 2014).

33. D. Adam, G. Atfield, A. Green, and C. Hughes, *Cities, Growth and Poverty: Evidence Paper 3: Case Studies,* The Work Foundation (February 2014), 20–4.

34. Moretti, *The New Economy of Jobs,* 195–7.

35. See e.g. H. Etzkowitz and L. Leydesdorff, 'The endless transition: a 'triple helix' of university–industry–government relations', *Minerva* 36/8 (1998), 203–8.

36. P. Aghion et al., *Exploiting States' Mistakes to Identify the Causal Impact of Higher Education on Growth,* UCLA online papers (2005).

37. Walter McMahon, *Higher Learning, Greater Good: The Private and Social Benefits of Higher Education* (The Johns Hopkins University Press, 2009), 109.

38. Moretti, *The New Economy of Jobs,* 94–5. He estimates that 'The earnings of a worker with a high school education rise about 7% as the share of college graduates in his city increases by 10%' (p. 98).

39. Neil Lee, *Advanced Industries, Job Multipliers and Living Standards in Britain,* Resolution Foundation (2017). Conor Darcy led this work within the Resolution Foundation.

40. 'A 1 percentage point rise in the share of high-paid occupation workers in a travel-to-work-area increases the hourly wages of least-paid quintile occupation workers by roughly 0.23%' (Ioannis Kaplanis, *Wage Effects from Changes in Local Human Capital in Britain,* Spatial Economics Research Centre, London School of Economics, December 2009).

41. These figures are even more striking given that universities are of course counted by the ONS as part of the private sector. Percentage of all adults aged 16–64 in different types of employment in the Oxford local authority area, ONS, *Subregional Public and Private Sector Employment, 2010 Data,* November 2011.

42. The National Council of University and Business, on whose Board I sit, monitors university business links. See NCUB, *The Changing State of Knowledge Exchange: UK Academic Interactions with External Organisations 2005–2015* (February 2016), 8 and table on p. 31.

43. David Willetts, speech to AAAS in Chicago 15 February 2014.

44. Haskel, Hughes, and Bascavusoglu-Moreau, *The Economic Significance of the UK Science Base,* Exhibits 19 and 20, pp. 32–9.

CHAPTER ELEVEN. THE UNIVERSITY IN THE MARKETPLACE

1. See e.g. Roger Brown with Helen Carasso, *Everything for Sale? The Marketisation of UK Higher Education* (Routledge, 2013), or, rather more historical and nuanced, Elizabeth Popp Berman, *Creating the Market University: How Academic Science Became an Economic Engine* (Princeton University Press, 2012).

2. Michael Oakeshott, quoted in W. H. G. Armytage, *Civic Universities: Aspects of a British Tradition* (Benn, 1955), 298.

3. Malcolm Bradbury, *Eating People is Wrong* (Secker & Warburg, 1959), 92–3.

4. Marina Warner, 'Learning my lesson', *London Review of Books* 37/6 (19 March 2015), 8–14 is a vivid if overwrought example of the unhappiness of some academics. Stefan Collini's books *What are Universities for?* (Penguin, 2012) and *Speaking of Universities* (Verso, 2017) are examples of the genre. The most engaging, because it is focused on the space academics need to be good teachers as well as researchers, is Maggie Berg and Barbara Seeber, *The Slow Professor: Challenging the Culture of Speed in the Academy* (University of Toronto Press, 2016).

5. Howard Jacobson, *Coming from Behind* (Vintage Books, 2003), 37–8.

6. David Hare, 'Why the Tory project is bust', *Guardian*, 8 March 2016.

7. Clark Kerr, *The Uses of the University*, 5th edn (Harvard University Press, 2001), 75.

8. Figures for first degree UK/EU domiciled students. HESA Table 3: HE student enrolments by HE provider, level of study, mode of study, and domicile for 2010/11, 2011/12, 2012/13, 2013/14, and 2014/15.

9. 'The majority of applicants (66%) cited improving their employment prospects or pursuing a specific vocation as their main reason for going to university...58% cited graduate employment rates as an important factor.' 'Choosing a university course: applicants' top five factors', *The Complete University Guide*, and Rebecca Hughes, 'Uni applicants 2014: how and why you made your choices', *Which University?*, 11 March 2014.

10. *Universities Terms and Conditions: An OFT Report*, OFT1522 (February 2014), 19.

11. Ibid. 21.

12. John Henry Newman *The Idea of a University*, ed. Frank Turner (Yale University Press, 1996), 105.

13. This is a consistent theme in the writings of David Palfreyman, e.g. David Palfreyman and Ted Tapper, *Reshaping the University: The Rise of the Regulated Market in Higher Education* (Oxford University Press, 2014).

14. *Privately Funded Providers of Higher Education in the UK*, BIS Research Paper No. 111 (June 2013), 7–8.

15. UGC, quoted in Palfreyman and Tapper, *Reshaping the University*, 6.

16. David J. Deming, Claudia Goldin, and Lawrence F. Katz, 'The for-profit postsecondary school sector: nimble critters or agile predators?', *Journal of Economic Perspectives* 26/1 (Winter 2012), 145.

17. Alternative providers were regulated under Section 22(1) of the Teaching and Higher Education Act 1998, which provides a power to designate a specific course so its students are eligible for support as well as a power to designate a whole institution.

18. Martin Wolf, for example, argues that this means universities cannot be for profit in 'Why universities are not supermarkets', *THE* 16 February 2017, pp. 44–9.

19. A QAA Briefing Note of 6 November 2015 entitled *CNAA and OUVS* states: 'The basic model of OUVS was not flawed.... The issues that led to limited confidence in the audit outcomes can be addressed, and this model could be renewed and

refined to provide an alternative pathway to validation and onto Degree Awarding Powers, without the need for legislative change.'

20. Instead others contributed to the debate, notably a report by the Higher Education Commission, *Regulating Higher Education: Protecting Students, Encouraging Innovation, Enhancing Excellence* (October 2013).

21. The 1988 and 1992 Acts cited in Palfreyman and Tapper, *Reshaping the University*, 12.

22. Ibid. 120–2.

23. The description of the three categories comes from *Success as a Knowledge Economy: Teaching Excellence, Social Mobility and Student Choice*, Department for Business, Innovation and Skills (May 2016), 24–5.

24. John Fielden and Robin Middlehurst, *Alternative Providers of Higher Education: Issues for Policymakers*, Higher Education Policy Institute Report 90 (January 2017).

25. Robert Anderson, *British Universities Past and Present* (Hambledon Continuum, 2006), 85.

26. A. H. Halsey, *Decline of Donnish Dominion: The British Academic Professions in the Twentieth Century* (Oxford University Press, 1992), 149.

27. The European University Association ranks British universities in the top three for the following autonomy measures: organizational (1st), financial (3rd), staffing (2nd), and academic (3rd). See T. Estermann, T. Nokkala, and M. Steinel, *University Autonomy in Europe II: The Scorecard*, European University Association (2011), chapter 3.

28. '(8) In this Part, "the institutional autonomy of English higher education providers" means—

    (a) the freedom of English higher education providers within the law to conduct their day to day management in an effective and competent way,

    (b) the freedom of English higher education providers—

        (i) to determine the content of particular courses and the manner in which they are taught, supervised and assessed,

        (ii) to determine the criteria for the selection, appointment and dismissal of academic staff and apply those criteria in particular cases, and

        (iii) to determine the criteria for the admission of students and apply those criteria in particular cases, and

    (c) the freedom within the law of academic staff at English higher education providers—

        (i) to question and test received wisdom, and

        (ii) to put forward new ideas and controversial or unpopular opinions,

        without placing themselves in jeopardy of losing their jobs or privileges they may have at the providers.'

    Source: The Higher Education and Research Act 2017, Clause 2, Section 8.

29. The provision is in the Education Act (No. 2) 1986, section 43, 'Freedom of speech in universities, polytechnics and colleges': '(1) Every individual and body of persons concerned in the government of any establishment to which this section applies shall take such steps as are reasonably practicable to ensure that freedom of speech within the law is secured for members, students and employees of the establishment and for

visiting speakers. (2) The duty imposed by subsection (1) above includes (in particular) the duty to ensure, so far as is reasonably practicable, that the use of any premises of the establishment is not denied to any individual or body of persons on any ground connected with (a) the beliefs or views of that individual or of any member of that body; or (b) the policy or objectives of that body.' It is important that strategies to deal with Islam extremism on university campuses respect this provision.

30. Interview with Sir David Bell, *Insight: The Magazine of HMC* 3 (November 2014), 15.

31. Immanuel Kant, *The Conflict of the Faculties* (Abaris Books, 1979), 29. Kant mischievously goes further in applying Adam Smith's ideas to a university: 'Whoever it was that first hit on the notion of a university and proposed that a public institution of this kind be established, it was not a bad idea to handle the entire content of learning (really, the thinkers devoted to it) by *mass production*, so to speak—by a division of labour, so that for every branch of the sciences there would be a public teacher or professor appointed as its trustee, and all of these together would form a kind of learned community called a *university*' (ibid. 23).

32. John Henry Newman, *Discourses on the Scope and Nature of University Education: Discourse V* (Cambridge University Press, 2011), 139.

CHAPTER TWELVE. WHERE: GLOBALIZATION

1. David Lodge, *Changing Places* (Secker and Warburg, 1975), 1.

2. *International Comparative Performance of the UK Research Base—2013* (Elsevier, 2013), table 3.1, p. 26.

3. Ibid. 59.

4. 'The European Commission revealed that 27% of the 3 million students who have taken part in its Erasmus exchange programme since it began in 1987 met their long term partner while studying abroad, potentially resulting in about a million bilingual babies' (*THES*, 2 October 2014, citing *The Erasmus Impact Study*, EU Commission, September 2014).

5. There are 17,581 higher education institutions across the world of which 10,476 in 184 countries have 'university' in their title, according to the World Higher Education Data Base maintained by UNESCO.

6. UNESCO Institute for Statistics, Enrolment by Level, Levels 6–8.

7. Rather peculiarly the statistics indicate 4,211,845 outbound and 3,936,609 inbound students—the rest presumably ending up on Mars. 4,000,000 seems a reasonable average (ibid., 'Inbound internationally mobile students by country of origin').

8. See the discussion and the diagram in Susan Reynolds, 'The Rise of Nations', in John Hutchinson and Anthony D. Smith (eds), *Nationalism* (Oxford University Press, 1994), 138–140. She does not accept the claim that the medieval university is actually the origin of the concept of the nation.

9. Alan Cobban, *English University Life in the Middle Ages* (UCL Press, 1999), 50, and also see *A History of the University in Europe*, Vol. 1: *Universities in the Middle Ages*, ed. Hilde De Ridder-Symoens (Cambridge University Press, 1992), chapter 2: Jacques Verger, 'Patterns', p. 40.

10. Provided there is no tightening of migration controls then one forecast is that the fall in the pound yields a potential net gain of 20,000 overseas students and a boost to university income of £227m. However this is offset by Brexit leading to a reduction in EU student numbers of 31,000 and a loss of £40m. The net figure is 11,000 fewer students but £185 million more tuition fee income. See Gavan Conlon, Rohit Ladher, and Maike Halterbeck, *The Determinants of International Demand for UK Higher Education*, HEPI Report 91 (2017).

11. BIS published a useful review of all this evidence during my time as minister. See *The Wider Benefits of International Higher Education in the UK*, BIS Research Paper No. 128 (September 2013).

12. 71% of total full-time Master's students are non-UK. The Chinese alone at 23% of the total are not far short of home entrants at 29%. See HESA Student Record 2014/15.

13. John Van Reenen, 'Growth must be the goal', *The Times*, 27 April 2012.

14. There were 8,200 overseas students in Sheffield of which 43% were from China. They brought in £105m in fee income plus £100m of subsistence spend and £6m of spend by visiting friends and relatives. After deducting the cost of services this brought a net benefit of £140m across the region. See *The Economic Costs and Benefits of International Students in Sheffield*, Oxford Economics (January 2013).

15. US research suggests that a 10% increase in foreign graduate students raises university patent grants by 4.5% and non-university patents by 6.8%. See Gnanaraj Chellaraj, Keith E. Maskus, and Aaditya Mattoo, 'The contribution of international graduate students to US innovation', *Review of International Economics* 16/3 (August 2008), 444–62.

16. *What do Prospective Students Think about International Students?*, HEPI Report 74, (March 2015).

17. 'Now that's what we call soft power', HEPI blog, 1 October 2015.

18. 'A person who moves to a country other than that of his or her usual residence for a period of at least a year (12 months), so that the country of destination effectively becomes his or her new country of usual residence. From the perspective of the country of departure the person will be a long-term emigrant and from that of the country of arrival the person will be a long-term immigrant' (United Nations Statistics Division, 'International migration', B. International long-term immigrant/ long-term emigrant).

19. Enoch Powell, speech of 20 April 1968.

20. 'In 2015, former immigration minister James Brokenshire said "it is important to recognise that net migration by the student route was 91,000 according to the latest Office for National Statistics figures, so there is an issue with students coming here and not going again" (Hansard 2015)', cited in Marley Morris, *Destination Education*, Institute for Public Policy Research (2016), p. 16.

21. 'The four least important factors for international students when considering study abroad are ... distance from home country, ability to get permanent residency in the destination country after study, exposure to culture or life in the destination country, better job prospects in the destination country', *Beyond the Data: Influencing International Student Decision Making* (Hobsons, May 2014), 20.

22. The Home Office did not release the report but an account was leaked to *The Times*: 'Ministers hide report on migrant numbers' (*The Times*, 13 October 2016, p. 1). Migration Watch and the Home Office claimed about 110,000 overseas students 'vanish' annually whereas the study suggests perhaps 1,500 do.

23. 'Government ministers have claimed on... that many non-EU international students (around 90,000) are not leaving the UK after completing their studies.... However, this claim is not supported by other evidence... that the IPS could be overestimating the number of students who stay on in the UK after completing their studies by many tens of thousands. The Home Office's visa data suggests that only around 40,000 non-EU individuals who came to the UK on student visas still have valid leave to remain or settlement five years later. The Annual Population Survey suggests that only around 30,000–40,000 non-EU migrants who previously came as students are still in the UK after five years' (Morris, *Destination Education*, 3–4). See also Office for Statistics Regulation '*The quality of the long-term student migration statistics*', July 2017.

24. Phil Honeywood in conversation with the author, 15 April 2013.

25. OECD website: *Migration and the Brain Drain Phenomenon*.

26. 'Brain drain as Britain's brightest students are lured to the US', *The Sunday Times*, 10 November 2013.

27. UNESCO Institute for Statistics, Inbound Internationally Mobile Students by Country of Origin.

28. 'Student voices', *The Independent*, 15 August 2013.

29. NOKUT, the Norwegian Quality Assurance Agency, recognizes Bachelor's, Master's, and PhDs as well as 'university college degrees' (2 years or 120 credits degrees) as long as 'the foreign qualification must be a completed degree, or a completed programme of study in the country of origin'. See NOKUT's criteria for general recognition of foreign higher education.

30. 'How Phil Hammond could turn £1 of spend into £22 of saving', HEPI blog, 12 November 2016.

31. A good example is *Universities and International Higher Education Partnerships: Making a Difference* (Million Plus, 2009).

32. 'All new police officers in England and Wales to have degrees', *BBC News*, 16 December 2016.

33. 'India's supply-demand gap in education expected to drive international mobility', *ICEF Monitor*, 28 October 2014.

34. Claudio E. Montenegro and Harry Anthony Patrinos, *Returns to Schooling Around the World*, World Bank Group Policy Background Paper for the World Development Report, 7. A separate report identified some of the implications. 'While our estimates are for private returns to schooling, the high returns to tertiary education will fuel demand for post-secondary education. Governments will need to consider the appropriate policy for financing tertiary education.' See Claudio E. Montenegro and Harry Anthony Patrinos, *Comparable Estimates of Returns to Schooling Around the World*, World Bank Group Policy Research Working Paper 7020 (September 2014), 19.

35. Percentage of bilateral aid for education going on post-secondary education: average 38%; Germany 69%; France 58%; US 8%; UK 6%. The percentage for multilateral is 15%. N. Gemmell, 'Evaluating the impacts of human capital stocks and accumulation on economic growth', *Oxford Bulletin of Economics and Statistics* 58 (1996), 9–28. It also shows developed countries in particular gain from more investment in tertiary education.

36. Measured by the membership of the main British international school networks: COBIS, BSME, NABIS, FBISA, and AOSBA.

37. Necat Berberoglu and Bahar Berberoglu, 'Grouping the mega universities according to their similarities', *Procedia—Social and Behavioral Sciences* 174 (2015), 2153–9; p. 2155. Also Open University website.

38. *International Education: Global Growth and Prosperity*, BIS, July 2013. Jo Johnson speech, 'International Higher Education', at Going Global conference, 1 June 2015.

CHAPTER THIRTEEN. HOW: EDTECH

1. Derek Bok, *Universities in the Marketplace: The Commercialization of Higher Education* (Princeton University Press, 2003), 87.

2. The Open University was due to take its first students in 1971. Ian Macleod, the incoming Conservative Chancellor, wanted to abort it but Margaret Thatcher successfully fought for it. At a Selsdon Park meeting of the Shadow Cabinet in early 1970 Mrs Thatcher rejected a claim that the proposed new university of Buckingham would be her 'Thatcher University Limited' with the words 'That is the Open University'. I owe this point to Nick Hillman, who cites John Campbell, *Margaret Thatcher*, Vol. 1: *The Grocer's Daughter* (Vintage Books, 2007), 204.

3. There is an alternative account—that universities increase costs to whatever they are funded for. These two explanations have been tested and the evidence is that 'the evolution of cost in higher education is very similar to the evolution of prices in other service industries that use highly educated labour and strongly dissimilar to industries producing standardised manufactured goods....Lagging productivity growth in personal services puts upward pressure on the relative price of these services because wage growth in this sector is not offset by higher labour productivity. More recently the rising wage premium for highly educated workers has put additional upward pressure on all personal services that rely extensively on educated labor. Higher education is one such sector.' See Robert Archibald and David Feldman, 'Explaining increases in higher education costs', *The Journal of Higher Education* 79/3 (May/June 2008), 268–95. Quotes from pp. 270 and 290.

4. William J. Baumol, 'Macroeconomics of unbalanced growth: the anatomy of urban crisis', *The American Economic Review* 57/3 (June 1967), 415–26; p. 416.

5. *Plato's Phaedrus*, trans. T. Hackforth (Cambridge University Press, 1952), 158.

6. Attributed to Einstein by Karl Popper in Karl Popper, *All Life is Problem Solving* (Routledge, 1999), 39.

7. A point I owe to Professor Van Schaack of Vanderbilt University.

8. Steve Kolowich, 'MOOC students who got offline help scored higher, study finds', *The Chronicle of Higher Education*, 7 June 2013.

9. Laura Pappano, 'The year of the Mooc', *New York Times*, 2 November 2012, and Steve Kolowich, '2014: the year the media stopped caring about MOOCS?', *The Chronicle of Higher Education*, 14 April 2014.

10. Anya Kamenetz, *DIY U Edupunks, Edupreneurs, and the Coming Transformation of Higher Education* (Chelsea Green Publishing, 2010) is a good example of the techno-optimism of the time.

11. Nicholas Negroponte, 'MIT Media Lab is vital to the digital revolution', *Wired*, 15 November 2012, p. 102.

12. I referred to this MOOC in a speech at a conference at the University on 15 May 2014. See also Louise Tickle, 'Are MOOCs the best chance we have to satisfy a global thirst for education?', *Guardian Education*, 20 January 2014.

13. See Robert A. Rhoads, *MOOCs, High Technology and Higher Learning* (Johns Hopkins University Press, 2015).

14. David Weinberger, *Everything is Miscellaneous: The Power of the New Digital Disorder* (Times Books, 2007).

15. Daisy Christodoulou, *Seven Myths about Education* (Routledge, 2014), and Daniel Willingham, *Why Don't Students Like School? A Cognitive Scientist Answers Questions about how the Mind Works and what it Means for the Classroom* (Jossey-Bass, 2009).

16. Stephen Balfour, 'Assessing writing in MOOCs: automated essay scoring and calibrated peer review', *Research and Practice in Assessment* 8 (Summer 2013), 40–7.

17. Dhawal Shah, 'By the numbers: MOOCS in 2016', *Class Central*, 25 December 2016. 'Registration' may not mean actual participation in an education programme.

18. See Ry Rivard, 'MOOCs may eye the world market, but does the world want them?', Inside Higher Ed. Blog, 25 April 2014.

19. Ryan Craig, *College Disrupted: The Great Unbundling of Higher Education* (Palgrave Macmillan, 2015), 76.

20. Ry Rivard, Inside Higher Ed. Blog, 18 July 2013, and John Douglass, 'Funding challenges at the University of California: balancing quantity with quality and the prospect of a significantly revised social contract', *California Journal of Politics and Policy* 7/4 (2015).

21. Gerald Ratner described the products in his jewellery stores as 'total crap' in a speech in 1991 and reduced the value of his company by £500m overnight.

22. Chen Zhenhao, Brandon Alcorn, Gayle Christensen, Nicholas Eriksson, Daphne Koller, and Ezekiel Emanuel, 'Who's benefiting from MOOCs and why', *Harvard Business Review*, 22 September 2015.

23. Chris Havergal, 'FutureLearn launches first Moocs offering academic credits', *THES*, 26 May 2016.

24. I owe this analysis to Simon Nelson of FutureLearn.

25. 2U, to whom I act as senior advisor, provides such courses.

26. *HEPI Student Experience Survey 2014*, 27.

27. Uri Triesman, cited in Bok, *Universities in the Marketplace*, 26.

28. Sarah Davies, Joel Mullan, and Paul Feldman, *Rebooting Learning for the Digital Age*, Higher Education Policy Institute (February 2017), 17.

29. Ibid. 17–18.
30. For a wider discussion see Jared Danielson, Vanessa Preast, Holly Bender, and Lesya Hassall, 'Is the effectiveness of lecture capture related to teaching approach or content type?', *Computers & Education* 72 (March 2015), 121–31; pp. 122–3.
31. Davies, Mullan, and Feldman, *Rebooting Learning for the Digital Age*, 13.
32. Kolowich, 'MOOC students who got offline help scored higher, study finds'.
33. Craig, *College Disrupted*, 195.
34. Conrad Wolfram, *Guardian*, 23 February 2014.
35. The Online Course Report, *The 50 Most Popular MOOCs of All Time 2017*, places the Duke course ('Think again: how to reason and argue') and Edinburgh ('Introduction to philosophy') as numbers 6 and 17, respectively. Number 1 is 'Learning how to learn' from UC San Diego.
36. Karl Kapp, *The Gamification of Learning and Instruction: Game-Based Methods and Strategies for Training and Education* (Wiley and Sons, 2012).
37. Craig, *College Disrupted*, 91.
38. See Mihaly Csikszentmihalyi, *Flow: The Psychology of Optimal Experience* (Harper Perennial Modern Classics, 2008).
39. An observation of Paul Feldman, chief executive of JISC (originally the Joint Information Systems Committee), which is promoting these innovative forms of learning.
40. *Improving Teaching with Touch Technology*, Economic and Social Research Council, November 2011.
41. Robert Axelrod, *The Evolution of Co-operation* (Penguin, 1984).
42. Davies, Mullan, and Feldman, *Rebooting Learning for the Digital Age*, 22–3.
43. Niall Sclater and Paul Bailey, *Code of Practice for Learning Analytics*, JISC, June 2015.
44. *From Bricks to Clicks: The Potential of Data and Analytics in Higher Education*, Higher Education Commission (March 2016), 41.
45. Davies, Mullan, and Feldman, *Rebooting Learning for the Digital Age*, 32–3.
46. Nottingham Trent University is a leader with a Student Dashboard. The University of Huddersfield has done work monitoring the attendance of students. The Open University developed their own OU Analyse. The Higher Education Commission is not aware of any Russell Group institution doing such work. See *From Bricks to Clicks*, 22.
47. Ibid. 18.
48. John E. Hunter and R. F. Hunter, 'Validity and utility of alternative predictors of job performance', *Psychological Bulletin* 96 (1984), 72–98.
49. Craig, *College Disrupted*, 123–5.
50. Lisa Ramsden, Delia Fuhrmann, Ashok Sakhardande, Fabian Stamp, Maarten Speekenbrink, and Sarah-Jayne Blakemore, 'A window of opportunity for cognitive training in adolescence', *Psychological Science Online First* (4 November 2016), 1620.
51. Ibid. 1628.
52. Craig, *College Disrupted*, 115.
53. Ibid. chapter 6.

CHAPTER FOURTEEN. WHAT: A BROADER EDUCATION

1. Eric Ashby, *Technology and the Academics: An Essay on the Universities and the Scientific Revolution* (Macmillan, 1958).
2. Simon Crowther, *The Crowther Report: 15–18*, A Report of the Central Advisory Council for Education (England) (London: Her Majesty's Stationery Office 1959).
3. Ibid. 245. I am grateful to Gary McCulloch for advising on its significance.
4. Ibid. 297, para. 441.
5. Sir Peter Swinnerton Dyer, former Vice Chancellor of Cambridge University and Chair of the University Grants Committee, The Rede Lecture, 1991, *Higher Education Quarterly* 45/3 (Summer 1991).
6. David Lodge, review of Brian Boyd, *A Passion for Particularity: Vladimir Nabokov: The American Years*, *Los Angeles Times*, 29 September 1991.
7. See *Higher Education: Report of the Committee Appointed by the Prime Minister under the Chairmanship of Lord Robbins 1961–63* (October 1963), Cmnd 2154, pp. 76–7 for discussion of specialization, and also pp. 94ff.
8. Tristan Bunnell, 'The rise and decline of the International Baccalaureate Diploma Programme in the United Kingdom', *Oxford Review of Education* 413 (2015), 387–403.
9. *Informed Choices A Russell Group Guide to Making Decisions about Post-16 Education*, 2013/14 edn, p. 29.
10. Adam Smith, *An Inquiry Into the Nature and Causes of the Wealth of Nations* (Oxford University Press, 1979), Book I, chapter 10: 'Of wages and profit in the different Employments of Labour and Stock', p. 126.
11. The Rathbone/Nuffield *Engaging Youth* Enquiry, 2008.
12. Ricardo Sabates, Angel L. Harris, and Jeremy Staff, 'Ambition gone awry: the long-term socio-economic consequences of misaligned, uncertain ambitions in adolescence', *Social Science Quarterly* 92/4 (December 2011).
13. 11% definitely agree and 22% agree maybe they would have chosen a different course if they were to have their time again. Jonathan Neves and Nick Hillman, *2016 Student Academic Experience Survey*, Higher Education Policy Institute and Higher Education Academy, data tables, question 12B.
14. Michael Teitelbaum, *Falling Behind: Boom, Bust and the Global Race for Scientific Talent* (Princeton University Press, 2014), 184.
15. A point made by Paul Connolly, Director of the MCA think-tank.
16. UKRC analysis of the European Labour Force Survey 2007, and Engineering UK, *An Investigation into why the UK has the Lowest Proportion of Female Engineers in the EU* (April 2011).
17. Tom Sutch, *Progression from GCSE to AS and A level*, Cambridge Assessment, December 2013.
18. Laura Spence was one of 22 applicants for 5 places to study medicine at Magdalen College, Oxford in 2000 and did not get a place. Gordon Brown, the then Chancellor, attributed her rejection to 'an old establishment interview system'. She

had excellent A levels but so did the other candidates. She went to Harvard instead and praised its 'broader, more balanced curriculum'.

19. He is referring to the Royal Society in its previous incarnation, to Imperial College and the Science Museum in South Kensington, and the Chelsea Arts Club.

20. C. P. Snow, *The Two Cultures*, with an Introduction by Stefan Collini (Cambridge University Press, 1998), 17, 19, 34.

21. Cited by President of the Royal Society Venki Ramakrishnan in the *Observer*, 28 February 2016, p. 35. He also observes in that article: 'all of us should enjoy science and mathematics which are a triumph of human achievement and are as much part of our culture as history, literature, art and music…we force students to choose between sciences and humanities too early.'

22. Academics from the humanities would tell me they had been unfairly treated in the allocation of resources. This was not correct: funding for research in the humanities and social sciences was protected from cash cuts just like the other research budgets. And when it came to teaching, the fees of £9,000 brought more funding in to humanities than any other disciplines because under the old system they had only been eligible for a teaching grant of £2,700, which together with the then fees of £3,300 added up to about £6,000 of teaching resource, as we saw in Chapter Three.

23. Howard Jacobson, *Coming from Behind* (Vintage Books, 2003), 37–8.

24. According to the 2013/14 DLHE the median salary for full-time, first-degree maths graduates was exactly 10% higher than the aggregate median salary (all subjects). See *Destinations of Leavers from Higher Education 2013/14*, Higher Education Statistics Agency, table 7. A similar effect can be found at other stages of education too.

25. Anita Klesch, *A Golden Age or Crisis? The History of Art in the Age of Information Technology*, DPhil thesis, Birkbeck, University of London 2011.

26. Eric Ashby pointed out that technology is about applying science to the needs of man and society and hence is what links science to the humanities/liberal arts. See his book *Technology and the Academics: An Essay on the Universities and the Scientific Revolution* (Macmillan, 1958).

27. *Why We're Behind: What Top Nations Teach Their Students But We Don't: A Report*, US Common Core (2009), p. iii.

28. The UK has the second youngest average age of first-time tertiary-level graduates in the OECD—23. This is second only to Germany (21). OECD, *Education at a Glance, 2016*, table A3.2, 'Profile of a first time tertiary graduate (2014)' (OECD Publishing, Paris).

29. David Bell, speech to Association of Science Education annual conference, 9 January 2015.

CONCLUSION

1. The campus novel itself reveals this way of thinking: 'Despite their apparent diversity, almost all British university novels play modest variations on one of three linked

stories: how an undergraduate at Oxford (usually) or Cambridge came to wisdom; how a don at Oxford (usually) or Cambridge was stabbed in the back physically or professionally, sometimes surviving to rule his college: and how rotten life was as student or teacher outside Oxford and Cambridge' (Ian Carter, *Ancient Cultures of Conceit, British University Fiction in the Post War Years*, quoted in Merritt Moseley, *The Academic Novel New and Classic Essays* (Chester Academic Press, 2007), 99).

2. Edmund Burke, *Reflections on the Revolution in France* (Penguin, 1986), 181.

3. Alfred Marshall, 'The future of the working classes' (1873), in A. C. Pigou (ed.), *Memorials of Alfred Marshall* (Macmillan, 1925), 121.

4. See discussion in A. H. Halsey, *Decline of Donnish Dominion: The British Academic Professions in the Twentieth Century* (Oxford University Press, 1992), 23–5.

5. 'This leaves us with some small but significant differences in university outcomes between pupils attending schools with different proportions of pupils eligible for free school meals that cannot be explained using the characteristics at our disposal. For example, conditional on their prior attainment, as well as the university they attend and the subject they study, pupils attending schools in the fifth quintile group (with the highest proportions of pupils eligible for free school meals) are 4.5 percentage points more likely to graduate with a first or a 2:1 than pupils attending schools from the first quintile group (with the lowest proportions of pupils eligible for free school meals)' (Claire Crawford, *The Link between Secondary School Characteristics and University Participation and Outcomes*, CAYT Research Report, Department for Education, June 2014, p. 69).

6. John Gill, *THES*, 28 January 2016, p. 5.

7. This point is made in Bill Readings, *The University in Ruins* (Harvard University Press, 1996), 11.

8. See e.g. Sheldon Rothblatt's shrewd essay 'The idea of the idea of a university and its antithesis', in Sheldon Rothblatt, *The Modern University and its Discontents: The Fate of Newman's Legacies in Britain and America* (Cambridge University Press, 1997). Some useful investigations on which this discussion draws include a restatement of the classic view of the university in Jaroslav Pelikan, *The Idea of the University: A Reexamination* (Yale University Press, 1992). A more troubled post-modern account is Readings, *The University in Ruins*. Gordon Graham, *Universities: The Recovery of an Idea* (Societas, 2002) is another contribution to the genre.

9. T. S. Eliot, *The Literature of Politics* (Conservative Political Centre, 1955), 13–14. I have substituted university in italics for Eliot's references to political parties.

10. Quoted in Pelikan, *The Idea of the University*, 181.

11. Jacques Derrida, *Eyes of the University, Right to Philosophy 2* (Stanford University Press, 2004); Jean-François Lyotard, *The Postmodern Condition: A Report on Knowledge*, trans. Geoff Bennington and Brian Massumi (Manchester University Press, 1984).

12. Immanuel Kant, *The Conflict of the Faculties* (Abaris Books, 1979). The key documents in the debate are in Ernst Anrich (ed.), *Die Idee der deutschen Universität. Die 5 Grundschriften aus der Zeit ihrer Neubegründung durch klassischen Idealismus und romantischen Realismus. Texte von Schelling, Fichte, Schleiermacher, Steffens und W. v. Humboldt* (Darmstadt, 1956).

13. F. R. Leavis, *Education and the University* (Chatto & Windus, 1943).

14. Kant, *The Conflict of the Faculties*, 27–9.

15. Readings *The University in Ruins*, 57.

16. Otto Kruse, 'The origins of writing in the disciplines: traditions of seminar writing and the Humboldtian ideal of the research university', *Written Communication* 23/3 (July 2006), 331–52.

17. Quoted in Pelikan, *The Idea of the University*, 129.

18. See Roger Kimball, 'Heidegger at Freiburg 1933', *New Criterion* 3/10 (June 1985), 9. 'The Self-Assertion of the German University', the address that Heidegger delivered in May 1933, to mark his assumption of the rectorate, and 'The Rectorate 1933/34. Facts and Thoughts', an *apologia* that he wrote in 1945, appear in *The Review of Metaphysics* 38/3 (March 1985).

19. Elaine Showalter, *Faculty Towers: The Academic Novel and its Discontents* (Oxford University Press, 2005), 124.

20. See the illuminating but pessimistic book by Bill Readings, *The University in Ruins*.

21. Chris Brink, 'On supply and demand in the knowledge economy', 14 February 2010.

22. Quoted in Readings, *The University in Ruins*, 77.

Bibliography

BOOKS

Amis, Kingsley, *Lucky Jim* (Gollancz, 1954).

Anderson, Robert, *British Universities Past and Present* (Hambledon Continuum, 2006).

Anrich, Ernst (ed.), *Die Idee der deutschen Universität. Die 5 Grundschriften aus der Zeit ihrer Neubegründung durch klassischen Idealismus und romantischen Realismus. Texte von Schelling, Fichte, Schleiermacher, Steffens und W. v. Humboldt* (Darmstadt, 1956).

Armytage, W. H. G., *Civic Universities: Aspects of a British Tradition* (Benn, 1955).

Arum, Richard and Roksa, Josipa, *Academically Adrift: Limited Learning on College Campuses* (University of Chicago, 2011).

Arum, Richard and Roksa, Josipa, *Aspiring Adults Adrift: Tentative Transitions of College Graduates* (University of Chicago, 2014).

Ashby, Eric, *Technology and the Academics: An Essay on the Universities and the Scientific Revolution* (Macmillan, 1958).

Axelrod, Robert, *The Evolution of Co-operation* (Penguin, 1984).

Axtell, James, *Wisdom's Workshop: The Rise of the Modern University* (Princeton University Press, 2016).

Barnett, Ronald, *Being a University* (Routledge, 2011).

Barr, Nicholas and Crawford, Iain, *Financing Higher Education: Answers from the UK* (Routledge, 2005).

Bate, Jonathan (ed.), *The Public Value of the Humanities* (Bloomsbury Academic, 2011).

Becher, Tony and Trowler, Paul, *Academic Tribes and Territories*, 2nd edn (Open University Press, 2001).

Becker, Gary, *Human Capital: A Theoretical and Empirical Analysis with Special Reference to Education*, 3rd edn (University of Chicago Press, 1993).

Bennett, William and Wilezol, David, *Is College Worth It?* (Thomas Nelson, 2013).

Berg, Maggie and Seeber, Barbara, *The Slow Professor: Challenging the Culture of Speed in the Academy* (University of Toronto Press, 2016).

Berman, Elizabeth Popp, *Creating the Market University: How Academic Science Became an Economic Engine* (Princeton University Press, 2012).

Berube, Michael and Ruth, Jennifer, *The Humanities, Higher Education, and Academic Freedom: Three Necessary Arguments* (Palgrave Macmillan, 2015).

Blakemore, Sarah Jayne and Frith, Uta, *The Learning Brain: Lessons for Education* (Blackwell, 2005).

Bok, Derek, *Universities in the Marketplace: The Commercialisation of Higher Education* (Princeton University Press, 2003).

Bradbury, Malcolm, *Eating People is Wrong* (Secker & Warburg, 1959).

Bradbury, Malcolm, *The History Man* (Secker & Warburg, 1975).

Brewer, John, *The Public Value of the Social Sciences* (Bloomsbury, 2013).

Brock, M. G. and Curthoys, M. C. (eds), *The History of the University of Oxford*. Vol. VI: *Nineteenth Century Oxford*, Part I (Oxford University Press, 1997).

Brown, Philip, Lauder, Hugh, and Ashton, David, *The Global Auction: The Broken Promises of Education, Jobs, and Incomes* (Oxford University Press, 2011).

Brown, Roger with Carasso, Helen, *Everything for Sale? The Marketisation of UK Higher Education* (Routledge, 2013).

Bruer, John, *The Myth of the First Three Years: A New Understanding of Early Brain Development and Lifelong Learning* (The Free Press, 1999).

Bush, Vannevar, Director of the Office of Scientific Research and Development, *Science, The Endless Frontier, A Report to the President on a Program for Postwar Scientific Research* (July 1945; reprinted 1960 National Science Foundation).

Butterfield, Herbert, *The Whig Interpretation of History* (Norton and Co., 1965).

Bynner, J., et al. *Revisiting the Benefits of Higher Education*, Bedford Group for Lifecourse and Statistical Studies, Institute of Education, University of London 2003.

Callender, Claire and Scott, Peter (eds), *Browne and Beyond: Modernizing English Higher Education* (Institute of Education Press, 2013).

Carswell, John, *Government and the Universities in Britain* (Cambridge University Press, 1985).

Christodoulou, Daisy, *Seven Myths about Education* (Routledge, 2014).

Clark, Gregory, *The Son also Rises: Surnames and the Laws of Social Mobility* (Princeton University Press, 2014).

Clarke, Ann and Clarke, Alan, *Early Experience and the Life Path* (Jessica Kingsley Publishing, 2000).

Coaldrake, Peter and Stedman, Lawrence, *Raising the Stakes: Gambling with the Future of Universities* (University of Queensland Press, 2013; 2nd edn 2016).

Cobban, Alan, *English University Life in the Middle Ages* (UCL Press, 1999).

Collini, Stefan, *What are Universities for?* (Penguin, 2012).

Collini, Stefan, *Speaking of Universities* (Verso, 2017).

Craig, Ryan, *College Disrupted: The Great Unbundling of Higher Education* (Palgrave Macmillan, 2015).

Crawford, Matthew, *The Case for Working with your Hands: Or why Office Work is Bad for us and Fixing Things Feels Good* (Penguin Random House, 2009; in the US *Shop Class as Soulcraft: An Inquiry into the Value of Work*).

Cook, Philip and Frank, Robert, *The Winner-Take-All-Society: Why the Few at the Top Get so much more than the Rest of us* (Penguin, 1996).

Crow, Michael and Dabars, William, *Designing the New American University* (Johns Hopkins University Press, 2015).

Csikszentmihalyi, Mihaly, *Flow, The Psychology of Optimal Experience* (Harper Perennial Modern Classics, 2008).

Curzon, Lord, *Principles and Methods of University Reform* (Clarendon Press, 1909).

Derrida, Jacques, *Eyes of the University, Right to Philosophy 2* (Stanford University Press, 2004).

Dweck, Carol, *Mindset: The New Psychology of Success* (Random House, 2006).

Edgerton, David, *Warfare State: Britain, 1920–1970* (Cambridge University Press, 2006).

Eliot, George, *Middlemarch* (1871–2; Oxford University Press, 2008).

Evans, G. R., *The University of Oxford: A New History* (I B Tauris, 2010).

Evans, G. R., *The University of Cambridge: A New History* (I B Tauris, 2010).

Flexner, Abraham, *Universities: American, German, English* (Oxford University Press, 1930).

Floud, Roderick and Glynn, Sean (eds), *London Higher: The Establishment of Higher Education in London* (The Athlone Press, 1998).

Flynn, James, *Are we Getting Smarter? Rising IQ in the Twenty-First Century* (Cambridge University Press, 2012).

Frank, Robert, *What Price the Moral High Ground? How to Succeed without Selling your Soul* (Princeton University Press, 2004).

Friedman, Milton, *The Role of Government in Education* in *Economics and the Public Interest*, ed. Robert A Solow (Rutgers University Press, 1955).

Galenson, David, *Old Masters and Young Geniuses: The Two Life Cycles of Artistic Creativity* (Princeton University Press, 2006).

Gibbon, Edward, *Miscellaneous Works of Edward Gibbon with Memoirs of his Life and Writings, Composed by Himself*, ed. John Baker Holdroyd, Vol. I (1796; reproduced Cambridge University Press, 2004).

Gibbon, Edward, *Memoirs of my Life*, ed. Betty Radice (1796; Penguin, 1964).

Golden, Daniel, *The Price of Admission: How America's Ruling Class Buys its Way into Elite Colleges—and Who Gets Left Outside the Gates* (Random House, 2006).

Goldin, Claudia and Katz, Lawrence, *The Race Between Education and Technology* (Harvard University Press, 2008).

Goodman, Nelson, *Fact, Fiction, and Forecast* (Harvard University Press, 1983).

Graef, Gerald, *Beyond the Culture Wars: How Teaching the Conflicts can Revitalize American Education* (Norton & Company, 1992).

Graham, Gordon, *Universities The Recovery of an Idea* (Imprint Academic, 2002).

Green, V. H. H., *The Universities* (Penguin, 1969).

Halsey, A. H., *Decline of Donnish Dominion: The British Academic Professions in the Twentieth Century* (Oxford University Press, 1992).

Hardy, Thomas, *Jude the Obscure* (1895, Everyman's Library Classics, 1985).

Heckman, James, *Giving Kids a Fair Chance* (Boston Review Books, 2013).

Hesse, Hermann, *The Glass Bead Game* (1943; Penguin Modern Classics, 1975).

Hilton, James, *Lost Horizon* (1933; Pansing Hotels for Shangri La Hotels).

Howard, Thomas, *Protestant Theology and the Making of the Modern German University* (Oxford University Press, 2006).

Howson, Susan, *Lionel Robbins* (Cambridge University Press, 2011).

Hume, David, *Essays Moral, Political and Literary* (Oxford University Press, 1963).

Ives, Eric, *The First Civic University: Birmingham 1880–1980. An Introductory History* (The University of Birmingham Press, 2000).

Jacobson, Howard, *Coming from Behind* (Vintage Books, 2003).

Johnson, Steven, *Everything Bad is Good for you: How Today's Popular Culture is Actually Making us Smarter* (Penguin Riverhead, 2005).

Jones, Ken, *Education in Britain: 1944 to the Present* (Polity Press, 2003).

Kagan, Jerome, *Three Seductive Ideas* (Harvard University Press, 1998).

Kamenetz, Anya, *DIY U Edupunks, Edupreneurs, and the Coming Transformation of Higher Education* (Chelsea Green Publishing, 2010).

Kant, Immanuel, *The Conflict of the Faculties* (Abaris Books, 1979).

Kapp, Karl M., *The Gamification of Learning and Instruction: Game-Based Methods and Strategies for Training and Education* (Wiley and Sons, 2012).

Kay, Ronald, *UCCA: Its Origins and Development 1950–85* (Universities Central Council on Admissions, 1985).

Kerr, Clark, *The Uses of the University*, 5th edn (Harvard University Press, 2001).

Layard, Richard, King, John, and Moser, Claus, *The Impact of Robbins* (Penguin, 1969).

Leavis, F. R., *Education and the University* (Chatto & Windus, 1943).

Locke, John, *An Essay Concerning Human Understanding* (1690; Fontana Library, 1964).

Locke, John, *Some Thoughts Concerning Education* (Dover Philosophical Classics, 2007).

Lodge, David, *Changing Places A Tale of Two Campuses* (Secker & Warburg, 1975).

Lodge, David, *Small World: An Academic Romance* (Secker & Warburg, 1984).

Lodge, David, *Nice Work* (Secker & Warburg, 1988).

Lodge, David, *Deaf Sentence* (Penguin, 2008).

Lyotard, Jean-François, *The Postmodern Condition: A Report on Knowledge*, trans. Geoff Bennington and Brian Massumi (Manchester University Press, 1984).

McCarthy, Mary, *The Groves of Academe* (Harcourt Brace Jovanovich, 1952).

Macintyre, Alasdair, *A Short History of Ethics* (Macmillan, 1966).

Macfarlane, Alan, *The Origins of English Individualism* (Blackwell, 1978).

McMahon, Walter, *Higher Learning, Greater Good: The Private and Social Benefits of Higher Education* (Johns Hopkins University Press, 2009).

Mann, Thomas, *The Magic Mountain* (*Der Zauberberg*, 1924; Penguin, 1960).

Marginson, Simon, *The Dream is Over: The Crisis of Clark Kerr's California Idea of Higher Education* (University of California Press, 2016).

Mazzucato, Marianna, *The Entrepreneurial State: Debunking Public vs. Private Sector Myths* (Anthem Press, 2013).

Mettler, Suzanne, *Soldiers to Citizens: The G.I. Bill and the Making of the Greatest Generation* (Oxford University Press, 2005).

Mischel, Walter, *The Marshmallow Test: Understanding Self-Control and how to Master it* (Transworld Publishers, 2014).

Moberly, Sir Walter, *The Crisis in the University* (SCM Press, 1949).

Mokyr, Joel, *Gifts of Athena: Historical Origins of the Knowledge Economy* (Princeton University Press, 2002).

Moretti, Enrico, *The New Economy of Jobs* (Houghton Mifflin Harcourt, 2012).

Morgan, K. O., *Labour in Power 1945–1951* (Oxford University Press, 1985).

Moseley, Merritt, *The Academic Novel: New and Classic Essays* (Chester Academic Press, 2007).

Nabokov, Vladimir, *Pnin* (Heinemann, 1957).

Newman, John Henry, *The Idea of a University*, ed. Frank Turner (Yale University Press, 1996).

Newman, John Henry, *Discourses on the Scope and Nature of University Education* (Cambridge University Press, 2011).

Oakeshott, Michael, *The Voice of Liberal Learning*, Foreword and Introduction by Timothy Fuller (Liberty Press, 2001).

OECD, *Education at a Glance 2011, 2012, 2013, 2014, 2015, and 2016*.

OECD, *Improving Health and Social Cohesion through Education* (2010).

Owen, Geoffrey and Hopkins, Michael, *Science, the State, and the City: Britain's Struggle to Succeed in Biotechnology* (Oxford University Press, 2016).

Palfreyman, David and Tapper, Ted, *Reshaping the University: The Rise of the Regulated Market in Higher Education* (Oxford University Press, 2014).

Parkin, Frank, *The Mind and Body Shop* (Atheneum, 1987).

Pascarella, Ernest and Terenzini, Patrick, *How College Affects Students: A Third Decade of Research*, Vol. 2 (John Wiley & Sons, 2005).

Pelikan, Jaroslav, *The Idea of the University: A Reexamination* (Yale University Press, 1992).

Pirsig, Robert, *Zen and the Art of Motorcycle Maintenance* (William Morrow and Company, 1974).

Plumb, J. H. (ed.), *Crisis in the Humanities* (Penguin, 1964).

Prest, A. R., *Financing University Education* (IEA, 1966).

Putnam, Robert, *Our Kids: The American Dream in Crisis* (Simon & Schuster, 2015).

Rees, Martin, *University Diversity, Freedom, Excellence and Funding for a Global Future* (Politeia, 2012).

Rhoads, Robert A., *MOOCs, High Technology and Higher Learning* (Johns Hopkins University Press, 2015).

Ridder-Symoens, Hilde De (ed.), *A History of the University in Europe*, Vol. 1: *Universities in the Middle Ages* (Cambridge University Press, 1992).

Ridder-Symoens, Hilde De (ed.), *A History of the University in Europe*, Vol 2: *Universities in Early Modern Europe (1500–1800)* (Cambridge University Press, 1996).

Robbins, Lionel, *The University in the Modern World* (Macmillan, 1966).

Robbins, Lionel, *Higher Education Revisited* (Macmillan, 1980).

Rothblatt, Sheldon, *The Modern University and its Discontents: The Fate of Newman's Legacies in Britain and America* (Cambridge University Press, 1997).

Rousseau, Jean-Jacques, *Emile or On Education* (Penguin Classics, 1991).

Royal Society, The, *Science as an Open Enterprise* (2012).

Ryan, Alan, *John Dewey and the High Tide of American Liberalism* (Norton, 1995).

Rylance, Rick, *Literature and the Public Good* (Oxford University Press, 2016).

Sanderson, Michael, *The Universities and British Industry 1850–1970* (Routledge and Kegan Paul, 1972).

Schuller, Tom and Watson, David, *Learning through Life: Inquiry into the Future for Lifelong Learning* (NIACE, 2009).

Scott, Peter, *The Crisis of the University* (Croom Helm, 1984).

Sennett, Richard, *The Craftsman* (Penguin, 2008).

Seyd, Matthew, *Bounce: The Myth of Talent and the Power of Practice* (Harper Collins, 2010).

Shattock, Michael, *Making Policy in British Higher Education 1945–2011* (Open University Press, 2012).

Showalter, Elaine, *Faculty Towers: The Academic Novel and its Discontents* (Oxford University Press, 2005).

Simpson, Renate, *How the PhD Came to Britain: A Century of Struggle for Postgraduate Education* (Society for Research into Higher Education, 1983).

Small, Helen, *The Value of the Humanities* (Oxford University Press, 2013).

Smith, Adam, *An Inquiry Into the Nature and Causes of the Wealth of Nations* (Oxford University Press, 1979).

Snow, C. P., *The Two Cultures*, with Introduction by Stefan Collini (Cambridge University Press, 1998).

Sparrow, John, *Mark Pattison and the Idea of a University* (Cambridge University Press, 1967).

Stephan, Paula, *How Economics Shapes Science* (Harvard University Press, 2012).

Stokes, Donald, *Pasteur's Quadrant—Basic Science and Technological Innovation* (Brookings Institution, 1997).

Taylor, Charles, *Hegel and Modern Society* (Cambridge University Press, 1979).

Teitelbaum, Michael, *Falling Behind: Boom, Bust and the Global Race for Scientific Talent* (Princeton University Press, 2014).

Thatcher, Margaret, *The Path to Power* (Harper Collins, 1995).

Trow, Martin, *Twentieth Century Higher Education: Elite to Mass to Universal* (Johns Hopkins University Press, 2010).

Truscot, Bruce, *Red Brick University* (Faber and Faber, 1943).

Veblen, Thorstein, *The Higher Learning in America, A Memorandum on the Conduct of Universities by Businessmen* (Dodo Press, 1918).

Vernon, Keith, *Universities and the State in England 1850–1939* (Routledge, 2004).

Vinen, Richard, *National Service: Conscription in Britain 1945–1963* (Allen Lane, 2014).

Wilson, Angus, *Anglo Saxon Attitudes* (1956; Faber and Faber 2008).

Woolf, Virginia, *A Room of One's Own* (Penguin, 1945).

Watson, Peter, *The German Genius* (Simon and Schuster, 2010).

Weinberger, David, *Everything is Miscellaneous: The Power of the New Digital Disorder* (Times Books, 2007).

Whyte, William, *Redbrick: A Social and Architectural History of Britain's Civic Universities* (Oxford University Press, 2015).

Willetts, David, *The Pinch: How the Baby Boomers Took their Children's Future and why they should give it Back* (Atlantic, 2010).

Willingham, Daniel, *Why Don't Students Like School? A Cognitive Scientist Answers Questions about how the Mind Works and what it means for the Classroom* (Jossey-Bass, 2009).

Wolf, Alison, *Does Education Matter? Myths about Education and Economic Growth* (Penguin, 2002).

Young, Michael, *The Rise of the Meritocracy* (Transaction Publishing, 1994).

ARTICLES, ESSAYS, AND RESEARCH REPORTS

Abel, Will, Burnham, Rebecca, and Corder, Matthew, 'Wages, productivity and the changing composition of the UK workforce', *Bank of England Quarterly Bulletin* 2016 Q1, 12–22.

Adam, D., Atfield, G., Green, A., and Hughes, C., *Cities, Growth and Poverty: Evidence Paper 3: Case Studies*, The Work Foundation (February 2014).

Agar, John, 'Thatcher scientist', *Notes and Records of the Royal Society* 65 (2011) 215–32.

Aghion, P., et al., *Exploiting States' Mistakes to Identify the Causal Impact of Higher Education on Growth*, UCLA on-line papers 2005.

Aiken, L. H., et al., 'Educational levels of hospital nurses and surgical patient mortality', *Journal of the American Medical Association* 290/12 (24 September 2003), 1617–23).

Aitken, Linda, et al., *Nurse staffing and education and hospital mortality in nine European countries: a retrospective observational study*, Lancet on-line, 26 February 2014.

Amis, Kingsley, 'Lone voices: views of the 'fifties', *Encounter* (July 1960), 6–11.

Amis, Kingsley, 'Why Lucky Jim turned right', *National Review* (October 1967).

Angrist, Joshua D., and Krueger, Alan B., *Estimating the Pay Off to Schooling Using the Vietnam-Era Draft Lottery*, NBER Working Paper No. 4067 (May 1992).

Archibald, Robert, and Feldman, David, 'Explaining increases in higher education costs', *The Journal of Higher Education* 79/3 (May/June 2008), 268–95.

Armytage, W. H. G., 'The conflict of ideas in English university education 1850–1867', *Educational Theory* 3/4 (1953), 327–43.

Arrow, K. J., and Capron, W. M., 'Dynamic shortages and price rises: the engineer-scientist case', *Quarterly Journal of Economics* (1959).

Austin, David, 'The Flexner myth and the history of social work', *Social Service Review* 57/3 (September 1983), 357–77.

Balfour, Stephen, 'Assessing writing in MOOCs: automated essay scoring and calibrated peer review', *Research and Practice in Assessment* 8 (Summer 2013), 40–7.

Bandira, Oriana, Larcinese, Valentino, and Rasul, Imran, 'Blissful ignorance? Evidence from a natural experiment on the effect of individual feedback on performance', *Labour Economics* 34 (2015), 13–25.

Baumol, William J., 'Macroeconomics of unbalanced growth: the anatomy of urban crisis', *The American Economic Review* 57/3 (June 1967), 415–26.

Bekhradnia, Bahram, *The Academic Experience of Students at English Universities 2012* (HEPI).

Bellavia, Andrea, et al., 'Fruit and vegetable consumption and all-cause mortality: a dose response analysis', *American Journal of Clinical Nutrition* 98 (2013), 454–9.

The Benefits of Higher Education Participation for Individuals and for Society: Key Findings and Reports 'The Quadrants', BIS Research Paper No. 146 (October 2013).

Bensman, Stephen, *Eugene Garfield and Page Rank: The Theoretical Bases of the Google Search Engine*, ArXiv, 2013.

Berberoglu, Necat and Berberoglu, Bahar, 'Grouping the mega universities according to their similarities', *Procedia—Social and Behavioral Sciences* 174 (2015), 2153–9.

Besley, Timothy, Coelho, Miguel, and Van Reenen, John, 'Investing for prosperity: skills, infrastructure and innovation', *National Institute for Economic and Social Research* 224 (May 2013), R1–R13.

Bibby, David, et al., *Estimation of the Labour Market Returns to Qualifications Gained in English Further Education*, Department for Business, Innovation and Skills, Research Paper No. 195 (2014).

Biotech Industry Association, *The Biomedical Catalyst: Making the Case to Continue* (2015).

Blanden, Jo, Del Bono, Emilia, McNally, Sandra, and Rabe, Birgitta, *Universal Pre-School Education: The Case of Public Funding with Private Provision*, CEP Discussion Paper, No. 1352 (2015).

Bloom, Nicholas, Dorgan, Stephen, Dowdy, John, and Van Reenen, John, *Management Practice and Productivity: Why they Matter*, McKinsey and LSE report (July 2007).

Bloom, Nicholas, Genakos, Christos, Sadun, Raffaella, and Van Reenen, John, *Management Practices across Firms and Countries*, NBER Working Paper 17850 (2012).

Blundell, Richard, Dearden, Lorraine, and Sianesi, Barbara, 'Evaluating the impact of education on earnings: models, methods and results from the NCDS', *Journal of the Royal Statistical Society*, Series A, 168 (2005), 473–512.

Blundell, Richard, Crawford, Claire, and Jin, Wenchao, 'What can wages and employment tell us about the UK's productivity puzzle?', *Economic Journal* 124 (May 2014), 377–407.

Blundell, Richard, Green, David A., and Jin, Wenchao, *The UK Wage Premium Puzzle: How Did a Large Increase in University Graduates Leave the Education Premium Unchanged?*, Institute for Fiscal Studies Working Paper W16/01 (June 2016).

Bogain, Ariane, 'Erasmus language students in a British university—a case study', *The Language Learning Journal* 40/3 (2012), 359–74.

Boliver, Vikki, 'Are there distinctive clusters of higher and lower status universities in the UK?', *Oxford Review of Education* 41/5 (2015).

Bologna Working Group Report on Qualifications Framework, *A Framework for Qualifications of the European Higher Education Area* (2005).

Bonjour, Dorothe, et al., 'Returns to education: evidence from UK twins', *American Economic Review* 93 (2003), 1799–812.

Brabon, Benjamin, 'Talking about quality: massive misalignment: the challenges of designing and accrediting MOOCs', QAA Issue 8 (May 2014).

Brennan, John, Patel, Kavita, and Tang, Winnie, *Diversity in the Student Learning Experience and Time Devoted to Study: A Comparative Analysis of the UK and European Experience*, Centre for Higher Education Research and Information (HEFCE, 2009).

Brennan, John, et al., *The Effect of Higher Education on Graduates' Attitudes: Secondary Analysis of the British Social Attitudes Survey*, BIS Research Paper No. 200 (November 2015).

British Academy, The, *Crossing Paths: Interdisciplinary Institutions, Careers, Education, and Applications* (July 2016).

British Social Attitudes Survey 28th Report, ed. Anna Zimdars, Alice Sullivan, and Anthony Heath (December 2011).

British Social Attitudes Survey 32nd Report, ed. John Curtice and Rachel Ormiston (March 2015).

Britton, Jack, Shephard, Neil, and Vignoles, Anna, *Comparing Sample Survey Measures of English Earnings of Graduates with Administrative Data during the Great Recession*, IFS Working Paper W15/28 (2015).

Britton, Jack, Crawford, Claire, and Dearden, Lorraine, *Analysis of the Higher Education Funding Reforms Announced in Summer Budget 2015*, Institute for Fiscal Studies, July 2015.

Britton, Jack, Dearden, Lorraine, Shephard, Neil, and Vignoles, Anna, *How English-Domiciled Graduate Earnings Vary with Gender, Institution Attended, Subject, and Socio-Economic Background*, IFS W 16/06.

Buckley, Alex, Soilemetzidis, Ioannis, and Hillman, Nick, *The HEPI-HEA Student Academic Experience Survey 2015*.

Bunnell, Tristan, 'The rise and decline of the International Baccalaureate Diploma Programme in the United Kingdom', *Oxford Review of Education* 413 (2015), 387–403.

de Burgh, Hugo, Fazackerley, Anna, and Black, Jeremy (eds), *Can the Prizes Still Glitter? The Future of British Universities in a Changing World* (University of Buckingham Press, 2007).

Bynner, J., and Egerton, M., *The Wider Benefits of HE*, Report by HEFCE and the Smith Institute, HEFCE Report 01/46 (2001).

Bynner, J., et al., *Revisiting the Benefits of Higher Education*, Bedford Group for Lifecourse and Statistical Studies, Institute of Education, University of London, 2003.

Callender, Claire, *It's the Finance, Stupid! The Decline of Part-Time Higher Education and What to Do about it*, Higher Education Policy Institute (November 2015).

Card, David, 'Education matters', *The Milken Institute Review* (Fourth Quarter, 2002), 73–7.

Carneiro, P., and Heckman, J., *Human Capital Policy*, NBER Working Paper 9495 (February 2003).

Carreiras, Manuel, et al., 'An anatomical signature for literacy', *Nature* 461 (15 October 2009).

Ceci, Stephen J. and Williams, Wendy M., 'Understanding current causes of women's underrepresentation in science', *Proceedings of the National Academy of Sciences of America* 108/8 (22 February 2011), 3157–62.

Cerqua, Augusto, and Urwin, Peter, *Returns to Entry Level, Level 1 and Level 2 Maths/English Learning in English Further Education*, BIS, 2016.

Chelleraj, Gnanaraj, Maskus, Keith E., and Mattoo, Aaditya, 'The contribution of international graduate students to US innovation', *Review of International Economics* 16/3 (August 2008), 444–62.

Chevalier, A., Harmon, C., Walker, I., and Zhu, Y., 'Does education raise productivity or just reflect it?', *Economic Journal* 114 (2004), 49.

Chevalier, Arnauld and Lindley, Joanne, *Over-Education and the Skills of UK Graduates*, CEEDP, 79 (London School of Economics and Political Science, 2007).

Coe, Robert, Aloisi, Cesare, Higgins, Steve, and Major, Lee Elliot, *What Makes Great Teaching? Review of the Underpinning Research*, CEM, Durham University, and The Sutton Trust (October 2014).

Conlon, Gavan, Ladher, Rohit, and Halterbeck, Maike, *The Determinants of International Demand for UK Higher Education*, HEPI Report 91 (2017).

Cosslett, V. E. (ed.), *The Relations between Scientific Research in the Universities and Industrial Research: A Report on Conditions in Great Britain*, International Association of University Professors and Lecturers (1955).

Cutler, David M. and Lleras-Muney, Adriana, 'Understanding differences in behaviour by education', *Journal of Health Economics* 29/1 (January 2010), 1–28.

Danielson, Jared, Preast, Vanesssa, Bender, Holly, and Hassall, Lesya, 'Is the effectiveness of lecture capture related to teaching approach or content type?', *Computers & Education* 72 (March 2015), 121–31.

Davies, Sarah, Mullan, Joel, and Feldman, Paul, *Rebooting Learning for the Digital Age*, Higher Education Policy Institute (February 2017).

Dearden, Lorraine, McGranahan, Leslie, and Sianesi, Barbara, Centre for Economics of Education, Paper No. 46 (2004). It is cited in Alison Wolf's *Review of Vocational Education*, March 2011.

Dearden, Lorraine, et al., 'The impact of training on productivity and wages: evidence from British panel data', *Oxford Bulletin of Economics and Statistics* 68/4 (August 2006), 397–421.

Deming, David J., Goldin, Claudia, and Katz, Lawrence F., 'The for-profit postsecondary school sector: nimble critters or agile predators?', *Journal of Economic Perspectives* 26/1 (Winter 2012), 139–64.

Dodgson, Mark, and Gann, David, 'Forget the start-up garage myth. We need golden triangles and super clusters', *World Economic Forum*, 3 November 2016.

Douglass, John, 'Funding challenges at the University of California: balancing quantity with quality and the prospect of a significantly revised social contract', *California Journal of Politics and Policy* 7/4 (2015).

Edgerton, David, *The 'Haldane Principle' and other Invented Traditions in Science Policy*, History and Policy, Policy Papers (2009).

Eliot, T. S., *The Literature of Politics*, Conservative Political Centre (1955).

Ercolani, Marco G. et al., 'The lifetime cost to English students of borrowing to invest in a medical degree: a gender comparison using data from the Office for National Statistics', *BMJ Open* 2015; 5. e007335.

Estermann, Thomas, Nokkala, Terhi, and Steinel, Monika, *University Autonomy in Europe II: The Scorecard*, European University Association, 2011.

Etzkowitz, H. and Leydesdorff, L. 'The endless transition: a 'triple helix' of university-industry-government relations', *Minerva* 36/8 (1998), 203–8.

Farla, Kristine and Simmonds, Paul, *REF 2014 Accountability Review: Costs, Benefits and Burden*, Technolopolis, 2015.

Feinstein, Leon, Budge, David, Vorhaus, John, and Duckworth, Kathyrn, *The Social Benefits of Learning: A Summary of Key Research Findings*, Centre for Research on the Wider Benefits of Learning, 2008.

Fielden, John and Middlehurst, Robin, *Alternative Providers of Higher Education: Issues for Policymakers*, Higher Education Policy Institute Report 90 (January 2017).

Fisher, Steven and Hillman, Nick, *Do Students Swing Elections? Registration, Turn-out and Voting Behaviour among Full-Time Students* (HEPI, 2014).

Frank, Robert, Gilovich, Tomas, and Regan, Dennis, 'Does studying economics inhibit cooperation?', *The Journal of Economic Perspectives* 7/2 (Spring 1993), 159–71.

Friedman, Esther M. and Mare, Robert D., 'The schooling of offspring and the survival of parents', *Demography* 51 (2014), 1271–93.

Gemmell, N., 'Evaluating the impacts of human capital stocks and accumulation on economic growth', *Oxford Bulletin of Economics and Statistics* 58 (1996), 9–28.

Gibbons, Steve and Machin, Stephen, *Valuing Primary Schools*, CEEDP, 15, Centre for the Economics of Education, London School of Economics and Political Science, London (2001).

Gibbons, Steve, *Valuing Schools through House Prices*, Centrepiece, LSE (Autumn 2012), 2–5.

Gibbons, Stephen and McNally, Sandra, *The Effects of Resources Across School Phases: A Summary of Recent Evidence*, CEP Discussion Paper No. 1226 (June 2013).

Gibbs, Graham, *Dimensions of Quality*, The Higher Education Academy (September 2010).

Gladwell, Malcolm, 'The order of things what college rankings really tell us', *New Yorker* (14 and 21 February 2011), 68–74.

Grant, Jonathan, *The Nature, Scale and Beneficiaries of Research Impact: An Initial Analysis of Research Excellence Framework (REF) 2014 Impact Case Studies*, King's College, London and Digital Science (March 2015).

Green, F. and Henseke, G., *The Changing Graduate Labour Market: Analysis Using a New Indication of Graduate Jobs*, LLAKES Research Paper No. 50 (2014).

Grendler, Paul, 'The universities of the Renaissance and Reformation', *Renaissance Quarterly* 57 (2004), 1–42.

Harmon, C. and Walker, I., 'Estimates of the economic return to schooling for the United Kingdom', *The American Economic Review* 85/5 (1995), 1278–86.

Harmon, C. and Walker, I., 'The returns to education: microeconomics', *Journal of Economic Surveys* 17/2 (2003), 115–53.

Haskel, Jonathan, Hughes, Alan, and Bascasvusoglu-Moreau, Elif, *The Economic Significance of the UK Science Base: A Paper for the Campaign for Science and Engineering* (May 2014).

Hattie, J. and Marsh, H. W., 'The relationship between research and teaching: a meta-analysis', *Review of Educational Research* 66/4 (1996), 507–42.

Hayes, Sarah, *MOOCs and Quality: A Review of the Recent Literature*, QAA MOOCs Network (July 2015).

Heckman, James, *Policies to Foster Human Capital*, NBER 7288 (August 1999).

Heckman, James and Masterov, Dimitriy, *The Productivity Argument for Investing in Young Children*, NBER Working Paper No. 13016 (April 2007).

Heckman, J. J., Moon, S. H., Pinto, R., Savelyev, P., and Yavitz, A., *The Rates of Return to the High/Scope Perry Preschool Program*, IZA DP No. 4533 (2009).

HEFCE, *Differences in Degree Outcomes: The Effect of Subject and Student Characteristics*, September 2015/21 Issues paper.

Heidegger, Martin, 'The self-assertion of the German university' and 'The Rectorate 1933/34. Facts and thoughts', in *The Review of Metaphysics* 38/3 (March 1985), 461–502.

Higher Education Commission, *Regulating Higher Education: Protecting Students, Encouraging Innovation, Enhancing Excellence* (October 2013).

Higher Education Commission, *From Bricks to Clicks: The Potential of Data and Analytics in Higher Education* (March 2016).

Hillman, Nicholas, 'From grants for all to loans for all: undergraduate finance from the implementation of the Anderson Report (1962) to the implementation of the Browne Report (2012)', *Contemporary British History* 27/3 (2013), 249–70.

Hillman, Nick, *Unfinished Business*, HEPI Report 65 (February 2014).

Hillman, Nicholas, 'The Coalition's higher education reforms in England', *Oxford Review of Education* 42/3 (2016), 330–45.

Hillman, Nick and Robinson, Nicholas, *Boys to Men: The Underachievement of Young Men in Higher Education—and How to Start Tackling it*, HEPI Report 84 (May 2016).

Hoare, Anthony and Johnston, Ron, 'Widening participation through admissions policy—a British case study of school and university performance', *Studies in Higher Education* 36/1 (2011), 21–41.

Holland, D., Liadze, I., Rienzo, C., and Wilkinson, D., *The Relationship Between Graduates and Economic Growth Across Countries*, BIS Research Paper No. 110 (August 2013).

Holmes, Craig, 'Has the expansion of higher education led to greater economic growth?', *National Institute Economic Review* 224 (May 2013), 29–42.

Howson and McNamara, 'Teacher workforce planning: the interplay of market forces and government policies during a period of economic uncertainty', *Education Research* 54/2 (June 2012), 173–85.

Hughes, Alan, 'Open innovation, the Haldane principle and the new production of knowledge: science policy and university–industry links in the UK after the financial crisis', *Prometheus* 29/4 (December 2011), 411–42.

Hughes, Alan, Kitson, Michael, and Probert, Jocelyn, *Hidden Connections: Knowledge Exchange between the Arts and Humanities and the Private, Public and Third Sectors* (AHRC, 2011).

Hughes, Alan, et al., *The Dual Funding Structure for Research in the UK: Research Council and Funding Council Allocation Methods and Pathways to impact of UK Academics*, a report to BIS by the Centre for Business Research (April 2013).

Hunter, John E. and Hunter, R. F., 'Validity and utility of alternative predictors of job performance', *Psychological Bulletin* 96 (1984), 72–98.

IFS, *Living Standards, Inequality and Poverty in the UK 2014*, chapter 5: 'Young adults and the recession', pp. 103–7.

International Comparative Performance of the UK Research Base—2013 (Elsevier, 2013).

Jewell, S., 'The impact of working while studying on educational and labour market outcomes', *Business and Economics Journal* 5/3 (2014), 1–12.

Kaplanis, Ioannis, *Wage Effects from Changes in Local Human Capital in Britain*, Spatial Economics Research Centre, London School of Economics (December 2009).

Keep, Ewart and Mayhew, Ken, 'Inequality—"wicked problems", labour market outcomes and the search for silver bullets', *Oxford Review of Education* 40/6 (2014), 764–81.

Kenkel, Douglas, 'Health behaviour, health knowledge, and schooling', *Journal of Political Economy* 99/2 (1991), 287–305.

Kimball, Roger, 'Heidegger at Freiburg 1933', *New Criterion* 3/10 (June 1985), 9.

Kirby, Philip, *Levels of Success: The Potential of UK Apprenticeships*, Sutton Trust (October 2015).

Klesch, Anita, *A Golden Age or Crisis? The History of Art in the Age of Information Technology* DPhil thesis, Birkbeck, University of London, 2011.

Knoll, Lisa, Fuhrmann, Delia, Sakhardande, Ashok, Stamp, Fabian, Speekenbrink, Maarten, and Blakemore, Sarah-Jayne, 'A window of opportunity for cognitive training in adolescence', *Psychological Science OnlineFirst* (4 November 2016).

Knowland, Victoria and Thomas, Michael, *Educating the Adult Brain: How the Neuroscience of Learning can Inform Educational Policy*, Centre for Educational Neuroscience, Birkbeck College, 2014.

Krueger, Alan and Lindahl, Mikael, 'Education for growth: why and for whom?', *Journal of Economic Literature* 39 (December 2001), 1101.

Kruse, Otto, 'The origins of writing in the disciplines: traditions of seminar writing and the Humboldtian ideal of the research university', *Written Communication* 23/3 (July 2006), 331–52.

Kuh, George and Pascarella, Ernest, 'What does institutional selectivity tell us about education quality?', *Change* (September/October 2004).

Kuntsche, E., Rehm, J., and Gmel, G., 'Characteristics of binge drinkers in Europe', *Social Science and Medicine* 59/1 (July 2004), 113–27.

Kutney Lee, A., Sloane, D. M., and Aiken, L. H., 'An increase in the number of nurses with Baccalaureate degrees is linked to lower rates of post-surgery mortality', *Health Affairs* 32/3 (2013), 579–86.

Lazear, E. P., 'Entrepreneurship', *Journal of Labor Economics* 23/4 (2005), 649–80.

Lee, Neil, *Advanced Industries, Job Multipliers and Living Standards in Britain*, Resolution Foundation, 2017.

Leigh, J. Paul, 'Accounting for tastes: correlates of risk and time preferences', *Journal of Post Keynesian Economics* 9 (Fall 1986), 17–31.

Little, A. N., 'Will more mean worse? An inquiry into the effects of university expansion', *The British Journal of Sociology* 12/4 (December 1961), 351–62.

Lockett, A., Wright, M., and Wild, A., 'The co-evolution of third stream activities in UK higher education', *Business History* 55/2 (March 2013), 236–58.

London Economics, *The Outcomes Associated with the BTEC Route of Degree Level Acquisition*, Report for Pearson (May 2013).

Machin, S., Vignoles, A., and Galindo-Rueda, F., *Sectoral and Area Analysis of the Economic Effects of Qualifications and Basic Skills*, DfES Research Report (2003), 42–3.

Machin, Stephen and Vignoles, Anna, 'Educational inequality: the widening socio-economic gap', *Fiscal Studies* 25/2 (2004), 107–28.

Maiworm, Friedhelm and Teichler, Ulrich, 'The students' experience', in *Erasmus in the Socrates Programme: Findings of an Evaluation Study*, ACA Papers, 2002.

Mandemakers, J. J., and Monden, C. W. S., 'Does education buffer the impact of disability on psychological distress?', *Social Science and Medicine* 71/2 (2010), 288–97.

Meadows, Pam, *National Evaluation of Sure Start Local Programmes: An Economic Perspective* by the National Evaluation of Sure Start Team led by Pam Meadows, DFE Research Report DFE-RR073 (July 2011).

Michail, Konstantina, *Dyslexia: The Experience of University Students with Dyslexia*, PhD Thesis, University of Birmingham, April 2010.

Mina, Andrea, Connell, David, and Hughes, Alan, *Models of Technology Development in Intermediate Research Organisations*, Centre for Business Research, University of Cambridge, Working Paper No. 396 (December 2009).

Montenegro, Claudio E. and Patrinos, Harry Anthony, *Comparable Estimates of Returns to Schooling Around the World*, World Bank Group Policy Research Working Paper 7020 (September 2014).

Moretti, Enrico, 'Workers' education, spillovers, and productivity: evidence from plant-level production functions', *The American Economic Review* 94/3 (June 2004), 656–90.

Moretti, Enrico, 'Estimating the social return to higher education: evidence from longitudinal and repeated cross sectional data', *Journal of Econometrics* 21 (2004), 175–212.

Morris, Marley, *Destination Education*, Institute for Public Policy Research, 2016.

Narin, Francis, Hamilton, Kimberly S., and Olivastro, Dominic, 'The increasing link between US technology and public science', *Research Policy* 26/3 (October 1997), 317–30.

Naylor, Robin and Smith, Jeremy, *Schooling Effects on Subsequent University Performance: Evidence for the UK University Population*, Department of Economics, University of Warwick Economic Research Paper No. 657 (November 2002).

Naylor, Robin, Smith, Jeremy, and Telhaj, Shqiponja, *Graduate Returns, Degree Class Premia and Higher Education Expansion in the UK*, CEP Discussion Paper No. 1392 (November 2015).

NCUB, *The Changing State of Knowledge Exchange: UK Academic Interactions with External Organisations 2005–2015*, February 2016.

Neves, Jonathan and Hillman, Nick, *The 2016 Student Academic Experience Survey*, HEPI and HEA.

Negroponte, Nicholas, 'MIT Media Lab is vital to the digital revolution', *Wired*, 15 November 2012.

Noble, K. J. et al., 'Family income, parental education and brain structure in children and adolescents', *Nature Neuroscience* published on-line 30 March 2015.

Nybom, Thorsten, 'The Humboldt legacy: reflections on the past, present and future of the European university', *Higher Education Policy* 16 (2003), 141–59.

OECD, *Looking to 2060: Long-Term Global Growth Prospects*, OECD Economic Policy Papers No. 3 (November 2012).

O'Neill, Onora, 'Integrity and quality in universities: accountability, excellence and success', *British Academy Review* 20 (Summer 2012).

ONS, *Measuring National Well-Being, Education and Skills* (2011).

Orchard, Janet and Winch, Christopher, *What Training do Teachers Need? Why Theory is Necessary to Good Teaching*, Impact, Philosophical Perspectives on Education Policy No. 22 (Wiley Blackwell, 2015).

Parker, Miles, *The Rothschild Report (1971) and the Purpose of Government-Funded R&D—A Personal Account* (Palgrave Communications, 2016).

Pascarella, Ernest, et al., 'Institutional selectivity and good practices in undergraduate education: how strong is the link?', *The Journal of Higher Education* 77/2 (March/April 2006).

Perez-Arce, Francisco, *The Effect of Education on Time Preferences*, Rand Working Paper WR-844 (March 2011).

Perkin, Harold, 'Dream, myth and reality: new universities in England, 1960–1990', *Higher Education Quarterly* 45/4 (Autumn 1991).

Pew Research Centre, *The Rising Cost of not Going to College* (2014).

Poschke, Marcus, *Who Becomes an Entrepreneur? Labor Market Prospects and Occupational Choice*, IZA Discussion Paper No. 3816 (November 2008).

Purcell, Kate, et al., *Futuretrack Stage 4 Transitions into Employment, Further Study and other Outcomes*, HECSU and Warwick Institute for Employment Research, 201.2.

Ramsden, Sue, et al., 'Verbal and non-verbal intelligence changes in the teenage brain', *Nature Letter* published on-line 19 October 2011.

Robinson, S. and Griffiths, P., 'Scoping review: Moving to an all-graduate nursing profession: assessing potential effects on workforce profile and quality of care', National Nursing Research Unit, King's College London, November 2008.

Rose, M., et al., 'Opportunities, contradictions and attitudes: the evolution of university–business engagement since 1960', *Business History* 55/2 (2013), 259–79.

Royal Society, The, *Science as an Open Enterprise*, June 2012.

Sclater, Niall and Bailey, Paul, *Code of Practice for Learning Analytics*, JISC, June 2015.

Shah, Dhawal, *By the Numbers: MOOCS in 2016*, Class Central, 25 December 2016.

Skolnick Weisberg, Deena, et al., 'The seductive allure of neuroscience', *Journal of Cognitive Neuroscience* 20/3 (2008), 470–7.

Steven, Kathryn, Dowell, Jon, Jackson, Cathy, and Guthrie, Bruce, 'Fair access to medicine? Retrospective analysis of UK medical schools application data 2009–2012 using three measures of socioeconomic status', *BMC Medical Education* 16 (2016).

Stone, Lawrence, 'The educational revolution in England', *Past and Present* 28 (1964), 41–80.

Sutch, Tom, *Progression from GCSE to AS and A Level*, Cambridge Assessment, December 2013.

Sylva, Kathy, *Sound Foundations: A Review of the Research Evidence on Quality of Early Childhood Education and Care for Children under Three—Implications for Policy and Practice* (Sutton Trust, 2014).

Tight, Malcolm, 'The golden age of academe: myth or memory?', *British Journal of Educational Studies* 58/1 (March 2010), 105–16.

Tight, Malcolm, 'Institutional churn: institutional change in UK higher education', *Journal of Higher Education Policy and Management* 35/1 (2013), 11–20.

Towle, Angela, *Undergraduate Medical Education: London and the Future* (King's Fund, 1992).

UCAS, *End of Cycle Report: Analysis and Research* (December 2016).

UNESCO, *Trends in Global Higher Education: Tracking and Academic Revolution* (UNESCO, 2009).

Universities UK, *Supply and Demand for Higher-Level Skills* (December 2015).

Universities UK, *Working In Partnership: Enabling Social Mobility in Higher Education: The Final Report of the Social Mobility Advisory Group* (2016).

Universities UK, *Higher Education in England: Provision Skills and Graduates* (September 2016).

University Grants Committee, *Report of the Committee on University Teaching Methods* (HMSO, 1964).

UUK and British Future, *International Students and the UK Immigration Debate 2014*.

Valero, Anna and Van Reenen, John, *How Universities Boost Economic Growth,* CentrePiece (Winter 2016), London School of Economics.

Vernon, Keith, 'Calling the tune: British universities and the state, 1880–1914', *History of Education* 30/3 (2001), 251–71.

Wadhwa, Vivek, Aggarwal, Raj, Holly, Krisztina, and Salkever, Alex, *The Anatomy of an Entrepreneur: Making of a Successful Entrepreneur* (Kauffman Foundation, 2009).

Walker, I. and Zhu, Y., *The Impact of University Degrees on the Lifecycle of Earnings: Some Further Analysis*, BIS Research Paper No. 112 (August 2013).

Watson, David, 'The coming of post-institutional higher education', *Oxford Review of Education* (2015).

Willetts, David, *Robbins Revisited: Bigger and Better Higher Education*, Social Market Foundation (October 2013).

Willetts, David, *Higher Education: Who Benefits? Who Pays?*, King's College London, 2015.

Zhenhao, Chen, Alcorn, Brandon, Christensen, Gayle, Eriksson, Nicholas, Koller, Daphne, and Emanuel, Ezekiel, 'Who's benefiting from MOOCs and why', *Harvard Business Review*, 22 September 2015.

Zimmerman, Seth, 'The returns to college admission for academically marginal students', *Journal of Labor Economics* 32/4 (2014), 711–54.

OFFICIAL GOVERNMENT REPORTS AND STATISTICS
(IN CHRONOLOGICAL ORDER)

Scheme for the Organisation and Development of Scientific and Industrial Research Cd 8005 (July 1915).

Report of the Machinery of Government Committee, The Haldane Report, Cd 9230 (1918).

The Barlow Report, *Scientific Manpower*, Report of a Committee appointed by the Lord President of the Council, Cmd 6824 (May 1946).

Simon Crowther, *The Crowther Report: 15–18,* A Report of the Central Advisory Council for Education (England) London: Her Majesty's Stationery Office (1959).

Anderson Report, *Grants to Students*, Ministry of Education Cmnd 1051 (1960).

The Trend Report, *Committee of Enquiry into the Organisation of Civil Science*, Cmnd 2171 (October 1963).

Robbins Report, *Higher Education: Report of the Committee appointed by the Prime Minister under the Chairmanship of Lord Robbins 1961–63*, Cmnd 2154 (October 1963).

Report of the Committee on University Teaching Methods, chaired by Sir Edward Hale, UGC (HMSO, 1964).

The Organisation and Management of Government Research and Development, 1971, Cmnd 4814 (1971).

Framework for Government Research and Development, Cmnd 5046 (July 1972).

Education: A Framework for Expansion, Cmnd 5174 (December 1972).

Review of the Framework for Government Research and Development, Cmnd 5046 (March 1979), Cmnd 7499.

The Development of Higher Education into the 1990s, DES (1985).

Advisory Board for the Research Councils, *A Strategy for Science Base* (May 1987).

Realising Our Potential, A Strategy for Science Engineering and Technology, Cm 2250 (May 1993).

Dearing Report, *Higher Education in the Learning Society: Report of the National Committee of Inquiry into Higher Education* (HMSO, 1997).

The Future of Higher Education, Department for Education and Skills, Cm 5735 (2003).

Lambert Review of Business–University Collaboration: Final Report (HMSO, December 2003).

Fair Admissions to Higher Education: Recommendations for Good Practice, Report of the Admissions to Higher Education Steering Group chaired by Professor Steven Schwartz (2004).

Growing the Best and Brightest: The Drivers of Research Excellence, BIS (March 2004).

Race to the Top: A Review of Government's Science and Innovation Policies Lord Sainsbury of Turnville (October 2007).

Aspiring to Excellence: Final Report of the Independent Inquiry in Modernising Medical Careers led by Professor Sir John Tooke (MMC Inquiry, 2008).

Higher Ambitions: The Future of Universities in a Knowledge Economy, BIS (2009).

Browne Review, *Securing a Sustainable Future For Higher Education: An Independent Review of Higher Education Funding and Student Finance* (2010).

Alison Wolf, *Review of Vocational Education* (March 2011).

Higher Education: Students at the Heart of the System, Cm 8122 (2011).

Tim Wilson *A Review of University–Business Collaboration* (February 2012).

Privately Funded Providers of Higher Education in the UK, BIS Research Paper No. III (June 2013).

A UK Strategy for Agricultural Technologies, HM Government (July 2013).

International Education: Global Growth and Prosperity, BIS (July 2013).

The Wider Benefits of International Higher Education in the UK, BIS Research Paper No. 128 (September 2013).

The Benefits of Higher Education Participation for Individuals and for Society: Key Findings and Reports 'The Quadrants', BIS Research Paper No. 146 (October 2013).

Universities' Terms and Conditions: An OFT Report, OFT1522 (February 2014).

CMA Report UK Higher Education Providers—draft advice on consumer protection law (November 2014).

Shape of Training: Securing the Future of Excellent Patient Care, Final report of the independent review led by Professor David Greenaway (2014).

Our Plan for Growth: Science and Innovation, HM Treasury and BIS, Cm 8980 (December 2014).

The Dowling Review of Business-University Research Collaborations (July 2015).

The Metric Tide: Report of the Independent Review of the Role of Metrics in Research Assessment and Management, chaired by James Willsdon, HEFCE (July 2015).

Fulfilling our Potential, Teaching Excellence, Social Mobility and Student Choice, BIS, Cm 9141 (November 2015).

Ensuring a Successful UK Research Endeavour: A Review of the UK Research Councils by Paul Nurse (November 2015).

Success as a Knowledge Economy: Teaching Excellence, Social Mobility and Student Choice BIS (May 2016), Cm 9258.

Building on Success and Learning from Experience: An Independent Review of the REF, Nick Stern, BEIS IND/16/9 (July 2016).

Building our Industrial Strategy, Green Paper, HM Government (January 2017).

The Higher Education and Research Act (2017).

Office for Statistics Regulation *The quality of the long-term student migration statistics* (July 2017).

Illustration Credits

Figure 1: Radharc Images/Alamy Stock Photo.

Figure 2: Indiana University Archives (P0024329).

Figure 4: Prixnews/Alamy Stock Photo.

Figure 5: is based on *The Benefits of Higher Education Participation for Individuals and for Society: Key Findings and Reports 'The Quadrants'*, BIS Research Paper No. 146 (October 2013), 6. Also see David Willetts, *Robbins Re-Visited: Bigger and Better Higher Education* (Social Market Foundation, 2013), 20.

Figure 6: 'Graduate' by Jamie Charteris, © Paperlink 2017.

Figure 7: Moviestore Collection Ltd/Alamy Stock Photo.

Figure 8: is based on Markus Poschke, *Who Becomes an Entrepreneur? Labor Market Prospects and Occupational Choice*, IZA Discussion Paper No. 3816 (November 2008), 24.

Figure 9: painting by Laurentius de Voltolina, Staatliche Museum, Berlin/ART. Collection/Alamy Stock Photo.

Index